The Book of Awareness
Clear Mind New Planet
Interpretation Guide

Written by Genie O'Malley
2010

H&V Publishing

The Book of Awareness,
Clear Mind New Planet Interpretation Guide
Copyright © 2010
by Genie O'Malley.

Disclaimer: Information presented in this book is not intended to be a substitute for professional medical advice, diagnosis or treatment. Never disregard professional medical advice or delay in seeking it because of something you have read in this book.

Printed in the United States of America.

H&V Publishing
81 Newtown Lane, Suite 162,
East Hampton, NY, 11937.
T: 888 515 0444

www.clearmindnewplanet.com

ISBN 978-0-615-37739-1

Dear Mary.

'Welcome Home'

Love Genie

The nature of the conscious mind is to dissolve the unconscious mind so as to reveal the presence of love...

Genie

Contents

Introduction

Welcome to the Book of Awareness! As you journey throughout the pages, you will be presented with many interpretations that support the process of dissolving the unconscious mind. To assist you in your journey through Clear Mind New Planet, the Book of Awareness was written to further clarify Clear Mind New Planet and the importance and opportunity of dissolving the unconscious mind.

The Book of Awareness is a comprehensive interpretation of potential. Prompting you to ponder, "What would it be like to live upon a planet that did not have the capacity to live within negative interpretations or needs? Why is humanity being invited to experience this potential today while inviting you to discover how the unconscious mind is acting out in your life with the solution and means in which to reinterpret the world in which we live."

In speaking of love throughout the Clear Mind New Planet and the Book of Awareness, one speaks not of the human interpretation of love, but an unworldly, profound, conscious perception of love about yourself, others, life, opportunities, and the world around us. What Clear Mind New Planet can reveal to you is that the planet is today within a moment of awakening that is allowing and providing each of us with the means and opportunity to redefine life in a manner that some only dreamed possible.

There appears at times to be so much to heal within the world, so much destruction across the world that competes with opportunities of peace, innovation, and conscious awareness to love. The gift of the Clear Mind Experience and the pages of this book is that here is the means in which to release the potential that is in front of you and within you simply, quickly, effectively, and today!

As the pioneer of the Clear Mind Experience, I can honestly say that Clear Mind New Planet with the Book of Awareness is the most comprehensive body of work that I have been honored to put together to explain the need, opportunity, and practice of the Clear Mind Experience.
For myself as the author, pioneer of the Clear Mind Experience, there was a unique process that came together for me in the writing the Book of Awareness interpretation guide which was that each word of the interpretation guide was scribed from spoken tapes. Thousands of words spoken from myself into a small dictaphone then typed into the written word. It is because of this process of discovering and revealing the information within the interpretation guide that I have maintained that the editing process of the interpretation guide was slight; ensuring within each paragraph to not in any way change the flow of any sentence or paragraph and particularly not add any words into its definitions. It is within great humility that I support what is written within the interpretation guide, as there is a great amount of information that was revealed through its spoken compilation that was new to myself. All information presented about the Clear Mind Experience and the purpose in which an individual would practice it are conversations that I have had many times over in thirteen

years. I have developed many workshops, training programs, and presentations pertaining to the importance, function, and practice of dissolving the unconscious mind throughout the years.

However, the written interpretations that discuss the potential of this earth and the importance of its release upon the planet, particularly at this time, were new to myself. It was in the discoveries made that this work, the need for humanity to dissolve the unconscious and what happens when we do has moved to a new level.

One of the most beautiful revelations that I had at the end of writing this book is that it spoke to many. It spoke to many varied interpretations of life, love, spirituality, interpretations of the mind, living and, most important, our potential. What this means is that no matter what your interest is or why you are compelled to read Clear Mind New Planet, you will move through the information at a comfort level. This is because there is something magical in its pages. A nurturing presence that makes this book a companion, a friend that is embracing you upon a new journey into dissolving the unconscious mind. You can be assured that the energy presented within these pages seeks and wants for you to be successful in your journey to dissolve the unconscious mind.

You are encouraged to take your time so as to digest what is being said, to discover and dive into your journey. As you progress through the pages, you will experience opportunity that is void of the unconscious mind. It is in feeling this that you will feel the freedom of living without it. Through the combination of Clear Mind New Planet and the Clear Mind In-Home Experience, your life will be void of acting, absorbing, or being directed by the unconscious mind.

Enjoy the Book of Awareness. It is a special friend within the Clear Mind Community, your friend and invitation into living life free of the unconscious mind which allows humanity to live within a Clear Mind revealing a New Planet. You will see within the Book of Awareness that some pages are filled with written interpretations and some pages provide questions or activities for you to practice that allow you to experience the interpretation. You will see upon the question pages that you are encouraged to answer the questions three times over different dates. This allows you to witness your new interpretations as you move into conscious mind interpretations on your journey of dissolving the unconscious mind.

No matter what you are lead to discover within these pages, it will be just what is needed within the moment to comfort your new levels of awareness or potential. Enjoy your discoveries and, most important, enjoy your journey of the Clear Mind Experience and dissolving the unconscious mind. As you move throughout the pages, throughout the Clear Mind Experience, the language of love will awaken the presence of love and allow your life to resonate the essence of self-appreciation within yourself, your life, and the lives of others.

Enjoy!

The Book of Awareness

The Book of Awareness is the interpretation guide to Clear Mind New Planet. Please enjoy the beauty of these two books and how they move in and out of one another to define the presence of love and the incredible momentum of living free from the unconscious mind.

To order **Clear Mind New Planet,** *please visit*
www.clearmindnewplanet.com

Enjoy!

Chapter One

Sunshine

1.1 Walking along the beach with the shadow bouncing off the light – the light being the sun, there is awareness to the fact that this is how most people walk through life. Into and towards the shadow-self. Always placing through thoughts, actions, and ideas the shadow in the front of them, meaning pushing it into the forefront of their life and how they define themselves. This is done because humanity in the past has believed that it is the shadow that must be overcome, confronted, and reflected upon which places it in front of us. However, the importance of this statement is that whatever we see or perceive as being in front of us has us feel suppressed, confronted by, or controlled by what is in front. Therefore, in facing the shadow, there is a 'perceived powerlessness' that it is in control.

Within our minds, we have the shadow and the light. The light is called the conscious mind, it is what perceives life in love, either action of love, statements of love or movement of love. Always thoughts (vision) within the conscious mind have the intent of preserving the qualities of love. Also within the mind, we have a direct mirror image of the light which is defined within the Clear Mind Experience as the unconscious mind. The unconscious mind is not able to perceive love and hosts thoughts, actions, and emotions that are there to challenge the presence of love through its inability to perceive love. Both aspects – the light and the dark come from the one mind - which is the personal mind of the individual. They are the mirror image of the same life experiences that happened within the first seven years of your life. The shadow aspects of the mind are the thoughts, feelings, and emotions that accumulated within the first seven years of life that are not able to perceive love. The shadow being called the unconscious mind, that which cannot perceive love. Then we have the conscious mind, which is our capacity to move perceived love into life through actions, words, and experiences.

The personal mind also has as a direct mirror, which is the collective mind.

The shadow because it cannot see love perceives that it is all that exists. If you think for a moment, if negative unconscious thoughts believed that there was love and they could support love, then the unconscious mind could not exist because it would know love. So the shadow to support itself has not the capacity to heal, to awaken, to let go to love because it does not see love as being available within life and will work against you in allowing yourself to discover love. The unconscious mind is programmed to preserve itself by denying love, potential, and expression of wisdom, just like the conscious mind operates to preserve love.

This is what the conscious mind serves love. The greatest deception that is played out within humanity when attempting to shift or transform their lives is that individuals perceive the unconscious as something that can be healed or supported and within this support it will let go. The unconscious will not ever 'let go' because it is programmed to preserve itself through control and protection which fuels denial.

2.2 The shadow-self will speak endlessly of itself. Seeking answers to itself. Using each moment within life to give itself definition so that it has greater and more expansive energy and thoughts available to define itself within your perception. It will jump from thing to thing, experience to experience continually seeking to define itself. Asking incessantly who and what it is because it is only able to define itself through outer perception, outer things.

It has no connection to inner understanding or perception, so it attempts to randomly define itself over and over by what is presented within how an individual feels within each moment. For example: let's say that IAM feeling love. The shadow because it cannot feel the love, will feel a void, so it will say I feel nothing. Then the rational mind will ask; "well do I feel love?" Then in that moment because feelings do not speak and wisdom does not save the mind from anything because it does not host the capacity to judge, the next answer if it is given through thought will be one that supports the unconscious mind because upon engaging in the thoughts, there is no longer awareness to the feeling of love. The power in the Clear Mind Experience is that when you are invited to speak to the unconscious mind to reaffirm its detachments from love, because it cannot perceive or feel love, rather than speaking with the unconscious thoughts, you are encouraged to practice three Clear Mind breaths and the Clear Mind Support Mantra. This is because the three breaths which keep you engaged in the feeling of love allow the unconscious thought to move on.

2.3 When the shadow is in front of us, meaning when

our negative thoughts, feelings and emotions are what we follow throughout the day either through destruction or seeking to heal from them, then the rational mind is more encouraged to give valid permission for the unconscious mind/shadow to be supported through our feelings. The rational mind will allow this to happen because we are walking behind the shadow catering to its demands of a better life, better partner, better job, more money, more medication, more opportunities, and more energy that is needed to heal it. The shadow will demand you to be engaged within it, and the rational mind when confronted with it, allows it because it 'feels' the energy of the unconscious acting out through past ideas, thoughts, feelings and emotions. Because the rational mind only rationalizes the moment, from moment to moment, if the feelings are not good in the moment or life is contradicting love then the rational mind will support the destruction and separation that is revealed by the unconscious.

The unconscious mind will seek to destroy inner connection by denying it, outer connection by controlling it or rejecting it and overall happiness because it cannot give control over to love. The unconscious knows that the rational mind is the gatekeeper and will seek endless ways itself to be reinforced by the rational mind. It will do this by presenting past feelings to the rational mind that can be supported within current experiences.

2.4 When the rational mind engages in supporting the unconscious mind it will validate past thoughts or experiences presented by the unconscious mind that awaken old feelings that allow the unconscious to come further into play. This is because the feelings have potential to be supported by life experience and through this the rational mind will validate and activate the perception of the unconscious.

It will do this impersonally to support the moment. The rational mind can be seen as the gatekeeper by the fact that, it is either allowing the process of love to dissolve what is not love within the mind, or allowing the unconscious mind to have residence by allowing it to retrieve negative feelings within the body, mind, emotions or supporting the conscious mind by presenting the feeling of stillness into each perceived moment.

3.1 Wisdom will listen, it will not act but become a witness to what is not love, as it is within the stillness that the noise is dissolved because the stillness if it does not respond, react or take the experience to the next level will dissolve and dissipate the experience. The wisdom aspect of the mind – the conscious mind will witness the unconscious mind not seeking to fix it because a quality of the conscious mind is that it is allowing of life of each moment. It will only move to preserve life and love within each moment. One would have to know that when we live in conscious awareness there are not moments of distrust, harm, deception, violence or untruth so there is nothing to protect only each moment to preserve.

3.2 When unconscious thoughts are allowed to pass, the wisdom aspect of the mind will speak and what it says will follow on from where the unconscious mind spoke, as wisdom will state the opposite. Always acting to preserve love by speaking the words that have the power to move the perception into love.

3.3 The unconscious mind asked questions so that it could be defined. Asking for definition and clarity of its identity. Seeking within each moment to further define the personal identity. However when it was allowed to make these statements and there was not feeling from the rational mind to support or define what was being said then wisdom was able to move into the conversation. Which is the moment where love moves to dissolve what is not love – as love within its divinity is programmed to find itself. So when non-love presents itself, love will move to say,"Oooh here I am!" Within this process then what is not love disappears into what is love. The Clear Mind three-part breath and Clear Mind Support Mantra serve to allow this process of love finding itself.

The Clear Mind Support Mantra provides an individual with an awareness to life without the unconscious mind. It is the Clear Mind Support Mantra that engages consistency within the Clear Mind flow within the brain by assisting the feelings to detach from thoughts and allowing the mind to experience each moment within a conscious perception. It is the Clear Mind Support Mantra that is consistently centering one's mind within the presence of love. The Clear Mind Support Mantra is what supports the experience of clarity and the momentum of dissolving the unconscious mind until the clearing has been fully achieved; however, it is always allowing one's awareness to be directed to that of love and not that which is not. It reveals itself as love drawing love within itself.

3.4 When there was no validation to define the unconscious mind, the conscious mind stated its existence. IAM it said, and within the IAM the unconscious mind could not respond. It could only move onto another thought. The process of awakening the presence of love happens within our minds spontaneously when we allow the rational mind to be still. To encourage and support this stillness of mind, rather than choosing thoughts, we take three Clear Mind breaths and within that moment, the rational mind engages in the feeling of the breath which is the perceived stillness. When it engages in the stillness then wisdom can present itself by speaking the opposite of what was stated by the unconscious. It is in this moment, this flow of inner conversation that the unconscious mind is not present. Activating this spontaneous flow of unconscious thought being dissolved by conscious thought is supported and brought into solid momentum through the Clear Mind Experience which activates the karmic equation between the unconscious mind and the conscious mind and the flow of movement within the mind that has them become one mind. It is the Clear Mind Experience that allows the 'union of one mind'.

4.1 The unconscious mind is always speaking outside of itself. So when it replied to wisdom, it did not perceive wisdom as within itself, as itself, it perceived wisdom as being an outside voice so then it asked wisdom to confirm that it liked it therefore, being the outer existence. When wisdom stated IAM, the rational mind was able to receive it because the unconscious mind believes it is all that exists. It is the IAM which is the statement of the rational mind, and moves the gatekeeper (rational mind) into the feeling of love. When wisdom replied, it made reference to feeling because it was drawing the rational mind into the presence of love. The conscious mind participates this way with the rational mind because it is spontaneously supported by the rational mind to preserve love. It moves the rational mind into love through words because that is its action of preservation. Right here it is just acting as itself. Not saving the unconscious just activating the movement needed to dissolve the unconscious into love.

4.2 The shadow cannot be drawn into love simply by making statements that are love to the unconscious mind because the unconscious mind is made up of single words and perception needs sentences to articulate information clearly. So what happens during this process without dissolving the unconscious mind is that there will just be an ebbing and flowing between the conscious and unconscious mind. The benefits of 'dissolving' the unconscious mind are valuable and important on the path of self-discovery because it awakens the feelings of love needed to bring the rational mind on board with the conscious mind. Once this has been achieved it is time to release and dissolve the unconscious mind and start the next level of realization of love.

4.3 The thoughts spiraling through the unconscious mind are fairly minimal and host only 49 negative feelings that are then reinterpreted through 49 positive feelings from the conscious mind. As much as we think that the unconscious thoughts can be unlimited, they are not because they only act to engage 49 negative feelings.

5.1 The shadow, meaning the unconscious mind, will speak incessantly about what it wants, always seeking immediate gratification. It has an insatiable desire for control and the next thing. Never feeling whole or defined by one thing, it seeks multiple experiences as it tries to mimic the simultaneous presence of love. As it craves one thing after the other, it is not able to fully engage in each thing so it will attract experiences that feed of one another and they are always a disassociation of love. As it seeks to create these experiences, it will attempt to rationalize each of them by incessantly speaking about what could be, should be, or will be.

5.2 Love spoke of itself to the unconscious as it moved to dissolve the unconscious questions and demands of the unconscious mind. The conscious mind is programmed to dissolve what is not love through wisdom. The conscious mind will move towards negative thoughts, when the rational mind is able to move still, and when it moves towards these negative thoughts, it is to dissolve them. To bring perception back within itself. Whenever love is faced with what is not love, it will move into the experience to discover itself. It is when the feeling of love moves into thoughts that are not love as statements of wisdom that love realizes its power and presence, because when it hears statements that are not love, it is given the power to find itself. That is the beauty of the unconscious mind that it is a constant invitation to love to discover itself.

5.3 In life we will reach a certain point within our lives where the shadow is walking in front of us and we will turn back around. We will turn around and head back through our lives within our minds, to the point where we are able to perceive life as a child. In the simplicity and beauty of a child. It is when we turn around to discover the child-mind. The first seven years of our lives that are living as thoughts, feelings and emotions that are continually defining us daily. When we turn back around, it is our journey home, some of us turn around sooner than others, but it is the moment that we turn around that we make a choice that the shadow will fall behind us. The importance of its questions, its needs and its direction is no longer important to us and not something that we wish to be lead by. It is when we turn around that we make a choice that the unconscious mind, the shadow is not important and we walk forward into the light, into the sun and within the fire of the sun the unconscious mind is dissolved. The Clear Mind Breath is the fire that will dissolve the unconscious mind. It is bestowed within humanity with the power to burn up what is not of the light, not of love and within the burning, the alchemy of love is revealed. When we turn around and walk back the way we came, this represents us walking back through the unconscious mind, its structure and rather than dismantling it we dissolve it through a new perspective. One of Love. We have the power through the Clear Mind Experience to dissolve the unconscious and the interpretations that we made along the way that the shadow walked in front of us. We have a choice to honor life living within love and the Clear Mind Experience can take your journey home to love to the moment where you will live perceiving life within the child-mind – effortless and filled with joy.

5.4 When we turn around, towards the light then the shadow when we are looking at the light will naturally position itself behind us. When we are looking away from the light, then the light falls behind us and the shadow in front of us. When we choose to walk in the direction of the light, the shadow becomes insignificant and we cannot hear it any longer because it automatically begins to follow us – not lead us. Within this change it will lose power within our lives, because it is behind us as and our perception is nurtured and embraced within the light. The shadow represents the unconscious mind, when we walk towards the light within a conscious mind, meaning when we support thoughts of the conscious mind then the unconscious mind will lose power in our lives and be following thoughts, actions and emotions of the conscious mind. It is when this happens that the conscious mind is able to continually disengage from the limitations of the unconscious because the unconscious mind is not leading life, not leading in thought but trying to counteract the conscious mind, wipe out suggestions and momentum of the conscious mind. The conscious mind cannot be confronted by the unconscious, it will always move upon the unconscious to dissolve its conflict but cannot be directly confronted because it is always walking away from it. The unconscious always perceives when you dissolve it through the conscious mind and expression of love that it is trying to get power, but not living within power. When it does that, then it will retract, decompress and dissolve.

5.5 When we take the steps to head in the opposite direction the light will nurture the mind, wisdom will nurture the mind. Once we take these steps the further we walk within a conscious mind, without turning back towards the shadow, without supporting unconscious suggestions or thoughts, then the greater our awareness of love becomes. The conscious mind when supported by each step we take in life will provide greater and greater awareness to wisdom which will permeate all life with a profound and penetrating light.

5.6 Once we continue to support the light, to support the conscious mind through our actions to allow it to operate within our lives then we will activate our rational minds to support love. The rational mind can be perceived to be within the center of the brow which is also where we host our perception. When we allow ourselves to engage within wisdom by supporting it within each step that we take within life, then the rational mind will feel nurtured, honored and supported and will center itself within our perception to provide clarity and peace. This is all happening within the center of the brow, where truth, wisdom, peace and love are engaged as IAM.

5.7 The conscious mind does not think in matter or limitations. It perceives life as a movement, visions of images that are created and presented within vibrations of light and color. When we live life within the perception and experience of the conscious mind the mind will interpret potential within color, images and vibration and engage in the essence of joy, because it is the feeling of joy that will carry the conscious mind into reality in a manner that preserves life. When we live within the unconscious mind the mind will think in a density, that will host limited ideas, that will engage the perception of 'rigid views'. The unconscious mind will seek to create for things, and measure matter, measure life as what is gained. It will create and force rather than receive and allow. The unconscious mind will seek the light, seek what is conscious all with the motive of complaining that it is exhausted in attempting to get to the light. However the unconscious mind is not ever going to see the light, as the light is love and the unconscious mind cannot perceive love. The further we activate the conscious mind, realize the presence of love the more silent the unconscious mind has to become because it has not a role in speaking within a conscious mind, it can only be taken over by the conscious mind, as it is the conscious mind that dissolves what is not love to realize what IS.

6.1 When we live, walk and express the conscious mind great power and strength will fill the body. As we will feel supported through the conscious mind. Not only will the conscious mind awaken such strength within the body but it will also ignite the mind with the unlimited potential of love. The mind will perceive unlimited opportunities to express itself as love. As love will move through the mind, through the perception in a spontaneous flow of self-expression, as it moves in rhythm to reveal itself from moment to moment.

6.2 When the mind is actively hosting the conscious mind within its perception, that is all potential to express, receive and define love in action then the language will be born. A language will move through the mind that is spontaneous and the language will engage the rational mind through the IAM statement and principal. E.g. IAM love, peace, joy and freedom will spontaneously express life through the mind. When this happens, outer experiences needed to realize the presence of love through these statements of the conscious mind will become active within life.

7.1 Once we allow ourselves to walk effortlessly in life, within no judgment about what is right, what is wrong, then we allow ourselves to turn in the direction of the conscious mind and when we do this we will realize the gifts that we have always had, the gifts that have allowed us to effortlessly and spontaneously awaken a new life experience.

7.2 The conscious mind is not able to perceive or operate in judgment. It can only respond to what is not love by attempting to move love into the moment, but it is a movement, a drawing into, where love draws what is not love into itself so as to dissolve it. The shadow is not able to articulate statements from the conscious mind, it is only able to continue to speak in questions that attempt to deny the conscious mind. The conscious mind will continue to speak in sentences that invoke the IAM. IAM love, IAM peace, IAM joy. The gift of the Clear Mind Experience is that it is the bridge that is able to cross the conscious mind into the unconscious mind. So love is able to dissolve what is not love, so conscious beautiful words can dissolve thoughts, feelings and emotions that are not love into itself. When this alchemy awakens then love will realize itself by serving to dissolve what is not. Both the unconscious mind and conscious mind are impersonal, it is the rational mind that perceives the personal identity.

7.3 When the shadow was following rather than being in front, then one is able to experience the beauty of the conscious mind. It is within the conscious mind that the feeling of love, the feeling of peace and the feeling of freedom is perceived because that shadow is behind. It is in it being behind that the conscious mind will perceive a stillness, that it is walking through life within the freedom of its own perception. Because the shadow is not out in front speaking, meaning the unconscious mind is not creating and speaking incessantly about life, its needs and what must happen to serve it, then the mind will perceive a freedom, a stillness, a peace and within this the presence of love will be experienced. Once we are able to achieve this within our perception then the overall feeling becomes self-appreciation. It is the freedom from the shadow speaking and acting in our lives that gives us this sense and awareness of self-appreciation because our thoughts, feelings and emotions are conscious, and within them being conscious we are expressing the presence of love as vision, movement and opportunity, it is within this perception that great joy moves through our lives.

8.1 - 8.2 The conscious mind and the unconscious mind make the One Mind, the Universal Mind. The gift of the unconscious mind is revealed in the process of dissolving it through the conscious mind. As when we do this we are able to fully realize the presence of love within our emotions, feelings and mental perception. What is new in this discovery and revelation of the Clear Mind Experience is that we are moving the conscious mind into the structure of the unconscious mind so as to dissolve the unconscious thoughts, feelings and emotions. The Clear Mind Experience reveals the divine criteria of the unconscious and conscious mind integration. The process is refined, accurate and has momentum that is beyond emotional or human integration. This is because there is a folding into effect. Where love folds what is not love into itself. It is within this process that true magnificence of the one mind is revealed in the momentum of wisdom, realization of love and beauty that is revealed.

8.3 Individuals wonder if we are living unconsciously within each moment of the days so that we can discover the conscious mind. What is true within this statement is that the unconscious mind is operating within each moment of the day, it is operating continuously all of the time. However we do not have to live within it, perceiving it as us. We can simply hear it, remain still within the Clear Mind breath and allow wisdom – the presence of love to respond spontaneously dissolving the unconscious and aligning the conscious mind to each perceived moment.

9.1 The conscious and unconscious mind are gifted to us because when they are ONE, moving in and out of one another, the momentum that is created and revealed within the mind through the dissolving of the conscious mind, creates an inner harmony because the momentum is so soothing, empowering, vulnerable, profound and peaceful.

9.2 It is within their integration that great wisdom awakens. Our greatest insights, spiritual gifts and awakenings become present within our mind when what is not love, meaning the unconscious mind is moved upon by the conscious mind. When the conscious mind moves into the unconscious mind and begins to energetically merge with it through the Clear Mind Words and Clear Mind Breath then realizations will occur within the perception. All of the dysfunction that exists within unconscious thoughts will be dissolved by the conscious mind and peace, joy, harmony, union and love will be present to shape new thoughts, new ideas and new visions. When the conscious mind and unconscious mind meld together and pop, realizations of love occur and love passes through our feelings because we are realizing when the shadow is dissolved how powerful love is and realize that IAM love.

10.1 The beauty of nature, the elements of nature are continuously speaking to us about unlimited potential. They are also placing our perception within the structure of nature. The beauty of nature is that it is able to gift us with the ability to stay within the moment. As when we truly honor a moment in nature we will be revealed with an interpretation of our lives and our current awareness and feelings. This is because nature is a transparent mirror and when the conscious mind is operating, the mirror is crystal clear to the point that the experience seems almost surreal.

10.2 When wisdom walks within life, and the unconscious mind is the shadow that follows, wisdom is always perceiving direction. Within a conscious mind Wisdom is always what brings life into action because it is what receives life, articulates life, acts within life. When the unconscious is continually walking behind the light, into the light, where all perception is created within the light, then the unconscious mind will no longer have footing within somebody's life, within their interpretations, so it will not be living. The Clear Mind three-part breath is what creates one to walk forward in wisdom and the unconscious mind to become the shadow that follows. When we walk towards the light, within the light, feeling the light, we cannot feel the shadow, we cannot hear the shadow, and the shadow dissolves within the light.

10.3 The shadow is following the light, and the light is leading within life. The unconscious mind slowly dissolves and dissipates and becomes silent because the conscious mind becomes so present it is not able to articulate any thoughts, words, or actions that are not within the state of love. It is when the conscious mind becomes clear of the unconscious that the unconscious becomes silent because the unconscious is no longer attached to the personal identity. The unconscious mind is brain matter within the brain. The Clear Mind Experience clears/dissolves this brain matter from being able to create perception within a person's existence. That action alone creates the silence.

10.4 At times on this planet, prior to this day, it has been advised by seekers and advised by some forms of psychotherapy that the unconscious is to be walked towards that one must understand how the shadow perceives life to be able to understand and articulate wisdom. This is true to the extent that the unconscious must be dissolved into love. Love cannot be dissolved into the unconscious. If we are walking towards the unconscious, there is the feeling within the perception that one is moving love into the unconscious. The unconscious must be drawn into love. Love must be the stable factor and draws into itself what is not love to realize love. There was time upon this planet to follow the unconscious, to study it, to seek it, look for it, reveal it. However, today, with the speed in which humanity awakens, there is not time to follow behind the unconscious attempting to place conscious thought. Now, upon this planet, is the necessity to walk as the light, void of anything that contradicts that light, anything that challenges that light, anything that does not serve that light, and anything that is unconscious to the perception of love. When you walk forward with the Clear Mind Experience, your mind is clear. It cannot perceive the unconscious, it cannot perceive the collective unconscious, and within that perception alone is the new planet.

10.5 For many lifetimes, many have walked towards the

shadow, behind its shadow, wondering and pondering and aching to discover the beauty of the Clear Mind, the unlimited potential of visions, and the union of love and stillness within one mind. Light workers have ached to feel supported by life, supported by abundance, potential, prosperity, and opportunity. However, they have walked their missions into the frequency of the unconscious. They are to walk forward now leading life, leading opportunity where there is nothing in between what is seen and what is unseen. There is the union of one mind. When the unconscious is no longer able to participate, then great clarity will come of the mind; great clarity to embrace visions, great clarity to know truth, great clarity to represent, express the beauty and unlimited potential that exists within the presence of love once it is revealed within the living presence of life.

The light workers have suffered their light quotients; being their balancing act as they have had to sit within an unconscious existence and maintain to know truth, to live truth, to reveal truth, to celebrate truth, and ultimately reveal the magnificent presence of love that is upon and within each state of awareness. Now it is time for them to walk forward. It is time for the everyday man to walk forward free of the unconscious as it follows with no feed, connection, or energetic flow within the brain, within the body, within the emotions, within the perception. As we walk forward toward the light as the light, within a Clear Mind, there is no perception of the unconscious, therefore, the unconscious is not able to function as it serves and has no role because it is unseen.

It is within, while allowing the unconscious mind to walk in front of us, that we are bombarded with mind chatter. As someone sits and meditates to find truth, they are bombarded with mind chatter because the meditation is to wit-

ness what is not. If the unconscious mind is placed behind
as the shadow within one's personal perception, the meditation becomes the union with the light. Within the light is
the presence of love. The condition within the presence
of love is the stillness. The one discipline within, no longer
allowing, perceiving, experiencing mind chatter, is the discipline to know that IAM living free.

11.1 It has been discovered throughout the history of this
planet that the unconscious serves strongly those within
human form to awaken to the magnificence of love by
moving beyond the limitations of the unconscious mind.
This has been achieved by very few, and when it is
achieved, it is because the karmic condition within the individual's existence is that they pop through the unconscious mind and become witness to it, and that is to be
able to deliver work, or condition, or awareness to what it
is to live within the higher mind or the conscious mind.

Today, however, within humanity is the opportunity for all
men to live within the conscious mind and the perception
of love, and it is within this, that no longer must one pop
through due to karma, but one must walk free of the unconscious mind. It is to be dissolved from the brain, and
when it's dissolved from the brain, then the individual is
able to perceive life within a conscious mind and live and
express the presence of love effortlessly. There is, however,
a divine criteria between the conscious mind and the unconscious mind. It is the need for the unconscious to be
dissolved that reveals to the conscious mind what it feels
like to experience love. Without the unconscious mind there
is no feeling of love because conscious mind is already
aware of the presence of love, living as the presence of
love. It is when the unconscious is dissolved into love that
the feeling of love becomes present within the individual

and the feeling is the IAM. It is the IAM that allows us to express love, create within love, perceive love, live within a vision of love. The unconscious is the gateway to the feeling of love, the revelation of love, and the realization of divine love. However, if we walk towards the unconscious, we are living within the unconscious attempting to be free of it. If the unconscious becomes the shadow that follows, we clear the mind so the brain is not able to perceive the unconscious. The unconscious will energetically let go. The unconscious expression will be dissolved within the brain so the individual is free to perceive love and live within, most important, the feeling of love.

11.2 When the unconscious mind is directing life, meaning the perception of all that we feel that we are, is walking within how the unconscious mind perceives life, then great suffering will occur within our lives. Our bodies will break down with disease and disharmony. What we have attempted to achieve within our lives will become our stress and confusion and what we fear the most to lose. Our friendships will break down and be meaningless. Our emotions will be suppressed or out of control. The feelings of who we are will not be in balance or harmony. We will have great disharmony because the unconscious mind is forever attempting to define itself, to redefine itself. Every time that you feel that you have reached a place of harmony, it will seek to redefine itself again to move that harmony over into the expression of the unconscious. It is a never-ending battle if one is to walk within an unconscious state or one is to harbor the unconscious mind within the mind.

11.3 When the unconscious mind is dissolved, all suffering that does not preserve life, allow life, allow one to live in self-appreciation is dissolved with it. The purpose of the Clear Mind Experience is not to say that the unconscious mind is bad, or to negate its presence, or to negate the importance of its existence. It is half of the whole. It is what allows light to know itself. Because it is when one turns darkness to light that light can experience its light. What you will discover through the Clear Mind Experience is that the unconscious provides us with an incredible union of beauty when it is dissolved, not dismantled. In dismantling the unconscious, it becomes uncontrollable and cathartic. However, when it is dissolved, it becomes effortless. The Clear Mind Experience is the experience of sugar and water.

11.4 Take a moment to sit very peacefully. Take a moment within your breath to practice the Clear Mind three-part breath. As you practice that breath connect to it, connect to the middle breath. Feel within the middle breath the freedom of no longer living within the unconscious, of no longer being able to receive information from it, of being free of the mind chatter, of being free of the emotional disharmony, of being free of the collective unconscious. Contemplate on the power of allowing yourself this moment.

11.5 When one enters the discipline to dissolve the unconscious mind, life is created through the mystical presence of love, joy, peace and wisdom. Each opportunity being interpreted through a conscious mind. When life is walking towards the unconscious, allowing the unconscious to be active within our lives, then the individual is continually seeking answers as to why the presence of the unconscious mind is so disassociated from the presence of love. Human beings spend a great amount of time within the human condition attempting to define life beyond the unconscious mind. At times this can be pointless because the unconscious mind has no desire to let go of you. It cannot let go of you. It doesn't want to let go of you, and it is not programmed to do anything but preserve itself as you.

When you walk within a conscious mind dissolving the un-conscious mind, your mind becomes a place of deep com-passion. Each moment, each thought, and each breath becomes an opportunity to embrace what is not and to dissolve into what IS. There are very powerful moments within the process of this union because what could have been perceived as your most painful moment in life be-comes your most profound celebration of love within your brain. Within the perception of how you see yourself, each moment of each day becomes a celebration of the mysti-cal presence of love. When you allow yourself to live within this mystical presence of love, it will define itself through all aspects of your life because your outer experience will be an experience of how the universe perceives you within the presence of love, not within the presence of seeking. It is within a conscious mind, when the unconscious mind is being contained within the process of dissolving itself into love, that one will experience great momentum and transformation within their lives, and there will be great consistency and clarity surrounding their life, and no longer with their life become a journey of discovering what is truth, but they will be living within the realized presence of truth.

12.1 The beauty of dissolving the unconscious mind is that it will make the conscious mind realize itself. The conscious mind without realizing itself will simply operate in life. It can seem quite lifeless, quite disconnected within the stillness with no real mission or purpose as it is detached from the personal identity, and there may present a lifelessness to the condition. It is when the dis-solving the unconscious mind into the conscious mind that the conscious mind goes through an activation process where the vibration of resolve/solution is placed within the essence of the conscious mind and it becomes what is driven by purpose and understanding of itself. When the conscious mind moves to dissolve the unconscious, it 'realizes love'. The joy of realizing love through the five senses and the living experience is ecstatically blissful to the heart, the solar plexus, and the root. It is within realizing the presence of love that sexuality is redefined, union within man and woman, woman and woman, and man and man is redefined. It is in realizing love as the conscious mind, it is within the conscious mind realizing that it is the expression of love that true personal freedom is attained from the collective unconscious, and life becomes the harmony and rhythm of the three-part breath and the awareness to the unconditional state of love.

12.2 When we experience life within the unconscious, it becomes and aspect of each of our five primary relationships. It becomes the inegative self-talk of the child-mind. It becomes the iiself-judgment within the self-love perception. It becomes the iiilimitations of the living self. It becomes ivthe cathartic expression, and vimbalance and suppression of the emotional self; and the viconfusion and exhaustion of the spiritual self. When you merge within a conscious mind, the five primary relationships within your perception will be free to experience love. The child-mind will embrace self-discovery within the perception of unconditional love. Feeling supported within the presence of trust, within knowing that wisdom lives within each moment, self-love will be an expression of union with others, within relationships, within the relationship to oneself. Sexuality, the condition of self care, and the beauty of union will be refined through the expression. The living self will be an expression of the unlimited potential of wisdom, abundance, and joy when they make union and celebration of the spiritual self. The emotional self will be the vehicle in which one creates the perception of how they not only perceive reality, but how reality perceives them. The emotional self will become the expression of the IAM, and not the I'm not. The spiritual self will be the realization of love where each moment of each day is freedom as there is no perception of the unconscious.

12.3 When an individual becomes free of the unconscious mind, they also become free of the collective unconscious. It is within the dissolving of the unconscious that profound insight is moved and realized within the perceived mind of the individual. There is a refining process that happens within the five primary relationships that when refined redefines perceptions of the mind to that of the conscious mind. It is within the clarity and momentum of life that an individual knows that they are love, living love, expressing love, and it is within saying that 'IAM Love' and feeling the presence of love that profound insight about the rebuilding the union of one mind, the creation that exists and moves upon this planet will also be revealed. This planet has prepared itself for profound insight to be revealed to humanity. It can only be revealed within a Clear Mind, within a mind that is no longer associated with the unconscious mind, within a mind that is not plugged in to the collective unconscious. It is this refining process that will release humanity into the ascension of the profound insight and union of love.

13.1 "Why now?" Why is it important for this accelerated process to be able to dissolve the unconscious rather than living within the unconscious expression? And the reason is that the activation that has happened upon the planet is that thoughts manifest as quickly, and as fast and accurately as the unconscious mind has. That being said, there is a battle being drawn between the conscious mind and the unconscious mind, with one aspect of the planet moving forward to rebuild life within a conscious state of awareness, there is also the unconscious that is moving forward to take away from that experience and to encourage less effort and less articulated experience in a rebuilding of the planet. It is because of this that the time is now that one cannot walk behind the shadow attempting to get around it. One cannot have the shadow within their brain interfering with their visions. One does not need to understand what this shadow says or even hear its voice. The importance of this time is that we do not manifest and create thoughts that create the unconscious to create power on the planet. It is within this knowing that one must be released immediately from the unconscious; where it is dissolved, discarded, and not created from. The unconscious mind has pushed itself into every aspect of existence. It is present within everything; within money, within government, within health, within environments, within education, within development, within the earth, within resources, within nutrition, within spirituality. Its limitations are perceived daily. It is critically important that it be immediately dissolved; not engaged, not looked at, not engaged in through conversations in thought, word, or action. This is what has become as to what will take us into the new momentum for this planet. This new planet is a planet free of the unconscious.

13.2 It is important to realize is that this gift has been presented to humanity because it has been called forth because the light quotient of transformation has awakened beyond the unconscious. Now it is simply about sweeping it out of the planet. Humanity has spent many lifetimes struggling to go beyond its limitations, struggling how to understand how to transcend its limitations. It has been within that struggle that grace has engulfed the planet, has enfolded into, as love moved towards this planet to dissolve what isn't love just like your brain. Consciousness is the universal mind, and within the universal mind is the same process as the personal mind. There is the dissolving where conscious love moved towards what is not love and dissolves it into itself. The Clear Mind Experience is that love that has now descended upon the planet to dissolve into itself what is not love. It is here to dissolve the unconscious, both personal and collective. It has taken many lifetimes to descend upon the planet, but now it is here, and all that separates its mission being successful are the thoughts within the unconscious that speak to say that the unconscious is needed, claiming control through ideas that an individual may have gotten rid of enough of it that they shouldn't get rid of the rest, or that they need the unconscious because it gives them their identity. Holding on to it does nothing to serve anything but itself. It does nothing positive to hold onto it and create from within it. The realization comes in letting it go. It is in dissolving it that we are able to realize the pure essence of love. Universal mind has breathed the Clear Mind Experience onto the planet as a process that will draw love back into itself.

13.3 Within the Clear Mind Experience is the new way, is the pathway, where we are no longer walking into the shadow struggling to interpret what its suggestions mean to us. Then, once interpreting it one will at some point be set free so the conscious mind is able to speak. Within the Clear Mind Experience, conscious mind speaks all day to the unconscious, releases itself within the brain as thoughts, feelings, and emotions that become an expression of life that create within your family, that create within your career, that create within your opportunities in your life. The ultimate gift of the Clear Mind Experience is that in dissolving the unconscious, you receive tremendous clarity, tremendous insight that has tremendous momentum that is beyond human expression and limitation. The Clear Mind Experience is a rhythm that occurs within the brain. Once wisdom is activated within that rhythm, every single moment of existence becomes an opportunity for love to realize itself effortlessly through the feelings, and not feelings that are negative or experiences of loss and suffering, but feelings that are joyful, abundant, and unlimited. The Clear Mind Experience is programmed to awaken humanity through joy, no longer through suffering. The Clear Mind Experience is programmed with the knowing and the frequency that thoughts create, and within its expression, it will connect the individual to this power immediately because it is safe. The individual will no longer, through dealing with the unconscious, risk creating anything that is unconscious in the quest to understand the unconscious. When an individual mind activates into the Clear Mind Experience, an individual is set free to experience life within thought, within creation because it is safe, because their perception is aligned solely to the conscious mind while practicing the Clear Mind Experience.

13.4 The Clear Mind Experience is the inheritance of those that have worked so hard to transcend and go beyond what doesn't engulf the entire of humanity into love. The Clear Mind Experience is the gift of every man and woman and child that has sat within the light, prayed, walked within the darkness and prayed and believed that within every moment there is a moment beyond the darkness. It is within this call that the Book of Awareness has been gifted, that this sacred practice is now revealed into 'experience'. The Clear Mind Practice allows an individual to feel every molecule of love moving through to discover itself. It is the most profound romance within, upon, the planet.

13.5 Because of the frequencies upon the planet, and the fact that life is co-creating within every moment instantly, it is very important that those us that are here to awaken into the new perception do so immediately because we have to maintain the momentum of love continuously, otherwise, the other will be created and fed. Every time we allow ourselves to live within an unconscious expression, we feed the unconscious collectively, we create more within the unconscious in which it can act upon the planet. It is critically important at this time that we are aware, that we can live in love, that we are only love, that love is revealed within knowing, that we are free of what isn't. The Clear Mind process is an experience. It is the Experience to know that IAM.

13.6 Previously, when dealing with the unconscious, individuals have been able to clear aspects of it through realizations that occur within their life when questioning the direction, flow, and experiences that they are having within their life. They will be in an experience and look for higher meaning, and it has been through that discovery that individuals have been able to successfully dismantle the unconscious and remove aspects of it. The problem with this, and dissolving aspects of it, is that the brain is made up of electricity when we have the unconscious activated within it. It is because of this that we will be going along within our day to day and, all of a sudden, someone who was in a conscious state of awareness will move into an unconscious state of awareness, which is called an unconscious trance state, where they are not aware of how they got there, they become disassociated from their feelings, and the unconscious mind begins to co-create within their lives. This happens because the unconscious has been dismantled. When you dismantle the unconscious mind, it does not decompress. It forms potholes within the brain, so when the electrical currents are running through the mind, through the brain, they will slip into one of these potholes. It is within a pothole that you become a trance state. When you practice the Clear Mind Experience, the unconscious aspect of the brain, the neuro-pathways within the brain dry up like raisins, they decompress. In this decompressing process, the electrical currents within the brain cannot activate them, and because the entire unconscious has been decompressed, there are no potholes. The mind becomes conscious. The unconscious becomes contained within a decompressed, dried up state of brain matter that is not able to send signifiers through the feeling system to be acted on.

13.7 It is important within this current flow and condition of humanity that the divine criteria between the conscious and the unconscious mind be revealed, released, and activated within each being's individual perception. That the divine criteria of the conscious mind moving upon the unconscious mind to dissolve it be activated, as it is within this activation that the collective unconscious, all thoughts, feelings, and emotions that are created within humanity to represent the whole, will be dissolved as they will be deactivated. It is not about fixing the world. It is not about looking at the problems and the conditions and changing them. It is about disengaging from the collective unconscious so it will fade away. We are the electrical currents that feed it. If we dissolve the personal unconscious, we will not be able to see the collective unconscious. We are able to see it because we have the means in which to perceive it through the individual unconscious. Due to the position of humanity at this time, the frequency of the earth at this time, the karmic condition in which the earth is moving, it is important that the personal unconscious be dissolved so as to disengage from the collective unconscious so the new planet can live - breathe. It is already functioning. It is already living. Many perceive it, many don't. Many sort of perceive it, some long for it. It is simultaneously operating at the same time. It is not about fixing an unconscious world. It is about perceiving a conscious world.

14.1 Due to the rise in consciousness on the planet, there is not the time available to live within the unconscious mind. Every moment that we live within the unconscious, we allow it to create within perception, and within this creation, it affects relationships, opportunity, ourselves, and others. It limits our ability to receive. It limits our ability to be able to live within vision, and within this vision, create, allow, and bring forth all that is needed for our new planet. The unconscious is what does not want this planet to wake up because within its awakening, it has no role. You cannot convince it to join you, or heal it so it gets out of the way. You must walk in the opposite direction. Clearing it from within your brain does not allow you to magnetize it within your life from the unconscious collectively. When it is clear within the mind, it is clear within life. We are clearing the universal mind of the unconscious. The Clear Mind Experience has descended upon the planet as the expression of love to fold the unconscious into it. It is in allowing yourself to do this that you will spend all of your life within a conscious mind, living within the frequency of love that can co-create and live love within each moment of life, within each moment of your day, within your career, relationships, parenting, relationship to nutrition, relationship to abundance, within your perception of the first seven years of your life, within your emotions, within how you allow wisdom to define itself within your life. When living without the unconscious, all of these expressions will be free and clear to be defined by love.

14.2 It has been through the focus on wisdom, light, transformation, and awakening that the activation of the quickening has occurred upon the earth. The next phase for us is to within the quickening, use the quickening to dissolve the unconscious. The unconscious mind has moved itself into the same speed as wisdom. It is running very fast. Many ways in which is expresses itself have now gone to the internet, to media, television, and different forms that allow it to have great speed upon the planet. Where immediate gratification of an unconscious experience is accessible within each moment. The unconscious mind has attacked the minds, it has attacked sexuality, it has attacked the perception of loving oneself. Wisdom is able to move as quickly as the unconscious within the Clear Mind Experience. Through the three-part breath, wisdom moves at great speed. It is within that great speed that it is able to move into, fold into, and dissolve the unconscious. The quickening of our transformation has provided us with the grace of this freedom. This is the day of tremendous freedom; where we as a generation do not have to host the unconscious, do not have to be in battle with the unconscious, do not have to live within the unconscious, but allow the magnificence and mystical presence of love to descend and awaken and enlighten the mind so the perception is one of profound light and insight that honors the experience, the knowing, the relationship, and the beauty of the unlimited potential of love.

14.3 There are many of you upon the planet at this time who realize that there is a profound quickening that presents to each of us a sense of urgency. The urgency is to awaken beyond preconceived limitations, fear, control, harm, violence, disease, and lack. There is also the fact that many have attempted to heal the unconscious, to awaken abundance within its perception, to pray upon violence, to attempt to heal disease, to attempt to take those out of fears through positive affirmations. However, you cannot heal the unconscious. You cannot affirm anything to the unconscious that will allow it to perceive anything differently. You cannot heal a disease of the unconscious. You cannot teach violence to become peace, and you cannot get lack to awaken abundance. You can, however, dissolve these limitations. Like sugar and water, you can dissolve violence within the perception. You can dissolve disease and lack within the perception. When you dissolve it within the perception, you will realize abundance, realize peace, realize wellness, realize life beyond these limitations. Life is about realizing these new perceptions and dissolving the old.

14.4 Within the quickening, we have incurred a tremendous karmic gift upon this planet. The quickening is to dissolve the personal unconscious which dissolves the collective unconscious by deactivating its presence on the planet. This planet has always had to live within the unconscious; has spent lifetimes attempting to get beyond it, to understand it, to know how to work with it, to be resolved to it. Today we get to create and awaken a new planet, to go beyond the unconscious interpretation of this earth, to not engage in it, to no longer see it, to no longer perceive it, to not have to live healing it; to be in the current state of 'IAM the presence of love within life now', not as a thought, not as a desire of the unconscious, but as a 'conscious feeling'. Because the conscious mind realizes itself within the feeling when the unconscious mind is not there to challenge the feeling, to challenge the knowing, to challenge the present, to challenge the realization. Then the conscious mind will activate the feeling. 'IAM the presence of love within life now' will be the feeling of the moment. This is our karmic gift upon this planet: to realize love now.

15.1 Dissolving the unconscious mind is a commitment to get on with business of the light. It is a commitment to no longer sit within the idea that we can be light, we can be conscious, and we can shift this earth. It is about finding the presence of love within through clearing the mind of the unconscious; standing up within the universe and saying, "IAM the light. Within the light, IAM creating, living, knowing, expressing, and revealing each moment of wisdom that is able to live within the presence of love." When we dissolve the unconscious mind, we no longer look at what isn't. We no longer try to get beyond what isn't. We no longer try to heal what isn't. We don't sit in suffering with a story of how to overcome. We have overcome. We are in knowing, as there is an activation of memory that occurs within the flow of the three-part breath and the rhythm of the experience, the rhythm of the invocations that invoke conscious awareness within the mind. It becomes the discipline. As within a conscious state of awareness, there is a profound discipline to only be within the conscious mind. There is no discussion. There is no seeking. There is no looking to be. There/here is IAM.

15.2 Clearing the mind of the unconscious allows us to create. It allows us to live within the perception and birth new ideas, concepts, structures, and movements at a speed that's able to elevate us into the next level of this conscious awakening. Within life, within our awareness, within the transformation of this planet at this time, there is the request and the need that the awakening happen at lightening speed. There is no longer the casual walk through life, the pondering, the questioning, the sitting within the meditation for the reflection. This has left. What is available now is the revelation, the realization, the moving forward, the creation, the knowing, and the living.

The union of this life for us is to be the living expression of love. Life at this point is the alchemy of human incarnation and realization of a conscious mind living as an expression of love. It is the generation of ecstatic bliss. The generation of celebrating consciousness, where consciousness is revealed as the celebration of love taking form, of love living within form, of love expressing wisdom as a parent, of love expressing wisdom as a child, of expressing wisdom in union with self-love, in union with the body, in union with the emotion.

Life at this point is about perceiving the unlimited expression of love in so many, so many, so many forms as what exist upon this planet. It is the time to honor the earth as she is our environment, she is our mother. She allows us to live within her potential as our potential, as love. When we place our hands within the soil, within the oceans, within the sky, within the sun, within the wind, we are living within the realized expression and beauty of what love IS, and what is available to us at this time. We have spent so many lifetimes seeking love, standing behind a wall of illusion that says, "What's love? Where are you going to find love? How do you become love?" The Clear Mind Experience dissolves that wall within a moment, collapses it to ash upon the ground, at which you walk away and say, "IAM love." Turning around from the wall, not walking through the wall, but turning in the opposite direction, walking back in the path in which you came, and each step you take within the Clear Mind breath provides a realization of where you once stepped within thought, word, action, or emotion. And as love steps upon that ground, steps within the rhythm of your life, it defines where you have once been within your mind, within your feelings. And within that re-definition, there is a realization of IAM.

15.3 It is when we walk upon the path as 'IAM', we have entered a state of being. It is the Clear Mind Experience that clears the mind to have the realization, over and over and over, IAM. When we create from the perception of IAM, we create an opportunity for all life to be preserved, honored, awakened within the presence of love.

15.4 When an individual mind creates from the perception of IAM, they become one; where their personal mind becomes one with the collective and they express life as the universal mind, so within they are the presence of love stating, "IAM humanity." It is in realizing that each man is of the other that love is cultivated; that the mystical beauty and presence of grace that is available upon the planet to restore, elevate, and re-create our earth is preserved. The beauty of our existence is the self-appreciation to honor the magnificence of love. The beauty of our earth is to honor the momentum of abundance, and it is within honoring the momentum of abundance by believing 'IAM the unlimited potential serving within humanity' that creates within our lives the freedom to live within a new planet. It is not an expectation of each man upon this planet to somehow fix it. It is, however, the calling of this planet to let go collectively as one body of the unconscious which is every thought, feeling, and emotion that does not serve love. When we do this, then the planet will be free of these thoughts.

16.1 This is the collective shift that we are making at this time; to dissolve the unconscious both personally and collectively. The role that has been undertaken within the Clear Mind Experience is that this opportunity to clear the unconscious will be brought to the forefront of spiritual and psychological communities, as it is these two communities that are pioneering new developments and opportunities within living within a perception that does not allow us to live within the dysfunction of the unconscious. The Clear Mind Experience is the bridge into this new experience because it dissolves what hangs on to these communities.

16.2 The role of the Clear Mind Experience is to create personal freedom within the mind of the individual so they can realize the presence of love within their own perception, and within that perception, dissolve the unconscious collectively by disengaging in it and no longer serving within it. And then, within the collapse of the unconscious, the individual and humanity are able to rise up within the celebration of consciousness and live a new life. The Clear Mind Experience is the moment, the middle breath, for the spiritual communities of the world and the psychological communities of the world to take a moment to clear what is not, to live what IS.

The Clear Mind Experience is about bringing union within one mind. Let's look at that for a minute. It is about bringing union within the personal mind, where the conscious mind dissolves the unconscious into itself, and the personal identity dissolves with that because the personal perception becomes a conscious expression of love. Within that process, the unconscious mind is dissolved into the presence of love within humanity and can no longer function as the unconscious. It is at that point that the unconscious mind has dissolved into the universal mind. What this means is the universal mind has restored all of these parts to the presence of love, and within that has become one mind again. As the universal mind created life, it created separation. It created the unconscious as a means in which to rediscover itself by realizing itself as the thinking essence of creation that has thought us into being. And in thinking us into being, it has returned its thoughts to that of love, and realized 'IAM love.' Within this realization, humanity will exist within a celebrated awareness of consciousness; celebrating life, celebrating every molecule of human existence as an expression of discovery, revelation, and the living presence of love.

16.3 The beauty of this moment is that we have as humanity been given permission, have been activated, have the karmic awakening that it is time not to seek love. It is time, as love is revealed.

16.4 The magnificence of this moment is that this awakening of love is upon the planet, and all upon the planet are included within the opportunity to experience this profound shift of love. It is the unconscious mind that keeps us separate; unconscious thoughts that separate individual mind from love. This is the most magnificent opportunity to be alive, as it is the moment where love realizes itself as every individual living being upon the planet. Allowing yourself to reside within a still mind, allowing yourself to dissolve the personal mind into the presence of love, a conscious mind that then dissolves into the universal mind as celebrated consciousness is your calling.

16.5 As nature allows herself the re-creation, re-growth, to be re-energized within each moment, to celebrate her beauty, where one part dies and another part is reborn, so does humanity, so does the brain. When you allow the unconscious thoughts to decompress, dry up, and dissolve, you allow for re-growth, re-birth, re-energized awareness within your perception of life. So many beings are disheartened at this time, confused, fearing 2012 and what will take place. So many beings look at the world, look at the problems, look at wars, look at pornography, look at addictions, look at limitations, look at our youth, and feel overwhelmed within the lossness of preservation of good-ness. But you are only witnessing the unconscious. Walk in the opposite direction. Drop it now. Take three Clear Mind breaths. Move back. Turn around. Walk back through your life, and every footstep that you take will be a re-creation, re-growth, re-energized awareness, and as you step, the beauty of nature will support you. She will re-energize your life, just as she is re-energized. You will allow magnificence to be born within your courage to move through life as an expression of the unlimited potential of love. Love can re-create. Love can awaken. Love can prosper. Love is the wisdom to live within the beauty and the stillness of allow-ing the season of life, the moment of life, to breathe.

16.6 - 16.6i Just as nature, so is our mind. The nature of the mind is that one perception dies and another one is born. That is what is available within the human mind; one perception can be no longer, and a new perception can be experienced. The beauty of the Clear Mind Experience is that it does not tell you who you are, who you are going to be. It allows the frequency of wisdom to define itself as you. It allows you to dissolve what thinks it's you. It allows the limitations to die. It allows the expectations to die. It allows the disease, the lack, fear, the control, the distrust, the disharmony, shame, the blame, the anxiety to die. And within dissolving these qualities: the birth of trust, support, a feeling of being nurtured, the feeling of being embraced, the realization of Inner Knowing will occur. It is a spontaneous awakening within the human perception, where the human perception becomes no more, where the human perception becomes the spiritual knowing where there is no me. There is IAM, and IAM the next man, and the next woman, and the next child. IAM within my expres-sion to these beings honoring, loving, revealing, and know-ing all that IAM; all potential, all love, as each living moment is one breath moving into the next breath; love folding in and out of itself from one man to the next; the beauty of human perception.

Birthing Wisdom through a Clearing of the Unconscious

17.1 The unconscious is always dismantling itself; every time a man has sat to meditate, a woman has sat to meditate, someone has entered self-development, someone has entered the realm of wisdom, someone has spontaneously awoken, someone has felt their calling home, they are dismantling aspects of the unconscious. There are always the moments within every moment of existence where the perception is moving slowly, some quicker than others, into the new identification, the new level of awareness, the new perception. However, when you're walking towards the unconscious attempting to figure out how to become free of it, it is continually manifesting and presenting itself within actions, thoughts, desires, creativity, education, awareness, and assistance. It is going into each of these perceptions and redefining it to wisdom that has allowed humanity to wake up at the speed in which a person can experience transformation within their living experience everyday. When you have to translate awakening into physical objectivity of living and functioning within your life, the awakening can be slowed down. It can be a laboring process. When the transformation happens spontaneously within the brain and it's activated to the rhythm of the breath, then the transformation and awakening is happening within every single moment with no repercussions to the outside of your existence. The outside will move at the speed in which you breathe, will move at the speed at which you realize love through the three-part breath. Therefore, great momentum, speed, clarity, and rhythm will become your life. Life will not be hindered. Awakening will not be slowed down, but the awakening process will be accelerated, and the acceleration sustained within the momentum that wisdom is unfolding at the speed in which you breathe. When you connect this to the three-part breath, there becomes no personal choice, no energy needed, no day where one decides, "Should I' or 'Will I' experience wisdom today?" "Will I let go of something today?" It becomes a spontaneous movement where every single moment of every single day, you are awakening within the conscious mind, within the presence of love.

17.2 The transformation of the Clear Mind Experience does not warrant a belief structure that it will work. Transformation happens extremely fast because the unconscious mind does not believe that you will change because it believes that it's you. It does not believe that you will fold into love because it believes that it is you, and it knows that it is seeking love, seeking to understand what the conscious mind is speaking about. It is in this seeking of what the conscious mind is speaking about that it moves close to it, but does not fold into it. When you do the Clear Mind Experience, the conscious mind engulfs the unconscious, swallows it up, dissolves it, like sugar and water.

So much of the transformation that is happening upon the planet is moving through the judgment of the unconscious. It seeks to fix, reflect, look at, ponder, contemplate, understand, continually revisits what love could possibly be to it while creating the limitations within the outer experience, always allowing an individual to be pushing up against what they wish they were, what they would long to experience. The gift of the Clear Mind Experience and the birth of this process is that the shift in awareness is able to happen as quickly as a person is prepared to practice it. The practice is accumulative. It is not based on time. It's based on number of times practiced because within the Clear Mind Experience, the unconscious mind is the structure that is dismantled from the top to the bottom.

When you practice the Clear Mind Experience, you are not encouraged to fix. You are not encouraged to change. You are immediately activated into a state of being. It is just about creating and allowing the space within your mind; that you are a state of being, and it is life experience becoming harmonized, filled with clarity, supported within a rhythm of love that allows the perception to let go.

18.1 The unconscious mind has always been fascinating to the planet. To those upon the planet, they have spent many hours seeking ways to understand its conditions. The unconscious mind fills a great portion of this planet. It fills a great amount of time of each person upon the planet. Within each day, people are either engaging within it, from the perception that they are the unconscious. They are suffering from it. They are seeking separation from it. They are being controlled from it. They are being held captive within their perception that the unconscious mind and what it perceives is the only way for them to live. The unconscious mind has taken great resources of this planet. It has taken great time for those who have discovered new ways to understand it, great resources in researching how it plays out within each person's life within each day. It is within this discovery process that there have been great strides made in ways to maintain the unconscious, supporting the ideas of why it should remain here. People will openly defend why it's needed, why it serves, why they should maintain relationship to it. It is this story that comes from the unconscious. The unconscious being separate from the presence of love believes it's all that is. So within every turn, within every statement, within every thought, experience, and opportunity, it is defending its role within the lives of individuals. The unconscious mind is present personally within a person's perception, and collectively within life. It is the personal perception and the collective unconscious that form union. The unconscious mind collectively will create lifestyle, will create experiences, relationships that will reinforce the personal perception of the unconscious. It is this overwhelming union that those of the light, those that have begun to separate and remove their perception of the unconscious feel overwhelmed by. Even light workers today are consumed in servicing the unconscious; how to heal people in its repercussions, how to show people what it's saying to them, with no real solution on how to get out of it. It has been this quagmire that has had light workers, within the light quotient of transformation, feel bogged down. "How do we set ourselves free?" they say. "How do I experience personal freedom?" they repeat. But they are speaking to the unconscious, so in response, the unconscious will present what will hang onto them, of ways they can't move, of limitations of abundance, of limitations of opportunities. The unconscious mind has been studied upon this planet for lifetimes. Kingdoms, governments, countries have been built on its belief structures. However, you cannot fix the unconscious. You can only walk away from it. And within walking in the opposite direction, where it is behind, will slowly dissolve, disappear and no longer be. As an individual it is important to perceive, "How have I supported the unconscious mind? Where do I defend its presence? Where do I say, 'Oh, but I need to look at the part of myself. Oh, I need to protect that part because this is how I feel. Oh, this is how it's serving me.'" Where, within life, is that experience being had? And through the use of the Clear Mind Experience dissolving the thought right now within the moment; no longer co-creating, living within the life that is an expression of the unconscious. It is our role on the planet within this generation that we no longer study or seek to understand this condition, or seek to understand the unconscious. It's irrelevant. It's dead. Walk away. Create, awaken, know, live, liberate into the presence of love.

18.2 The unconscious mind is the fantasy, is the aspect of the brain that perceived the separation to love. It is the aspect of mind that lived within the separation from love. It is what karmically incarnates us into the next lifetime. What we believed within the unconscious brings us into form. It is what allows us to continue to accumulate light quotient because it has been previously in overcoming its perceptions that one is to believe that they are not that, so each lifetime incarnating to have these future, further, progressive realizations that 'IAM love.' The unconscious mind has stored what does not perceive love. And because love is the seeming reality, the unconscious mind is the fantasy. It is continually stimulating perception to say, "'Well, what if?' 'But how do you know?' 'But what if it doesn't?' 'But can I?' 'But can you?' 'But will you?' 'But do you?'" It's continually questioning. It's programmed to question as the mirror so one says, "IAM." If you are walking behind the shadow, towards the shadow, you will be exhausted saying "IAM" because you will always have the perception that the unconscious mind is out in front. When the unconscious mind is placed behind you through the process of the Clear Mind Experience, you are walking towards the light, as the light, in the knowing of IAM. It is this presence, this strength of virtue, this knowingness that doesn't allow the unconscious to be heard. It becomes irrelevant. It cannot challenge, will not encourage. Because a question will come before a statement. However, walking behind you, within the Clear Mind Experience, the unconscious asks the question of the statement; which gives one the feeling that IAM.

18.3 Within the first seven years of our lives, we are witness to our environments with a program running within the perception that says, "Who am I?" It is during those first seven years of our lives that we develop the feeling center. We develop the feeling center that will generate thoughts from a conscious or unconscious perception. When the feeling moves, the perception engages the unconscious or the conscious mind. The difficulty with this aspect of creation for overcoming the unconscious when it is not being dissolved is that the unconscious mind runs down into perception so gravity will pull it into play. Once an individual is continually moving in and out of the unconscious at a rapid rate, the unconscious mind will take over perception. This happens to 99.9% of humanity up until 1997, and now it happens to 79% of humanity, decreasing continually as the new incarnates join the planet. The new incarnates joining the planet don't have the capacity to let go of the unconscious mind because it feels etheric to them. There is no grounded electrical current running for them. They have to move outside of themselves to process the unconscious which is another discussion. However, for most of the population of the planet in the first seven years of their lives, they witness reality, and within the witnessing of reality they have the feeling within themselves, "IAM Love" the statement "IAM Love, IAM All, IAM Love." Each moment that they experience reality and the feeling, of not being within the presence of love, is experienced, that feeling moves within them as one of the 49 unconscious perceptions of love. Once age seven comes, there is an articulated expression, a movement that happens within the brain through development that they believe that they have a stronger personal will and need less supervision. Then the childhood up through adolescence to adulthood becomes about fostering that lack of supervision, that not needing of supervision, that "I am old enough. Let me go. I can do this alone." Once a child really expedites this process and they become an adolescent, then the unconscious mind and the conscious mind express themselves as the child engaged within reality where the collective unconscious will return favor and speak to the child's mind through how they are perceiving. The greater number of the population are perceiving through the unconscious. So it is the unconscious that will be co-created. Every time a child is born, or has been born, that has lived through an unconscious first seven years primarily, where their predominant expression is unconscious, meaning they are not able to perceive truth, they are not able to perceive the ultimate love, then the planet has further collective unconscious created. Further energy to overcome. Further energy to engage in. Further unconscious expression that now can be believed in. To clear the planet, we must clear the collective. To clear the collective, we must clear the personal. To clear the personal, we must feel within the feeling center 'IAM Love.' In the first seven years of life, the 'IAM' becomes distorted because we are saying, "Who am I?" As a child stands within the environment and witnesses all that participates within the environment, the child will internalize the feelings of what it feels like to be in that environment, storing always interpretations of the 49 qualities of feelings that create thought and expression. The 49 feelings when negative attract thought and interpretation and experience. The 49 qualities when conscious express vibration and allow movement that celebrates the vibration upon the planet. There is no collective unconscious when everybody is within the conscious mind because we just become lightbody frequency movement, having an experience of the conscious mind, perceiving the unlimited potential of its creation. As the speed and vibration of the conscious mind increases on the planet, form will change. There will be less density within the form. Rather than the body being made up of such high quotient levels of water, the body will have less water, less matter, high frequency. The conscious mind creates the heaviness upon the planet of physical form to hang onto itself. That will change. Obesity on this planet is not from the personal unconscious, it is from the collective. The collective unconscious creates it as its anchors. It is said by humanity that it is the spiritual, emotional and physical responsibility of the person that is overweight to heal the form. However, it is the collective unconscious that is creating within their form so as to feed itself of negative, self-loathing, judgmental thoughts within humanity. This being said it would be more productive for the individual if the population, if humanity cleared their thoughts to allow the personal freedom to those that suffer within the collective. We are all affecting one another within each moment, within each day. Every time a question comes, "Should I clear the unconscious?" think of a child. Think of someone suffering within the collective. Ask yourself again. It is time to let go, to honor the process, to honor the unconscious by giving it its defined role, the purpose in which it was created. It was created to help us align to the light. It is the greatest gift given to humanity when it is not studied, adored, worshipped, or allowed.

The first seven years of our lives give union of the unconscious. It presents it. It is the most sacred time of our development. It is where the karma of why we came to the parents we came, the environment in which we came, who we will become, what the unconscious will define as us is all created, accumulated within the first seven years. It is our bridge to love.

18.4 If you take time to reflect upon the unconscious mind, it speaks only in the negative. Within each moment, it seeks transformation, seeks change, seeks for life to be different, seeks for life to have new meaning, seeks for life to change, seeks for form to change, seeks for the mind to change, seeks for the people around it to change, seeks for everything to be different, and it does this because it seeks immediate gratification within the moment. If you took everything that the unconscious mind stated to you and created it within form, all the ways it said you would have happiness, you would get to the point of what you had created, you would be sitting within the creation and the unconscious mind would say, "But are you really happy?" The unconscious mind can't sit in peace. It can't celebrate consciousness. It can't say, "Look there's a creation." It can't say, "Look, there's a moment." It can't say, "Look, I'm in an experience." And within that experience is radiance, is love, is allowing, is knowing, is oneness, kindness, compassion, union, and love. It has no capacity to do this. If you listen to the thoughts of the unconscious, it's all about moving out of, moving away from, retraction because every suggestion of the unconscious is to take you out of love, and when I say 'you' I mean 'the perception.' 'You' is the perception. You are only a perception, a perceived experience of life living in a conscious or unconscious expression. Thoughts allow perception to create. Thoughts within the unconscious create through perception. When living within a conscious mind, frequency, vibration, color, and insight experience itself. It doesn't create because it lives within as the creation. It lives within perception as the IAM. So the outside is the validation of the Inner Knowing. Whereas when you are within the unconscious mind, the outside is continually trying to define you through limitation; closing you down, down, down, down, down. Even when you are connected to the light and wisdom, there is always the collective unconscious trying to get you to believe something else. If you listen to the unconscious mind, it's a retraction from love that will tell you all the ways that you cannot feel love, feel trust, feel beauty, feel knowing, feel wisdom, feel compassion, feel joy, feel nurtured, feel honored, feel supported. It will not allow you to have these experiences, and it will create around you all that is needed so you forget love.

18.5 Conscious mind, conscious expression is what is able to perceive, articulate, experience, receive, and give the 49 qualities of love. It is a refined process of expression. The conscious mind does not think, it perceives. The perception moves through feeling. It moves feeling within perception, awakens wisdom to express the validation of the IAM presence that is living outside as life. The conscious mind is the gift, the vibration, the movement, the expression, the color, the light that lives clear, transparent awareness to love within thought, action, speech.

18.6 The unconscious mind are all thought, feelings, emotions that are not able to articulate, receive, express love. It is all thoughts, words, and actions that do not preserve the beauty, the magnificence, the radiance, the integrity, the divine code of love and life. The unconscious mind is dense, but subtle. It is revealed, but hidden. It is expressing, but retracting. It draws life into itself in a greed consumed to re-create, to seek identity within each moment to say 'look at me.' It cannot say 'IAM.' It will say 'I am here.' It does not have humility. It has longing. It does not have kindness. It has self-judgment. It does not allow for the man alongside of you as it sees itself and what it wants to achieve to be. It harbors resentment for life, frustration for what it cannot do, cannot have, and cannot will into being. It believes it's the creator. It does not celebrate creation, but it feels entitled to receive, to live, to be, to get.

19.1 The unconscious mind will always present different levels of interpretation that present the struggle to perceive love and question love. It will be continually seeking the means in which to find love so as it can finally engage in love. The unconscious mind has created a spiritual identity for itself known as 'the seeker.' "I must find the truth. I must become the truth. I must learn how to live within the truth." It will have you create rituals. It will have you feel separate from the world. It will have you see the world, despise the world, and see the world as the obstacle. It will have you perceive children, noise, experience, career, responsibilities, progress as what creates a separation from truth. However, this is an unconscious interpretation because the interpretations within the wholeness do not preserve life. When we speak of preserving life, we mean preserving love within how I am perceiving each moment. You cannot preserve life within an outer interpretation, experience, relationship, or person. You can only preserve love within your own perception, and within that preserving of love within personal perception, you will only create, live, attract experiences that honor that within the conscious mind expression.

The unconscious mind will have one believe that it needs to seek love, to be on a quest to find love, and the whole time that the person is seeking and is upon on the quest to find the truth, the unconscious mind is contradicting their experience, asking them are they really having the experience? Does truth really exist? Does that teacher really provide it to you? Is it really going to happen to you? Are you ever going to find love? Is all of this really real? These are all statements of the unconscious. To perception, while you have perception as human experience, life is real. The unconscious mind is the lie. The conscious mind the expression of creation is the expression and experience of love.

Love can be real through form because it must be taken through the feelings. You have the hands, the feet, the finger pads, and the foot pads that touch the earth that believe within that moment 'IAM human expression.' It is within being and living as human expression that you are having an experience and it is real to touch. When you say to the mind 'none of this is real', the mind perceives a loss of life. It, after years of that statement, will become lifeless, will despise responsibility because that is what the unconscious mind wants you to believe. The first statement is "None of this is real. None of this matters. I don't have to engage. It doesn't matter. I will retract." When the individual perception retracts, it moves into a shadow. Within that shadow, it moves into a darkness. Within that darkness, it feels a separation. Within the separation, it experiences resentment. Within the resentment, it experiences lifelessness. Within the lifelessness, it experiences blame. Within the blame, it experiences further separation from those that it blames. This is a cycle. It is a one-way street into an unconscious separation from love. As my feet walk upon the earth, as my hands touch the soil, as my body swims within the ocean, as my eyes perceive the stars, as the sun warms the crown, as my sun warms the body, life is real. As I see a child cry, as I see a child laugh, as I see the beauty of nature, as I see a bud return upon and grow within the heart of releasing a leaf from a tree, life is real. When we tell the mind that life is not real and it does not matter, we remove the beauty of creation that within every moment there is something growing, something moving, something breathing, something living, and it is within our control as human perception to perceive each of these moments in conscious awareness, dissolving what wishes for you to retract.

19.2 The most sacred offering of the Clear Mind Experience is the divinity and the divine order encoded within

the unconscious mind. The unconscious mind is a structure. It is a set structure of commands. The commands
when creating the unconscious mind are a set of sequences that activate the perception to perceive 49 negative interpretations that separate the perception from love,
that develop the identity of the individual to believe that
it is a limited expression of love with limited qualities that
need to be redefined, recalibrated, and reawakened to understand that there is difference and opportunity within living as a man or a woman. However, the beauty of the
Clear Mind Experience is that we know it is a structure, so
when we go in to dissolve it, we dissolve it within the structure. We walk backwards through the set of commands
dissolving each piece one at a time. Each of the 49 signifiers that are created within the unconscious mind are dissolved every 21 days. It is a set of sequences that dissolve
the unconscious. The gift of dissolving the unconscious as
a perceived structure is that the structure stays erect and
does not flood the entire brain matter which then articulates mass animation of an unconscious perception. There
can be great pain in dismantling the unconscious because
it will flood itself through the seven key emotions that
allow thoughts, words, and actions to be carried forth upon
the planet.

If you think of dismantling a structure, if it's not dismantled in order, if we don't take the roof off but blow up
the floor, then the building will explode. It will fill the
neighborhood with dirt and dust. No one will be able to
see. Everyone will be inhaling the pollution, and life within
that neighborhood for one moment will be a dust cloud
of destruction. And no one will be able to see what has
happened until the dust settles. It is much the same of
the unconscious. If you go and randomly try to dismantle
aspects of it, it will collapse. Within the collapsing will be

trance states of the unconscious where it will animate itself. The individual will feel that they are regressing spiritually rather than progressing spiritually. The unconscious mind will not have decompressed. The unconscious mind through the Clear Mind Experience decompresses, which means it loses all electrical current and flow into itself, dries up much like a raisin. Then the process itself moves backwards through the 49 signifiers that have been created through the language of the planet and it is dissolved. It is in knowing this that it makes the unconscious mind doable, accessible, understandable, and irrelevant. This technology is very vital. It's important to the new direction of frequency of this planet. Dissolving the unconscious mind is critical in the next step. However, knowing that its 49 signifiers that you are going in to dissolve every 21 days is simple. The Clear Mind Experience is accumulative. It does not depend upon belief structure to be successful. If we were to present you with a solution to the unconscious, and say you had to believe it would be dissolved, that would be foolish. Basically, we would be saying that the unconscious mind had to believe that it could get rid of itself. The process itself operates. It operates as the experience to dissolve what is not love. It is like the Creator is placing a droplet of water every time that you breathe on the unconscious and dissolving it. That is the grace of the unconscious mind, that it's there to be dissolved, and it is within dissolving it that new feelings are born, that the presence of love is born, that the expression of love is revealed, and the realization of why one would incarnate into form living as the presence of love to be able to look, perceive, understand, express, and experience life in such magnificence is all revealed within the dissolving of the unconscious mind. It is the gift. It is the moment without the struggle. It is the beauty. It is for all those that hang on to the unconscious, guarding it, protecting it. All the children, all the adults that were the children that had to hang on and protect themselves from the pain can now put down their weapons that protect them, can drop their thoughts that protect them, and merge within the magnificent rhythm of love, allowing the mind to awaken to the perception that 'IAM the living expression of love.'

Together

20.1 When one is teaching or experiencing or practicing the Clear Mind Experience, they are taught to perceive reality within two halves. All of a sudden, the mind goes from being the individual mind into two minds where one mind speaks to the other mind. This is encouraged to awaken the child-mind. It is done so the child-mind can perceive that it is not stuck behind the unconscious thoughts. It is taught to slowly engage and look and perceive the unconscious thoughts and say, "Well, I am not you. I am not going to perceive life as you. IAM Love. I do not need to have this negative experience. That's a limitation. I am not that. IAM Love." And we do this to create the separation to the unconscious firstly. This is very important, not because it is this change in perception that shifts the unconscious. It is because this change in perception activates the permission for the unconscious mind to be dissolved. If the individual is acknowledging within the universe and within the universal contract they no longer need the unconscious mind, that they are bearing witness to the unconscious mind and that it is time to be set free from the unconscious, it activates on many levels the freedom that one needs to experience, that one needs to pertain to express to become free from the unconscious. It gives practice to the fact that everyday that the unconscious mind is dissolving, an individual has given the permission. It is a powerful expression because as the Clear Mind Experience begins to create movement within the brain, the individual is allowing the movement by continually staying within the stillness that 'IAM Love.' It is at this point that the rational mind gains feeling of what it feels like to feel love and then allows the transformation to move incredibly quickly.

We separate the mind into two halves. We are allowing the coming together. We are placing on one side of the perception what is not love while activating the conscious mind within the other aspect of perception, and through the process of the Clear Mind Experience, the conscious mind is moving in and dissolving the unconscious mind. This can only happen when they are perceived to be separate. There has to be a moving into and moving from.

20.2 It is through the conscious and the unconscious minds appearing to be separate and folding in and out of one another that the perception of love increases in awareness because each time the conscious mind enters the unconscious and the unconscious seeks the validation of love and love says IAM, there is a feeling associated with what that feels like to have dissolved an aspect of the unconscious that has almost kept the mind as a slave to its story, and then within that feeling, an individual is set free. It is the feeling of being free that creates the realization of love to occur. It can happen many times throughout a day. Typically, a person can feel that feeling two or three or four or five times in one lifetime. Through the Clear Mind Experience, it is happening multiple times throughout a day because it happens every single time you dissolve one of the 49 signifiers, and you're dissolving one every 21 days that can occur upon any day within the 21 days.

20.3 Defining love within the process of the Clear Mind Experience, within the process of this book is important. When we define love, we define love as universal love. Universal love is one mind, the universal mind. Within that universal mind are the conscious and unconscious perceptions. When we talk about ultimate love, we talk about the conscious mind realizing the presence of love that exists within the universal mind; taking what is unconscious into itself, and through the feeling of that entering its expression, love is realized which can then express itself.

The primary quality of universal love is unconditional love. It is the unconditional love that allows love to find itself because it unconditionally draws the unconscious mind into itself. It does not have a means in which to protect itself because it is there to experience both as one. The overriding mission of love is within us. It is the feeling, the purpose, and the realization of love's presence. We realize the presence of love through the conscious and unconscious mind union. It is realizing this love through their union and coming together that allows us to feel the presence of love. Once the unconscious mind has dissolved into the conscious mind, the IAM will become an expression of universal love. The unconditional qualities of love that see no darkness, see no shadow, see no difference because it has dissolved what kept the shadow experiencing life into itself so it has no fear of its existence. It has no fear that the unconscious can create because it has transformed it, transmuted it into a perception of the universal mind.

21.1 Humanity has lived and created and experienced, aligned and supported perceptions of the unconscious mind since the start of time because within the birth of this planet, there was always the duality. The karma of this planet is to rediscover the presence of love within living.

Humanity upon this planet is the IAM living expression of love. There are planets that do not take form, they merely think. There are planets that are pure frequency of light that experience creation upon it. This planet karmically took form to realize love, to express life. Nature is the expression of life; the birth, the beauty, the structure, the flow. This is all available within the minds of individuals within their perception. Seasons, they exist within the mind. The beauty of living within life, within this earth is that the earth did start with the dual thought, "IAM. Am I?" And from that, the earth has created itself, its perceptions. It has been creating within an unconscious mind since the start of time with us, with the earth, with humanity attempting to understand it for this day because as individuals practice the Clear Mind Experience to dissolve the unconscious mind, to dissolve the perceptions, the earth breathes the three-part breath. As the earth breathes the three-part breath, the collective unconscious is dissolved. This planet is on the cusp of pure magnificence where it will breathe and realize the presence of love within itself from its core. Mother Earth will ascend into the magnificence and unlimited potential and frequency that will exist within a thousand suns. This the most magnificent moment upon this planet because it is not knowing that IAM the presence of love, it is the moment of realization which is the ecstatic bliss of creation. We are on the cusp of this ecstatic bliss that will last approximately five years upon this planet as each person realizes 'IAM Love' through the Clear Mind Experience and allows the collective to be dissolved and the realization and the presence of love to live beyond any human condition. The ecstatic bliss within humanity will rise up, will rise louder than the loudest volcano, the loudest clap of thunder, the loudest of any natural expression on the planet. The noise will be heard through multi-dimensions as love continues to pop and realize itself within the consistency and clarity to never be separate from any individual mind. The realization within these pages is to know that the time to understand is beyond us. It is now the time to be.

21.2 The foundation of the unconscious mind both collectively and personally is the level of responsibility that an individual feels to support its condition. We either feel addicted to what it says to us and what the immediate gratification in which that it presents to us sexually, through addiction physically, mentally, emotionally, or we feel repelled by it and seek to fix the problems it which it creates; on our knees, cleaning and scrubbing the floors of its destruction. The foundation of the unconscious has been solidly defined by philosophers, spiritual leaders of the earth. For thousands of years, individuals have contemplated over the role of the unconscious, supported it, whispered words of encouragement of its purpose, shared their wisdom on living within it, moving out of it, trying to be happy within it, defining it, redefining it, what's it saying, how's it creating, how do you get out of it, how you should move into it, what does it mean, walking behind it, walking towards it, living within it, understanding it, what's it saying, where'd that thought come from, where'd that feeling come from, who said that to me, what should I do with it, what does that mean? All of these conversations from the foundation of the unconscious which keep it erect come from the unconscious. It is simply telling you what it is there for. It is simply telling you what created it. It is simply telling you what is serving to destroy within your life within the perception of love. That's painful. That says, 'I'm stuck.' That says, 'I'm suppressed.' That says, 'I'm limited.' That says, 'I'm not love.' It will have you seek love through the idea that you're not love by what you have to fix. You'll run after it, agreeing. Within the rational mind, "Oh, I see.

That's why I'm not love. That's what I need to change to find love. Oh, I understand." So the rational mind in your life becomes a vehicle in which to follow IT running after IT, letting IT randomly entertain you as to why and how you should become different. The foundation of the unconscious mind is your experience and connection to living upon it. When you support the foundation of the unconscious mind, you are really are only talking about what holds you up. You're really only talking about your relationship to it, defining why you love it, defining why you feel enslaved to it, defining why you think it has a hold of you. All of this is made up. It has hold of the mind. It has hold of the perception. It is the Clear Mind Experience that separates this hold, cuts it off, dissolves it.

21.3 The Clear Mind Experience is just that: the experience. When you have an experience of something, you are able to create a new foundation of perception. When you are seeking an experience, you will be on the old foundation seeking to erect new life upon it. The Clear Mind Experience is the foundation. It's what holds up your new house, supports you, creates trust, safety, sense of being nurtured, sense of being embraced, and it is within that support that wisdom will escalate, reveal itself, expand, and the unconscious mind will do what it does best, retract. See that? The unconscious mind is programmed to retract. What that means is, if you're walking backwards through it, dismantling it through the 49 signifiers, we need it to retract because in retracting, it's decompressing. All the qualities you are afraid of within the unconscious? They're our gift because we use them. We allow it to still operate and act, and it destroys itself, dissolves itself, gets rid of itself. Because the unconscious mind believes so strongly in form, it believes so strongly in the house that it has erected, a wise man will walk on water, the unconscious mind will say you need a boat. The unconscious mind believes the foundation in which you stand if dissolved will have you collapse. However, it won't because perception will become an expression of love. The qualities of love will be that you will be supported by what is unknown. The unconscious mind does a lot to protect its structure. The first thing it did was it created drug companies. And then within the drug companies, it spoke of fear. And within the fear, it said, "What would life be without it?" And then within that expression, it said, "You can't be without it." And then it said, "Do you have anxiety? Do you have depression? Do you have disease? Do you have a condition? Well, here, swallow this. Validate the condition. Validate the disease. Validate the anxiety. And then the foundation will be strong." Medication is the trance state of the unconscious. There is medication that is important to the planet. It is important to preserve life through transformation and awakening the presence love. There are illnesses that people experience daily, conditions of the body that people experience daily through the process of waking up to the presence of love. It is difficult to stop this from happening, and the progress of medicine allows this progress of spirit to be achieved because it will act as the bridge to cross the being over by protecting their body to stay upon the planet. However, the greater portion of drug companies is the trance state of supporting the foundation of the unconscious, keeping you asleep, getting you to believe in the fear, the control, and the delusion that you are suffering. The unconscious mind is taking the medication to keep itself alive. Not only are there drug companies, but people scramble daily to suppress the unconscious. They learn to manage its anger. They learn to redefine its emotions. They learn what it feels and thinks, and they hold it deep within themselves as pain; as a thought, feeling, and emotion that they will never be free of. They condition their lives to live within this pain, condition their lives to live separate from the presence of love because they believe they have lost love, lost the ability, and lost the beauty to truly resonate within the beauty of love. Most individuals don't realize that the unconscious mind has a hold of them because the rational mind rationalizes the experiences of the unconscious mind because it did feel, at times, in the experiences of accumulating the unconscious that the experience was real. Therefore, the rational mind says, "This is who you are. You have anxiety. You have depression. You have addiction. You have concerns. You are vulnerable." The greatest enslavement of man is to believe that they are vulnerable to addiction. Addiction is the unconscious expression of itself. Addiction is when the immediate gratification program within the brain activates itself to a speed that defies rational thought and action. It is perpetuated through fear and terror. However, it is an unconscious addiction. Without the unconscious, addiction cannot exist because the conscious mind is an expression not a retraction. Addiction is a retraction. It's about accumulation.

22.1 Then a very subtle holding onto the foundation of the unconscious is the spiritual seeker that believes in truth and that they are right; that the unconscious mind serves to awaken the perception to love. Where there is delusion is that one believes one must participate in it and understand it and figure it out. That is not true. The same activation principles are received, and the same levels of wisdom are achieved and ignited within the perception through the dissolving process. The fact is, because the dissolving process takes an accumulative amount of time, the process of awakening happens quickly and within tremendous clarity, and one doesn't feel exhausted through the process but enlivened through the freedom of what is being felt when one is dissolving the unconscious. It is a great time upon the planet for spiritual seekers to become free of the unconscious because their light bodies will become free, engulf the earth, and help to become a vehicle of the mass shift in consciousness. When the unconscious collectively is no longer operating within the life of the light worker, tremendous realization will exist upon this planet. Through the Clear Mind Experience, what was once perceived as a spiritual teacher, that will now become an expression of the living love and will be born within seconds of one another upon the planet. They are all activated and ready to be untied, set free within the presence of love, to express love as a vehicle of support, as a midwife to those that are beginning their journey. The Clear Mind Experience has dissolved the teachers, the need for spiritual teachers as we are all one, all living within the presence of love and within a Clear Mind are living within the expression of self-,mastery. The Clear Mind Experience is awakening the mystic pioneers that through innovation, wisdom, knowledge, resources, communities will awaken a world that is beyond human condition, and beyond time and space of human creation. The world is free, neutral, allowing, receiving. It's time for light workers to be free of the unconscious. It's time for light workers to be free of the collective unconscious. It's time for humanity to receive the gift of this generation and that is freedom from the unconscious. We are the generation of ecstatic bliss.

22.2 The unconscious mind has a divine criteria, a structure. It is a pattern of 49 signifiers that can be dissolved as one follows into the next, much like dominoes. It is this structure that is also available within the collective unconscious. The collective unconscious is also a set of signifiers that when not engaged upon within the personal perception will dissolve and disappear very, very, very quickly. The unconscious collectively is a mirror of what exists within the brain of the human. If within the brain of the human there is the expression of the conscious mind, then the outer experience will be expressing the fluidity of the conscious mind. If the unconscious mind is active within the personal perception within the brain of the individual, then collectively what is perceived by the individual will be the unconscious mind as the same structure as the perceived personal unconscious. In knowing that both are a pattern and structure, we are able to go into the pattern and structure and dissolve it in a frequency and order that is not harmful, not destructive, not cathartic, not painful. It doesn't raise question as to when it will be over, how it will be different, why it is going to be different, why it needs to be different, because the awakening within the Clear Mind Experience is based on the principle of universal love which is the unconditional expression of love.

22.3 The science of the Clear Mind Experience that has been released into planet earth at this time is one of profound formation. It is a science that is laid upon the unconscious as a holographic, energetic field of consciousness that is lifting and drawing the unconscious mind into position for its release. The unconscious clearing is one of formation. It is one where what is formed is released into what has no form. Within the conscious mind, there is not the structure of thought. Perception is an expression, a movement of each moment. There is nothing contained within it that has identity to say, "This is what was. This is what can be, but this is what is now." The formation of the unconscious mind is limited. It does not contain huge amounts of information, as everything that is experienced within life unconsciously is filed within a filing cabinet, in a drawer, and there are only 49 files. The formation of the Clear Mind Experience is to dissolve each of the files so the mind becomes one container, one vessel of expression that through feeling engages 49 interpretations of love that are expressions of 'state', meaning 'states of being'.

23.1 Jacques Lacan, amongst many famous psychiatrists and philosophers, studied the unconscious mind. In one text he revealed that the unconscious mind is created through language and signifiers. He was correct. That is only the unconscious mind. Everything created above it is created from the language or signifiers. The language and signifiers are the basis in which the unconscious mind is created. The dream states, the archetypes, they are all images of the thoughts that have come from the language and are activated through the signifiers. The signifiers are part thought, image, vibration of touch, senses. The fives senses are an aspect of the signifiers. It is the five senses that activate the unconscious mind to become present through the signifiers, by engaging the signifiers.

23.2 There is great joy in the revelation of the Clear Mind Experience because it is the accumulation of many lifetimes of work for many individuals that came to the planet to begin implanting holographic implants of information that are now activated to allow the karmic value of the Clear Mind Experience to take form upon the planet. Jacques Lacan is one of those individuals. There is great ecstatic bliss in the revelation that the unconscious mind is made up of language and signifiers because that is the formation of the unconscious and the structure in which it was erected. It is also the structure that dissolves it. The Clear Mind Experience dissolves signifiers through feeling, but it also provides the language that dissolves the unconscious. The Clear Mind Experience has 149 different formations of words that have up to 600 words in one formation. Their language, the self-love language, the language of love, the language of the conscious mind, which is frequency, is what is passed through the unconscious to draw it into the conscious mind for dissolving.

23.3 The Clear Mind Experience is made up of word sequences and the unique three-part breath. It is the combination of these two that create movement within the brain. The breath is the movement, the vehicle that carries the word sequences to the unconscious, retrieves the word sequences that are stored within the structure of the unconscious, and dissolves it within the realization of love within the conscious mind. It is the rhythm of the breath that is moving the words that allows movement from what is unconscious to conscious because the conscious mind would never see reason to fix the unconscious. We move the power of perception of the conscious mind into the unconscious through the rhythm of the three-part breath. The middle breath within the three-part breath is what bypasses the rational mind's interpretation of what should be moved out of the unconscious and what should be retained so the mind becomes a vehicle of dissolving love within itself. When dissolving the unconscious mind within the conscious mind through the three-part breath and the language of love word sequences of the Clear Mind Experience, the participant is dissolving all thoughts, feelings, and emotions that are unconscious within the unconscious mind that allows us to perceive life through an unconscious perception into what is perceived as conscious. It is upon the unconscious perceptions bypassing the rational mind and entering the conscious mind that the realization occurs within the conscious mind perception not attempting to occur within an unconscious perception as previously attempted to achieve here on the earth.

23.4 The earth at this time has an elevated consciousness operating upon it. There has been a quickening of the energetic field of the earth. When you move transformation into the rhythm of breath and you place the realization of love to the speed of the unconscious, then you are moving at the frequency in which the unconscious mind is being dissolved through the realizations of love. The earth at this time is realizing the presence of love through the frequency shift on the planet. When we are in the unconscious, we believe we are separate to that. When we practice the Clear Mind Experience and dissolve the personal unconscious, we are moving at the speed of that frequency, therefore, shattering the mirror of the collective unconscious at the same speed in which the earth is taking her ascension, and the same speed that the unconscious mind is operating.

23.5 What has been so disheartening to light workers upon the planet has been the lack of harmony between the conscious and the unconscious. What has been the lack of harmony between the collective unconscious and the personal unconscious, that one will awaken aspects of the conscious mind within their perception, but the collective unconscious is still operating within their lives. This is because the unconscious mind personally has been dismantled so aspects of the unconscious that are currently operating and active and alive will create within the mirror and that is all that is seen. While an individual has the unconscious within its perception that is currently activated within the electrical current within the brain, it is impossible to create aspects within life that allow a flow. Life and the outer experience represent the inner experience and perception of the brain. If there are aspects of the unconscious operating within the brain, then those aspects of the unconscious will operate outside so there will be the same discrepancies and disruptions within someone's life. So if they're creating within the vision of reality, if they're creating within the vision of life, then the outer experience will have the challenges that the unconscious mind is feeling within the perception from the aspects of the unconscious that are still active. What is so powerful about the Clear Mind Experience is that it brings complete harmony between clearing and dissolving the personal unconscious, and clearing and dissolving the collective unconscious because the unconscious mind personally is retracting into and decompressing, and not activated within electrical currents, then it's not able to create on the outer, so where it was connected to the outer, where it was feeding the outer, it will now dissolve, and the outer will not represent the struggle. There will be consistency and clarity throughout each experience throughout each day because the unconscious mind is not being perceived within outer experience.

24.1 Speaking of union, the most sacred union at this time is within Mother Earth, as it is her ascension we are upon and within her operating as her, and what is important to this ascension process is that the collective unconscious be dissolved. The way that this happens is that we create the same light frequency shift within the personal mind/brain that is currently functioning upon the earth which is achieved through the Clear Mind Experience because we are dissolving the unconscious mind, decompressing it, deactivating it, letting it retract and move out of life through the process which enables the light frequency shift that can be perceived within a conscious mind to take form within somebody's personal perception and the frequency of the conscious mind to become one with the earth. The conscious mind will see potential, opportunity, abundance, and love through the personal perception because the conscious mind will have the same light frequency that is currently functioning on the earth for this transformation on the planet.

24.2 Within the Clear Mind Experience, there is tremendous union with the earth because the speed of our awakening, the speed of which the unconscious mind dissolves is happening in the same flow and presents the same opportunities and the same frequencies and potential that the earth is experiencing at this time. This is about knowing that IAM one with the earth. IAM one within nature, rebirthing within the beauty and the expression of unlimited potential that is available within the presence of the earth.

24.3 – 24.3i In reflecting for one moment upon the earth realizing that as individuals and movements, we are assisting to awaken the earth in one mind. If you look at the earth at this time, there is great innovation, great focus, great ways and means in which to protect and cultivate her resources, support her resources to live in harmony within her beauty, and a desire and need deep within the core of humanity of those that are awakening and are continuing to awaken within a conscious mind to preserve love and life and peace within humanity because the condition of the presence of love is that we, as individuals, wish to live within the process and flow of self-appreciation which allows love to breathe to be preserved.

The innovation of the planet that is available and continuing to evolve at this time is preservation of life. How do we assist the earth, honor the earth, allow the earth, experience the earth, and move her expression into one that is preserved because if the thought within our own mind is to preserve the presence, the perception of love so that the life experience is one of love, then the earth does not have to be cared for. We do not have to be implementing the discipline of care because we are already in the expression of preserving life and love which allows it to be an unfolding. There will not be a thought of how we have to live. We will say, "IAM Living."

24.4 The karmic release of the Clear Mind Experience has been gifted to the earth at this time because the earth is not able to support a transformation that comes about by one trying to integrate the unconscious into life experience through personal choices and evaluation. In dissolving the personal unconscious, we are, at this time, dissolving the structures, thoughts, conditions, and experiences of the unconscious that exist upon the earth. If we do not dissolve the unconscious, we will not dissolve these structures of the unconscious that operate within the collective, and that will not allow the earth to take her ascension. We are not primary, we are secondary. Humanity is secondary, earth is primary. The collective unconscious has to be dissolved for the personal conscious mind to exist upon the planet because without that Mother Earth cannot ascend, and without ascending she cannot BE. In the past, there has been a moment of grace where we have sat within evaluating the unconscious perceptions, creating within the collective unconscious to understand how it operates within its form, but that has only been established for this miracle. Without it being established, there would be no miracle to perceive. As Mother Earth takes her ascension, she must be free of the collective unconscious. That means all of the structures, all of the means in which the unconscious is supported through thoughts, experiences, and conditions. We dissolve them by dissolving our need to have them. We dissolve the need to have them by dissolving the personal unconscious mind, the aspect of the mind that feeds on having them in place to live life. We are honoring the earth by clearing our minds. It is the next step. It is the key in the success of the mission for earth to transcend, to ascend into the presence of love, and the ecstatic bliss of celebrated consciousness.

25.1 As Mother Earth is transforming, through our commitment to her at a rapid rate, we must also do the same within our personal minds as to be in union with her awakening. It is important that we are not feeding the earth in which we assist and clear and clean and process and restructure for her awakening, that we are not polluting the earth through the personal unconscious mind. We are to be in union with her awakening, to be walking along within her. She is the womb in which we live, and the womb in which we are creating is one that will nurture the conscious mind. Without the form, the baby cannot be born. She is the form, we are the baby. Without the form, it is all but a thought. She is the form. We are thinking who we wish to be, but she is the form in which to give birth to us. If we set her free through our own personal freedom to be reborn, then magic will take place upon the planet, and the birth of a new consciousness will have occurred.

25.2 The ascension of the earth at this time is that of the earth. Within the activation of the conscious mind, we are ascending previous limitations of how wisdom will present itself. Wisdom does not think about what it is. It does not think of how it can contribute. It does not plan identity. It does not plan what it should be. Wisdom is a spontaneous flow of information that is activated within each moment of creation because it activates itself within the field and the realm of vibration, and the vibration has to be present for the wisdom to be present. When the unconscious mind is no longer present, wisdom will redefine itself again in means and ways in which we have not even dreamed possible because the unconscious mind is not able to perceive wisdom and not able to perceive the magnitude in which it can create in such a limited timeframe. It is timeless. It has no limitations of what could be, or what potentially must be, it just is.

25.3 Within this current reality, there are many practices and modalities and healing phenomena that exist. The purpose of these healing modalities is not a means in which to dissolve the unconscious interpretations, but a means in which to celebrate consciousness. The many modalities that are present upon the earth at this time, if perceived through celebrating consciousness, will be realized by humanity that these practices celebrate consciousness by revealing the light. These practices are powerful when the unconscious mind has been resolved because they cultivate perception, they cultivate perceived love and the presence of love. Using these modalities on a quest to heal, conversations, suggestions, thoughts, and actions of the unconscious remove the celebration from the modality. The unconscious mind convinces the rational mind that it is learning through the modality. However, one is revealing one's truth, one is revealing the presence of love within the modality, and celebrating the modality will connect the individual to abundance so the modality becomes their expression of potential, prosperity, wisdom in an abundant flow of unlimited potential. Many individuals and light workers who have entered their path of discovery and are practicing these modalities, at times, complain that the flow of abundance is not present within their day to day. This would be because exhaustion has taken over as an interpretation of self-development and spiritual practice. The ideas "IAM Tired. Am I going to arrive? Have I arrived yet?" would surface and speak out language into the universe. This is the unconscious mind. It believes it is going somewhere. The IAM presence knows that it exists within this moment, within each moment, within each breath. It does not have to arrive anywhere, or go anywhere. When the IAM presence is living within the presence of the living mind, then abundance, prosperity, and flow will move through it as a celebration of consciousness. Celebrating consciousness within these modalities is key within the realization of love and momentum of love upon the planet. The Clear Mind Experience is able to gift this awareness because a practice is no longer done in seeking, on a quest to discover what is conscious and what is love. The practices will be initiated and practiced through a stillness, and within the stillness, the presence of love will be. These modalities will offer consistent, clarity, insight, perception, and celebration, and within the celebration of life, of wisdom, and the presence of love, one will be able to live within the expression of these modalities as a practitioner or a client from the perception of joy and celebrating higher consciousness, higher visions, higher knowing, higher purpose, and revelation.

25.4 There is an under swell of excitement within humanity at this time. There is a focus that the tipping point will be reached the day in which the personal and collective unconscious mind has been dissolved. It will be when we celebrate through the dissolving of the unconscious into celebrated consciousness that love will be expressed endlessly and effortlessly within thought. Individuals will not suffer within the limited perceptions of mind chatter. Mind chatter is the perception and expression and endless questions of the unconscious. When the unconscious mind is dissolved, there is no mind chatter. When there is no mind chatter, love is an endless expression that is timeless and always present within each moment, within each breath. There is an under swell of excitement that the potential to live within the perception of love is going to be available upon this planet. The Clear Mind Experience has been gifted to the earth at this time to accelerate this process. Within accelerating the process by dissolving the unconscious, rather than confronting it, the earth can make the shift in awareness and the shift in consciousness within a very short period of time. If the unconscious mind was left to be dissolved within the normal practice of life, where it was reflected upon through outer action, then some of us within this lifetime may not celebrate consciousness. However, that was not the karmic calling of the earth. The earth has been programmed with a time to release various components that enable the ascension of the earth. The release of such information is at this time within the Clear Mind Experience. Dissolving the unconscious mind is a sacred gift within humanity that is available right now to allow perception to live within love, not through longing, not through ideas, not through the need to change, but through the practice that is the revelation of the IAM presence of love.

Gift

26.1 The beauty of this time upon the earth is that there are energies that have been released and activated upon the earth that amplify thought at a rapid rate. Many light workers make reference at this time that thoughts are manifesting within the moment and this is true potential. It is because of this amplified awareness that it is important that the personal awakening come from within the conscious mind dissolving the unconscious mind, and not the unconscious mind seeking a conscious mind. This is because the thoughts of the unconscious and its lack can manifest immediately upon the earth, which will labor the birth of our new planet. If we are dissolving the unconscious mind within the conscious mind, then the conscious mind is the thinker. It is the one that creates, awakens, activates, and allows perception within each moment of life. It is within allowing the perception of the conscious mind that we activate perception and within the presence of love. It is within activating the presence of love that we allow the amplified energies to serve the awakening and not create harm, blockage, and destruction through an unconscious perception.

26.2 For many, the concept of dissolving the unconscious within a conscious mind has been challenging because it turns around, turns inside out, the ways that the personal mind, that the individual has been influenced both within psychology and spiritual practice. Both say, we need to integrate the shadow. This perception has led people to act upon following the shadow to understand it. However, integrating the shadow is achieved by dissolving it. The shadow meaning the unconscious. Dissolving allows no repercussion of action. Does not allow the unconscious mind to live in present time. This is now, in these new times, a myth that the unconscious mind is needed. It is not needed. It is an aspect of the brain that when activated through the dissolving process provides profound insight, provides opportunities, experiences, thoughts, feelings, and emotions that activate the realization of love. When the conscious mind dissolves the unconscious mind, it will intuit interpretations that awaken perceptions of love.

26.3 Great discoveries in these two areas of psychology and spirituality have presented to us the philosophy that the unconscious mind is there to assist us to wake up, and in essence it is true. People have studied dreams, believing that the archetypes within dreams will tell them what the unconscious mind is thinking and how it's perceiving reality. Each time that someone reflects upon the uncon-

All children are born to live within love. It is only the thoughts, feelings and emotions of an adult within the unconscious mind that encourages them otherwise.

scious mind, they are taken into earlier thoughts, patterns, and ideas that were created within the first seven years of their lives that have allowed them to integrate a loss of love within their lives. This is a powerful process to understand the unconscious, but does it dissolve it? Does it dissolve the behavior? Does it awaken the presence of love to look at the unconscious? Unfortunately, it does not, and what this looking at the unconscious actually does to the mind of perception is encourages the perception of the powerlessness associated within understanding what the unconscious mind is thinking because feelings will activate the rational mind to agree. It is upon reflecting on the unconscious continually that this integration and suppression and condition of belief of the unconscious is subtly happening within oneself. Continually looking at what is not from the sense of wondering, pondering, understanding how to move out of IT will only put you further into IT because you are validating within the human perception that the unconscious is where you are within that moment. The human mind is a combination of conscious and unconscious expressions and thoughts. At times there is a movement into the conscious mind that believes that what happens within the moment is all that there is, and then there is the expression or the activation or knowing or understanding of thoughts and projection of the unconscious mind which will validate that you should feel certain feelings within each moment because that is what has come up in that time. This is the mechanism of the mind to live within the moment. Living within the moment is not something to 'seek'. It is a natural state. The mind can live in the moment when it is free from unconscious thought. The mind will only live within the moment when it is free from unconscious thought because it is there to serve the moment through intellect, assimilation, understanding, and most important by delivering the presence of love and wisdom into outer experiences in which to awaken further into the understanding and presence of love.

27.1 What is distinctly different with the Clear Mind Experience is that you are, within perception, aiming to pass the unconscious mind through the conscious mind, not seeking to pass the conscious mind into the unconscious mind. Individuals in the past have chosen to seek to pass the conscious mind into the unconscious mind in a hope to have revelation and at some instances, and in some points, there has been a slight awareness and revelation, but it has not dissolved the unconscious mind. It has just created a dual mind, a mind that perceives light, love, peace, and union, and an aspect of the mind that is not able to seek this, and within separation they exist, where one moment the unconscious mind will animate itself into reality, and another moment the conscious mind will present itself as an awareness to life. What gets the unconscious mind to become active when an individual is able to perceive reality within a conscious mind are limitations that present themselves within the unconscious collective mind, which validates to the rational mind a feeling of powerlessness to the old. The outer experience struggles to transform when the unconscious mind is not dissolved within the personal mind because the collective unconscious is in relationship to the unconscious mind within the personal mind. If it is not dissolved, then the outer experiences will continue to move the presence and the present state of the mind and awareness into unconscious perception and limitation.

27.2 What is very important to note in the revelation and discovery and release of the Clear Mind Experience is that the very process itself places the shadow behind and not in front, meaning the unconscious mind is not leading life and creating within life but being dissolved within the presence of the conscious mind, and the conscious mind and how it perceives reality within the unlimited potential of love, joy, and wisdom is what creates, leads, and lives within each moment of expression. That is the gift of the Clear Mind Experience, that the unconscious mind is following. It cannot initiate or instigate any blockage or action that will slow down progress, will slow down visions, relationships, opportunities and potential experiences to celebrate the expression of consciousness and love.

27.3 What is primarily important at this time is that we use the energies on the planet for healing and awakening to support inspiration, potential joy, and preservation of love. When we use the unconscious mind to realize truth, we can do so within a path of destruction. Surrounding our epiphanies can be broken relationships, broken homes, broken opportunities, lack of vision, a feeling of a lack of support, a lack of abundance. If we are not using the energies of the planet, meaning the accelerated consciousness that is being amplified across the planet that allows thoughts to manifest. If we are not using this energy from the conscious mind perspective, then we have great potential to create great destruction, great distraction from awakening and supporting love within a conscious mind.

27.4 When we are able to engage within a conscious mind in the manner in which dissolves the unconscious and doesn't allow the unconscious mind to create and live in destruction, suffering, and separation of love actively within our lives, experiences, thought, feelings, emotions, and actions, then what we gift ourselves is outcomes that we can use as beings of light that support our future and the vision of our times. In speaking of outcomes, what is meant is structure within the universe, systems of operation within our day to day, structure within our day to day that allows us to live within a conscious expression of love. It is important within these times that we create outcomes that can be used within the light because we have great opportunity within front of us, within us, surrounding us that allows us to wake up very quickly within each moment, where from one moment to the next, reality will be perceived differently. It is important to use this energy in a manner in which honors love, preserves love, to use the presence of love that is able to activate great awareness of what is able to BE as innovation for our future and the vision of our times. The presence of love is what supports all vision. The presence of love is what is able to create new ways, new pathways, a new journey within life, that love allows us to live within a conscious mind and support activities, thoughts, feelings, emotions, opportunities, and experiences that speak the language of love into life. Speaking the language of love into life is what is existent with the Clear Mind Experience. When a participant engages within the language of love and it is spoken within their minds through the practice, it becomes apparent within the universe that this is the experience, and the universe has a moment where it hears, engages, witnesses, and creates from the conscious perception because the language of love is speaking within the universe. When a participant experiences the Clear Mind practice, what is amazing to them initially is how magnificent it is to hear words moving through their brain, moving through their perception, awakening their feelings of how magnificent the potential of their life, their love, and their knowing and wisdom and presence of the IAM is. It is important within our commitment to the earth that we allow the magnificence of love to be a language upon her. That when we speak it is in a means that supports the 49 qualities of love. It is within speaking in this way that we no longer engage within the unconscious, not speaking about what we must become, not speaking about what must be different, but allowing each moment to live within the beauty, unlimited potential, expression and radiance of love.

Chapter Two
Union of One Mind

28.1 The question that raised the contents of this book, Clear Mind New Planet and the birth of the Interpretation Guide the Book of Awareness, is the question, "Do we need to live our lives within the unconscious mind to realize the conscious mind?" And the answer is, "Absolutely not!" It is deception of the unconscious to believe that IT must be the pathway. Our need today is to live within a conscious mind dissolving the unconscious mind, dissolving its presence and how it is active within life. The epiphanies that one believes one has if it lives within an unconscious mind seeking the conscious mind are few and far between. The realizations that one has when living within a conscious mind dissolving the unconscious mind are rapid, fluid, a movement, a revelation, the realizations at the speed of the breath. The conscious mind connects through the Clear Mind Experience to the 'life flow', to the chi, because the awakening of the conscious mind is happening within the breath. It is the breath that carries the language of love to dissolve the signifiers and the language within the unconscious mind. The breath becomes the bridge, becomes the union of one mind.

28.2 Let us ask ourselves, what does the question really mean to live without the unconscious mind? Well, to an individual it can mean less stress, less anxiety, no stress, no anxiety, no feelings of suppression, no emotional imbalance, no lack, no limitation, no fear, no control, no failure, no expectation, no misunderstanding, no questioning of 'what if', limited disease, limited of disharmony. All that does not serve love, does not serve peace, knowing, union, oneness, kindness, compassion, stillness, the presence of love, or what does not serve the presence of love, preserve the presence of love, exists within the perception coming from and within the unconscious mind. Dissolving the unconscious mind takes with it all that it harbors to distract the mind from the presence of love. Once the unconscious mind is dissolved, a reconfiguring of perception through the feeling center will take place within the being, and this will allow all that has been witnessed within life to be redefined through the presence of love. This is an exciting process and sometimes breeds impatience within participants and those that seek the solution and the answers of personal freedom. Within the Clear Mind Experience, impatience is not an aspect of practice. The transformation is too quick. It moves through breath. If one were to question transformation, one would not be breathing in the rhythm of the three-part breath. When one breathes within the rhythm of the three-part breath, one will experience profound stillness. It is within this stillness that mind chatter becomes obsolete. It cannot exist because there is no belief structure operating to know that it is purposeful. The unconscious mind is being dissolved and the purpose within its function along with it.

It is within the importance of the realization process that of which the Clear Mind Experience pertains that one is able to understand, integrate, embrace, and form union within the benefits of the unconscious mind. It is not that the unconscious mind creates benefits. It is just that when a signifier that which expresses a lack of love is taken within the conscious mind and dissolved, then a realization will occur, but the gift is not within the unconscious, it is perceived within the conscious mind. The benefits one will receive from the unconscious mind are integrated within the conscious mind. What the unconscious mind is filled with are thoughts, feelings, and emotions that have been given permission to disassociate from love through the feeling center and what one feels within life, within love, within experiences within the first seven years of life.

28.3 In simple terms, this book is asking us, do we need to live within darkness, negativity, and ideas that separate us from love, and most would answer no. Do you have the belief structure to believe you can no longer participate or access these negative interpretations? No. While there is an unconscious mind, one is always able to perceive that they would be able to integrate their thoughts into darkness and negativity if the right experience were to present itself. When one participates in the Clear Mind Experience, they do not necessarily do it through the belief structure that they believe that it will work. It is the unconscious mind that typically puts the person into the practices. It is within joining with the practice, they have been seeking some type of freedom within who they are.

29.1 Throughout our lives, many of us have been aware that hard times bring great insight. It is within hard times that individuals perceive new opportunities. It is within the feelings that come about in hard times that activate within the mind the opportunity to perceive a newness that activates the perception of the conscious mind. This has happened and been the way in which many have merged within the presence of the conscious mind. However, today through the quickening and realizations of earth energies, individuals realize that this does not need to be. Individuals seek to be free of the unconscious, free of the extreme circumstances that awaken the conscious mind, and they quickly look for means in which to not engage within what the conscious mind is telling them they need to experience to awaken wisdom. It is the unconscious mind that tells us we must suffer to experience wisdom. It does this to trick the personal will. First it sets up the experience where one is not living within wisdom. Then, one will seek the conscious mind. The unconscious will allow the conscious mind to present a feeling that one has left a sense of powerlessness or story of the unconscious, but remember the experience, the thoughts, feelings, and emotions of the unconscious in this circumstance have not been dissolved, so the unconscious mind will present an experience outside of ourselves that will awaken feelings of powerlessness that were there at the beginning that originally initiated one to seek the conscious mind, and the unconscious does this to be able to say and reinforce its foundation, and that foundation is that nothing exists outside of itself.

As one struggles within the unconscious perceptions, it creates experiences that are difficult to cope with. The unconscious mind is reinforced. The powerlessness of the struggles is reinforced. The unconscious mind if not dissolved is virtually impossible to escape. It is the sole creator when it exists within the mind because it does not allow the conscious mind to exist within its freedom. It is in control because the aspect of the unconscious can be controlling. It will control the perceptions within the mind to support itself and its existence. To support its foundation and the presence within life, it will create opportunities to depend upon its stories, such as addictions to medication, drugs, and alcohol.

29.2 Previously, before the Clear Mind Experience, when one has been able to articulate the unconscious through suggestions and guidance of the conscious mind, one will be able to realize profound insights that provide new and wise perceptions of life. The problem of not dissolving the unconscious is that it will become partly dismantled and still be active providing the limitations and suppression that it has always been in responsibility of within our lives. If, however, we dissolve the unconscious, and all thoughts, feelings, and emotions that live within its structure, the conscious mind will realize profound insights, but it will have no unconscious expression to challenge it because the Clear Mind Experience is about the union to create one mind. It's the bringing together, the folding in and out of, from the conscious folding, drawing, swallowing of the unconscious into itself to realize the presence of love, which does not allow for unconscious mind perception to be a leader within one's life. When this happens, there is profound momentum in the realizations and insights that occur that provide these new and wise perceptions of life.

29.3 It is within the realization process of the Clear Mind Experience that a participant can simply articulate that they are receiving benefits daily through the dissolving of the unconscious mind. They are not questioning the unconscious mind. They are not seeking for it to support the process of the Clear Mind Experience. It is in the dissolving into love experience that one will feel the wholeness, the awakening, the allowing, and the presence of love within life. It is within this expression that one feels the benefits.

30.1 One important realization that awakens within the union of the conscious and the unconscious mind is that one is able to receive profound gifts and wisdom. This is because conscious mind is what is creating within expression. The unconscious mind is no longer thinking of its destruction and creating these experiences of destruction within reality. The conscious mind, however, has become an expression and within the conscious mind becoming an expression, it is providing an opportunity within life that others merge within the preservation of all life through action. One is able to receive profound gifts within a conscious mind because the conscious mind will preserve the gift. The unconscious mind will attempt to rationalize, seek, improve, or understand its gifts; what it seeks to be gifted from a conscious mind. It will try to come in and take action over ideas or experiences of gifts by defining how it should work, what it is for, what can happen within it, how it needs to be. The conscious mind when presented with gifts of wisdom will seek to preserve the gifts by expressing the gifts, and within expressing the gift, one will receive gratitude, and within that gratitude, one will celebrate consciousness.

30.2 It is in knowing that there are deep insights within the conscious mind through the Clear Mind Experience that we are benefited through a smooth, rhythmic, free and comforting expression that allows the rational mind to exist within life, supporting the dissolving of the unconscious. Typically, when we dismantle the unconscious mind, the rational mind is challenged by this and will present ideas, thoughts, feelings, and emotions from the unconscious by allowing the unconscious to speak because it can reinforce what the unconscious mind is saying through feelings that it can correlate due to past experience and present experience that support the reawakening of the past. However, through the Clear Mind Experience, the rational mind is primarily engaged within the rhythm of the Clear Mind process through the three-part breath and the assimilation of the language of love. It is difficult and impossible to dissolve the unconscious mind through thoughts of affirmation, ideas of what we think we can become, recollec-tions of the past, and healings of energy. This is because the unconscious mind is created as a structure that is cre-ated through words and signifiers, meaning emotional per-ceptions that contain relationship to feeling. When we have union of one mind, we allow the perception to be smooth, rhythmic, allowing us to be free of the unconscious, slow-ing the rational mind to be comforted, allowing beauty to be born through the knowing that I am living within deep insights and allowing the presence of love to perceive.

31.1 Clearing the unconscious both personally and collec-tively is beneficial to ourselves and not only ourselves, oth-ers and the world. When we clear the unconscious mind, we are building a global community of like-minded individ-uals that perceive reality within the conscious mind that are able to host new ideas of innovation to create life and structure within a conscious mind. When we dissolve our personal perception of the unconscious mind within our own mind, our personal mind, then we will be gifted to see the beauty of love within life because the collective unconscious will not have any way to feed into the per-sonal experience of the individual which will allow it to be dissolved.

When we dissolve the personal unconscious, we benefit tremendously because we have within our own contribution to ourselves dissolved the unconscious collectively. Be-cause what will happen within a Clear Mind is one will per-ceive love, one will perceive the momentum of love, and the understanding of love, and life will present the actions that allow love to fulfill itself through a lifestyle, environ-ment, career, relationship, or outer life experience.

31.2 The union of one mind is when the unconscious mind

is dissolved into the conscious mind. It is within this process that we are revealed tremendous beauty of the conscious mind as what it gifts us is the realization of our capacity to live in love, honor love, and perceive love within each moment of life. When we are able to perceive the conscious mind within feelings, then we are living within the IAM presence in the awareness acknowledging the presence within through all life expression.

31.3 The sacred gift of the Clear Mind Experience is not that it teaches wisdom. It is that it dissolves the unconscious mind. Once the unconscious mind is dissolved personally and collectively upon the planet, the Clear Mind Experience will no longer exist. It simply exists within this moment to achieve the level of work that it must achieve to clear the earth of all perceptions and ideas, thoughts, and feelings that keep her separate from the idea that 'IAM love living within the radiance and knowing of IAM love now.' There is great importance on this gift and the fact that it dissolves the unconscious mind. Dissolving the unconscious mind has not ever been an alternative on this planet until this day, and dissolving the unconscious mind at the speed in which the Clear Mind Experience does so is a gift of grand proportion for humanity. If humanity wants to honor the presence of love, the greatest way in which to do so is to dissolve the one obstacle within the personal mind that does not allow the perception of love, and within that, the obstacles for others and life and creation and movement and momentum of this planet will be dissolved within the dissolving of the collective unconscious mind.

31.4 Another gift of the Clear Mind Experience is that when we have a sense that there is a momentum of dissolving of the unconscious mind into the conscious mind, there is a deep sense of peace where one form dissolves and disappears into the other. The rational mind will chase the unconscious mind into the conscious mind. Once the unconscious mind has been dissolved by the conscious mind, great love, passion, insight, awareness, knowingness, beauty, peace will be revealed because what wasn't able to operate as these qualities but contradicted these qualities will have disappeared into the presence of the other—love.

31.5 Within the simplicity of dissolving the unconscious mind awakens incredible momentum in which realizations of love can occur randomly, consistently, and with profound fluidity and clarity. It is within the process of dissolving rather than dismantling the unconscious mind that our most incredible momentum will be living within the mind as oneself. When one reflects upon the qualities and participation of the Clear Mind Experience it will be revealed as a simple, free-flowing expression of childlike energy which awakens the perception of the child-mind. It is important within today's time that we are not dismantling the unconscious mind because the dismantling of the unconscious mind will limit, without doubt, the perception of love that one feels one is here to integrate within life.

31.6 If one takes a moment to reflect on how one would be embraced, supported, honored, and allowed within the presence of love, doesn't a conscious mind feel wonderful? Doesn't a conscious mind act within life as a gift? And doesn't dissolving what isn't, allowing the conscious mind to reveal itself, feel a way in which to honor such raw, beautiful insight and wisdom of the conscious mind?

31.7 The Clear Mind Experience will remove effortlessly the cathartic unknown struggle of 'awakening' because within the union between the conscious and the unconscious minds, there can be no struggle within the Clear Mind Experience. As each draws themselves into one another, there is no struggle because the unconscious mind is not verbalizing itself as being different and is not able to initiate action that is able to contradict love.

31.8 When we speak on dissolving the unconscious mind, the unconscious comes about with many questions. It will be speaking about dissolving the unconscious. Is one using the technique to turn their backs on the divine purpose of why one has lived through unconscious pain within their lives? However, this could not be further from the truth. When one awakens within the Clear Mind Experience, they are able to catalog word sequences within their mind, within their lives that allows them to speak love into the lives of all that choose to experience love.

32.1 An interpretation that has circulated this planet for many years is the thought that we need the unconscious. If we don't experience our lives through its perception, then we will inhibit our growth because it has been believed that the essence of what we awaken into has come from the structure of the unconscious mind. However, this is actually not true. This is actually an interpretation created by the unconscious mind in which to maintain itself. When you dissolve the unconscious mind, growth can never be inhibited because as you dissolve the unconscious mind into the conscious mind, then the conscious mind realizes its magnificence in transmuting what is dark to light. It is within the Clear Mind Experience that this momentum is revealed and celebrated.

32.2 It has also been stated by these individuals that the unconscious mind exists of both positive and negative experiences. The unconscious mind cannot exist of positive experiences because positive experiences are that of the presence of love. Once the negative experiences are dissolved into love, then the unconscious mind does not exist. The unconscious mind does not take residence within the conscious mind, it is dissolved into the one mind,

32.3 The questions that need to be answered within the study guide will be how the structure and role of the unconscious mind is playing out in our day to day. This is obvious to see. It is very clearly identifiable where love is not serving because where love is not, unconscious perception will be. Because if we are able to accept and acknowledge the unconscious conditions on the planet, and accept our role in dissolving the personal unconscious mind so as to move through life effortlessly with an experience of self-appreciation. Being within the unconscious and the conscious mind is a divine alchemy. The conscious mind when activated to move into the unconscious mind through the three-part breath and the language of love will draw the unconscious mind into itself from where it stands. Through the three-part breath, it will just expand into the unconscious mind and draw the unconscious mind back into itself. Because when the conscious mind energetically meets the unconscious, the unconscious attempts to take over the experience and what it does to do this is retracts however it does not realize that it is being encouraged and pushed by the conscious mind to retract into itself. Because love always prevails and love is programmed within the alchemy to return home. So it is this spark that happens in between when the conscious mind meets the unconscious mind that is the alchemy, the fire that dissolves what is not love, into love.

33.1 What needs to be openly discussed is the fact that the unconscious mind is what is contained therein when moved into a conscious mind will reveal higher states of consciousness and spontaneous awakenings to light, love, and wisdom. There is an important aspect to each person's evolution and that is that of a teenager. It is very important when one is a teenager to reconcile feelings with parents. It is within the reconciliation process that a child will be set free either through interaction with the parent or through practicing the Clear Mind Experience. When one reconciles with past experiences, they gain permission from those within the experiences to allow the unconscious mind to reveal itself so that it is able to be dissolved. It is a powerful moment, the rite of passage in which an individual will begin the process of returning to the child-mind.

33.2 A gift revealed within the Clear Mind Experience is that it is a process in which to integrate the unconscious mind, what some call the shadow. The conscious mind empowers an individual to feel profound stillness.

33.3 Where most of us agree is that we do need to integrate the unconscious mind or shadow into the conscious mind to realize the truth of life to understand the profound and simple things about ourselves. It is valuable to the planet to clear the unconscious within the personal mind. It is valuable beyond words because it will be within the awakening of light that great transformation will occur.

33.4 It's safe to say that the unconscious mind is developed as a means in which to define the perceptions within how the conscious mind dissolves thoughts, feelings, and ideas because within the process of dissolving the unconscious mind, the unconscious mind is able to let go of what it believes within a conscious mind. Then the conscious mind will, through purpose, understanding, and allowing the process to evolve, define the unconscious mind and these experiences through a conscious mind perception by using the language of love to define the condition of each experience.

34.1 The unconscious mind is the key to love. As when we place it within the keyhole of the conscious mind, and we turn it through practice, then all conversations that are not supporting love dissolve in that moment. However, when we do this, we also awaken the conscious mind to be able to express itself randomly without plan which awakens higher truth of healing, realization, insight, innovation. All the while the conscious mind is moving within the divine radiant knowing that one is in service to humanity. When the unconscious personal mind is being dissolved within an individual's personal practice, that is service to humanity. Every thought that you moved within the mind that does not allow the mind to be clear is in some way playing out within humanity. It is simultaneously happening within the life of another. It is important that we clear the unconscious to allow the realizations and innovation for humanity to be revealed.

34.2 The speed in which the Clear Mind Experience dissolves the unconscious is suitable to these times. If one focuses on the unconscious and how one is meant to overcome its thought, it seems almost archaic in form. It is important that when living within a conscious mind, a structure is implemented within the environment that allows you to be honored within the perception of a conscious mind.

34.3 When you spend a great number of hours within one lifetime attempting to be released from unconscious perceptions by life experience then attempting to define the unconscious feels too long. When you are beginning to perceive new potential from within and that new potential is not operating within the planet knowing of itself, it can seem restricting, constricting within the heart that one feels that one has been secluded from, excluded from, and placed within a suspended moment that has enabled them to disconnect and disassociate. One can spend lifetimes preparing to be released from the perception of the unconscious.

34.4 It is very important in honoring the relationship to the earth where we are forming union within one mind. Meaning the conscious mind is merging within the universal mind and becoming one mind because the personal unconscious dissolved into the collective unconscious which revealed the conscious mind which allowed the expression of the conscious mind to move through life that of which all was dissolved into the universal mind.

It is our joy and service to Mother Earth to experience the means in which to provide a faster method of understanding higher truths, witnessing higher truth from within the mind as what has happened through this release of this process is that we have enabled the earth to take her ascension, and within her taking the ascension, all that needs to be present to serve her are able to be because within a Clear Mind, humanity will be living with her and not polluting her essence, not polluting the ideas, not polluting the expression of nature, but allowing all within this beauty to move through life.

34.5 Today's current experience where there is a rise in consciousness is one of astounding capacity. Everyone within this moment is focusing on what has to be let go of in which to be different. However, that is the trick of the unconscious because we do not let go, we dissolve. When we dissolve, it is happening spontaneously, and it is the spontaneity of the conscious mind that is the alchemy of awakening. When we are able to through human perception connect to higher thoughts of the conscious mind, it allows us to escalate the process of union of one mind because there is no judgment or separation that can be fulfilled within the expression of love that exists.

34.6 It is the awakening of the earth at this time that defines us. If we allow ourselves to be defined by the unconscious mind, there will be great conflict and disharmony. However, if we allow ourselves to be an experience and expression of the conscious mind, then we will be allowing consciousness to rise within astounding capacity. Reflect for one moment on ways in which you support a rise in consciousness. It is the awakening that the earth is having that defines our commitment to the awakening and to the transformation that one is provided through the Clear Mind Experience because one is awakening within the Clear Mind Experience within a new perception of love, not love that is acquired, not love that is trained to perceive, but a love that is revealed within dissolving what is not.

34.7 The ascension of the earth is within each moment. It is 'the moment'. The ascension, union of one mind, is when the collective unconscious mind has disappeared into wisdom and the conscious mind has been invoked through the personal freedom to let go of what is not serving the expression of love.

35.1 Within this moment, what is realized and offered and brought forth is that humanity is going through the same shift in awareness as the earth. They have been walking separate paths. The human being has been looking at the ways in which the earth will serve us, however, the role today is to allow us to serve the earth through the preservation of love within, allowing the perception of love to be. When we allow the perception of love to be, the earth will be supported through the shift in awareness that is happening.

35.2 It is in the profound unity of joining within awakening love within a conscious mind and dissolving what is not able to perceive love within an unconscious mind that we take the journey. Our earth is defined on how we move through our awakening. It is not the earth moving us, it is us moving her through our minds. If we clear the mind, we will clear the pathway in which she will also discover her divine radiant magnificence. Her beauty will be revealed as a deep richness within the presence of all that IAM within.

35.3 It is so incredibly important in reviewing all benefits of dissolving the unconscious mind and the alchemy that exists between the conscious and unconscious minds. The time that it takes to confront and attempt to understand the unconscious mind through life experience is what labors the birth of our new planet. When you are in the process of birthing, you are not reading books on how the process will take shape. It is within the moment of going into labor that the body takes over and begins the process of birthing the child. There is beauty because within life, one is committed to not having life overfull within an over-expectation but within a freedom. When we allow ourselves the freedom, then we will no longer be attempting to understand the unconscious mind through experience, but we will be allowing ourselves the moment to experience life with all dissolved into one.

35.4 When we attempt to have the unconscious mind define the conscious mind and what the path is of seeking, we create destruction because the nature of taking life into the unconscious mind to find truth is that we are by nature invoking a battle so life becomes the battleground, one where the unconscious will hang onto itself out of fear and loss, but the conscious mind will allow itself in the need to express. As it is within the need to express that the conscious mind is able to expand and expanding is its purpose, as it expands from the personal conscious mind into life, into others, into opportunities, experiences, and most of all, into the awakening of a vision. Each being has a vision of life, has a divine criteria of how the conscious mind will present itself within their life, as their life. It is this divine criteria that will awaken within a conscious mind when the unconscious mind is no longer engaging within the day to day.

35.5 The Clear Mind Experience is able to mimic to the unconscious its past condition of self-discovery. When an individual answers a question as part of the Clear Mind Experience, there is an igniting of the unconscious which in past times was a previous interpretation of a rising up of the unconscious. Then, through the person answering the question, there is a discussion within reality on what the unconscious believes. In the past, we would call this an animation into reality. Then, once an individual has breathed the three-part breath and moved the unconscious into the conscious mind, the conscious mind will in time, over the next seconds, moments, or hours, release a definition of what has taken shape in what has been dissolved. When this happens, there is an awakening, a sense of victory.

35.6 We are all encoded with the divine awareness to release the unconscious. Throughout this process, there will be times of limitations, hardships, and perceived bumpy roads, but they come from a disassociation to love. And while the disassociation is operating upon the planet, the unconscious mind presents all thoughts, feelings, and emotions that will allow the individual to perceive the difference of structure. When one is processing the Clear Mind Experience, it is not negative from the perspective that one is able to envision past experiences that were painful. There are thoughts, feelings, and emotions that surface that are awakening to help create boundaries, solution, and condition of new life where one is preserving love within life. Disassociation from love is operating on the planet exponentially. There is a greater number of the population that is not able to assimilate love and one becomes disassociated when one feels the feelings of how love will express itself within knowing.

35.7 When one dismantles the unconscious mind rather than dissolves it, there are many disheartening moments. Initially, the individual mind perceives that it is free of the unconscious when there is a similar epiphany to its function and what it believes in. Once we have this realization, there is a feeling of self-appreciation for one's courage to face what is not love. Within higher consciousness, innovation can thrive and limitations of the unconscious can disappear. However, there are times when the limitations will reappear and attempt to impersonally remove, limit, restrict, or stifle the expression of higher levels of consciousness. The unconscious mind when not dissolved will appear and attempt to impersonally remove, limit, restrict, and stifle expressions of the conscious mind. It will be continually questioning what if, why, when, regarding what is happening within. Reality becomes difficult when the unconscious mind has animated itself to be validated for existence. The unconscious mind appears to impersonally remove, limit, and restrict higher levels of consciousness. This is because it has been dismantled. There is no inner mastery as there is no master within the unconscious mind animation.

35.8 – 35.8i The unconscious mind when confronted with

the loss of itself through spiritual practice, self-development, inner inquiry, or seeking to go beyond its limitations is confronted and becomes territorial to its position within your life. It will at that point intervene with ideas, thoughts, and feelings of what you should become, of what should happen, of ways you should become free. If there is not some divine intervention of grace from within the conscious mind, within that moment, then the unconscious mind will lead the individual on a path of self-discovery. Self-discovery along the pathway will be made. There will be moments where the conscious mind is revealed, but the unconscious mind feels no threat of the conscious mind. It feels its fluidity, and within the fluidity, it has no structure therefore it is not real. Within the unconscious mind believes that all that it perceives and all that it defines as itself is the only thing that is real. What typically happens within the seeker or the light worker or the individual seeking to overcome the unconscious is that they begin along the pathway of discovery only to discover that the unconscious mind places them right back within the feelings that they first started out to address. This is because, along the way, the unconscious mind has not been dissolved. It has granted access for perception to move further into it, around it, through it, but has not dissolved it. To dissolve the unconscious mind, one must dissolve the 49 signifiers through the language of love. The rhythm of the Clear Mind breath helps an individual remain within the process and not disassociate, so within that is the power that the unconscious mind cannot create the individual to disassociate through feeling. It is the story of many who have sought to overcome the unconscious that through their seeking, they have tried and attempted to mentally protect themselves from acting out, all the while suppressing the unconscious mind to the point that one day it will create a situation within life that will blow the lid off, and there it is, fully animated, fully there, claiming its position, placing perception and rational mind back within its seat so it can restore the power of itself within the perception of the individual.

35.9 With so many modalities available upon the planet for people to awaken inner reflection, this struggle is more apparent than ever. Daily, individuals struggle to be free of the grasp of the unconscious, free of the connection and the direct mirror of the collective unconscious, struggling to let go of the unconscious as if it were an octopus wrapped around their free will holding them back in position and not allowing them to move forward. This is because the greater majority of modalities that are upon the earth at this time are there to assist the light. They are there to assist the light be current and active and present within all aspects of reality. This being said, there are not practices available that can effectively dissolve the structure of the unconscious mind in the order in which it was created. Dismantling it through the rhythmic process and rhythmic awareness of love just gently piece by piece in which the order of signifiers follows along to one another. The Clear Mind Experience is this gift. It will go in and dissolve the unconscious mind signifier by signifier aligning each of the emotions, the seven emotions: self-acceptance, forgiveness, silence, compassion, celebration, inner knowing, and gratitude, to that of love. Within this, the five primary relationships within the perception will also be aligned to the presence of love; which is the child-mind, the perception of self-love, the living mind, the emotional mind, and the spiritual mind. All perceptions will be living within the presence of love, able to assimilate the expression of love and not pushing forth the projections of the unconscious. It is when this whole integration happens, within the perception, that the individual is living free from the unconscious and the struggle is no more. Throughout times, people have talked about this final moment, this final moment to let go of what isn't the truth. There is no such final moment. The unconscious mind would have one believe that because it would like the individual to be chasing that moment, forever trapped within its domain of thought. There is one moment to the next, the moment where the unconscious mind is in front of the individual leading, creating, and moving life within its projection, and then there is the moment where the individual turns perception inward and walks away with the unconscious mind following and not creating, but being dissolved in insignificance.

It is when the individual is able to make this effective awakening by walking through life within a conscious perception of love that the struggle cannot be. Through the Clear Mind Experience, there is no struggle. It does not exist because the function of the process is continually dissolving the structure of the unconscious, and from the moment that it is practiced daily or it is practiced several times a day, there can be no more interpretations of the unconscious moving forth as the personal mind becomes witness.

35.10 More than ever at this time, individuals are striving to release themselves from the unconscious mind through pain, lack, hurt, loss, limitation, fear, disease. They look to the unconscious mind, look at its behaviors and how it is driving thoughts of who they are without knowing that it is the unconscious mind. Individuals believe through the language of the unconscious that it is them personally that is experiencing these hardships and these disassociations from love, but all that is happening is that the unconscious mind is speaking throughout the day and operating within one's life thinking it is the individual. So when the rational mind hears the language of the unconscious presenting itself within the day to day, it is perceived that the individual

Children – the unlimited potential of love that if allowed to live in love will discover the beauty of living, creating, inspiring, and discovering all that allows love to prosper.

is talking about themselves from the 'I' perspective. Through the Clear Mind practice, the rational mind becomes witness to the unconscious looking at it through the practice witnessing it speaking about itself as a disassociation from love. Through the Clear Mind Experience the rational mind moves into the feeling of love, therefore, turning itself into 'IAM.' It is within this process that the personal identity begins to break away that was created through the unconscious. The personal identity within a conscious mind does not exist. There is just a fluid expression of love being defined within each moment, each experience, just as nature. One year a tree can grow a leaf, and that leaf fall away, and the next year grow a different leaf that looks, feels, and is within texture is different. That is the same for the birth of the conscious mind from the unconscious. As the unconscious mind draws and falls away, a birth will take place of a new perception, which is that new leaf, and as much as it is upon the same tree, it will feel different from the year before. There is a fluidity to nature. The leaf will fall again. It will grow back, but it will not be the same leaf. It will be another interpretation of the same tree. That is the fluidity of the conscious mind, fluidly creating without thought of what one must be.

The conscious mind speaks as an affirmation of what already exists. To support the conscious mind, one must invoke the conscious mind into the unconscious. When an individual is practicing the Clear Mind Experience, they practice the language of love which is also what we call invocations. We are moving single words into the unconscious to dissolve the signifiers invoking the presence of love as it is dissolved and moved into the conscious mind. The unconscious mind speaks in definite principle of what it believes it is, should have, and will create and do. If the rational mind is not able to see separation within this voice, it will believe that the voice is the life that is operating. The Clear Mind Experience moves the rational mind into the perception of love through feeling. Immediately that the rational mind becomes witness to the unconscious mind, it will work effectively with the conscious mind continually moving every feeling, all 49 feelings, into the perception of love because the rational mind supports feeling before thought.

36.1 There are a great number of light workers upon the planet that have done many energy work practices, studies, and ceremonies in a plight to awaken the mind beyond the preconceived ideas of the unconscious, and this they have. They have awakened tremendous accelerated bodies of light and are able to perceive tremendous levels of consciousness in celebration of consciousness. However, the unconscious mind weighs around them like concrete boots pulling them continually down when they feel to be elevated. The way that the unconscious mind is typically dealt with in this situation is through suppression. However, the light worker has guilt associated with 'why have I not become free of this?' This is a statement of the unconscious mind. It is saying to the mind of the light worker, "How are you not free of me?" How are you not free of these feelings of negativity? How are you not free of the limitations of the collective unconscious and the fact that you feel it is holding you back from your true visions? It is the gift, the ultimate gift of the light worker to return home, to re-embody the light quotient in which they were activated to experience upon the earth. When the unconscious mind is dissolved, the light quotient increases rapidly to the point where the light worker may have to take physical rest to allow the process to occur. The Clear Mind Experience is the ultimate gift to the light worker. It will place them upon the earth fast. It will place abundance within their hands quickly. It will place union amongst one another profoundly. And it will take all work that they have been practicing to new levels of 'celebrated consciousness'. It will restore the power within the lower back region. It will remove all feelings of exhaustion, and, most important, it will return full memory of the IAM.

The greatest benefit of the light worker once practicing the Clear Mind Experience is that their lives become a consistent clarity of frequency and vibration where each moment is being perceived as the conscious mind, and each moment is being celebrated within the collective within a conscious interpretation that supports the conscious mind's visions. There will be no lack of continuity. The greatest gift at this time is for light workers to be placed strongly upon their feet as pillars of light anchoring the earth through this transformation speaking nothing of unconscious thoughts and disassociations from love. It is that of the light worker that must first turn and walk away from fear, the ideas of control, lack, limitations, suppression, the questioning of 'what if'. The light worker through fatigue can speak of limitation of what holds on within humanity. This is feeding the unconscious to hold on. It is important that the light worker not acknowledge the unconscious mind either collectively or personally at this time, that they represent the light in which they stand and that the Clear Mind Experience through dissolving the unconscious mind will present this realization within their being, within their knowing, within their perception, and within their work they will be living as the radiant celebration of consciousness.

36.2 The light worker at this time is being called. The earth energy has accelerated itself in service to humanity. It is of a critical nature that the unconscious mind be dissolved to help humanity be rid of the repercussions and creation of the collective unconscious. The way that humanity will achieve this is by dissolving their personal unconscious mind which will no longer allow them to personally perceive the collective unconscious which will allow it to dissolve and fall away. There is a tremendous calling to light workers, a calling to truth, love, freedom, peace, and rhythm that they move into the new perception one without the unconscious mind that will allow all transformation to be sustained; where life upon this planet can be sustained. For one moment, as a light worker you reflect upon the unconscious mind and say, "Well, I have done the work. It is gone." That very statement proves that it is not. Within a conscious mind, one would comment differently.

There is a great gift at hand within the Clear Mind Experience, and it is important to be in honor and humility for that freedom. This is that gift. This gift has presented itself through the walk-in that has come to deliver the message; as the messenger is the book: The Book of Awareness. It is the book that speaks within these transcriptions of this Interpretation Guide telling of this gift. If this gift were to be rejected, it would be rejected by the unconscious mind protecting itself, protecting its identity, saying, "I am already something. I am already somebody. I have already achieved." It is guaranteed within the gift of this process that not a soul upon this earth has dissolved the unconscious mind effectively. They have dismantled it, but it has not been dissolved because it is the grace of the Clear Mind Experience that is lifting if from humanity, the program in which it is running. The unconscious mind at times will attempt to mimic this process, but they will be mimicking a karmic pattern that will engulf those that believe that they should oppose. This process is a calling upon earth as an activation. It is a calling upon the earth for

Mother Earth. It is to set her into freedom. It is released by the Karmic Board, the Ascended Masters, the Pleiadian Sisters. It is released from Helios, Vesta, in union of one mind. It is released into humanity within the perception of Christ, Buddha, the presence of love. It is released within all realms, within angelic realms, within the Great Divine Orchestrator, within the Ashtar command, all sits and waits at this time for the Clear Mind Experience to lift the unconscious; the cloud of energetic field that covers and hosts place upon the planet. This is the gift of many lifetimes. This is the gift of thousands upon thousands of years traveling to arrive at this planet. This is the GIFT. If this gift is challenged, it is only ever challenged through ignorance of the unconscious. If this gift is challenged, it is only challenged through the unconscious mind that in which is perceived by the walk-in delivering. There is pure freedom within this practice as there is no attachment to what must become of it. What speaks within these pages is the book that stands before humanity as a woman and speaks of the transformation of this planet in the clarity, because each page of this book turned within her intent to merge humanity into love in which love is revealed. This transformation has happened on other planets. It has been orchestrated within the realm of the same being that is within this woman. It has been successful many times over. It will be successful now. Those that hang on to the unconscious mind will remain within its perception. That is the journey that they will take. This is the gift that will test, will test many, will ignite the free will of many to say, "No I won't." For those that have interpreted the final doorway, this is the final doorway, the moment in which: "Will I continue to walk towards the unconscious, or turn and walk towards within the knowing that IAM Love?" Within the courage to make these steps, within the courage for this new order, great gifts will be bestowed to participants. Great gifts will be bestowed to this planet. This is the time to let go of the unconscious to move in order, to move in presence, to breathe union within one mind.

37.1 It is within dissolving the personal unconscious that the individual no longer needs the collective unconscious to realize that the personal unconscious is playing itself and acting out. So many people at this time look around the world, look at the destruction, the mayhem, the great loss, the greed, the poverty, the abuse, the pornography, the addictions, the immediate gratification, the loss of values. They witness this upon the earth, and they say, "How will the earth rectify these problems? How is this fixed?" The answer is that these things cannot be repaired. They cannot be fixed. They are unconscious presentations of the unconscious mind within the collective. However, if one does not host capacity to live within an unconscious perception, then the unconscious mind will be forced to dissolve. It will die, shrivel up, no longer exist because its stages will be empty, its theatres will be empty, its ideas will not be paid for, its greed will not be hosted, its fears will not be allowed. All that it offers in experience will be denied. Not through suppression, through the void of being a witness. Humanity will stand and look at the unconscious mind as it breathes the three-part breath as it dissolves the personal unconscious. And as it dissolves the personal unconscious, the unconscious mind will fall away like ash, and underneath that ash will be the birth of new life, will be the buds of a new humanity, will be the spring and the bulbs and the creation and the knowing and the color and the beauty of a new garden of life in which we live.

It is not about fixing the unconscious. It is not about telling it that it needs to go away. It's not about being consumed within the judgment of why it exists because it is within this idea that the unconscious mind has you believe in it, which allows it to function. The unconscious mind does not need your support, it needs your attention. If you are going to give it attention by analyzing it, looking at it, and judging it, it still has your attention, it's still being fed; even if you disagree with the unconscious and stand up against it. Light a candle in a vigil. Stand out front of the store and say, "I don't believe in you." It still has your attention. Where you could have been sitting within the peace and the presence of love, and it's standing there alone with no audience, you are standing within the front of it. It loves that. All the unconscious mind aims to do is create your perception to live within it. Take your time. Take your belief systems. Take the structure that houses your soul. Take the structure of your mind. Take the grace and gifts that are available within the beauty of spirit and keep them trapped in the idea that you have to find truth, find who you are, find freedom, heal a wounded mind, heal a wounded childhood, heal the pain, understand the pain, understand the parents, understand what happened, understand reality, understand why you are suffering. You can never understand the unconscious mind. There is no understanding. It is for immediate gratification, and within the immediate gratification, all it seeks is your attention. It just wants you to partake in conversation with it endlessly about what could be, will be, may be, shall be, should be. The Clear Mind Experience and the process of dissolving the unconscious mind will keep you separate from this. It will keep you separate from thinking that you should partake in such activities with the unconscious mind because, again, through the feeling of the experience of the Clear Mind Experience, you will be witnessing the unconscious.

37.2 - 37.3 The earth at this time is calling for men and women and children of the earth to become free of the unconscious so as to dissolve within the beauty of love. Within the earth at this time is the divine radiant expression of love that is unseen or seen intermittently by those that seek to realize love. If you are able to perceive love in any form today, you would acknowledge that we are on our way into the existence of divine radiant love. What is needed at this time is that humanity would take the calling to dissolve the collective unconscious mind and the personal unconscious mind so the union of love can form upon the earth. It is the calling at this time that pride be placed upon the ground. That ideas of what I should be be placed upon the ground. That addictions and wounds be no longer ignited within the actions of thoughts, feelings, and emotions. Upon this day, there is a calling within the earth that the unconscious mind be lifted that it be transmuted and taken from the earth through the breath of man. It is within humanity that love is being restored through the realization that I AM receiving the unlimited potential of love awakened within all moments of life, love, purpose, and union. It is within this moment that the earth calls forth in great humility for freedom to be restored as love upon this radiant earth. For many, many years, thirteen to be exact, from September 27, 1996, an activation occurred upon the planet where the walk-in of the Book of Awareness came into form within the woman. The Book of Awareness at that time healed and soothed and dissolved within the brain and perception of that woman the unconscious mind that had perceived all horrendous acts in which the unconscious mind would have one believe. The Book of Awareness has moved through the being, cleared the feelings, cleared the unconscious mind, allowed the being to integrate into the presence of love, and within this time, this book is revealing itself as it has integrated into form. Throughout the past thirteen years, it has been witnessed by Ascended Masters, by realms of consciousness visiting.

There is tremendous momentum of light upon the earth as she takes her ascension. September 22, 2008, the being in which is speaking was instrumental in removing and releasing within the twin flame the collective core of the collective unconscious. Much like an apple, the core has been removed from the planet, returned to the sun, where it disintegrated into the ashes of new life. Now upon the planet, the collective unconscious mind is an apple without a core that rots daily. As individuals align the present state of mind to love, to the perception of love, by releasing the personal unconscious mind, there will continue to be great momentum of light upon the planet. There are many levels of consciousness witnessing this transformation at this time. There is tremendous potential that we face in living free of the unconscious mind, and that potential is living within action at this time. The battle of the unconscious mind has already been won because the book is now present. If the battle of the unconscious mind had not been won, if the conscious mind had not removed the core of the unconscious, this book would not be present today. This book is the birth of realized beauty upon the planet. It is the answer to the prayers of those that have asked, "Please may I ascend into the freedom, into the personal freedom of unconditional love and the presence of knowing that IAM the presence of all light prevailing, living, breathing, and knowing life on earth." This book is this gift. It is anchored within the womb, within the throat, within the voice, within the knowing, within the perception of the woman that carries it, the author of these pages. Her assimilation is your gift within this moment. Her assimilation is one of freedom as she is aware that she, the author, is the embodiment of the book. She is not within her mind consumed in human identity. She is not someone who seeks adoration. She is one that does not stand on a platform. She is one that stands within humanity and whispers within the presence of their perception, "IAM Love." She is the memory, the recall, the awakening, and within that awakening, you are being honored by a tremendous gift that is uplifting humanity, holding humanity, restoring profound tremendous light upon this earth. The greatest gift that you can present at this time to the work of this being and the Clear Mind Experience and the legion of light that releases it within humanity, is to stand within your own light, free of the unconscious mind, in union with the earth, witnessing the collective unconscious as it drops away into ash. In celebration, you will encourage light. In celebration, you will honor others. In celebration, humanity will rise up in union. All within celebration. Each one within humanity will form an aspect of a global community that will celebrate the rhythm, touch, beauty, and qualities of light and wisdom that move through each. The Clear Mind Experience is not the practice to practice for integration of wisdom. It is your freedom from the unconscious that will set you free and cross you over into the practices that support the light quotient and wisdom. This is the gift to move you into a full, engulfed knowingness and presence of love and light.

38.1 It is important at this time to share the story in which how the Clear Mind Experience entered the earth realm. It entered the earth realm within a transformation of a woman. One day, a woman sat broken, her body filled with disease, her mind filled with interpretations of pain, deep pain. As she sat, she died. Within a living body, the soul left. And within that living body, the book moved within. As the Book of Awareness is also a soul from another dimension of reality, from another planet within our sacred universe. When the book arrived and took form as the woman, it turned the pages, it spoke, out loud, to the mind of the woman. As the mind listened, the conscious mind activated. It began to work in union with the book, and slowly, the unconscious perceptions fell away within the rhythm of the Clear Mind breath and the language of love. This radiant woman was awakened within a conscious mind and merged within union with the soul – the book and within her this expression became her wholeness. The book restored her value, her insight, her vision, her knowingness, her capacity to feel love, her capacity to nurture. As within each moment of existence, this woman was preserving life. No longer did she have the disease of death within her womb. She was aligned to the presence of love, her perception, and within wholeness, she lives as the book. The pain of the moment was the cloudiness, it was being able to turn the pages within rhythm because the unconscious mind did not want those pages turned, and every way that it could present itself over those thirteen years to stop those pages from being turned by the conscious mind of that woman, it did. That book initiated an army of light on every dimension. It called forth on every dimension that earth be victorious, that earth claim victory, that earth win in all light, in all union, and that the unconscious mind be dissolved, and that book raised up within that woman the self-worth, the knowing, and the presence to know that the unconscious mind cannot wound, it cannot take away, it cannot take life, it has no place, and through her passion to live within the freedom of the book, the book was born and all that was challenged, and all ways that she was challenged turned to dust. Within the dust that woman, the author of the written pages, released herself as the book and the Book of Awareness was released to interpret living a Clear Mind for a New Planet.

38.2 – 38.3 When the book entered the beauty entered the beauty of this woman, the need within humanity to be free of the unconscious blanket was revealed on a daily basis, as the pages turned within the book, within the woman. To her mind was revealed what was needed. Each moment of training and education that needed to be available to humanity to allow this indescribable beauty to be revealed was placed within her mind, within her efforts, within her intent and birthed within life. Throughout the process, there was union within the brain, two sides of the brain. Magnificence was born. Two realities within the mind, passing in and out of one another, have awakened a perception of the universal mind, the conscious mind.

Within the creation of the Institute that holds forth this process, the initiatives of the Clear Mind New Planet, within the hearts of those that move into the process to serve others, there is always the presence of this woman. There is always the presence of the victory of her brokenness. As our community rises up and in one mind holds a victory to the light, that freedom of the unconscious mind is the calling at this time. There is always within the room the stillness of that what was once a broken woman, and that she was restored to the beauty and magnificence of light through the magnificent experience of the Clear Mind breath, and the language of self-love, and the pages of the book.

The book was gifted to the body on January 1, 1997 at 6:37am in Currumbin, Australia. The woman(the author of these pages) sat upon a balcony, looking out at the ocean, and within that moment, an Ascended Master let a dove loose, the holy spirit, that carried the book. As the book moved through multiple dimensions, it came metaphysically to the woman and flew into her stomach, into her solar plexus, and from the moment that her footpads touched the earth to walk away from that balcony, she walked into the journey of this day. Walking through the fires of tremendous calibration to light and personal freedom of the personal unconscious, the Institute is mirrored within reality from a conscious mind. It is a safe harbor in which one can sit and look out into the ocean of life and be restored because surrounding it is the presence of the Ascended Masters, the flame, the light, the sacred sun of Helios that shines upon the balconies, upon the oceans and rivers. Beloved Vesta, who entered the life of the woman and now lives as the woman is moving the Clear Mind Experience as the woman, within living rooms, within the life of those that sit and breathe the Clear Mind breath and become free within the words of the book. This grace was available as not one page was left unturned, revealing the magnitude of the healing that took place within the heart of the woman, within the mind of the woman, within the life and reflection of the woman, at such magnitude that the book used every page, every breath, every word of the language of love to release her into radiant freedom, into the presence of love and knowing. There is freedom to love.

Chapter Three
Clear Mind New Planet

39.1 It has taken thousands of years upon the planet to raise the consciousness of the earth to the potential that we are experiencing today. It was when the earth hit a frequency it was programmed to ascend in 1996 that the Clear Mind Experience was released into the earth field. It has been the momentum of the earth that has allowed the process to take thirteen years to be present in clear, precise accuracy, today accompanied by the book, to be able to transform and dissolve the unconscious mind both personally and collectively. This moment was predestined. However, it has been the prayers and actions of all light workers upon the planet that have brought the planet to this day. The expectation of this new era that we are entering is an era free of the unconscious mind. That is the only difference. Within the freedom of the unconscious mind, new life, new order, new laws will be written, will be present, will be activated and available upon the earth plane. This is, without doubt, a moment of tremendous transformation. It is the moment when love moves within itself; when love takes what is unconscious within itself and says, "IAM Love" in mass proportion across the globe where humanity becomes a village, and within one moment, love is realized.

39.2 The Clear Mind Experience is here on the planet for this time. It is this moment, this shift in consciousness that has called it forth. It could not have been available sooner. It could not have been revealed later. It is the alchemy of the moment of the revelation of its need, of where humanity is within this moment, that has moved it into being.

39.3 Because of the frequency of the earth, of the planet at this time, allowing the unconscious to be present, playing within allowing it, being indecisive through it, and delving into the darkness of it to attempt to see the light is not safe or required. The reason that it is not safe is that it will create prior to conscious mind. If it walks out in front of you, if you move into it to find truth, then it has already created. It is important at this time that it has no creation, and it is not allowed to progress in any way. Each person participating within the Clear Mind Experience has stopped the progress, and has attempted to stop the progress of the collective unconscious because the personal unconscious is deactivated. If an individual is pushing the unconscious out in front to understand who they are by continually reinforcing the statements of the unconscious mind that's seeking to heal it, innocently seeking to heal what cannot be healed, destruction can be created because the unconscious mind will connect to an outer experience within the collective unconscious to reinforce its position, create powerlessness within the perception of the individual, and then the individual will sit there and say, "Well, how can I be different. Look at my situation." This is not safe because of the frequency of the planet, and that thoughts are creating rapidly. What used to take months to happen will happen instantaneously. Within moments. A person will have an unconscious thought, within moments, an outer experience will have reinforced that. It is because of the speed in which the planet operates at this time that it is critically important that those of the earth to serve Mother Earth and her ascension process are dissolving the unconscious mind within every breath and not activating it to take action upon the planet because it will create suffering of an insurmountable proportion.

39.4 A new awareness that has happened upon the planet, it is a calling within humanity, that the personal unconscious mind be cleared because many things are manifesting simultaneously, both from the conscious realms and the unconscious realms. There is great talk amongst light workers, amongst people of the planet that we will come to a head as a planet, if there is not a gravitating shift in awareness of the personal mind then this may be so. If this were to happen, it would not be enjoyable to be on the planet. Those that have made a conscious shift of love may not really want to be on the planet. If the Clear Mind Experience and Experience was not on the planet, one would say that was the potential. But because it has been revealed, the book would have to be never read, the practice never practiced, the person carrying it not on the planet for this transformation to be lost. This cannot happen. The victory has already been won. As individuals turn the pages, practice the Clear Mind Experience, listen to the language of love, and take the three-part breath, it has already been won. The planet has made the shift, is continuing to make the shift. It has been many lifetimes, many realms, many moments that have created this moment. This moment is a pure activation of consciousness that has been accumulating. It is important that humanity become free. It is important that humanity be in love. It is important that humanity not feel that love is a choice but presence, and a sense of knowing within each moment. It is important that earth be safe to experience an open heart, an open mind, and the perception of love. There are many light workers that have become sick within the body as they have pushed away the unconscious mind, but let it be told that victory is here; that every three-part breath that is taken, every word that is assimilated within the brain, the freedom to live free of the unconscious mind is there operating within that action. It is time to heal those great masters that are upon the planet by setting them free from the unconscious mind. It is time that love be revealed within the simplicity of dissolving what isn't.

40.1 Many ponder daily within vulnerability of just how the world would support such a collective shift of consciousness. The world at this time feels divided. Light workers are on one bank saying, "This is the way in which we must live." The unconscious mind, dancing around like a fool on the other bank, creating profound suffering as the light workers sit and watch in the powerlessness of the non-judgmental still mind. As the light worker sits within compassion and watches the suffering upon the other shore, within the solar plexus, there is great delusion that is felt. There are ideas within the minds of the light workers that how could this possibly be? How could the unconscious mind leave when the belief system to support its demise doesn't exist within itself? This is the gift of the Clear Mind Experience. The unconscious mind will always seek. It will always seek to be better, and the Clear Mind Experience will play into that. It can't see that it will be gone, but as soon the individual feels within their solar plexus the feeling of love, and the rational mind feels the potential of that love, the unconscious mind from that moment on is essentially heading out the door; dissolved within every single practice, every single time the participant sits down to practice the technique, it is gone. The Clear Mind Experience specifically speaks to the unconscious. It speaks about its experiences of holding onto, and it loves that. It has the unconscious mind believe that it must change, that it must be different, and within that it will practice. As it practices, it is dissolving, and then one day, the greater mind is present. The greater portion of the mind is conscious, and the unconscious mind is just slipping away effortlessly. Beautiful revelations occurring daily within the conscious mind which encourages the rational mind to continue to always allow the process of discovering that is being revealed. There is such profound wisdom in this moment, in this practice. Such alchemy that allows the unconscious mind to be tricked within its own foolery of believing that it is control. The unconscious mind is impersonal. It is not bad, it is not doing the wrong thing. It is not evil. It is just a separation to love and the greater degrees in which it is separate will appear to be evil or bad, contained within great hardship, misery. As the world watches these darker parts of humanity, we sit in fear, in concern, and wonder, hopelessness, how this will ever be that we will be free. It is simple: don't look, turn away, move within, dissolve the desire to figure it out, dissolve the desire that it's your responsibility, dissolve the desire that you can hear it, believe it, see it, and think that it can harm, dissolve the desire to engage. And without your eyes looking upon it, without your feelings moving into it, it will be gone.

40.2 There is great destruction, poverty, abuse, violence, and wars upon the planet, there is not the time to sit and look at the suffering, it feels that it is everywhere, seeping through every crack within the universe within the planet. It feels to be the unconscious mind emits destruction. Now there is a perceived looming fate of 2012 where the light worker ponders, "Where can this really go?" Mother Earth is making her ascension. 2012 will come and go. Our thoughts will create, however, prior to this date. If we create destruction that we believe, then this is what will happen. The unconscious mind is telling you to fear 2012. It is telling you that there will be great destruction because there will be, if we believe in it. There will be great destruction if we think that it is the way. There will be great destruction if it impersonally operates within its agenda. However, if one is not engaged within it, there will be birth, not death. There will be harmony, not noise. There will be beauty and serenity because the greater portion of the population of the planet will be free of the unconscious mind. The collective unconscious will accumulate itself or it can destroy itself. The conscious mind will just witness it. The conscious mind will move into the destruction, and within the destruction, a birth will occur. 2012 is allowing us a great opportunity; not to support the fear of loss, not to support the fear of failure, not to support the fear of destruction. It is the unconscious mind that is saying to the light worker, "You are failing. You haven't prayed enough. You haven't done enough. You haven't meditated enough. You haven't integrated enough light. You're all going to fail." No. You did integrate the light because the Clear Mind Experience was birthed. It has come as a friend to humanity, to dissolve the unconscious mind. When you do this practice, you don't do it for yourself. You do it for the earth. You will be set free in the process, but you are doing it for the earth. You are doing it for the victory. When the unconscious mind looks at you and tells you that you are not love, you practice the Clear Mind breath in its face. Remain still within the words of love, within the language of love, taking three breaths, you just stare aimlessly, it will move on. And when it moves on, it never connected. It's less present from reality. Every time we connect to the unconscious mind, we bring it into reality. The Clear Mind Experience does not allow this connection to the unconscious to take place. If we sit in fear of 2012, the fears will be our reality. If we listen to the unconscious mind telling us that as a planet we are failing, and there will be great destruction and mayhem in 2012, this is what will happen. If we dissolve the means in which the uncon-scious mind can communicate with us, and the means in which the unconscious mind can be seen as the collective unconscious within reality, then 2012 will represent the celebration in consciousness and tremendous freedom upon the earth plane. Because thoughts create, it is im-portant that the conscious mind, that the light worker not verbalize any path of destruction. There is no end time that says that we are not responsible for what is here within our hands right now. Right now, we are given the opportunity to preserve life within love. This is our calling. Anything other than that is the suggestion of the uncon-scious, believing that how you show up in reality doesn't matter because it is not measured, because it will end anyway - which is delusion. The responsibility of the light is to act as the light. It only knows to act as the light. It is the unconscious mind of individuals that believes that it is in control of saying where light can disperse and when it cannot. This would be true, but that is the uncon-scious mind, and any rational feeling person would not play foolery, would not support the hopelessness of it, would step away and allow it to turn in on itself, would give permission for the conscious mind to admit to it, to resolve it. This is the path of life upon the planet to be a gateway in which love will find itself, be restored and live as you.

40.3 For some, this time is filled with tremendous oppor-tunity, transformation that is abundant with potential. There is excitement of the child-mind within the minds of the in-dividuals in which it is restored. Life becomes the path of discovery, self-discovery, where the child-mind is witnessing reality and saying, "Ooh, what could I experience next in love?" and it's through the feelings that the being says, "Ooh, IAM the presence of love."

At this time upon the earth, there are many that run along-side the destruction of the unconscious and build a con-scious mind structure in which the conscious mind will perceive reality. We will see great proportion that when the unconscious dissolves and falls away that standing erect and waiting is already a structure; financially a structure, a structure within wellness, a structure within education and development. These structures are not large and are not swallowing up the earth, however, they are enough that given the momentum of support through humanity, they will grow and foster and take over and create great and pro-found statements and opportunities upon the earth as ex-periences that support a conscious perception over the coming years. It is these beings that are being innovative in erecting these opportunities for others that support and cel-ebrate this transformation at this time that is filled with the unlimited potential of wisdom.

40.4 Then there are those that have ideas that there will be tremendous loss and suffering during this time. What they are perceiving is the death of the unconscious; the falling away and dissolving of the unconscious, and within all that is unconscious, it will dissolve. There will be no discrimination of protecting anything that is unconscious. The unconscious mind will just deactivate and disappear. This is the way the earth will heal. There is no fear of that unless you are un-conscious, then you would see that you would be going. The unconscious mind is always fearing its demise. It makes money, it fears its loss. It creates a business, it fears its loss. It creates an addiction, it fears not having the drugs. It creates an addiction through alcohol, it fears not drinking. It creates an addiction through sex, it fears not having inti-macy. It creates ideas of what it should have and only ex-periences the other. It creates expectation of a partner and loses its partner. It is always creating for loss. It believes in the loss. Right now as we perceive loss upon the planet of the unconscious, it is just the unconscious speaking out loud of itself; telling us that it's losing, telling us that it's disappearing, telling us that there will be great loss and suffering because it already is great loss and suffering.

40.5 This important contribution that individuals and humanity can make at this time is to get out of the way of the unconscious mind, and this is done by dissolving your connection within it. Within your personal awareness and perception, it is advised that one would dissolve the unconscious so the unconscious is not active within the being. Then within this, it is important that the individual no longer engaged within the collective unconscious so that it feels that it has footing and ways in which it creates. The unconscious mind needs human form to take life, just as a soul. Without human form, it cannot exist. Without a brain, it is not real. Without a body, a soul is not incarnated. Without a brain, the unconscious mind cannot function. Sweeping the brain of its perceptions, clearing the mind of its perceptions is you getting out of the way of the unconscious so it can dissolve.

40.6 In clearing the mind, we dissolve the thoughts, emotions, and feelings both collectively and personally that allow the unconscious to act. If we dissolve these thoughts, the unconscious will have nowhere to act upon the planet; not within the personal mind, and not within the collective. Ways in which it harbors thoughts, ways in which it harbors limitation will exist no more and what feeds its limitation will exist no more. And the individuals that are trapped within the suffering will no longer be trapped within the suffering but be set free. It seems like a grand plan, and it is, if you had to go and sweep the streets, but if you just, within your own mind, cleared perceptions, it won't exist.

40.7 It is perceived by some that wisdom comes from the unconscious, but this is not true. It is when the unconscious moves into the conscious mind that the conscious mind will realize love because it has dissolved what is not love. When it feels the unconscious mind being dissolved, it feels the victory of light and love, and within that feeling, can define the principles and feeling of love, the wisdom is contained within the conscious mind. When the unconscious mind is dissolved within the conscious mind, it will present many thoughts, feelings, and ideas that then are translated to become conscious awareness, insight, revelation, and expressions of truth and wisdom and love. It is these expressions of love that create momentum. The more that you experience awakenings and expressions of love, the more times they are presented within real time. The greater awareness to love is moving through life, and the greater momentum is apparent within the individual's movement and progress within each moment. But all of this comes from the unconscious being dissolved within the conscious, and the conscious feeling the victory of what it is to have drawn what is not love into love and dissolved what was not able to perceive love into love.

40.8 What the earth needs now at this critical time is momentum. We need to feel momentum within an individual's existence; Mother Earth needs to feel the disharmony of the unconscious field lifting off her. The further it lifts away, the more she ascends in frequency. The more density that is raised up and dissolved, the greater opportunity there is for her to raise in frequency. When the collective unconscious disappears, it disappears into the sun. It is Helios that purifies in his great magnificence. The collective unconscious will turn into ash. As we take this time to create this momentum through the Clear Mind Experience, a huge gift is manifesting upon the planet, and that is the potential that resources, innovations, support, love to be reflected into the personal perception of individuals. As the collective unconscious dissolves, so does poverty, grief, lack, destruction, control, and indecision. The unconscious mind will attempt to hold onto itself. The conscious mind, however, through the Clear Mind Experience will be presenting itself, expressing itself, and realizing itself beyond any voices, actions, thoughts, and deeds of the unconscious.

41.1 A gift of today is that through the Clear Mind Experience, love can be realized comfortably. Love can be realized as a celebration because one is awakening through the process of dissolving the unconscious mind, realizing love beyond the momentum of personal experience that one is not suffering at the hand of the unconscious mind through the awakenings. Revelations, insight, beauty, and love are being presented continually. An individual is not fighting to become free of the unconscious mind through outer experiences that keep reinforcing its presence.

41.2 Within dissolving the unconscious mind is the gift of tremendous clarity and the pressure to change. The thoughts that I must become, I must change, I must do are dissolved within the unconscious mind and what awakens is the knowing and simplicity of IAM. One through the Clear Mind Experience is not chasing or seeking the IAM, they are also not forcing stillness in an attempt to find IAM. The IAM – living stillness awareness awakens as it is simply revealed when the other is dissolved.

41.3 When the unconscious mind is dissolved, the presence of love becomes an experience that lives within the day to day. Each opportunity or experience in life becomes a moment in which love is operating as revelation or discovery

– consciously operating within the perception and awareness of the individual.

42.1 - 42.1i Our environment in which we live always speaks the language of our lives. If we are seeking the presence of love in no matter what interpretation, we will always be given situations that have us seeking to find, or validate the experience. Mostly, the experiences will be always leading us back to ourselves, speaking to reveal the wisdom that all love is a language within knowing that love is all that IS.

42.2 Unfortunately, when one seeks love, life will be a treadmill of expansion and retraction. Where we think that love is manifest and the qualities that are being defined as love living in revelation within our lives, within the awareness that we are operating at the time, then upon intrusion of the unconscious mind, love will retract, and the situation in which love retracted from will then be defined through the unconscious mind, as it validates that love is retracted at the time. When this happens, our environment will provide to us experiences that support the retraction and from this – separation of love – life can become stressful, confusing, and lonely which will fuel many behaviors that support separation to love.

43.1 All of the thoughts, feelings, and emotions that humanity moves through existence within our day to day – move through the earth. So this being said, imagine existing as the earth and all of the negativity and unrest that exists from unconscious thoughts, feelings, and emotions within humanity were playing out within your body mind on a day to day basis without any reprieve. This is what is happening with Mother Earth. Our personal unconscious is her greatest pollution, her greatest pain and her only separation to the fullness of love.

43.2 The time is now that humanity redefines life through the sacred opportunity of the Clear Mind Experience allowing the personal unconscious to dissolve throughout the next eighteen months to three years. Throughout this process, we are well on the way to merge as one mind, where we will live within one mind, living within a new life as a new planet, as a Clear Mind. This is the time now to let go. This is the sacred opportunity and the gift bestowed within the Clear Mind Experience. Such magnificence and such beauty is now born and allowing life to move in a new direction. The Clear Mind Experience is present upon the planet and has already cleared portals of existence. The portals that are clear are allowing creation to live within the conscious mind and not within an engaged relationship of the unconscious.

44.1 Take a moment within your mind to visit all the conversations that have been had within this Interpretation Guide, that there is a perception out in the world that we need the unconscious to wake up. This is true in part. Living within it, we do not need, the incarnation of its process we need. Take a moment to look at where the unconscious mind believes it is you and acts within your life. What relationships, experiences, opportunities, and life patterns and structures has it hosted, and where does it reside within life? Sit within the peace of this moment and within the vision of what you see, feel what it feels to be in those situations. It is those feelings, the capacity to have those feelings that will dissolve within the Clear Mind Experience, and the structures that are supporting the feelings will either be redefined to be able to operate within love or dissolved.

44.2 Within this moment, let's look at the visions that were created of the unconscious in 6.1. Let's agree that the unconscious mind is at play in different areas of life, and let us go a step further into that feeling; awakening the statement: IAM Love living within the capacity to feel love. Within that statement, there is a choice. The choice is to dissolve the unconscious and live within the presence of love, or to move back within the unconscious mind and allow it to live as you.

44.3 Frequency of a conscious mind is all-knowing, all-knowing of love and wholeness. There is no perception of the personal being, in the sense, attachment to personal identity. Because of this, there is no one that is seeking to wake up as there is no definition of awake or asleep. Life to the unconscious mind is the movement of love expressing itself to rediscover its potential. When we live within the idea that we are not love seeking to wake up, we are hosting an idea from the unconscious. One would say, "Who needs to wake up?" It is the unconscious mind that perceives this, but it also the unconscious mind that has no capacity to awaken. It will have you practice many things to wake up. Each time one is practiced, it sends further clarification to the unconscious that one needs to seek. To be within love is a process of realization, not acquiring. The conscious mind does not acquire, it expands. The unconscious mind acquires knowledge, acquires process, acquires what is needed to keep itself stuck within the idea that it has failed in what it initially set off to do. The conscious mind is expanding, ever-present and all-knowing. If it moves within a dark place within the universe, it will simply move forth as light. And as soon as love is hosted within that space of darkness, there is only light. The conscious mind is a movement not a projection. It is an expression not a thought. It is a state, not a condition. And it is a revelation, not an idea.

44.4 In accepting 'IAM Love,' within our perceived aware-ness we are already within one mind. The Clear Mind Ex-perience allows the conscious mind to dissolve the unconscious mind. Within this process, the realization of love occurs as a state fully operating. Because there is no separation between the conscious and unconscious mind, they are not singularly operating within perception. Through the Clear Mind Experience, they are joined within the rhythm of the breath, merging and dissolving, and drawing and moving into, expanding and retracting, within each mo-ment, thought, condition, idea, and knowing of each mo-ment of each day. It is a continual flow from one moment to the next of realizations, presence, knowing, love.

44.5 When there is no separation between conscious and unconscious, love is prevailed, accessed, experiences lived within, and as a perceived higher frequency. When the un-conscious mind is dissolved into the conscious mind, the perception of love becomes very centered within clarity. There is clear insight unfolded into each moment of reality. There is no guessing. There is only the full expression of IAM, which makes life move within minimal action, but will achieve great and substantial movement. Love, being the higher frequency lives clear, balanced within an expression of profound clarity.

45.1 – 45.1i Let us take a moment to review. When an in-dividual is working with the unconscious mind to realize it throughout their day, and how it is operating and perceiv-ing reality, and creating within relationships, experiences, opportunities, and life, then one would ask: Are they rein-forcing its importance of existence by always calling forth its presence by wanting to determine how it perceives re-ality? The Clear Mind Experience does not allow you to in-dulge within perception of what the unconscious mind thinks, feels, seeks, creates, or says. The Clear Mind Experience creates opportunity for the participant to become free upon practice. When one is delving in to the unconscious trying and attempting to define what it is saying, one is within an engaged experience with the unconscious mind, and one would ask in that situation, has one brought it forth? And the answer would be yes.

45.2 When we are seeking to understand the unconscious mind and how it is active within our present day, it is the shadow walking along in front of us as on the beach. The unconscious mind is creating questions: What if? What do you think? Maybe? Could we? Do we? Can you? Will you? Do you? Then, depending upon the individual's perception of conscious reality, the individual will either feel overwhelmed by the unconscious mind and consumed in stress, anxiety, depression, and a powerlessness, or they will be continually speaking the conscious mind towards it, feeling frustrated that what the unconscious mind is repeating is not leaving, just redefining itself as another experience.

45.3 – 45.3i When you are walking towards the unconscious mind participating within its play, it will present numerous ideas. And wisdom, being the presence of love and always moving to where love is not present, will continually give an interpretation of love to counteract it. That is the beauty of the wisdom, and the conscious mind is that it will continue to speak to the unconscious, continue reminding it of the beauty and the presence of love, so the two aspects of the mind will be running simultaneously alongside of one another; unconscious mind speaking and conscious mind speaking, but not folding in an out of one another. When an individual pays the unconscious mind this special type of attention to discover it and speak to it, it loves it. It has the attention. It will become melancholic, controlling, suddenly needing your attention and then pushing you away to face the pain of its creation. When you are facing within its direction, it will have you follow endlessly; listening to its stories, ideas, listening to its play.

The conscious mind loves to communicate in the presence of love. It loves to speak and delve and dive and experience the beauty of love and allow it to unfold in magnificent presence. And when the unconscious mind needs loves, the conscious mind will not try to get rid of the unconscious because the conscious mind does not see any reason or any fault of the unconscious mind. The conscious mind is just an expression. The unconscious mind will project its concerns and failings and questions of 'what could be better to make a better life?' The conscious mind will just express love within each moment being relative to what the unconscious mind says, but the unconscious mind will not receive it because it has no capacity to receive the conscious mind through personal will. It can only negate the conscious mind, believe that it is not there. And the conscious mind will not force connection because it is in essence 'stillness.' When you practice the Clear Mind Experience, the structure of the experince and the wisdom behind its program allows these two aspects to move in and out of one another. It gives stillness movement, and it ceases the unconscious mind from being able to project and moves into it to allow its retraction. When the unconscious mind retracts, it draws love into itself. When the conscious mind realizes that it is moving into the unconscious, it does what it does, returns home into itself, which draws the unconscious mind into itself.

46.1 One would ask that if one were to have a spontaneous realization of a higher state of wisdom or if one were to meditate for years and years and realize truth, would it be fair to say that the conscious mind in one moment dissolved all capacity within the mind to believe the opposite? What would be fair to say in this situation is that the conscious mind realized itself to a greater capacity than the unconscious mind. It is at that point that the personal unconscious becomes the collective unconscious perception within the individual's mind. This allows them to connect to the conscious mind and create within their lives a message within the lives of others that awakens individuals to higher states of consciousness. It is not fair to say that the conscious mind has the capacity to believe the opposite. It does not have the capacity to believe the opposite because it never did. It believes nothing. It is a transparent golden frequency of light that moves and operates as a movement. It is an expression of love that forms images, shapes, essence outside of itself, outside of the human mind, within form. Within the human mind, it is the stillness of golden light that moves through feelings to create oneness within self-acceptance, forgiveness, silence, compassion, celebration, inner knowing, and gratitude.

46.2 Throughout the process of awakening the presence of love within the mind, the mind is not conscious mind. It is not saying, "Ooh, there's the darkness and I need it to wake up." It does not say anything or take any position of right or wrong, or better or worse. The conscious mind is an expression. It exists within the moment as the natural state of love.

46.3 Within the realm of human perception, when the conscious mind works to dissolve the unconscious mind, there is a movement, a merging into. Through the process of the Clear Mind Experience, an individual through a question that they answer daily is moved into the unconscious. Then the individual participates through the CD or the Clear Mind breath track, which is a combination of the language of love and the three-part breath. It is within this movement that the conscious mind enters the last point of reference within the mind, within the brain, the neuro-pathway in which the individual accessed to answer the previous question. It is within that moment that the words that move through the three-part breath on the Clear Mind Breath track work to dissolve and swallow the limitations, limited ideas, thoughts, and feelings that operate as brain matter within the unconscious mind. How that is perceived within the essence of energetic means is that the darkness is dissolved into the light. That is what light does; dissolves darkness into itself, transmutes all into light.

46.4 Those times that one faces what exists within the unconscious, there is an internal debate over the perception. There is a loss of trust within understanding where the perception is coming from: Is it a thought that protects and awakens wisdom? Is it a thought that retracts and takes wisdom away? Within the Clear Mind Experience, there is no separation of the two aspects of the mind. They are forming union by folding in and out of one another. So what the participant will experience is love speaking about love. There will be no confusion and distrust cannot be supported because distrust can only be supported within human perception through the unconscious. If the unconscious is dissolving through the process, then love will be what speaks.

46.5 When love speaks, it speaks in kindness. It allows honor and awakens life within humility. Love is expressed within union and wisdom when speaking about life, love, past, present, and concepts. The Clear Mind Experience because it is dissolving the unconscious mind gives great clarity to concepts. Think of those concepts that you have awakened, and thought or reflected upon within your life, both past and future, prediction and vision. Think of life within this moment. How is love being expressed? Is there kindness, honor, humility, and union? And is wisdom moving life as an expression? These are the questions one must ask to understand. Am I walking within the shadow?

46.6 The collective unconscious has an unlimited amount of ways in which to present limitation in the thought that one can live free from the unconscious mind. It will also blur the lines between what is conscious and what is unconscious mimicking stillness, mimicking love. One cannot guarantee to know if one thought or experience or emotion or condition or relationship or opportunity is unconscious or conscious. The only way that one can know is if the perception is free of the unconscious, is when one knows they only have the capacity to view life within love. Dissolving the unconscious mind into the conscious mind is just light dissolving darkness into light. It is an effortless process that only serves to honor the structure of the mind. When light moves into your seven primary emotions, your seven primary perceptions, and ignites the feeling of 49 positive, awakened, Clear Mind feelings, then love is living, breathing, expressing, and being. You cannot choose this experience. One cannot choose to find love or feel love or live in love. One can only open the divine alchemy within the personal perception and within the human brain to be able to live and create and awaken the opportunity in which the alchemic reaction will take place within human perception to allow such love to be present.

47.1 For a moment, let us reflect upon life, relationships, children, opportunities, experiences, and let us perceive that no longer are questions, thoughts, feelings, or emotions seeking to be free from the idea that you are not love, that you are not able to live, serve, and celebrate, and create within radiant consciousness. Imagine if life was free from these perceptions. Imagine if not for one moment of any day a thought arose that was separate from love. What would have been created? What would exist? What does exist under the thought? If the cloudiness of the unconscious mind is removed, the fog is removed then what will one perceive?

48.1 Like anything, things must evolve. This planet has been on a path of evolution and continues to do so. Throughout the evolution of the planet, there have been interpretations that one must hold onto darkness in a way that was powerful. It was important. It was important to spend decades understanding how the unconscious mind was developed, why it was developed, how it acted and played out within life, and it was also important to give it the opportunity to fully emerge upon the planet. It was important because for love to truly realize itself in its fullest potential, it must dissolve the opposite. There must be equal portions upon the planet for this to happen. For love to truly realize itself, it must have truly dissolved what isn't. What is important to realize within today that living within the darkness, living within the shadow, living within an unconscious mind is dead weight. It cannot progress. You are not able to progress. It will have you remain stuck and question, "Am I there yet? Where am I? I can't. I'm not going to make it. I can't live within life." The unconscious mind has been verbalizing on the planet, "I can't live here." It is the unconscious mind verbalizing this that has led to huge amounts of suicide amongst teens. The unconscious mind knows that there is no room for it on the planet, but the problem lies within people believing that the unconscious thoughts are their own. The unconscious mind saying, "I can no longer live" it is just verbalizing exactly what is happening to it. As the light accelerates upon the planet, the unconscious mind must retract. When it speaks within personal perceptions and says "I cannot stand it. I cannot live. I have to retract." It is interpreted by the rational mind as death. All of these things are critically important to understand. Drug companies have created ways in which to shut down the mind, the conscious mind, to numb it, to dull it, giving all power to the unconscious. In a state of confusion, people walk the streets believing that they are asleep, and that their sleeping state is them living. Individuals fear life through anxiety, fear living, fear choices, fear emotions, fear the body, fear their identity, fear their careers, fear one another, fear wars, fear terrorism, fear attacks, fear addiction, fear food, fear for animals, fear for presentation of life. Fear has attached itself to everything. If we allow ourselves to be confused, and understand and believe that the unconscious mind speaking is us, we allow it to operate as us. Then at times, for different people, based on outer circumstances, it is difficult to create separation. The Clear Mind Experience through practice creates this separation so the realization can occur, not through personal choice, but through a chemical shift and reconfiguration of the brain.

48.2 On the planet at this time is profound potential. The karmic release commanding consciousness to let go of itself, meaning the unconscious mind, has occurred. Once an individual is free from thought that the unconscious mind is their only perception of self, they are free. There is a process of allowing new consciousness; the birth of the conscious mind within life to celebrate life within the mind as the person's personal potential. Letting go, letting go within the Clear Mind Experience is the sacred gift of this moment, as there is no choice to let go. There is just the spontaneous realization that one has.

48.3 Making the choice to let go of the unconscious mind may never happen. However, the rational mind will support the process of the Clear Mind Experience if it can understand the qualities of the unconscious and conscious minds, as it will choose which experience it wishes to participate in because it will have foresight in the feelings it will experience within each condition of the mind, meaning conscious versus unconscious. The purpose of this book, the Book of Awareness, is to create the awareness to this discussion. Creating a foundation in which the realization can occur. Creating a safe and transparent opportunity to let go. One will never choose to let go in fullness. One may just choose to participate. There need not be a belief structure that believes the unconscious mind can be dissolved. However, the action of doing the process will awaken the process within the brain, and the spontaneous action of the process will awaken the individual into the presence of love beyond the unconscious as it is dissolved.

49.1 – 49.2 The unconscious mind has for lifetimes been confusing. Doctors, professors, spiritual teachers have spent lifetimes discussing it. The unconscious mind is not discussed in the Book of Awareness. It is revealed as being what will be dissolved. The purpose of the Book of Awareness is to create the foundation of trust so one may ignite the process within their personal mind. One can never figure out the unconscious mind because thought is an unlimited potential. It can define itself and redefine itself. The beauty of the Clear Mind Experience is that it is created within a structure, and within the structure, it is very easy and simple to understand which removes confusion. The unconscious mind loves to be confusing. It loves to be randomly placing thoughts, feelings, and emotions that contradict one another into play. Through the Clear Mind Experience, it is not able to do this because it is fairly silent. It is the conscious mind that is continually speaking to the unconscious. It is the conscious mind that is educating the rational mind, and it is the conscious mind that speaks out into the universe as an expression to create ways and means in which the conscious mind can function upon the planet. In this process, and once this happens, there is no confusion of the unconscious because there is one thought: Goodbye.

What has been most frustrating to individuals has been the spontaneous, cathartic expressions, thoughts, ideas, experiences, and relationships that the unconscious mind will bring into play. People have felt powerless to personal choice, feeling that they never chose to experience the unconscious mind, and, in part, this is true. The personal choice comes in the idea of releasing it and dissolving it but not in its creation. It has been most frustrating to individuals, and that is how medication has come on board with so much force because it increases the opportunity to have personal choice not to deal with it. The unconscious mind within the realm of the Clear Mind Experience is dissolved through the personal choice because the personal choice becomes the practice, the medication, in which one does not have to engage within the unconscious mind. There are some individuals that have lived within the unconscious mind that have risked their lives, created deep and unwavering pain and physical discomfort. It has created trauma and grief. It has revealed great depth of fear within an individual. When someone has experienced this level of fear in an unconscious state, it is virtually impossible to make a choice that one must be free of the unconscious because the unconscious mind interprets itself as the protector. It says, "I must be in control to be safe." Therefore, that statement alone reinforces the presence of the unconscious mind and that it needs to exist to be able to create a safe haven for the mind and for the life of the individual. It has been this cycle and this merry-go-round that has been most frustrating - A: to the person suffering within its hold, and B: to the people who are attempting to clear the person of the unconscious interpretations. However, within the Clear Mind Experience, the personal choice to be free of the unconscious is not made by standing up against it or opposing. It is made through moving the language of love into the unconscious mind and having it dissolved within the presence of love. The personal choice becomes the five minute practice per day. So there is no direct confrontation for the fear. Once the rational mind is able to integrate the peace within the process, it is very much allowing the flow of all love to flow through to the unconscious because it understand that it is creating a feeling of love within the mind and the overall expression of life.

49.3 Throughout the pages of Book of Awareness, we will travel together into the unconscious, into the structure of how it is perceived. The unconscious mind will not know of our journey, but you will know of how it thinks, feels, acts, and moves within life; not as a perception of condition meaning how you are suffering within it, within your life, but you will understand how it thinks, and within understanding how it thinks, you will achieve the freedom to feel at peace with the Clear Mind Experience.

49.4 The unconscious mind has a structure, a very clear, defined structure that consists of 49 signifiers that are attached to feelings that were accumulated during various experiences within the first seven years of life. Each of these signifiers contains a certain number of word sequences in which forms language of the unconscious which enables the unconscious mind to express itself. It is in knowing that the unconscious mind has structure that has created such profundity in the work of the Clear Mind Experience because it is taking the guesswork out of the experience of dissolving it. This is the gift to humanity; the revelation of its structure. Within humanity, humanity understands the level of destruction that can be created through the unconscious mind, and, now, we must walk in the path of understanding how the conscious mind is able to dissolve the unconscious mind to birth profound beauty upon the planet as this is the moment of birth. This is the moment of ecstatic bliss where what is not seen meets what is seen, where what is not love or not perceived as love meets love, where what is not known meets all-knowing. This is the moment of all oneness within the wholeness to be revealed within the now.

49.5 Throughout the Book of Awareness, how the unconscious mind works, how it moves into perception, how it creates limitation, how it can be accessed within personal choice and dissolved consistently within a timely and efficient manner is revealed. One must ask oneself: If upon everyday there was a clearing of the unconscious, what would the following day bring? If the Universe was not able to see the unconscious mind, what would the following day look like? There would be freedom, peace, stillness.

49.6 It is the mission of this book to openly reveal a new interpretation of the structure of the unconscious mind, and within revealing this structure, many gifts will unfold and unlock, both personally and collectively. What will be revealed is that we have the capacity to live within union between the conscious and unconscious minds as the conscious mind is dissolving the unconscious. The union is able to be fostered and lived within the moment of starting the process. One does not have to wait until the end. The union occurs at the beginning, and throughout the technique, one learns of the profundity of that union, and that is how a realization occurs rather than an education. You are not educated through the Clear Mind Experience and convinced into becoming something. Through the technique, the realization occurs of the union of one mind. Then, once the union of one mind has occurred, each day is a continued realization of how that union will be defined as you within your life. That is the gift. That the transformation happens at the beginning. And along the way from the moment of the transformation, from the moment of the awakening, there is just the realization as to what the awakening will translate to mean within the individual's perception and life.

49.7 The Clear Mind Experience is one of simplicity. It is provided to return the mind to that of the perception of a child. Through the expression of the Clear Mind Experience, one will awaken into love through new definitions that are revealed throughout the universal mind. The universal mind will become the perception of the individual as the individual will be living within union of the conscious and unconscious mind. When one is practicing the Clear Mind Experience, they are living within the one mind. How the one mind is interpreted as living as you will be the depth of your awakening and what is revealed to you within your profundity. The Clear Mind Experience is simply the vehicle in which you attain such a state within a timely, efficient clarity.

50.1 Throughout the journey of this book together, throughout the journey of the Clear Mind Experience, you are encouraged to allow love to pass through the mind. When limited perception and limited thought engage within the potential of what life could bring, you are encouraged to take three Clear Mind breaths as part of the Clear Mind Experience.

50.2 It is encouraged for individuals to be open to the beauty of perceiving life and love beyond the struggle. There is no path to find. There is no path to seek. When one thinks and feels they should seek what is lost, a natural struggle is what presents itself. Within the Clear Mind Expression and Experience, there is the revelation of knowing love, IAM Love. Sitting within love, IAM the expression of love. Allowing love, IAM allowing the beauty of love. Feeling love, as IAM allowing the feeling of all love to live within life, within the stillness, as all life is revealed within the potential of love. Being open to that journey is key to awakening to the presence of love simply. If one allows themselves to debate the purpose of awakening to love, then one will be lost within the debate. The two sides of the brain will oppose one another, and there will be no union. It is important through the process of the Clear Mind Experience that one allows union of the brain by not engaging in opposing thoughts that attempt to cancel one another out. The way in which to bring union of mind that empowers the process of the Clear Mind Experience is through the three-part breath.

50.3 If one allows the excitement of this book and its revelations, the excitement of the insights, they will escalate beyond judgment and limitation. Profound ideas of light will awaken and darkness will be dissolved. There will be no limitation and together through the words and breath of Clear Mind beauty, Mother Earth will experience the freedom from the collective unconscious, that of which she is attempting to transcend and ascend into. It is within the open-mindedness to participate that freedom will be birthed. The unconscious mind will always judge, review, seek to understand, or look for explanation. However, it is within the Clear Mind Experience that this cannot be because one must have had the experience to have cleared the unconscious. The words of this book will not clear this. It is the process itself that dissolves the 49 signifiers within the unconscious mind and dissolves the structure in which it is contained. It is also the process that turns the mind, the brain, raises it in consciousness, raises it in frequency, so all thought can be visions of light. It is also the process that creates a chemical change within the brain that does not allow thoughts to become lodged in thoughts of lack and what is not love. All perception is transformed within the experience. It is the experience of the program that gives this to the participant, not the book. The book, however, is for further understanding of the gift. The book is to awaken the lifestyle in which to support the conscious mind. The book is to awaken the environment within the brain that allows the conscious mind to function unhindered by questions. The unconscious mind can ask many questions through the process of the Clear Mind Experience, but the practice itself helps the individual not be hindered by mind chatter. Mind chatter is revealed as the unconscious mind from the moment of practicing. Mind chatter is not observed. Mind chatter is dissolved. If you look at the process of dissolving something, it is a chemical reaction; where one element dissolves another element into it. It does not take laborious effort. It is one moment in time, a dissolving, where one takes over the other. That is the beauty of this Experience. That is the gift to humanity.

50.4 One must ask, is it time? And maybe it is time. Maybe it's no longer difficult, and maybe it's here, the time to finally let go. For each being that practices the Clear Mind

Experience daily, there is a revelation. The revelation of love. It is within that revelation that profound peace, wisdom, and stillness is birthed upon the planet. It is within the revelation of love, there is the knowing that nothing can be done and nothing is to be done. It is the revelation within the presence of love that allows the personal freedom to give compassion, to allow to forgiveness, to align stillness, to live within self-acceptance, to celebrate life within joy, to live in the knowing and the presence of wisdom, all while exchanging gratitude within each moment of life within breath with life. Maybe it's time to just let go.

51.1 Within this moment, imagine that a new level of karma was recently activated upon the planet that is allowing a celebration to awaken. That this activation has removed what was once the struggle to become free. This is what has happened. A new level and interpretation of karma was recently activated, and now individuals are able to access celebration within their awakening. The struggle is no longer present as it has been dissolved into the unconscious mind and let go of from a person's personal perception. With the core of the unconscious mind having been thrown towards the sun, there is only the outer expression of the unconscious mind left. It has nothing to grow from. It has nothing to create from. All it can do is see itself within the mirror. If the personal unconscious mind dissolves, the unconscious mind outside has nothing in which it can be contained so it will be released. It's like breathing on the universal mirror of life and clearing how one perceives oneself.

51.2 Right now within your life, within this moment of reading these words is your gift. It is the personal freedom that is available and ready to clear your mind. The Clear Mind Experience is the language of love. It is the beauty of the

Clear Mind breath. It is the beauty of the unknown grace. It is the activation on multiple dimensions. It is the freedom of Mother Earth. It is the awareness of the conscious mind. It is that in which will live upon the planet. It is the beauty of this clearing of the unconscious that humanity has been walking towards, and right now, within this moment is this personal freedom that is available and ready.

51.3 Throughout time, upon this planet, there have been great teachers, philosophers, both within psychology and spirituality that have been able to reveal that there is a direct integration between what is dark and what is light. Within the process of the Clear Mind Experience is the discussion and the experience of this. It will be within this practice and within the wisdom of the book that under-standing and observation cannot be denied and will be re-defined into new opportunity. Within the pages of The Book of Awareness is the opportunity to attain new life, to perceive new life, to dissolve what isn't, and to reveal the union of the unconscious and conscious.

51.4 What will be revealed is the relationship to the two aspects, and their purpose and potential as one. That when we dissolve the unconscious into the conscious, something profound is revealed. Are you curious to reveal the potential within life when the unconscious mind dissolves into the conscious mind?

Curious to reveal the potential of the moment that the unconscious mind dissolves into the Conscious Mind.

52.1 Within the curiosity of dissolving the unconscious mind into the conscious mind is the question of how could this positively affect us? This is something for you to give consideration to. Where in your life, if you were able to perceive love, would it be different? When you feel powerless to situations, there is an interpretation that you are not going to be free of a certain experience. This, however, is not true. The unconscious mind does not have the capacity to let go of itself. But, take a moment to sit back and ask the conscious mind to reveal: what does love feel like within you?

52.2 What happened through the dissolving of the unconscious mind is very profound. As what awakens is for an individual to no longer have the capacity to engage in limited thoughts, feelings, and emotions, and a lack of love and potential. It is within this that freedom, expression of love, is revealed, not thought awakened and experienced. We do not know who we are. The humanity does not have expectation of what it would be without the unconscious mind. We can only dissolve it and wait for the discovery.

52.3 Dissolving the unconscious mind is an incredibly gentle process. As dissolving the unconscious mind within the Clear Mind Experience is done so within union with breath. You are, within the Clear Mind Experience, dissolving the unconscious mind through the living expression of how you are perceiving and living within life. If you are living with responsibilities and children and things that keep you active within life, you will dissolve the unconscious mind at the speed in which is gentle within how you can connect to love. Love does not seek to create destruction. It does not seek to create unrest and grief and loss. That is the unconscious mind's fear; that throughout the process of dissolving the unconscious mind that you will upend in some type of emotional turmoil. When, in effect, emotional turmoil belongs to the conditions of the unconscious mind. When you move into the conscious mind, you move into the rhythm of the stillness. You move into the rhythm of allowing each day to be, rather than trying to resolve each problem that you've interpreted may have arrived. The conscious mind will not interpret problems. It will interpret opportunities. It will not interpret ways in which it should behave. It will interpret a fluidity of how life is within each moment of each day. The rational mind within the Clear Mind Experience becomes profound stillness. Within that stillness what is revealed is that the conscious mind is just operating, and within the conscious mind operating, it is expressing love. When one is not practicing the Clear Mind Experience, the unconscious mind is operating. The individual will either be operating upon the commands of the unconscious and feeling deeply disconnected and deeply suffering and lost in tragedy of no longer expressing or feeling love, and maybe in some ways being pushed by the unconscious mind to feel loss. However, when one is living within a conscious mind, there is nothing to run out to save, to do. Life is happening through it, not because of it.

52.4 When love moves into the personal perception or the perception moves into the presence of love, it gives the individual a feeling of what love feels like. And, once one is feeling love, the universe will interpret this feeling and will set up experiences within life that honor the presence of that love because love is conditioned to preserve itself. So when love is magnified outward to the universe, the universe will magnify to love ways in which to preserve itself.

52.5 Once the feeling of love is registered as a perception of oneself, then your feelings are no longer attached to thoughts. Once the universe perceives that feelings are not attached to thoughts, it perceives the individual as a rhythm, as a flow, celebrating the beauty of consciousness and the presence of love. It will provide experiences, relationships, and opportunities to become present in life. So life becomes a new expression that is void of limitation, pain, hurt, confusion, exhaustion that was once structured within the unconscious mind. It is the unconscious mind that has us live within conditions and experiences that do not preserve love. When one practices the Clear Mind Experience, their life becomes void of the unconscious expression; not that they mindfully try to erase the unconscious. That is not encouraged. It is simply through the participation, like sugar and water, the unconscious disappears.

53.1 The beauty of this book is that it cannot be interpreted through levels of consciousness from the participant. The book is for the layman who is seeking individual freedom from the unconscious, and also the light worker who seeks union of mind and earth where their insights, wisdom, practices are calling and honored in the resources, opportunities, and abundance to serve. This book is interpreted through the personal perception of the participant. It is not here to tell you how to think, how to be, what you should be within life. It is here as a vehicle to accompany the Clear Mind Experience. As you move through the Clear Mind Experience, each page, each section will be reinterpreted, will present new meaning and different definition throughout your journey, and that is the gift in which it is bestowed and given and presented.

53.2 There is also the opportunity within the pages of this experience for professionals who seek to help others experience the dissolving of the unconscious mind. As within the pages are opportunities for participants to understand the importance of the journey. The Clear Mind Experience is a powerful experience, but when joined with a professional that has been given the assimilated perception and bestowed through the transmission the opportunity to take others through into new awareness of personal freedom, then it is a different experience again. There are some individuals that feel that they need the opportunity to experience this with another through training as a facilitator and that is encouraged. The entire work of the Clear Mind Experience is to open up an opportunity where one feels that they are being supported within the safety of a new experience. It is in feeling supported that the unconscious mind is easier to dissolve because it will not hang on in fear of protecting itself.

53.3 No matter what your purpose for picking up and reading The Book of Awareness, it is about you realizing the power of perceiving love within a Clear Mind. The book is meant to accompany the practice. This book is not another prescription of how you may choose to change your life. This book is to accompany the gift; the gift being the Clear Mind Experience. It is in practicing the Clear Mind Experience that you will be dissolving the unconscious, and what is written within this book will be companionship not an invitation or a direct challenge to the unconscious mind.

53.4 The Book of Awareness is for personal freedom. It is presented through this being in tremendous humility for your life. It is presented in aim to discover love, most important, to honor you as the divine presence of love. As it is within the book that liberation can be bestowed; liberating one from the unlimited perception of what is not able to contain liberation. All things that those desire to be free of what isn't the ultimate expression of consciousness celebrating consciousness, or consciousness realizing the presence of love, is available within the union of one mind, within the union of the written word and the divine experience of the Clear Mind process.

53.5 You are encouraged to go beyond the unconscious right now. Within this moment, you are the living potential of love that is realizing itself as a gift within humanity and in allowing yourself the beauty of the Clear Mind Experience, you will be celebrating the greatest potential of this realization. It is not about what is written, it is about the experience, and then what is written will speak to the experience, and within that, realizations will occur at a much more rapid rate within the clarity of what is perceived within the written word.

Spiritual Psychology

54.1 The Book of Awareness is the divine union of spirituality and psychology. If we look at this union closely, we can observe that psychology by nature is studying and looking to understand and potentially overcome the limitations of the unconscious mind. Psychology is what has revealed to the unconscious mind. Psychology is what has encouraged us to reflect upon to seek, to understand, to calibrate the unconscious mind's expressions and how and when they formed. Psychology, however, is void of the remedy in which to take an individual out of the unconscious mind perceptions. It has played with ways in which to do it; that the clarity and precision that is needed to dissolve the structure of the unconscious mind has yet to be revealed, but is revealed in its wholeness within the Clear Mind Experience. The unconscious mind structure has yet to be revealed in which it is in the capacity of the Clear Mind Experience. It is within the revelation of the Clear Mind Experience that psychology will redefine the approach of the unconscious mind as psychology will become what supports a conscious mind. Psychology of the new times will be a discovery of fine tuning perception of conscious thought. Psychology will open up means and ways in which a transparent mind can create. Psychology will be about shape-shifting, vibrational frequencies, light beings, how to perceive reality through that which is unseen. Psychology will be what supports the pineal gland. Psychology will be what expands perception into multiple universes. Psychology will be a container in which the mind is contained in light. Psychology will be, and continues to evolve into, a much greater experience of higher frequency. It is the Clear Mind Experience that, once moved through the planet, will have redefined psychology. All of a sudden, the people that enter the offices of psychologists will be seeking affirmation. Psychologists will no longer be invoking what isn't working but supporting what is. Speaking about potential is as important as speaking about non-potential, if not more. Speaking about what IS, is critically important because it enables the being to celebrate consciousness without the direct assimilated verbal assimilation or integrated physical integration of celebrated consciousness, if one is not able to manifest in life. One would become static.

55.2 Most times that an individual is seeking to find counsel of a psychologist, it is in a need for help. It is because they have assimilated or lived through an experience where they have felt victim to the unconscious mind, either someone else's or their own. The problem being is that the mass population of psychologists on the planet does not sit someone down and say, "Well that is the unconscious mind, not you. You are within your natural state the perception of love, and the unconscious mind believes that it is you." And then within that moment, they are not able to take them through a process that enables them to dissolve the aspects of the unconscious that have been presenting themselves. However, within the Higher Mind Institute and the Clear Mind Experience, this is exactly what is maintained and happens. Humanity is served to remain and support the nature of love. The unconscious mind is dissolved, discarded, and not given life through conversation. It would be more beneficial for an individual to talk about potential than destruction. Once reinforcing destruction within two people through a conversation, you have created it to manifest, or you have supported it to be present. One must always say, "Who am I if I am not that?" One must always say, "Who am I if I am not engaged within the unconscious thoughts of destruction?" This has more power for change. However, if one is not dissolving the unconscious, all this is mere based conversation, and just the mind randomly presenting thoughts, ideas, and desires of what potential could be, and what loss feels like.

56.3 The unconscious mind will have us spend a lifetime trying to process its interpretations. It will be screaming to become free of what it believes about itself. More often than not, the thoughts are painful, limiting, and lacking of unconditional love. The unconscious mind is always perceiving the suffering. It can spend endless hours within that suffering; creating it, living it, and talking about it. However, what is beneath that? What is on the other side of the mind? What is able to be perceived within the other aspect of the brain? This is what must be accessed and activated. Within the Clear Mind Experience, this is what is activated; the aspect of the brain that has the capacity to see life beyond what the unconscious mind limits us to believe. Within the other aspect of the brain is the conscious mind, who really doesn't look to know or understand any aspect of the unconscious. Every time the unconscious mind acts or speaks, once the conscious mind is activated, it will just speak in love all day to the unconscious. If, however, the rational mind is able to make connection with an unconscious thought, it will create the unconscious thought to become a reality through the feelings of what it feels like to receive the unconscious thought. The Clear Mind Experience does not allow the rational mind to make contact with the unconscious mind so, therefore, the rational mind becomes the witness. It is when it is the witness that it participates in listening to the conscious mind, and, of course, the rational mind is about feeling. When it listens to the conscious mind speaking, it falls in love, and then it begins to protect its true love: the conscious mind.

56.4 Spirituality upon this planet has those seek love, seek purpose, seek truth, destiny, and freedom from the actions of the unconscious mind even though someone may not perceive that the actions they are attempting to get rid of or escape from are unconscious thoughts.

57.1 Spiritual psychology for a beautiful mind which is what is given and bestowed from the Clear Mind Experience is the incorporation of the two needs.

58.1 Union of one mind is the union of two needs. The first need is the need to dissolve negative and limited behaviors, ideas, thoughts, feelings, and circumstances that are perceived from the unconscious mind that limit one from the perception of love.

58.2 The second need is to allow the conscious mind to awaken the experience of truth and love by perceiving the value of this feeling. The conscious mind, when it awakens and lives within the presence of wisdom and truth, is able to create within its feelings.

58.3 It is the unlimited expression of their merging within their union that is the beauty of the Clear Mind Experience; that what is seemingly opposing becomes one, what seemingly cannot merge becomes whole, and it is not done through the personal choice or the intent that this is what must happen. It is done through the action of the Clear Mind Experience.

58.4 The Clear Mind Experience is the oneness, the wholeness of mind. It is the oneness on how to move into the mind to know, to understand the mind, and the revelation and birth of the conscious mind, the oneness. Spirituality and psychology need to form union upon this planet. Everybody is attempting to wake up at this time, and some are interpreting their awakening as limitations of the unconscious mind as being their reality. Spirituality and its philosophies and psychology must merge together because people that are awakening need to go and sit with a psychologist to be able to talk about the potential of their lives without getting stuck within the projection of the unconscious and the powerlessness of the unconscious. The Clear Mind Experience will bring union between these two fields of thought and consciousness.

59.1 Allowing the conscious mind, the spiritual mind to dissolve the unconscious mind is union of self. It is the realization of love. It is the point of consciousness where true discoveries and revelations of love, purpose, wisdom, and destiny are unveiled to the participant. There is magic and beauty and mysticism within love. There is a way in which we do not understand what love perceives. However, the mind is a vehicle in which we can give love life, in which we can give love action, in which we can give love the opportunity to create what is its expression as a divine being upon the planet.

59.2 The divine alchemy of the mind is for these two aspects to merge as one, the conscious and the unconscious. The unconscious and the conscious mind are available within the one mind to go through this process. That is the alchemy of their incarnation; that the conscious mind will dissolve the unconscious mind into its presence and level of awareness. When one engages within alchemy within a feeling state, what is birthed is the bliss. Where life takes form, form knows no form and love expresses itself as nothing as it lives within the wholeness of all.

59.3 Living within the conscious mind is an effortless movement that allows life to be soothing, calming, nurturing, and within the expression of life is a beauty that awakens profound peace. Because there is no need to be, there is no personal identity to protect, there is no thing or object that could mean or present any greater opportunity than what it is to feel love alive within the perception of oneself.

59.4 The union of one mind awakens within a magical place within the mind. The pineal gland is what takes both aspects into one. It is within this pineal gland that one will feel youthful, invigorated, excitement, and joy. It is within the pineal gland that one will merge within the childlike nature of life. It is the magical place where unlimited universal perception meets world.

59.5 The child-mind lives within the pineal gland. It is the aspect of the brain that allows and invigorates life to be that of the unlimited perception of a child, where each moment is not found or pursued; each moment is revealed. A child moves effortlessly through life, free from judgment of what is not right, what is not good, until their perception allows it. When one activates the pineal gland and lives within the perception of the child-mind, one accesses life prior to the knowing that life can be separate, that love can disappear, and that each moment can create hurt. When the unconscious mind is dissolved, the pineal gland becomes the seat of perception. It is where all light is moved from within the mind. It is the portal between two worlds; the world in which you stand, footpads to soil, and the world in which is unseen, the universe in which one came. It is within the pineal gland that the alchemy of this moment is born. It is the beauty of the pineal gland that awakens, celebrates, lives within life, within the perception and union of love. The pineal gland is the seat, the ascension seat. Within the earth, there is the pineal gland, her ascension, where she will ascend from. The pineal gland of the earth is yours. You are carrying what will activate her ascension as the earth is the true bodhisattva. She is providing the opportunity for you to awaken, to liberate, in which she will follow.

60.1 To really assist with uncovering exactly how the conscious and unconscious minds define life, one is going to have to delve into the five primary interpretations, relationships to life. Human form is about relationships. Human form is given to master our relationships. However, relationships cannot be mastered while carrying the unconscious because true self-mastery is the expression of love. The five primary relationships upon the planet are: relationship to child, relationship to self-love, relationship to emotional self, relationship to living self, relationship to spiritual self. One will understand with great power of perception how the unconscious mind is being dissolved when they are able to clearly define how each relationship is operating within their lives. When each relationship operates within the unconscious, great turmoil and frustration fills life. When love moves into each of these primary relationships, and the unconscious mind is no longer able to present itself, then these relationships become harmonized, and within the harmony, tremendous love is again realized. When love is perceived, it is perceived on multiple levels and interpretations, evolving one after the other after the other. There is great beauty in perceiving life through love. Relationships, when they are hosted within a conscious mind, just become a vehicle in which to express the divinity of love and how love will find itself within each moment of life.

61.1 When one is living within the unconscious mind or with the unconscious mind active within perception and the day to day, one's life will be filled with negative self-talk. Most actions, experiences, opportunities, and relationships will be primarily moved and activated within life by self-defeating negative thoughts. These negative thoughts, 'negative self-talk' as known within the Clear Mind Experience, are accumulated within the first seven years of life. They are each thought, feeling, and emotion that makes up the unconscious mind. It is dissolving negative self-talk that is Level 1 of the Clear Mind Experience. To be able to move forward with dissolving the unconscious effectively and efficiently, one must gain trust within perception. One must re-connect with the inner knowing and inner awareness to wisdom and allow wisdom to integrate the journey of dissolving the unconscious. To be able to integrate the journey and integrate the presence of wisdom, one must dissolve negative self-talk. A lot of individuals report, "Well, I don't talk negatively." But their actions are subtly being invoked within their day to day by negative ideas that they have of themselves; that they must protect, seclude, control, change, invoke separation from others, be co-dependant, be attached, protect themselves by strategies and ideas. This is all motivated through negative self-talk. The negative self-talk generates a lack of self-appreciation so when activities, experiences, opportunities move forward from within the universe to acknowledge our presence upon the planet, they typically, if the unconscious mind is not dissolved, speak to the language of negative self-talk, re-inforcing thoughts, feelings, and emotions that leave one feeling suppressed, controlling, defeated, or misunderstood. If one takes time to listen to the unconscious mind when it is speaking, it is only speaking about itself. It is talking about its lack of ability to be able to integrate into love. It is talking about how it must find ways to be peaceful because it doesn't have the capacity. The issue comes within human perception when the person believes that's who they are, and it's not just the unconscious running like a tape telling you what it is. Once you start the Clear Mind Experience, you are able to witness this voice very clearly speaking about itself. Then all the ways that it has created feelings within the being associated with the neg-ative self-talk are cleared by dissolving the unconscious.

61.2 If an individual is living within the unconscious mind, it will live and operate within life through negative self-talk. One can still gain and accumulate and perceive success within negative self-talk because it can be achieved and acquired through the process of believing that others are negatively perceiving us or experiences need us to be in control. It is when we perceive reality through negative self-talk that we compete strongly against others. We do that to empower oneself for the win. The unconscious mind will speak endlessly of what it must do to overcome relation-ships with others. It will speak endlessly of the powerless-ness that it is experiencing within different relationships. It will speak endlessly, negatively of others because it needs to do that to be able to feel that it is greater than - within understanding, education, interpretation, so it can find itself to feel more powerful. It is within that that the unconscious mind feels a sense that it has achieved something greater than, so, therefore, it is fine. The unconscious mind seeks adoration to be able to hold onto itself. To believe in itself it has to disbelieve in others. It doesn't have the capacity to stand alongside, shoulder to shoulder, with great men and women. It wants to take one step further ahead. It believes in position, immediate gratification, of being served.

61.3 The unconscious mind will convince itself that a person standing before it that cares for it and wants the best for it, is there to be distrusted; that their motives of care are not transparent which is quite often untrue. The unconscious mind sees everything against it. It can have great friends but believe the friends are against it. It always creates separation within inner language concerning others. It has to. It is separate. There is no union. It cannot be in union. It can be in a forced union. But it cannot solely surrender to the experience. If an individual solely surrenders to an experience, it is the conscious mind that does so because it forms union with every experience. Relationship being an opportunity, it will either form union with an individual through like-mindedness and oneness, or compassion. The unconscious mind believes in separation because it has to, to exist.

61.4 The unconscious mind will believe in relationships that to be successful, celebrated, feel worthy within itself, it must push up against, or away from, what represents a unit, what represents its empowerment. The unconscious mind will feel empowerment by being in control. Most successfully, great people who believe they are great, who have achieved greatness through the unconscious mind will say they are incredibly lonely; that they feel great distrust for those around them, that they've never found a friend, that they've not been able to find a true partner, that they gained and gained and gained and were left to feel lonely with nothing. This is because the unconscious mind has created within their mind the negative self-talk and is operating within that to keep people at bay and to keep itself guarded because it does sit within distrust. It does not feel that it can support others or that others can support it.

61.5 When living within the unconscious and perceiving relationships, the individual can confuse itself to the point where everything in person that is perceived by the unconscious as a means not to support, not to honor, and not to love oneself or the other. The unconscious mind is continually speaking within separation. It is a vehicle of separation. It can only perceive separation. When one practices the Clear Mind Experience, the unconscious mind is decompressed; that means that the unconscious mind retracts within itself, no longer acts out within relationships, so when one is maintaining, honoring, and expanding within the conscious mind creating relationships, opportunities, and experiences to honor the presence of love, the unconscious mind cannot come in and define the distrust, disharmony, disunity, fear of their relationship. Within the Clear Mind Experience, it will remain decompressed, contracted, withdrawn into itself, unable to define each moment as itself.

61.6 The unconscious mind is impersonal. It is not acting out maliciously to control anything or anybody. It is impersonal. However, it does appear that way to the personal mind because the unconscious mind is not able to perceive love. When one is sitting within the presence of love, feeling love at different points within their life, and the unconscious mind appears, it will define the loss of love so it will appear to the perception that the unconscious mind is going to take, destroy, attack, manipulate a situation which will hurt somebody, but the unconscious mind is just operating. When you practice the Clear Mind Experience, you are able to witness the unconscious mind. It appears as a voice that just speaks, randomly talking. There is no feeling in any way to support, engage, heal, look at, review the voice of the unconscious. When one practices the Clear Mind Experience, they are living within a conscious mind allowing the unconscious to slowly dissolve.

61.7 The unconscious mind to protect itself will always speak about itself. It will speak about its needs, what has to happen, how it can be protected, what needs to change within life so it can feel peace, what needs to happen within life so there is no stress, the amount of money that it needs, the perfect partner that it requires, how that partner should be perceived physically, how children should behave, what life should present it, what should have happened within childhood, what would be better to have happened now. It will get, form attachment to, things that represent the false identity of happiness; meaning if the things disappear so does the happiness. The unconscious mind loves to speak about itself because within defining itself within the universe, it is more vast. It loves to imprint itself throughout all of life through talking. When one practices the Clear Mind Experience, it retracts and is unable to speak out loud. Therefore, the thoughts just pass, they are nothing; like clouds passing within the sky. It is the three-part breath that it is the wind, the wind of the Holy Spirit that blow those clouds across the sky.

61.8 The unconscious mind loves to speak about where there is no love. It loves to define the hopelessness of no love. It always defines the other person's lack of capacity, "If only they were different, I'd be different; if only 'this' was this way, it would be different for me; if only they had have behaved differently, it would be different for me; if only I had the capacity to love; if only I could change this, I would be in love; if only I had the money, I could be free; if only I was more financially secure, I could let go." It is just an endless conversation, "If I looked more beautiful, I will be happy; if I change 'this' about myself, there love will be; if I find the perfect partner, there love will come." Life is about a relationship to our own inner awareness to ourselves and the presence to love, 'ourselves' being the presence of love. When one feels the presence of love, all life represents that. When one is not able to feel the presence of love, then all life will represent this longing. The unconscious mind will present multitudes of experiences, opportunities, relationships, and thoughts that are continually seeking the validation of love as it is forever complaining that it is not able to find it.

61.9 At a point within life when the unconscious mind is speaking where there is a lack of love, one can ask oneself, "What do you feel in the current situation? What is the feeling of being within the experience?" Whether the feeling is a sense of distrust, whether the feeling is a sense of lack of support, whether the feeling is a sense of confusion, fear, self-doubt, and whatever the feeling it is the emotional payoff of why you are in the experience. It is the feeling that you receive and that you connect to, that the unconscious mind has initiated for the experience collectively so you can engage the feeling within outer experience so the unconscious mind can be reinforced. If you look at the feelings that you feel within these experiences, they will be reinforcing ideas of falsehood that the unconscious mind has to be able to keep you out of the presence of love. When using the Clear Mind Experience and you connect to these feelings, you are able to move your perception out of the unconscious feeling into the opposite/conscious feeling. What this does is allows the unconscious mind to be dissolved. Quite often when an individual faces an experience of this when they are doing the Clear Mind Experience, they are dissolving the signifier itself. That is the electrical field around a set of commands and the language that is active within the unconscious mind. These are powerful moments. To move one's perception consciously changes life forever because it says to the aspects of perception: IAM.

61.10 At times when one is clearing the unconscious, dissolving it, they will find themselves disengaging in negativity with other people within relationships. It is at that point that a person that you cared for may consider that you have abandoned them because you are no longer speaking about issues within the unconscious. If you look at this for a moment, it is the unconscious mind speaking about you abandoning it, no longer feeding into the stories that it has about who you are or how life is. It is at these points in time within relationships that it is important to verbalize and bring into the experience of the relationship the understanding and feeling of the IAM. This can be easily done by sitting with the individual speaking about the qualities that you find most beautiful about the person. Once you have spoken about the qualities that you find beautiful about the person, you speak about your own beautiful qualities. You then explain to the individual that your path in life is to honor those beautiful thoughts about oneself, and to allow the negative thoughts to drift away. It is within this moment that you may have integrated the process that is occurring within the brain through the Clear Mind Experience into physical relationship. However, a person can also feel completely abandoned that you are not supporting negativity and walk away from you to experience their negativity. No matter what happens within your life, through your life, around your life, when you are practicing the Clear Mind Experience, there is only ever the feeling to preserve love within which allows love to be experienced through life. Allowing this process is simple, freeing. When you are living within the Clear Mind Experience, there are no expectations of others. You are able to allow others their own experience because you are celebrating yours.

61.11 When one experiences the clearing of unconscious belief systems and structures within one's life, the unconscious mind will believe that the relationship, the experiences and how it is defined, is what you deserve to struggle against, the unconscious mind when there is a struggle is active as it is within the struggle called into play. The unconscious mind will create struggles because it ultimately believes there must be one for it to exist. The unconscious mind within life, when active, will define most of life as a struggle. Life will be a struggle. It will be a perceived struggle to make money as one perceives the fear to maintain and hold onto the money. It will seem a struggle to maintain a relationship when one longs and aches to be free of the relationship. It will perceive a struggle with one's health and wellness when one perceives that health and wellness is a struggle to maintain. Everything that the unconscious mind touches, it will confuse into a loss.

61.12 At different moments of discovering your feelings, you will be able to determine if the feelings you are having about an experience, relationship, or opportunity are conscious or unconscious. Feeling the feeling of the situation is often a great way to make a decision to understand, "Did the experience come through the unconscious or conscious mind?" because the feelings that will come up will show you what you are able to experience within what you feel. Sometimes the conscious mind will express itself and present a new opportunity and the unconscious feelings that want to protect one from experiencing what the conscious mind has placed in front will surface. But with those feelings, there will be a sense, a knowing that the feeling is holding one back, getting you to retract. Feelings are important in determining how one moves and experiences life. The Clear Mind Experience is about creating fluidity within feeling. It is within feelings that one can discover tremendous beauty within life. When feelings are suppressed, they engage great anger and corrupt one's motives. When feelings are allowed to be free, and they are feelings that honor and preserve love and life, then feelings become the conductors of how we experience life. The messages we receive, the relationships and how they are defined, everything becomes a feeling. It is within our feelings that the conscious mind becomes a movement, an expression. Feelings allow us to live within the ecstatic bliss of love. It is within the feelings that love dissolves the unconscious. Feelings allow us to radiate the pure joy and beauty of an awakened life. Feelings resonate our souls. Feelings resonate outward inward, creating unity between the outer perception and the inner knowing. Feelings, when calibrated to the unconscious mind, will create great harm to the body. There will be a feeling of retraction within the body, a feeling of control within the body, and the underlying motive of the body will be the fear to control the body and not celebrate the body in its ultimate movement and knowing. Feelings are what make us human. Feelings allow us to be spiritual. Feelings allow us to be a parent. Feelings engage us in being a child. Feelings engage us with another. Feelings engage us sexually. Feelings engage us within success. Feelings engage us within vision. Feelings engage us within other realms. It is our feelings that allow pure magnificence to be born. Suppressing feelings through medication, thoughts, feelings, ideas, television, music that suppresses the true feeling of love are harmful to life. They defrag an individual's energetic field, so an energetic field will be walking through life shattered unable to communicate with other beings, other realms. It is the feelings that we honor that support love to form union. Feelings are our enlightenment, our liberation. Feelings allow us to realize the presence of love. Feelings take us home. Feelings unite. Feelings awaken freedom. It is the feeling of moving within the ocean, the feeling of standing upon the mountain, the feeling of the sun, the feeling of the wind that speaks within us the language of the earth. It is the language of love of the Clear Mind Experience that speaks into the feelings to enliven, activate, and awaken feelings into the pure bliss and freedom of love.

61.13 If a relationship within your life is conscious, but being hindered by the unconscious expressions and fears of the unconscious or aspects of the unconscious or language of the unconscious, then dissolving the unconscious mind will release perceptions that one has of the relationship. If this is able to be achieved, then a time will present itself to either heal the relationship or release the experience of the relationship. Sometimes, we are able to bring things together in a beautiful magnificence once the unconscious mind is clear, and then other times, we will release life experiences just as the unconscious is dissolved. It is in releasing life experiences and allowing them to move away, move on, and redefine themselves that one may need the nurturing of another verbally. When an individual is making choices based on what feels right, a discussion about those feelings is important. The Clear Mind Experience has trained leaders, men and women of tremendous value and compassion, that are able to discuss feeling, are able to allow a safe space in a transparent portal of light that is of the Higher Mind Institute, in which they are able to discuss the flow if wisdom. When an individual is consulting with a Clear Mind Practitioner, they are entering one of these portals of light, and within the portal, they are experiencing themselves, while with the Clear Mind Practitioner, as being free of any feeling that is being interpreted through the unconscious that is of their primary focus at that time. Once they move out into their life from the appointment, the individual will feel the feeling and feel the time to initiate that it be let go. Clear Mind Practitioners are turning points, moments that assist to create one moment to the next. Within their portals, they sit within pure transparency. What sits them within the portal is the humility that they have engaged in to surrender their own story of the unconscious mind.

61.14 Clear Mind Practitioners are trained to determine limitations. They are trained to discuss limitations with those whose feelings become very strong, with those whose feelings have been suppressed, and there is fear in integrating them. The Clear Mind Practitioner will help in determining the limitations of the unconscious that one is experiencing and allowing within life to block feeling. The Clear Mind Experience can also successfully be practiced without the Practitioner by those who are able to create fluidity of assimilated feeling very quickly. The Clear Mind Experience is spiritual psychology for a beautiful mind. This is because the condition of the experience is one of unconditional love, compassion, and wisdom. Clear Mind Practitioners are trained to create space and awareness of an individual's experience, and within that, the individual will realize how the unconscious mind is playing out within life. It is very important when dissolving the unconscious mind that one can clearly determine its limitations early on, so when the energies get subtle at the later stages of entering into the spiritual mind, one is able to see the limitations in the subtle form.

62.1 As individuals practice the Clear Mind Experience, we do so for Mother Earth. As within the dissolving of our own personal unconscious, we are dissolving the collective unconscious which affects/defines her, similarly to how the personal unconscious mind affects/defines us. This year in celebration of this awareness, the Higher Mind Institute launched the Clear Mind New Planet Initiative. This was launched to be able to bridge those that are practicing the Clear Mind Experience into the collective unconscious and create and opportunity in which the earth was served in greater conscious perception.

62.2 It is the Clear Mind New Planet Initiative that will bring awareness globally to the power of negative self-talk, how it is affecting the momentum of our lives, and Mother Earth and her awakening. It is the motive and initiative of this year to bring awareness to individuals about the power of negative talk and how it is playing out within their lives, and in playing out within their lives, what is it doing to the earth and what limitations is it breeding within humanity?

Negative self-talk is Level 1 of the Clear Mind Experience. This means that in 2010, January 4th, Level 1 was released to Mother Earth. She is now clearing negative self-talk. She is able to do this through the participation of those within the Clear Mind New Planet Initiative. As part of this Initiative, there will be great outreach over the coming years to orphans, children who have been denied connection to the mother through the conscious mind. Mother Earth will call these children home within herself through the Clear Mind Initiative and the Baby Breath Program. It is Baby Breaths that awakens the sense of oneness with the mother, moves and dissolves all rejection within the unconscious, allows for embrace and opportunity and potential of love within self. As well as the Baby Breaths, the Clear Mind Initiative is available to youths so as to awaken the feeling within oneself of self-love; teaching the youths that preserving love is the key to successful living. Next there is the Suicide Prevention Program which is teaching those that are vulnerable that what they hear is not a command of death within themselves, but it is the unconscious mind dying collectively upon the planet. It is the unconscious mind losing traction, and in identifying with this conversation and practicing the Clear Mind Experience, they will become witness to the unconscious mind speaking of its demise. The Clear Mind New Planet Initiative is also moving within the lives of those that experience physical disease and disharmony. It is within the Clear Mind Experience that they will be able to witness the unconscious mind speaking of its loss of body awareness, its loss of traction upon the planet. The unconscious mind is moving away from its body, both personally and collectively. Within the collective unconscious, the body for the unconscious to hang onto, is the earth. Within the personal unconscious, the unconscious mind is hanging on to the personal body. As the unconscious mind is losing frequency and vibration to be able to attach itself to form, it speaks of losing awareness to body. When it does that, it perceives disease. Once the rational mind hears these conversations, it allows the unconscious mind to create ways in which it can be attached which is disease, disharmony, fatigue, and stress of the form.

62.3 It is the hope of all realms of consciousness that conduct the Clear Mind Experience upon the earth; to have others realize that this Initiative has not been set up as criticism, but more of a means in which to show and demonstrate how powerful the unconscious mind is when it speaks of itself, of the destruction and disharmony that it can cause both personally and collectively when it is speaking, especially when the rational mind believes it is a conversation of oneself. 2010 of the Clear Mind Initiative of the Clear Mind New Planet and Higher Mind Institute is about opening debate and discussion about life without the unconscious and how quickly it can be dissolved; removing the complication and the limitation out of the ideas that one should live within its perceptions.

62.4 There are so many unconscious interpretations and stories within the unconscious mind, both personally and collectively, that once you practice the Clear Mind Experience, you will notice that it is randomly speaking continuously within everyday. It will challenge peace within each moment of creation by presenting random conversations, negative conversations that lead to disharmony of oneself, about oneself, and others. Once someone engages within the Clear Mind Experience, it becomes very apparent very quickly that the unconscious mind will spend hours and hours and hours defining and redefining and redefining life and its needs and what it needs to be happy, peaceful, and allowing of each moment of life. Each time it presents an idea, within the idea is always a limitation. There is always an 'if only' or 'what if' attached to the idea that the unconscious mind will present. It speaks about oneself. When it speaks about others, it is speaking about itself. What gives the unconscious mind personal identity within the personal perception of the individual is that it is developed through the environment that the child lives in within the first seven years which connects to the feelings of what it was like to live within those first seven years, and within creating the unconscious mind, it takes hold of the feelings and says, "This is who you are." It is this fact that makes the unconscious mind feel personal. However, once the feelings engage within the presence of love, which happens very quickly upon practicing the Clear Mind Experience, then the feelings are no longer attached to the unconscious, and when they are not attached to thought, the unconscious mind has no way to engage other than through random conversations, and words, and sentences that are supposedly speaking of the individual. The gift of the Clear Mind Experience is that feelings are no longer attached to any thought, good or bad. Feelings just become spontaneous movements and expressions of love that move and are activated through perception within each moment. Feelings become clear of thought. So it is not the thought waking up the feeling, it is love being magnetized into the outer experience. When the feeling moved through the perception, it is registered within the rational mind.

63.1 The unconscious mind seeks very strongly to protect itself. However, what is important is to understand 'how' it is protecting itself. It will protect itself through co-dependant relationships. It will protect itself through suppression and powerlessness. It will create experiences within your life that you feel you cannot get away from. This is a story of the unconscious. It likes to live within these experiences so it can always talk about being trapped. It is the conversation that it has about being trapped that awakens the feeling that one is, but without the feeling being attached to the idea of being trapped, one is able to negate such statements. That is why when one starts practicing the Clear Mind Experience, it is important to realize how the unconscious mind is protecting itself, and it is quite doable because the thoughts and feelings are not attached. Thoughts of the unconscious are not attached to feelings.

63.2 When one practices the Clear Mind Experience, they are able to easily and effortlessly understand who the unconscious is in relationship with, what is it saying about others, how is it defining limitation within the world, what is it doing to act out and create within your life? Your understanding of the unconscious mind will happen very quickly. The conscious mind when it is witnessing these random conversations of limitation within the unconscious will be speaking continually throughout the day. As it continually speaks to move the unconscious mind into another experience, it will speak about the experience that the unconscious mind is in. It is within that moment that the rational mind will witness what the unconscious mind is perceiving and how it is engaging within life. As the feelings move into the presence of love, the rational mind will reinforce the direction of love. It will allow the conscious mind to speak of the importance of love because the rational mind is all about protecting the feeling of feeling good. The rational mind will protect the feeling of feeling good, of feeling happiness, of feeling joy, of feeling abundance, of feeling prosperity, of feeling union once it has experienced love. If the unconscious mind is active, the rational mind will protect the feelings of loss, abandonment, suffering, distrust, and hardship that come through the unconscious because all that the rational mind is there to do is to protect the feeling of the moment because the feelings are being cleansed within the mind, set free to experience love by dissolving the unconscious mind. The rational mind will end up working to protect the feeling of love.

63.3 – 63.3i Because we live within a world that has been created primarily through the unconscious mind for lifetimes, life is filled with daily expectations that function within the unconscious. These expectations are defined through media, education, and belief systems of each culture. At this time, western civilization amongst others are driven daily to want more, find more, and be more within the world. Because the unconscious mind has so much traction upon the planet, or seemingly so, it is very simple to spiral into a conversation with another or within yourself when you are carrying the unconscious mind that is not able to support love. Within the unconscious mind, if active, life will be filled with failed expectations of how life should show up, of how you should be nurtured to the point where the unconscious mind will define spirit as having failed, will define mysticism as being a lie, will define beauty as ugliness, will define grace as a seeming potential, will define spiritual opportunity as a sacrifice. The unconscious mind is always competing. It is competing within every moment to share space within your mind, within your life. The vibration of the unconscious mind is very fast. It is because of this fact that the Clear Mind Experience, the three-part breath and language of love, when an individual is initially practicing the program is integrating at great speed. This is because it is required that conscious mind move as quickly as unconscious mind. Then, once the conscious mind is moving as quickly as the unconscious mind, so as to bridge itself into the unconscious and draw the unconscious back into itself, then the breath is able to be slowed down. The program will slow down because it will be at that point that we will be drawing the unconscious into the conscious mind at the speed of the conscious mind and not the other way around. However, initially, to be able to make the activation, one must breathe and participate within the program and language of love at the speed in which the unconscious moves.

64.1 One would ask the unconscious mind 'what if it had to be still?' It would force the stillness. Then, it would complain about having to be still and then it would chatter away within the mind saying all the reasons why stillness isn't able to work. The unconscious mind can't be still. When we say to ourselves, "I must be still," we are saying, "I have to try." That is an unconscious statement. It is an unconscious command. Stillness is a state of being that cannot see itself. It is a state of mind that operates within fluidity of itself. It cannot seek itself. It cannot perceive to seek itself as it is a state of being. The Clear Mind Experience does not force stillness. The Clear Mind Experience draws the unconscious mind into stillness, meaning the conscious mind. Once the unconscious mind moves into the path of stillness, into the conscious mind, then the feelings will live within stillness. The unconscious will never have slowed down, but it will be not pulling life in its direction. It will be following the conscious mind, therefore, it will appear to have slowed down as it dissolves.

64.2 For a moment, contemplate on the idea, What if you could not accumulate anymore? What if you did not seek to be different anymore? What if you could change nothing about yourself within this moment? What would the mind say? How would the unconscious mind react? What would it create within the idea that there was nothing to gain, nothing to get, and nothing to do? It would act as a caged animal. It would complain and growl. It would beg to be fed to the point of insanity. It would feel suppressed and invoke anger, as it does not have the capacity in which to sit, to perceive that there is no measure of gain.

64.3 Contemplate again, if the unconscious mind is operating, how are you ever going to feel love? If the unconscious mind has no capacity to love, and it believes it you, how are you going to feel love?

64.4 If love cannot be measured from measuring gain, then how would love exist, and where would love present itself? This is how the unconscious mind perceives love. It knows that love has no capacity to increase itself through seeking gain, and that is where it thinks it can win. Because it will spend endless hours speaking about ways in which you should accumulate aspects of reality to keep you out of the expression of love. It feels the presence of stillness surrounding it. However, it cannot move into that stillness, so it will keep the mind busy to maintain itself so one is not sitting within the stillness.

64.5 Gain or loss within perception is a measurement. The essence of love is stillness, which means that it has no movement in its still state to be measured. The unconscious mind cannot see the essence of love because it only measures what is gained and what is lost. The ebbing and flowing of the unconscious mind happens through measuring life: weighing things up, increase, decrease, gain, or loss.

64.6 If one has the unconscious mind at all operating within the brain and has not dissolved it, then one will struggle with stillness, struggle to allow love to present itself, struggle to allow to self-love to define inner feeling because there will always be the mind chatter of questioning love and the qualities of love such as stillness. The unconscious mind will also question the practices in which to celebrate consciousness, to celebrate the conscious mind because it will be always questioning that you are not able to be still. It will sit within, while one is meditating upon the conscious mind and talk about how one can't sit within the conscious mind because one can't be still, but the one that it is speaking of, is itself, and it is right.

64.7 The unconscious mind will seek to control love through the addiction and need to have love. It will speak of all the ways that love must serve it, where it must find it, how it must look, how it must perceive reality, what it must live like, how it must appear in form, how it must appear within, how it expresses life. The unconscious mind will define love many ways; some appear to be beautiful, some appear to be very gross, ugly, and harmful. Either way, the expression of love that it seeks to define is its addiction. It is its payoff to celebrating itself, whether the payoff is an ugliness and a deprivation, or a co-dependency and greed.

64.8 The unconscious mind will at times allow a superficial happiness where there is gain. However, there will be an inner feeling of hopelessness for life, even within the gain. This is because the unconscious mind is always able to perceive some form of suffering. So in payoff for the gain, one will allow the suffering.

65.1 Attempting to change or improve the unconscious mind is an endless treadmill. The unconscious mind is not able to change. It will, however, allow you a payoff of feeling that you have changed, as it expects another one. It will make one change and then speak about the next one to come, and you will be continually moving through it, seeking these changes, and finally return back to the place in which you started because the unconscious mind's motive at that point is just to operate, just to gain the attention. If an individual within the first seven years of life lacked attention from parents, the unconscious mind will present itself having very fast mind chatter. The modus operandi of the unconscious mind will be to create attention for itself, to gain your attention, to gain the attention of the rational mind, to perform for it, because that is how it spent the first seven years of its life; that is in which the action it was created.

65.2 Take a moment to think about the times you have successfully changed an aspect of yourself, and how the feeling you had as the person you were prior to the change has now moved itself into another interpretation within your life. That is the unconscious mind. It is not dissolved, but it has moved like rock hopping.

65.3 How many times in your life have you successfully implemented a change and sat back and really thought that you had made it to a new place within your life. And then within what seemed a very brief moment, you were right back into old feelings that you had before the change was initiated. That is because the change happened within the unconscious. The unconscious mind was not allowing change, it was simply transferring feelings from one experience to another. The problem within that experience is that once an experience has been transferred from one situation to another, the powerlessness that comes over the individual as they believe that they will never be free of these aspects of themselves can, at times, lead them to medication or a type of practice or process that suppresses their ability to be able to be free; which will happen often with people with addictions where they spend their entire life fearing that they are no good and are not going to be able to return to goodness because they fear that the unconscious mind is who they are, when, in essence, once the unconscious mind dissolves, so does the addiction.

65.4 When the unconscious mind allows you to change, and you suddenly realize after the change that old feelings have surfaced, there will be a loss of that change. You may not return back, but there will be a loss of celebration because you will feel trapped by the unconscious. The unconscious mind will confiscate the happiness, love, support, and new vitality that you felt because the change was defined by the unconscious mind. This is a painful place for some individuals because it represents a loss of personal will and ability of happiness.

66.1 The trick within the unconscious mind is that it has an insatiable appetite for a better life. One is not able to cater to its appetite and ideas of how life should be better and serving it. One will be faced with an endless dialogue. Life will be defined within disharmony. There will be a fear of loss, control, addictions, and indecisions, and all ways that you had better change to improve conditions within your life. There will be great fear and powerlessness that you cannot change, but, again, that is the unconscious mind speaking of itself because it is not able to change. The unconscious mind will always seek to present thoughts, feelings, emotions, and ideas that cannot be achieved within a conscious state; love being a conscious state. The unconscious mind is there to prove to you that love cannot exist. It will take you out into experiences that have you define that. Then it will tell you that you cannot be free of the unconscious and you had better hold onto it, and it doesn't need to be gotten rid of because it is life, and where would you go if you didn't have it? When one seeks to create improvements and conditions that come from the unconscious, one will suffer. Because the final suffering moment will be the fear that one is trapped.

66.2 If the unconscious mind is not dissolved, then the rollercoaster, emotional, mental, and thought, makes total sense. As humans, we only have the capacity to live within an unconscious or conscious experience within each moment. Life is just the movement of conscious and unconscious expressions. If the unconscious is there, it has to move, you cannot deny it. Its birthright is to operate until it is dissolved within the conscious mind. That is why the Clear Mind Experience is so vitally important because it is the ultimate freedom. One who practices has clear motive, is allowing of awakening to the presence of love because the unconscious mind is dissolving. One is not choosing to be better. There is just an awakening to love which presents the feelings that awaken a heightened sense of joy, an inner awareness to happiness and surrender and peace, all because one has opened up the portals and the awareness, frequency, and vibration within the mind to live within the presence of love. The human condition becomes one of love.

67.1 Our capacity is to live in love when the unconscious mind is dissolved. Our capacity is to allow wisdom to create within life as a spontaneous movement and expression of love when the unconscious mind is dissolved. Our capacity is to dissolve the unconscious because the conscious mind is active within the mind, within the brain, from birth. It is our birthright, the alchemy, the karmic contract of the mind that the unconscious mind may be dissolved at any moment that the individual participates to do so.

67.2 If the unconscious mind is dissolved, life would be one of love. Life would be a reflection of higher calling, purpose, and destiny. It is a struggle to define purpose with an unconscious mind because the unconscious mind will allow the purpose to be revealed, but then it will attempt to confiscate it through the problems and the agony and the suffering of attempting to have the vision be birthed upon the planet. When one is free from the unconscious, there is a natural progression; an ebbing, a flowing, and an awakening of true abundant measure in which the vision can be birthed. When the unconscious mind is dissolved, love is a spontaneous movement within each moment. Compassion and unity of man is birthed within each moment. Life is nowhere but within the moment. Children are an opportunity to express self-love. Adults are an opportunity to live within love and compassion. Life is an opportunity in which love can fulfill itself in oneness and the rhythm of beauty.

67.3 The journey of the Clear Mind Experience is to discover love, is to awaken the beauty of love, is to realize that when love is present, how it will feel and present itself upon the planet. The beauty of this journey is that love is revealed within every breath. When one enters a spiritual mind within the Clear Mind practice, compassion is birthed as the final moment in which the unconscious mind is dissolved, and within this is the gratitude for all life that has been walked, for all life that has been experienced. A wholeness is born where the body, mind, emotions move as a physical, mental, emotional union of love.

67.4 Take a moment to reflect. Look within life. Look within. Feel for a moment. If right now, within this moment, there was nothing to do, nothing to become, only the feeling of love within, within this freedom of this love, how would you be defined? How would life present itself? What is freedom?

68.1 There are many that could say they have done great work in getting rid of interpretations of the unconscious mind. Many that would say this is true, and I am sure. However, within reflection of what is existent upon the planet at this time, one is not getting rid of the unconscious mind, one is understanding its story. Understanding its story allows you to avoid its story, avoid its presence. When we avoid the unconscious mind personally, it becomes very present collectively. It becomes present within the relationships to others. It becomes present in relationship to money. It becomes present in relationship to opportunity. In the practices that have existed prior to the Clear Mind Experience, one is simply becoming aware of the function and the presentation of the unconscious, however, not dissolving it. The language of love of the Clear Mind Experience has been released forth into the being through the book, into the being of this woman. The words have been written by many levels of consciousness. Many realms who are engaging within the unconscious daily have written the words to dissolve it. The words are not made up. They are the alchemy that dissolves the personal and collective unconscious mind that exists upon this planet within this moment.

68.2 The most powerful aspect of the Clear Mind Experience is that it is just that: a system. Consciousness, once it integrates into the planet, needs structure. That is why there are seconds, hours, minutes, seasons, elements of the earth. Consciousness can be defined clearly when it's in a structure. Its purpose becomes a refined quality. It is not left to random interpretation that dilutes the true form of its expression. The Clear Mind Experience has taken over thirteen years to be released in form through this being. This is because of the refining process. The structure was created first and then the magnificence birthed within the structure. It is in practicing the Clear Mind Experience that the unconscious mind is dissolved within structure. When we dissolve the unconscious mind within structure, we are creating an opportunity for great power to unfold within the process; where epiphanies, realizations, inner knowing are birthed spontaneously within each moment that the unconscious mind is dissolving. People are not waiting random lengths of time to have realizations. It is a continual movement of realization from moment to moment to moment integrated within the Clear Mind breath. The Clear Mind Experience becomes the pulse within the reality of the being. It becomes the heartbeat of truth. The Clear Mind Experience is the gateway to personal freedom.

69.1 The Clear Mind Experience is a journey. One dissolves the unconscious in sequence within order in which it was created working from the back to the front. When this happens and an individual is running through the same electrical current within the brain, the awareness moves within clarity. There is not a wandering, probing, flitting from one idea to the other within the unconscious. There is no contemplation on what a shift means because the conscious mind is integrating the awakening through clarity, through inner knowing, so there is an inner conviction and inner awareness to IAM that. Accessing the unconscious mind within a pattern, dissolving it, dissolving the pattern activates a profound alchemy within the structure of the unconscious that it is programmed to be released. As the unconscious mind is programmed to awaken, and within the dissolving process, both aspects of the mind are consistently moving, ebbing and flowing, in and out of one another.

70.1 The Clear Mind Experience is about dissolving the unconscious mind by dissolving its structure. In dissolving its own structure, it is not able to be contained. In not being contained, it is able to be released and dissolved into the conscious mind. Dissolving the structure of the unconscious mind is the gift of the Pleiadian nations. It is the gift of the galactic star systems. It is an encoded format that has been released into this planet. It is in honoring this that great transformation will abound upon this planet. Much love is bestowed within this being, the author that carries the code, and within this love, great transformation is transmuted and released upon the earth. This woman, who has taken the name that was bestowed by the Sun, named Genie, is just that. She carries the wish of humanity, and that is the personal freedom from suffering. It has been the sacrifice of all inner presence that has allowed this code to be released unto her after thousands and thousands and thousands of years in which traveling to this earth. As a radiant walk-in, she has taken form; walking in from a star, walking in as a sacred light in which to bestow the three-part breath and the beauty of its abundant light, love, peace, and freedom. In all magnificence, the Clear Mind Experience will be celebrated abundantly by nations as one movement, as one breath. The radiance of all giving, all knowing, all presence is activated, and the code bestowed. This woman is a sacred vault of information that walks the planet activating the presence of freedom of an earth calling.

70.2 The Clear Mind Experience is a powerful process when perceived within the mind. You are not only dissolving the thoughts, feelings, and emotions, but also dissolving a program that runs within the brain that anchors perception that says, "One must hold on. You must hold on and protect and maintain the unconscious mind." One is not able to hold on and protect the unconscious mind. The unconscious mind is only serving itself. When this statement is running, the unconscious mind is saying, "I must hold on and protect my state." The unconscious mind has ways of subtly presenting itself in spiritual form. The way in which to determine if it is the unconscious mind speaking is to listen to the language in which you speak. Is it love? Is it judgmental? Is it unconditional? Does it place condition? Does it have judgment, fatigue, concern, fear, stress? And, if so, it is the unconscious mind speaking. Even when an individual says, "I need peace to protect my spiritual awareness." That is an unconscious statement. The conscious mind seeks no protection. The conscious mind lives within each moment. The conscious mind is the present level of awareness and love that allows the beauty of all that is to shine in its magnificence with no measurement of what should be or what isn't. The conscious mind is the radiance of love and the all-knowing presence of beauty.

71.1 When an individual randomly dismantles the unconscious mind, it will create pockets because the unconscious mind will not have dissolved in a flow in which it was created within the sequence. It will be randomly disjointed. The unconscious will create what is similar to 'potholes/pockets.' It is within this experience that the electrical currents within the brain will enter these potholes/pockets of the unconscious which will create a profound drop in energy awareness and an almost trance-like presence within an individual. When an individual is primarily within the conscious mind, one will have to create means through the body-mind experience to place themselves back within the conscious mind.

71.2 A pothole within the unconscious is really just that. It is a hole that anchors an individual's awareness and perception into it; a null zone within the mind. For individuals who have done a lot of meditation, self-development, and spiritual work, they can have a number of these potholes or voids within the unconscious. When an individual enters a void, there is a sense of confusion, a loss of clarity, a loss of purpose, a lifelessness. What could be perceived as a slight depression, a confusion, their energy will feel static. They will start to question, '"Where am I? Where did I go? I was here one minute. I've disappeared. What happened to me?" This is because of the unconscious mind, because the perception has landed in the pothole, will interpret that it has lost contact with itself because the electrical current fell into the void and was not accumulating movement through the unconscious. As part of your study group, the instructor should draw a visual representation of what this looks like. At this time, take a moment to visualize, remember, or reflect on times when you have felt to be very conscious, very aware of your state, and then, all of a sudden, the state just disappears, and then there is a sense of loss, and a sense of not knowing, where am I, what happened to me? These are all the conversations of the unconscious losing conscious awareness of itself.

71.3 It is when the individual's awareness of oneself moves into the unconscious and disappears within one of these breakage points within the unconscious mind that the electrical current within the unconscious mind will randomly seek to select thoughts in an attempt to define oneself. When one is in this type of null zone and is able to host a conscious perception, the conscious mind will be drawing, drawing, drawing, and attempting to draw the perception back into itself. But what keeps one within the unconscious is reaffirming this negative self-talk of 'where did I go?' It is upon reaffirming this negative self-talk that the condition of disappearing into the unconscious mind is reaffirmed which builds greater awareness to the unconscious, lesser awareness to the conscious mind, and then an entire different experience within the unconscious starts to awaken through the validation that one is lost within the unconscious.

71.4 When an individual randomly releases the unconscious mind and dismantles it without dissolving it, it is very likely that the electrical currents will hit one of these pockets. It is at that point that the perception will fall into what is known as a 'trance state.' These states can be extremely destructive and disheartening for the individual. It wakes up the conversation, "Am I ever going to be free? Am I ever going to get there?" A huge lethargy can enter the body at these times; confused states within the mind; people can make major decisions within their lives to support the trance states and then have to repair what they have done from within the conscious mind. That is the beauty of the Clear Mind Experience that through dissolving the unconscious, you are not moving into these pockets. The gift of the Clear Mind Experience comes at the beginning for anyone who has created these pockets because initially, upon practicing the Clear Mind Experience, once the conscious and unconscious aspects of the mind are synchronized and moving together at the same speed, the unconscious mind decompresses, draws in on itself, and retracts. As it retracts, it closes up the pockets; retracting almost like a raisin, a grape that is drying into a raisin, so there can be no electrical current within the brain that is triggering unconscious perception.

72.1 At the point when an individual moves into a trance state, there is the experience of a mental numbness or fatigue; a disorientation within sequence of events and a loss of the current moment. Ideas, thoughts, and feelings will seem chaotic and overwhelming to the individual, and this is because at the backdrop of the feeling of all of these random feelings is the foundation that is fueling these feelings, questions, and concerns, and the foundation is: "Where am I? What happened to me? Where did I go?" This is the conversation that the unconscious mind has because within the trance state, it is not conscious. The individual is neither conscious nor unconscious. However, the unconscious mind realizes that the perception has disappeared within itself. This aspect of understanding of how the conscious mind and unconscious mind interact and work together, and how past works have created these formations within the brain that become these potential trance states which appear as pockets, or potholes, within the brain, is very comprehensive and takes a lot of discovery and questions and presentation. A Clear Mind Facilitator has studied these types of experiences and understands how and why these experiences occur. The Higher Mind Institute is built as an education facility that does take this type of discussion to the next level: the level of understanding. The Higher Mind Institute will over many years continue to prove and validate the statements of how the unconscious mind is dissolved and discussions like this one about the decompression of the unconscious and the trance-like states that occur in dismantling the unconscious. This discussion is one of the most key discussions for those that are seeking freedom through spiritual work. When one is seeking freedom through spiritual work, it is the freedom from the unconscious mind. One does not have to understand trance states, one just simply needs to decompress the unconscious mind to be free of the repercussions and the experience of these trance states. When a light worker is able to decompress the unconscious, and not move into trance states, their life becomes accelerated and the frequency of their outer existence begins to live as an expression of their inner. Becoming free of trance states awakens new vitality within those that have suffered by them for so many years. The 'dismantling' of the unconscious mind is the long way to the point of love. Because to get oneself out of a trance state or to understand how to dismantle the unconscious mind, one must live through multitudes of experiences and make decisions and choices to no longer support unconscious representations, actions, experiences, and opportunities within their lives. This can take a great amount of time. The same benefits that can be achieved by walking that long and difficult pathway to dissolving the unconscious mind are achieved within the Clear Mind Experience in dissolving the unconscious mind.

72.2 When an individual moves into the trance state of the unconscious, they will not be able to formulate clear thought. Normally what happens for an individual to be moved out of the pocket, they will get fuzzy in the head, a fatigue that may make them become sleepy, they may

Within dissolving the unconscious mind are new feelings, thoughts, and emotional expressions of ourselves so as to inspire and reveal a new world in which we will innovate a new living structure in which to experience ourselves.

crave a particular food, experience a headache or physical reaction, or become overly emotional. What is attempting to happen at this point is that the unconscious mind is seeking a reinterpretation of thought to restore the electrical currents of the unconscious that move through the brain to trigger the feelings, thoughts, and emotions that are released and transpire from the unconscious. All of these side effects of moving into the trance state are in an effort to move the individual's perception from the trance state back into the unconscious mind. An individual on the Clear Mind Experience is not able to move into a trance state because of a decompression of the unconscious. The conscious mind is not able to attempt to release somebody from a trance state because there is no need to fix or change, moving within the intent of the conscious mind. What will happen is a person will get pushed out of the unconscious mind through a symptom or side effect that will push them into the unconscious electrical currents, again more unconscious thought, and then the individual will choose to move out of the unconscious mind or attempt to get themselves out of the unconscious mind by working on a practice of the conscious mind. But, again, if an individual is able to restore perception to the conscious mind, the unconscious has not been dissolved. The individual has just chosen to enter the other aspect of the mind that cannot be maintained if not dissolving the unconscious.

73.1 Individuals that practice the Clear Mind Experience have accelerated and rapid awakenings because the pockets are not able to function within the unconscious because there is no dismantling and the decompression of the unconscious is able to reduce and not allow any experience of entering a trance state. This becomes very powerful in somebody's life because it can be the trance states that have an individual create disharmony within their lives when they are in a conscious perception, and they will look at their behavior within the trance state as being old behavior, and then self-defeating thoughts and ideas can come of oneself; negative self-talk which engages the unconscious.

73.2 To further clarify the decompression process, what it simply means is the neuro-pathways within the brain that represent the unconscious mind shrivel up and are not able to conduct activity within the electrical current that triggers unconscious thoughts and emotions within the brain. The electrical currents spontaneously trigger the unconscious one thought after the other after the other, which is how one loses personal perception to the unconscious. When practicing the Clear Mind Experience and the unconscious mind decompresses, one is not able to access these neuro-pathways which, in a sense, keeps one within the conscious mind. Again, take a moment to reflect on experiences that occur within your life where you enter a trance state and what comes of that trance state, what you create from it. Is it a repetitive argument? A repetitive emotional condition? Is it a repetitive problem within relationships? Is it a repetitive career change? It will be a repetitive experience that is coming from the trance state.

73.3 The benefits of decompressing the unconscious, and practicing the Clear Mind Experience for the decompression purpose, means that there are no pockets to experience because the unconscious mind is more or less deactivated as being the primary conductor of thought within the brain. This then stops all experiences that have manifested from the trance state which enables a profound clarity of mind within the stillness of thought, then a momentum of thought within the clarity, which enables the manifestation of vision, and the union of inner knowing and the outer world. This really does summarize the potential of dissolving the unconscious because they are the living components that are integrated within the process. Take a moment to reflect on these conditions within your life. What is an experience that could come as a trance state? When do you feel you have clarity of mind? If you had momentum from thought, how would it manifest as vision and union of wisdom within and within the outer world?

73.4 The momentum and clarity are the greatest gifts of the Clear Mind Experience because they are bridging the inner awareness to the outer experience, and the outer experience is becoming a celebration of inner awareness. And when the unconscious mind is active and perceiving reality, the outer world becomes a vehicle in which to demonstrate the unconscious mind, meaning life becomes insurmountable lessons that one must overcome to be able to understand who they are and how they're showing up within the world which can create pain and suffering. When life is perceived through the conscious mind, the outer experience becomes what celebrates consciousness, and celebrates the presence of love; creating new opportunities and life to become an abundant vehicle of vision, and inner knowing, and expression of love.

74.1 Taking a moment to absorb the information of this Interpretation Guide, reflect upon the unconscious mind, how it plays out within your life, and what other gifts that you feel await you within the conscious mind. You will be able to feel this by perceiving the thoughts. If you have vision of the unconscious and how it wishes to create within your life, then connect to the feeling of what it would feel if it were to fulfill itself, and write down those feelings. Those feelings are what the unconscious mind perceives as reality, and it will create anything within the unconscious field to support those feelings. However, knowing that you are not the unconscious mind but love perceiving itself as love, take a moment within your mind to have vision of a conscious mind and what you would perceive within reality from the conscious mind. Then connect to the feelings of this experience of the conscious mind and write them down, and any visions or moments of awareness that you had would be aligned to fulfilling those feelings. Upon this reflection, then one must ask oneself, "Why would one continue to support the unconscious?" The unconscious mind does not believe that the Clear Mind Experience works. It does not believe in the entity in which carries it. It does not believe in the story in which it was developed. It does not believe in the beauty that it pertains to behold within itself for humanity. However, this is irrelevant. Sitting down regardless and practicing it will release into the mind the feeling of which it is known and revealed; that within the experience of the Clear Mind Experience is the presence of love.

74.2 The aim of this book is to provide the information that can be nurtured and embraced to support the potential and revelation of dissolving the unconscious mind versus attempting to define life through its confrontation in hope of its destruction. Dissolving the unconscious mind is the sugar and water experience of awakening. There does not have to be the battle, as you are living already as IAM Victory.

74.3 Within the Clear Mind Experience, one is embarking on a magnificent journey; a journey that allows and awakens the inner vision and freedom that reveals the knowing of living clarity. As within the Clear Mind Experience, IAM an expression of love, and within the expression, many opportunities will awaken within the success of hopes and dreams. As within the Clear Mind Experience, IAM dreaming a dream of freedom, a dream of love, a dream of inner vision, a dream of union, a dream of beauty. As within the Clear Mind Experience, IAM living within the perception of a Clear Mind, awakened within the magnificent knowing that life itself is the birth of each moment, and within each moment, IAM revealed as the divine violet ray of love. As within the divine violet ray of love, I live as the earth; as the womb in that which nurtures the beauty that I know, that IAM a living expression of love. As within the conscious mind, IAM living, IAM expressing, IAM within life unconditional beauty that radiates the magnificence of pure, divine, radiant love.

74.4 So much of earth's reality is about discussing the potential of awakening into the freedom of living out of the unconscious mind. The Clear Mind Experience is just that. It is the experience. The Clear Mind Experience of awareness comes first; the practice. The reading is just the validation of the practice. If this book is read without the practice, it will be interpreted by the brain, by the perception, as another thing to do, as another potential outside of self. Then the unconscious mind in fear of what is being said is true will attempt to mimic itself as being one that does not need the practice. The practice is to be done first, tried, attempted, integrated, if only once. Then, from beginning the practice, the book may join. But it is the practice that is the joy, the practice that is the union, and it is within the practice that the book will be defined as confirmation of already achieved experience. So much of the earth plane is built on yearning; of beings yearning for the freedom, yearning for the freedom from the unconscious mind. This is your gift. It is through the yearning that this action has been birthed. This is your gift. The Clear Mind Experience is the gift. The gift of awakening. The gift of self-realization of love. Within the definition of self-realization, self is love. The gift of the Clear Mind Experience is the full realization of love, and that any thought, any need, any desire, any pain, any suffering, any limitation, any fear that wishes to take you out of this is simply the suggestion of the unconscious mind. The unconscious mind is what wishes to destroy itself. Within the destruction, it will tear down one's life to believe in its own powerlessness. However, it cannot function in any other form. It is simply running as a tape; running with a story of how life is, and how one perceives the limitations of love within the first seven years of life is what is written on the tape. It becomes the narration.

74.5 The beauty of the Clear Mind Experience is that it provides you opportunity to awaken within your day to day. It provides you opportunity to practice within your day to day. One is not confronted with life, with how to achieve what is written within this book because there is nothing to achieve. The Clear Mind Experience is a beautiful, gentle practice that dissolves the unconscious mind every time you practice it.

75.1 Without the Clear Mind Experience, this book is a concept, a discussion of potential that would prove frustrating and confusing. This would be because the unconscious mind would not be able to interpret it all, and what it couldn't interpret, it would mimic so one would feel that one had achieved this. The conscious mind has no need to interpret anything that is written here. However, the conscious mind can interpret the experience and, within the experience, create greater understanding of what already is. When one practices the Clear Mind Experience, the conscious mind will awaken within the presence of love. It will not be seeking the love. It will reside within the love because the chatter of the unconscious mind will be dissolving. It is in this process that the conscious mind feels a sense of freedom because it is becoming free of the limitations of the unconscious mind. This book is for validation of the experience, so one is able to understand why the experience has so much profound impact on their existence. This book is also to exchange the magnificence of the grace that is within the pages, within the language of love, within the three-part breath, within the birth of that which is the Clear Mind Experience.

75.2 Without the beauty of the Clear Mind Experience, the words within this book would be a dream, not a reality. The book is made to be reality when one is practicing the Experience. If one is not practicing the Experience, the book becomes a question. If one is practicing the Experience, the book becomes a validation. One must practice the Experience in means in which to embrace the book in the purpose in which it was written. If one is not practicing the practice and reading the book, one is seeking to find the distance between the Experience, the opportunity to dissolve the unconscious mind, and what is written.

75.3 The gift of the Clear Mind Experience is that it is an experience that defines a concept, which is the book not a concept of a book that seeks the experience. This is new for this planet, but it is timely, and it is impactful, and it is profoundly life-changing; changing the course in which humanity walks the planet. If we look for one moment that the universal mind is one mind in which we all reside, as each of us has perception and return to love, it is the one mind drawing itself into itself which is us. As people perceive the Clear Mind Experience, they begin to turn around on the beach and walk towards the sun. The Clear Mind Experience is an invitation of Helios. He is inviting those to use the expression that is bestowed within the Clear Mind Experience as the Holy Spirit, which is the breath, to restore all perception of feelings and thought to that of love. As humanity walks toward the sun, they will be embraced by the sun's rays. All that does not serve will be burned up as ash within its heat and fire, and each of us will be nurtured within the womb of this fire. The unconscious mind will be behind, being dissolved within the brilliant light of the sun. The Clear Mind Experience is the sacred invitation, the beauty that exists within the sun, as it is when we look towards the sun; that the mind becomes clear and transparent, filled with the heat, depth, and warmth of the light.

75.4 Not only is the Clear Mind Experience an experience, it is a profoundly simple, beautiful, daily process that works within your life in divine fluidity. It is a process that integrates effortlessly and seamlessly into your day to day existence, your home, and your adventures. It does not seek to control your daily experiences but seeks to bring opportunity to live within witness to the unconscious mind and not live within repercussions of how it represents life.

Structure

76.1 Let's take a moment to reflect upon consciousness. As much as we feel that consciousness cannot be defined, as much as some of us know that if we attempt to hold onto consciousness through one definition, it will shapeshift and move and dissolve into another. However, consciousness also fits within a structure. Consciousness moves through structure within physical form. The physical body is a vehicle in which consciousness is living within structure. The unconscious mind is an aspect of this structure that pertains to move consciousness in and out of itself as does the brain and human perception.

76.2 For a moment, let's reflect on all the ways that consciousness does fit in to structure. It fits into structure and is defined within structure through the human body, through the human mind, through human emotion, through human condition within the aspects of nature that are repetitive and cyclic. Consciousness represents itself in many forms and structures upon the planet that have been birthed through the miracle of life and the presence of love.

76.3 Some of the ways in which consciousness moves within structure are the seasons of the year, times throughout the day, times within future, present, and past, mathematical equations, alchemy, years, cultures, nature, countries, weather, currency, wellness, food types. These are all means in which consciousness is defined and contained within one essence to serve the purpose of the structure itself.

76.4 It is knowing that structure is able to operate consciousness within form that the Clear Mind Experience has been conceived. The Clear Mind Experience is consciousness that's able to move through structure. It within itself is a clear structure that moves within another structure to be redefined as its structure.

76.5 The Clear Mind Experience is higher consciousness defined clearly. It is defined within such clarity because it exists within structure. There are no random interpretations left to the moment. It serves purpose and is structured within a flow much like the alphabet. As it moves within this structure, it is clearly defined and within its definition provides opportunities for awakening within the presence of love that are referred to within the pages of this book.

76.6 It is because the Clear Mind Experience is so clearly defined within its structure that it provides incredible momentum within how it is perceived and moved and integrated within life. This is because it is a structure that represents living. It is a structure that supports human perception. It is within this understanding we are able to assimilate clearly how it will move within your life as it was developed through the perception of human experience.

77.1 - 77.2 The Clear Mind Experience has clearly taken the unconscious mind and been able to define it through interpreting 49 negative feelings and the ways in which it integrates into the seven primary emotions. The Clear Mind Experience is also able to define consciousness and the conscious perception of love through 49 positive feelings that move through the seven primary emotions. It is in identifying with this as you progress through the Clear Mind Experience that one is able to see ways in which the unconscious or conscious mind are moving within their life.

Freedom

78.1 As we continue to delve into the next phase of self-discovery which is the Clear Mind Experience, it is important to acknowledge that within life there is no right or wrong way to live. Within life, it is not preferred that one would live within a conscious or unconscious perception when one is witnessing life from the universal mind. However, due to the accelerated awareness upon the planet, there is a compulsion, a pushing forward, a momentum towards the light. The Clear Mind Experience, the pages of this book, and all statements are there to assist one within when propelling and moving within the direction of the light. The Clear Mind Experience is a means in which to accelerate consciousness through the path of non-suffering. It is when one dissolves the unconscious mind that suffering dissolves with it. And as one walks towards the light and one integrates the conscious mind, it has not done so from the perception of loss or suffering.

78.2 Within the Clear Mind Experience, there is no interpretation of failure or gain, and no measurement as to what should or could be because these are statements of the unconscious mind. From the first moment of practicing the Clear Mind Experience, it is very apparent to the participant that they are being drawn out of the unconscious mind, therefore, all suffering is being retracted; retracting into itself and love is moving what isn't love into itself so the individual being is able to feel that love is supporting itself upon its new journey to restore itself into the presence of love.

78.3 The Clear Mind Experience is not about change. The Clear Mind Experience does not perceive one way as better than the other. It is simply to provide clarity as to the duality that exists within the conscious and unconscious perceptions of reality, life, and what one seemingly believes is real. The Clear Mind Experience does not support the idea of change. However, it is the experience of realizing love and potential of love, and the Clear Mind Experience is provided in a means in which potential can realize itself.

78.4 The beauty of the Clear Mind Experience is that you are encouraged within your life right now to not judge what must be different but to find capacity within yourself to simply embrace your life right now knowing that you are living within your capacity of how the unconscious mind is operating within its present state believing that it is you. It is when you allow yourself this moment of grace that you allow yourself to be supported into the flow of love. If one supports negative interpretations of oneself, then one is not able to enter the flow of love because they are reinforcing the ways in which they are not there. Love is a vulnerable perception. It is a perception within life that takes tremendous courage to access because the unconscious mind has one believe that one must be protected from the pain that can be implemented within one's life when one, within its vulnerability, lets go of the stories that are not able to support the presence of love. When you enter the Clear Mind Experience, you enter the opportunity to say, "Right now, within this moment, IAM Love." You do not have any judgment of what is assimilated around you in any current time knowing that within that moment you are embracing life within the capacity in which you can.

78.5 Each human being is a vessel for conscious or unconscious expression and it seems collectively at this time this awareness has become apparent to most people that seek and strive to be a vessel for conscious thought. This is primarily how the Clear Mind Experience has been called into action because the greater potential for humanity to live within the conscious mind has been called upon, activated, and is moving into present time.

78.6 The magnificent joy in the realizations of the Clear Mind Experience is that you are not trapped within an unconscious mind. It is the realization that within the Clear Mind practice, you will be moving forward within life in a steady, clear path dissolving all ability of the unconscious mind to operate and its content able to become active within life. There is pure joy and magnificence within knowing that the beauty of the unconscious mind is that it is here to have love realize itself. There is beauty in the unconscious mind when you choose to walk away. That is why it behaves the way it does; to send you away. And as you walk towards the sun, as you walk towards the essence of all that is, you are walking each moment within love. Each moment that you walk with the unconscious mind following, you are preserving the presence of love because you are within that moment saying, "IAM the light of all knowing that lives within the beauty of living as a radiant expression of unconditional love."

Chapter Four
Relationship to Emotions

79.1 Humanity is conditioned through fear and control and suppression of many forms to suppress emotions. The gift of our emotions is that they are the key to how we integrate wisdom and present it within our lives through our perception. Within society, our emotions are often feared by ourselves. They are often overlooked in spiritual self-development and defined as something that needs to be curbed or controlled. We are often encouraged to "calm down" or suppress our emotions. However, the problem with this is that our emotions are the action of our perception. It is our emotions that bring an animation to how we are perceiving life. If our emotions are being moved by the unconscious, then our emotions will appear to be imbalanced, suppressed, not easily harmonized within each moment, filled with expectation. However, when our emotions are a vehicle to express the conscious mind, they will bring great character and dimension to who we are and our role within life.

79.2 To further clarify, if we were not to have emotions, our perceptions would remain static, meaningless in the realm of communication. It is our emotions that bring meaning, connection, depth, color, passion to our daily ideas, thoughts, feelings, aspirations, and interpretations. This allows us to form connection on many levels of perception with different experiences, with different individuals, and different opportunities. It is our emotions that assist us to experience many aspects of love because it is our emotions that form relationships within our perception and the outside world.

79.3 It is our emotions that act as our vehicle which moves the conscious and unconscious mind within life. It is within expressing life or projecting life through the conscious or unconscious mind that the universe is able to know how we are feeling about life and it is our feelings that we express within life that are fulfilled within our outer experience; meaning if we were feeling sad, if we were feeling rejected or abandoned, we would encounter experiences, opportunities, and relationships that provided us with a validation of that feeling. If we were, however, feeling happy, insightful, and wise, we would attract experiences that enhanced that feeling and allow that feeling to fulfill itself within our lives. It is our emotions that present our feelings to the universal mirror of life, and what is presented within that mirror being the expression of the conscious mind or the expression of the unconscious mind is what is revealed to us.

79.4 Our emotions being our vehicle to express our feelings and our feelings being what is reflected back to us within the universe is the flow in which we create outer experience within our lives. Changing our minds about how we feel by repeating new ideas or new ways in which we need to live within our current thought does not necessarily create change within our lives. Our feelings have to change to be able to support the conscious mind to be able to attract conscious experiences that reflect the presence of love.

However, our feelings are driven by our emotions that are a vehicle for the conscious or unconscious mind. So, again, going back into the conscious mind and the unconscious mind, one must dissolve the unconscious mind so the 49 feelings being given forth into humanity are feelings that will allow love to be expressed and experienced within life.

80.1 When one is perceiving love, feelings are free from thought because they become an expression of love. When you clear the mind of the unconscious, you clear all thought from feeling which then allows the universe to be in an exchange with your feelings that allows the perspective of love to live within your outer experiences. Take a moment to reflect on the experiences within your life, either relationships, experiences surrounding your career or living environment or situation, relationships to family members, relationship to past experiences, relationship to sexuality. If you take a moment to reflect on these relationships, and just sit within the feelings that come up within thinking about them, ask yourself what thoughts are attached to the feelings, are these thoughts negative? Or if any thought appears to be positive is it attached to expectation? So really witnessing any thoughts that surface while understanding which is conscious and unconscious will give you an idea of the language that is being presented through your feelings. Allowing you then to really identify with what is the powerlessness, or what are the experiences within life that are reinforcing those feelings of the unconscious?

80.2 - 80.3 What is witnessed within the Clear Mind Experience is an individual's capacity to attract consistent support within the universe once their mind begins to clear of the unconscious because the feelings become free to express and live within the perception of love, and living within an experience and expression of love allows the universe to present opportunities, relationships, and experiences that support vision, ideas, love, destiny, purpose, truth, and abundance. When someone has cleared the mind of the unconscious, they are not actually trying to manifest love, destiny, ideas, truth, abundance, and purpose. They are living as the expression of these qualities because all these qualities, when named, are of the conscious mind. When someone has cleared the unconscious, then these qualities become a natural expression of the being. It is in seeking these qualities that the unconscious mind attempts to say that one is 'not this' and must find it. However, these qualities are already an aspect of each of us. It is just that the unconscious mind has us believe that we must seek to become them. When in essence what needs to happen is that once the unconscious mind is dissolved through the practice of dissolving it, then the realization of purpose, truth, abundance, destiny, and various expressions of love, new visions of ideas are just the everyday unfolding. So whereas a person's mind was previously consumed in erratic mind chatter that was disempowering of someone's belief in peace, kindness, loyalty, love, abundance, prosperity, or any of the 49 positive qualities, or positive feelings, once the mind is clear of thoughts that are consistently not supporting the presence of love, then these beautiful qualities of love can be the only thing that lives or the only expression that lives within us. It's really not about seeking them. It's about seeking to allow the mind to unfold into this expression as it becomes free of what isn't love within the perception by dissolving the unconscious.

81.1 Understanding that feelings become free of thoughts is incredibly important because it is the thoughts that attach themselves to feelings that become the validation of our action. If one is within an unconscious state of awareness, then a lot of the thoughts that will attach to the feelings will be thoughts of protecting oneself, controlling various experiences, conversations of lack, disease, fear, and control. They will be suppression. They will be experiences that really don't foster a personal freedom and non-attachment from outcome which can often keep us enslaved through fear as to what must happen. However, understanding this point that feelings become free of thoughts is important because when feelings become free of thoughts, then rather than becoming an idea, a plan where feelings become an idea, a thought that plans out an outcome, then our feelings become an expression of love. And an expression is defined as a feeling of energy, a feeling of love, a feeling of any of the 49 positive mind qualities that are on the Clear Mind Feelings Scale. So, then an individual will be expressing the 49 conscious mind feelings that are on the Clear Mind Feelings Scale, and really taking the time to visit to understand those 49 expressions; expressions being what we move into reality through a feeling of what I am rather than a thought, and a feeling of what I am is something that moves through us as us. A thought is something that I am creating through a feeling of what I wish to gain, I wish to become, I wish to acquire, I wish to participate in; so it is always coming from a place of separation.

When one dissolves the unconscious mind rather than dismantling it by pushing up against it, you activate the gift of this outer experience that supports the inner presence of love so what is being expressed is being received, nurtured, and birthed from the outer, so every expression of love is being given back from an outer experience that takes the expression to the next level of awareness, the next realization of love. It is magnificent to witness how love manifests and speaks out loud within our everyday experience. Sometimes relationships, experiences, opportunities, and things that have happened in our lives will present themselves to be completely different to us than what they were previously. Within an unconscious mind, usually we perceive everything through suppression, loss, control, and fear. And when within the conscious mind, these same people that we had these interpretations from within our lives can actually appear to be very kind, loving, loyal, supportive, or they can appear to be afraid or appear to need compassion and love. And because we have shifted our awareness to the perception of love, we now have the capacity to allow people to be who they are within our lives without the expectation or necessity that they be showing up within life to serve us. But really life is an opportunity for each one of us to express the magnificence of love from within our own capacity. This is one of the most valuable gifts of the Clear Mind Experience is that it awakens your capacity to express the presence of love, and within that expression, it will be revealed in your everyday living life that you will witness love in action.

81.2 If we are expressing the unconscious mind within our perceived ideas through our emotions, then our emotions will be speaking out unconscious ideas of how we perceive life, others, experiences, and opportunities. We will be able to speak out these unconscious ideas emotionally because our feelings will have created outer experiences, relationships, and opportunities that support the unconscious feelings that we already have. The feeling state within who we are is perceived within the universal mirror of life through silence. It doesn't necessarily need to be spoken out. Our feelings are what make us real within the world. It's an energetic frequency that enables the universe to define us because it feels us through our feelings. Quite often what happens is an outer experience will happen, and then a feeling will come up of what it feels like to be in the outer experience second to the experience. So then what happens in that case is our feeling, negative feeling, unconscious feeling is then validated by the world. And that is the gift of the universal mirror or the detriment of the experience of living within the world if you are unconscious, because you will be having your feelings perceived that are negative and unconscious by the universal mirror of life, which will then make your negative feelings real within the collective unconscious which then can create profound physical, mental, and emotional suffering. But the gift of the universal mirror is that if you are living within a conscious mind and your feelings are clear of thought and expressing the presence of love, well then the outer environment, the outer world is able to create magnificent experiences within your life that enable you to celebrate consciousness in profound ways that could never be perceived within thought because they are beyond one's capacity to seek or desire to look for, but they are just miracles that appear before us because they are experiences that are being defined and attracted to us through our inner feelings which, when in a conscious mind, are the expression of love.

81.3 As we dissolve the unconscious mind and begin to experience moments where we are free from its interpretation, then the emotions will, through our perceived ideas, thoughts, feelings of love, begin to un-limit our interpretations of how we are living our life. And as we un-limit our interpretations and remove the suppression, control, and fear out of them, then we will inspire new opportunities within our lives because the universe will start to feel new ways in which we are feeling about life. It takes time for outer experience to be redefined when we initially start to shift our perception of how we perceive life. However, throughout the process what happens is an inspiration takes shape and begins to birth itself where aspects of how you feel for your life to be different and how you feel love within your perception of yourself begin to speak very subtly to the universe, and the primary experiences and relationships surrounding you at this time will subtly begin to shift in language and then more and more and more of this outer shift will occur. But, initially, it is where the current situations within life begin to subtly transform how life is being interpreted by you, because as you move into this clear state of the mind and your emotional perception becomes clear of thought, wisdom is able to act within life. It's able to communicate within life, and wisdom will become a cheerleader to these new, inspiring opportunities that are beginning to be birthed through the perception.

82.1 Our emotions are an expression of love. They are our most magnificent means in which to express the divine qualities of love in action. When an individual is clear within the mind through the Clear Mind Experience, emotions come alive to celebrate the beauty and magnificence of consciousness because the unknown is consistently revealed through the beauty of self-acceptance, forgiveness, silence, compassion, celebration, inner knowing, and gratitude.

82.2 Our emotions come alive when we are living within a Clear Mind because what is cleared within the unconscious is the fear of attempting to suppress or control emotions out of the fear of what they could manifest. It is so simple to allow ourselves to suppress emotion and listen to the stories of why we cannot trust our feelings and how we are perceiving life within our feelings, and our feelings can become overwrought within the expression of the unconscious that articulating life through the feeling and through emotion becomes very much what we attempt to suppress. It is when we practice the Clear Mind Experience that seeking to suppress the imbalance of our emotions is no longer present within our day to day or our life experience.

83.1 Our emotions when allowed to express the presence of love are simply a beautiful gift. They are our filter for love. They are what gives us character within life. They can be what presents our charm, what has the appearance of a nurturing warmth. They can be what presents inspiring insights. And, most important, our emotions and the freedom in which they express love become our invitation to others to join us within the day to day experience and expression of life.

83.2 If, however, we are living within the unconscious mind and the language that it speaks to separate us from the presence of love, then our emotions and how we interact with life emotionally will become an indicator that maybe we have problems or concerns within our lives, within our interpretations of ourselves, others, opportunities, and experiences, and, therefore, we will attract relationships and experiences and conditions within our lives that support the unconscious mind because the universe will match us to how we feel about ourselves and what we are perceiving about ourselves. It is when we attract experiences, relationships, and opportunities through the unconscious mind that these emotional interpretations of ourselves will become fulfilled within our various experiences.

83.3 Our emotions are a position of great vulnerability to us because if we are living within the unconscious, our emotions can reveal aspects of ourselves that we'd rather not see or allow others to see. It does not make our emotions bad. It just means that they are a filter and a representation and a mirror of our feelings to the universe because our feelings will move through our emotions. And if our feelings are not sustained within love, then our emotions will be perceived to be not within harmony within life by others.

83.4 The gift of our emotions is that if we, rather than suppressing or controlling them, seek to dissolve the unconscious mind, then they will be a gift in showing us ways in which to perceive life, ourselves, others, and potential that honor the presence of love.

83.5 Our emotions quite simply are an incredible gift of allowing consciousness to celebrate itself in form if one is willing to awaken the 49 positive feelings of oneself and clear the mind so the feelings are not attached to limited thought of the unconscious.

83.6 If, however, you are not willing to clear the unconscious mind, then you may have great fear about what you see within yourself emotionally. You may use great control within your life emotionally, and you may have a sense of feeling powerless to how you are emotionally interpreting life because the unconscious mind always has a perception of powerlessness to various interpretations of our emotional condition when the unconscious mind is in relationship to our emotions because our emotions, again, move through feeling. The unconscious mind will see that it needs to suppress feeling because the unconscious mind by nature likes to appear to be in control within each moment of life. Even if it is out of control, it will believe it is in control of the out-of-control-ness.

84.1 One of the first tools that was created to support the Clear Mind Experience was our Clear Mind Feelings Scale. This is because feelings are the most important indicators. They are our gift in awakening love because they give a means in which to create action within our story. Our feelings present the presence of love within our day to day, and through the qualities of the feelings, we are able to further understand the perceptions and awakenings to love that occur.

84.2 It is within an individual clearing the mind that harmonizes the feelings to the presence of love, and this is a spontaneous realization process that takes place simply through the dissolving of the unconscious mind. Once this spontaneous awakening to love occurs within the feelings, there seems to be a birth of inner conviction which is an inner strength that awakens a true power within how one perceives life, themselves, their opportunities, and their momentum of each day. And within this power, there is also tremendous vulnerability. And the vulnerability comes from the fact that an individual is expressing the presence of love through feeling, and feeling is being moved by wisdom, and wisdom is a spontaneous expression that occurs from moment to moment. So, when a person is void of control, suppression, and fear, then they will experience vulnerability, wisdom, and the presence of love and insight which will allow them to live within each moment defining each moment within the qualities of love. So as much as there is a profound inner conviction, inner awareness to a self-power of knowing oneself as IAM to the feeling of IAM, there is also a tremendous vulnerability that allows an individual to maintain a consistent awareness to love and awareness to the presence of the IAM.

84.3 It is actually the vulnerability of not being able to define oneself outside of the moment that awakens the inner conviction and the personal power. This is because living within the vulnerability of not being able to control how one is perceived by oneself or the world each time one lives through an experience of knowing that within that experience they perceived themselves within love, strength, and vulnerability, they feel more empowered to allow that process to live within how they are presented to the world. It is in living within the vulnerability, that as the unconscious mind begins to dissolve and the new feelings, the positive Clear Mind feelings, are being revealed in relationship to life, opportunities, and their perceived identity, that one realizes the essence of vulnerability.

Personal Attachment to Individual Identity

85.1 When an individual clears their mind of the unconscious, they clear the attachment to their identity. And this is what is dissolved within perception to allow a personal freedom where they are able to inspire themselves in and out of new directions and experiences within life that embrace the presence of love.

85.2 Dissolving one's identity once one realizes that this is what is unfolding within their lives, even though not perceived as a necessity by some is a valuable step when moving into the essence and expression of personal freedom. Maybe they've created huge success or circumstances and vision within their lives and they feel that they are happy with their lives. Or maybe the individual is seeking to be released from past identity due to emotional pain, or physical or mental anguish to past experiences as one would be seeking to shift that identity. Both pathways equally welcome the shift in identity. Because what happens is if you do have a successful life and you dissolve the personal identity through the unconscious mind, you awaken a new way in which to communicate who you are to the world, and who you are within what you are contributing to the world, and what your career is, and what your day to day tasks are which awaken new platforms within an individual's life to take them to a new level of their success or their ambition or vision for oneself. If you have lived through painful experiences or you have lived through disease or disharmony that has allowed your identity to become enmeshed within the powerlessness of the experience, then welcoming the clearing and dissolving of the unconscious will assist in releasing this identity that has had you perceive the pain of past experiences, which then allows you to experience the re-creation, rebirth of a life perceived within love and not the limitations of the unconscious.

85.3 The unconscious mind will have us be a slave to who we are, who we are not, what has been created, what we've lost, what we could potentially lose, what we long to experience, and that the idea of life is to be centered around our personal needs and desires. When we live within this condition within life mentally and emotionally, we are supporting unconscious ideas because they are being moved within and out of our perception through immediate gratification and seeking to gain and create identity surrounding who we are. No matter what is gained within an unconscious perception, the unconscious mind will always perceive that it will be lost at some point. Many great successful individuals have created profound success within their lives only to get to the point and wonder where their lives have gone and what was the purpose of gaining so much when they know so little and trust so little in who they are and who they would be if the success was gone. When you can live within a successful life knowing that you are an expression of love within that success, then that success can begin to inspire itself through new directions, new pathways, new ideas, relationships, and opportunities because there is a certain freedom to who you are because you are not attached to the being that started and created this success but more moving into a direction of allowing the freedom of how you perceive life to celebrate the success. This can be a profound moment within the lives of individuals that are clearing their minds within the realm of having been a successful person. When you have been in life struggling to awaken success, then it can be challenging at different times to be able to believe that there would be any other hope to experience life or experience inspiration or new directions, ideas, and opportunities. But within the Clear Mind Experience, you are clearing the unconscious mind which is not able to perceive success, not able to perceive new opportunities and experiences, and once those thoughts, feelings, and emotions have been dissolved, then the new opportunities and experiences, and the new flow of how you feel about yourself begin to fulfill itself because there is nothing opposing the feeling.

85.4 No matter what we expect that our successes or failures should feel to us or others, when our perception is being moved through the unconscious, then our personal identity will always seem to ourselves and others to present qualities of exhaustion, qualities of control, fear, expectation, loss, concern, suppression, desire, disassociation, and highs and lows of happiness, sadness, calmness, and anger. Success does not mean that we will naturally move into a conscious mind. It quite often leaves us struggling within an unconscious mind because the unconscious mind is developed within the first seven years of life and is, basically, thoughts, feelings, and emotions that activate as interpretations of ourselves based on life and our personal will. Our successes at times are created through the unconscious, and once we are living within the successes, then these are the qualities to support the disassociation from love will present themselves. For example, the exhaustion, the control, the fear of the success, creating some type of loss within our lives, or attempting to hold onto the success, expectations of what can happen around the success, and the fear of its loss. Many different dimensions of interpretations will be directed towards the success when one is within the unconscious.

85.5 However, when an individual has cleared the mind of the unconscious, then the perception is operating as a conscious mind that's living within the presence of love. The individual has the capacity within thoughts, feelings, and interactions to preserve life within each experience; 'life' being defined as 'love.' So an individual when they experience success or they experience just life, they will be preserving an interpretation of love and the celebration of consciousness within each interpretation.

86.1 A tremendous gift within humanity is when an individual is not attached to personal identity. They are able to operate from wisdom, feeling, and insight of the universal mind. This means there is no, or limited, personal motive in one's actions which enables the universal mind to create within form through the individual's wisdom, feeling, and insight.

86.2 When one is operating within universal mind, all life is a means in which to celebrate love. Within a knowing that IAM all life, and within this, gratitude, compassion, service, stillness, and beauty will express itself within form through the life of the being in a means and flow in which to honor humanity and the presence of life within all individuals, all life, all rhythm, all knowing, all experience, and all moments.

86.3 When an individual is not operating through personal identity, the perception will be that life is an opportunity, not the obligation. All emotions will operate as a fluid movement of feelings that are an expression of the 49 qualities, feelings of love. When an individual is operating emotionally within this experience, much within life can be created to support love, preserve life, and inspire innovation that allow wisdom to move throughout the world in tremendous momentum through many ways in which we engage in developing the nature, the minds, and the bodies of the experience upon earth.

87.1 The magnificence of emotions is the beauty of allowing their movement rather than forcing or suppressing them. When we allow emotion to be a flow within movement, it is much like the ocean; where emotion will move into an experience, wash through it in celebration, in self-acceptance, within compassion, allowing stillness, radiating forgiveness, allowing insight, and expressing gratitude. When emotions move through experiences as a spontaneous flow of the universal mind, there is profound beauty that exists within life as the emotions are the rhythm of the life force energy that moves through the being, moves through life. Rather than suppressing the life force energy that becomes blocked, and in an attempt to move itself forward, it will become cathartic.

87.2 When an individual is operating within the universal mind, and emotions are harmonized to the presence of love, and feelings that are being resonated through an individual's experiences, opportunities, and relationships daily are that of the 49 Clear Mind Positive Feelings, then tears and laughter are equal opportunities to experience life. The highs and lows are not driven by what should be or what wasn't, and there are relatively minimal, if any, highs and lows. There is within the individual an expression within the mind that appears as a movement, such as, more awareness, and a greater sense of stillness will be present within all actions and all expressions of love from within the feelings.

Structure of Emotion

88.1 There is great structure within the unconscious mind and an aspect of that structure is the structure of emotion. Within the Clear Mind Experience and Philosophy, emotions are interpreted as seven primary key emotions. It is the seven primary key emotions which are self-acceptance, forgiveness, silence, compassion, celebration, inner knowing, and oneness that an individual will express 49 positive or negative feelings that express the unconscious mind or the conscious mind.

88.2 Prior to dissolving the unconscious mind, an individual will act out within their lives and push forth within their day through the 49 negative feelings that will be expressed through the seven key emotions. The unconscious feelings meaning the feelings that are unable to perceive and express love will animate themselves within the life of the individual and create disharmony within relationships, experiences, opportunities, and expectations from moment to moment.

88.3 The beauty of the Clear Mind Experience and dissolving the unconscious mind is then that the 49 feelings that will be expressed through the seven key emotions will be the 49 feelings that express the presence and potential of love. This then will provide the individual with the opportunity to experience relationships, moments, experiences, and opportunities within their life that honor and preserve the momentum and potential of love.

Perception

89.1 Perception defined within the Clear Mind Experience and Philosophy is the act of creating life through the conscious or unconscious mind. It is the aspects of the mind that combine thoughts, feelings, and emotions into concepts of life. It is practiced within the Clear Mind Experience and Philosophy that all life and the knowing that we are born into life are encoded within the perception of the individuals. The encoding of the perception of the individual is first encoded within the first seven years of life to perceive oneness. As the individual perceives oneness, it interprets all thoughts, feelings, and emotions that are present within the day to day as thoughts, feelings, and emotions of oneself. After the age of seven, the perception is encoded to release all thoughts contained within the unconscious mind as an identity of the personal beingness that will then move forth within reality through personal will to create an experience and fulfill all relationship to the feelings that are within the unconscious mind. It is only the unconscious mind at this point that is operating within the personal will because the conscious mind is not stored with anything. It is expressing itself within the moment. The conscious mind is a flow of wisdom that will present itself from moment to moment. So the perception is mainly engaged to the unconscious because the unconscious is forever creating flow within the perception because it is always anchored within current present mind. Then, once an individual gets to a point that the unconscious mind is creating blockages within their lives that provides inner-discomfort from the feelings, emotional, or mental states, then a reconciliation process can take place to allow the individual to identify with certain things that were experienced within the first seven years of life that trigger the unconscious mind to retract and begin to reveal itself and its conditions to the rational mind. It is at this point that the conscious mind will awaken and begin to interpret how the unconscious mind is moving in and out of each moment of expression. When one practices the Clear Mind Experience, there needs not be the reconciliation process as the individual is able to clear, retract, and dissolve the unconscious mind through the process.

90.1 - 90.2 Perceptions are stimulated through our senses and packaged to be received by others through our emotions. It is our emotions that move our perceptions into reality from a conscious or unconscious perspective. Take a moment to reflect upon different perceptions that you hold within your life. Are they movements or expressions of the flow and wisdom, insight, and beauty of the conscious mind, or are the perceptions a retraction, withdrawing from life, control, fear, and confusion perception?

Perception of a Conscious Mind

91.1 Within an individual, when life is perceived within a conscious mind, then we perceive love. When perceiving love, it is our emotions that allow us to express 49 positive feelings that allow love to be an expression that honors all that is revealed as life. It is within preserving life through our perception that we allow profound potential and momentum to move through our day to day. It is within a conscious mind expressing 49 positive feelings that we are able to create synchronicity between the presence of love, perceived through the inner feelings, and life experience and how our engagement with life experience will allow us to feel the presence of love within each moment.

91.2 Within a conscious mind when we express ideas, visions, and potential, then love is directed within our lives towards others, within situations, and within the movement of different experiences.

91.3 It is within a conscious mind and allowing life to be directed within love that we allow profound visions and ideas to express potential within love, and within this position, humanity is able to reside to create great momentum where wisdom and innovation can take hold within our day to day and create unlimited opportunities to embrace and experience profound love and insight. It is within a conscious mind that limitations of the unconscious collectively are dissolved. For example, poverty, lack, abuse, pornography, addiction. These qualities are able to be dissolved within the collective when an individual is no longer feeding off them from their own personal perceptions.

91.4 There is great power within humanity and the momentum in which humanity is moving into higher levels of consciousness when the capacity to look at the struggle is no more. It is within dissolving the unconscious that an individual awakens the capacity to allow beauty to live, to breathe, to be, to honor, and to express the essence and mystical beauty of love that exists within all moments and that is the unveiled potential of life.

Perception of the Unconscious Mind

92.1 Life is perceived through an unconscious mind. The 49 qualities, the 49 feelings that an individual experiences life through will be limited, controlling ideas, thoughts, and feelings that do not allow an individual to live in hope, potential, or beauty. When one perceives life through the unconscious mind, the 49 feelings will always be presenting a feeling of controlling or retracting.

92.2 Within the unconscious mind, an individual can experience great fear and within this fear, controlling interpretations that limit one into rigidity, separation, disease, stress, and fear will become present within their life through thoughts, feelings, and emotions that are expressed throughout their life within opportunities, relationships, and experiences.

92.3 It is the 49 feelings of the unconscious mind that create physical discomfort simply because the body is filled within the heaviness of their interpretations. There is a slowing down within the being due to the fact that there is a lack of freedom within movement due to stress and anxiety, or there will be a racing imbalanced sensation that will also create the individual not to release themselves from stress and anxiety.

In Between Both

93.1 As much as it is perceived to be uncomfortable to live within the unconscious mind's various perceptions, what can give greater stress to an individual is to be between the two; where within life there is the experience of the conscious mind that is supportive, nurturing, allowing, and celebrating of wisdom, and then within another moment, there is the unconscious mind that is retracting within fear, control, and suppression. It is when an individual dismantles the unconscious mind rather than dissolving it that the in between phase within perception is very common and is why one will move out of the heart-centered awareness where they are able to perceive humanity within the heart because it is through this experience that they feel to be engaging with the collective unconscious and the collective unconscious is affecting them negatively through negative energies. But in essence, it is simply that the unconscious mind is dismantled and within the dismantling of the unconscious mind, the individual is moving in and out of trance state pockets, and within the trance state pocket is disappearing within their perception to the unconscious and then having to move themselves back into the conscious mind through perception. There is great questioning during this process because an individual will question if a transformation, realization, or awakening that they experienced prior to this trance state even happened, and this is the play of the unconscious mind; where it seeks to have you believe that your awareness has deteriorated, gone, or that you must do something else to connect to it, but simply if you watch and participate in such an experience and listen to the language of the unconscious, it will be saying, "I've disappeared. Where have I gone? What happened? I was here and now I'm here." And that is simply the unconscious mind losing footing. It's as if the carpet came out from underneath the person and they fell down a hole, and, all of a sudden, they're questioning what happened to them, and that is the language of the unconscious. It is the unconscious mind saying, "What happened? Where did I go? Where did my experience go? How was I in the conscious mind and now I've disappeared?" It is the unconscious mind speaking this because it has disappeared into a trance state and does not have footing.

93.2 If an individual has dismantled the unconscious mind, it is very difficult because they do not have a strong sense of clarity, and there is always the underlying fear and vulnerability of not trusting their position within life, of not being comfortable or nurtured within any type of stability because they are moving so rapidly between a conscious and unconscious perception. And because the unconscious perceptions are coming about based on the fact that the electricity within the unconscious is promoting a trance state, it is not perceived by the rational mind as being an act of personal will which sets up great fear and vulnerability in one's stability of mind.

93.3 When an individual is faced with the fluctuations of moving in and out of the conscious mind and the unconscious mind, which is what is happening to many, many light workers, there can be the experience of feeling very, very tired from transformation; where they feel that one moment is not sure within the next because there is this continual awakening to love and retraction from love. It is simply, again, the fact that the unconscious mind has dismantled itself and because we are only living perception and once we have activated the conscious mind, there is less desire to change or be different or to create change within who we are and how we feel about ourselves. Then what happens is through the lessening of the desires the individual is just moving in and out rapidly from a conscious to an unconscious awareness because of the dismantled unconscious mind. The more you dismantle it, the more potholes it has in which the electrical currents within the brain can perceive themselves, can perceive the individual as being lost and having disappeared within themselves which makes them not sure of how to define life. When an individual moves into a trance state of the unconscious, they will have a language about how they perceive the moment, "I am looking for myself. I'm not sure who I am. I'm not sure where I am. I'm not sure what I'm here to do. I'm not sure what's happened to me. I don't know what's happened to me. I'm not trusting of who I am. I'm not trusting of my capacity to have clarity. I have a lot of confusion." These are all trance state conversations because, again, impersonalizing what is said, it is purely the unconscious mind making statements about how it is perceiving itself.

93.4 When the unconscious mind is dismantled and you have not dissolved it, then a transformation of oneself can seem long and tedious. Bringing union of mind between how we perceive ourselves within life and how we are received within life by experiences, opportunities, and others can appear to be disjointed and not in union. This is because the trance states within the unconscious mind create, allow, and activate feelings within the unconscious mind that move through the emotions that set up a question on one's integrity and ability to integrate new awareness that they have perceived within the conscious mind into their day to day.

93.5 - 93.5i When an individual is constantly living through these fluctuations, and the vulnerability of these fluctuations, of moving in and out of love, then the collective unconscious mind will affect them energetically and will turn the vulnerability into a cynicism. The cynicism will awaken the perceived opinion that all the world is unconscious. It is this opinion that comes from within the unconscious mind because the unconscious always speaks to the individual as if it were the individual. However, it is only speaking about its experience. It will be saying to the individual, "you're unconscious" as it attempts to anchor the perception into its interpretation which is that of the unconscious.

94.1 When the perception is clear of the unconscious, wisdom, compassion, and support within humanity will pour forth because one has a profound capacity to love oneself. And what one realizes throughout the day is that they are seeing themselves each moment within the life of another. The individual with a Clear Mind perception will see themselves within the world. They will identify with aspects of the unconscious mind that they themselves are no longer engaged in, and in seeing the collective in this form, it is the compassion, wisdom, and support that will pour forth in an unconditional expression of love that gives them the realizations that they have themselves awakened beyond previous limitations of the unconscious. It is within the Clear Mind Experience that an individual will be continuously realizing throughout their day that they are communicating with aspects of themselves that are no longer present within their minds, and they will be encouraging the same levels of awareness that they are experiencing within themselves. It is through this exchange with others that the realization process of love fully activates because the awakening is conditioned within the essence of oneness, where an individual is able to interpret that the person within front of me is an aspect of my past self that has been set free through the Clear Mind Experience, and within this experience of now speaking to this person, I am setting myself free from the collective, while helping the person however I have been chosen to do that.

94.2 It has been perceived by those who are awakening within the presence of love or wisdom, or who on the path of self-realization, that an individual who is moving between the conscious or unconscious mind must live within a certain way to protect their state of awareness. In part, this is true. However, awareness wishes to be integrated into the everyday. Awareness wishes to be integrated into a role upon the earth that preserves love and life. There are times when an individual will have to move out of certain lifestyles or certain relationships to be able to preserve the presence of love. However, in most cases, an individual, as they are moving in the realization process of love by dissolving the unconscious mind are able to live within the day to day, the living beauty of life in form, and able to preserve the qualities of love within the expression of love. Because where there is not love, love will move to preserve itself within compassion, and where there is love, love will move to celebrate itself within consciousness.

94.3 When the unconscious mind has been dismantled and not dissolved, an individual will at times activate a trance state by awakening a feeling of needing to be protected within humanity from the collective unconscious because it is somehow affecting them. And what typically registers them to this process is how they have been affected emotionally and will interpret the feeling that this is the case; that the collective unconscious has taken them out of a perceived state of the conscious mind and placed them within the unconscious mind. And this is true in the sense that the unconscious mind has been activated, but it has not been activated because one has been attacked by the unconscious. It has been activated because the unconscious mind is speaking to the feeling of the individual and reciprocating based on that feeling which then has the individual enter the unconscious. And, if a person is practicing transformation upon the path, they will retract into a trance state.

95.1 It is true that before all perception is engaged within the presence of love through a Clear Mind, one that operates from a conscious state with little awareness of the unconscious, that the unconscious mind will be perceived as exhausting, and this is because exhaustion is a quality of the unconscious. It is a quality of the unconscious mind that has one give up on the path of transformation, on the path of self-discovery, on the path of healing, on the path of allowing one to feel good about oneself, on the path of marriage, on the path of education, on our career paths, within our relationships. It is the unconscious mind that wants to give up because it is exhausted, because it cannot be challenged any longer by the conscious mind.

And because of the rise of consciousness on the planet, the unconscious mind is challenged within many forms throughout many days, and because of this will perceive itself to be exhausted. It is only speaking about itself because it gains no sustenance from self-development work or any perceived conditions of the conscious mind. So when the exhaustion of transformation appears within the life of another, it is simply the unconscious mind speaking of itself because it is not able to gain footing within life. It is activating trance states, many at a time, to be able to gain that perception of exhaustion. And it is when an individual gets to this place that dissolving the unconscious will be rapid and create a huge energetic impact within their lives setting them free to live their purpose and destiny.

95.2 - 95.4 On the path of spiritual development upon the planet, people are guided into understanding how they are perceiving reality, often looking at experiences, relationships, and opportunities and seeking to find the blockages that exist in each of these aspects of life. When they find a blockage that exists within one of these aspects of life, then they begin to look at past circumstances that may have led to developing that blockage or that blocked perception. When one is awakening to wisdom through this form, it can be interpreted by the unconscious mind as exhausting because there is the constant physical interaction within reality to understand a new aspect of who one is and how one is seeing and perceiving life. When one is attempting to awaken through outer interpretations, and outer interpretations of how one is allowing or not allowing life experience, then the unconscious mind will measure effort versus result. Because the unconscious mind is not able to perceive love, then one's efforts to connect to love will be continually interpreted through the unconscious as a waste of time and time-consuming because the end result is love, and it is not able to perceive love, so it will say love does not exist. It will continually speak about the efforts that one must take to understand one's mind and how one is perceiving reality. When, in a sense, you are not dissolving the unconscious but interacting with it, you are just engaging the unconscious mind through looking for interpretations of outer experiences. You are engaging the unconscious mind to tell you and give you opinion as to what it thinks and believes you are. And coming from the unconscious, these would all be limitations of consciousness that do not allow the presence of love.

95.5 When the unconscious mind wants to express to the personal mind that is seeking the presence of love is too difficult, tiring, exhausting, takes too much effort for little reward, it will do this by projecting feelings into reality that present life experiences or thoughts of life, yourself, or others, and opportunities that make you feel that you are not gaining any momentum within awakening to new perceptions of life. It will present old patterns and cycles within life that attempt to have the perception moved into the unconscious and attempt to block the conscious mind from celebrating the presence of love that is being revealed. To be able to dismantle the unconscious mind takes tremendous amounts of work, of realization of what isn't love. That is subtly, however, empowering the unconscious to believe in itself because you are paying it attention. Then if you deny the unconscious mind by just blocking it out, then you will suppress it, and it will come back to life through animation, through the feeling that one will have of 'is it gone?' or 'is it going to present itself?' And through that vulnerability, the feelings will create an outer experience that will bring it back into play. The subtleties of awakening beyond the unconscious limitations really are difficult to translate into human form and human word because the subtleties are so minute and, at times, borderline transparent. The beauty of the Clear Mind Experience is that you are dissolving the unconscious mind, not by looking at it, engaging in it, or seeking interpretation from it, or seeking to understand it, but dissolving it mechanically which allows it to no longer reflect into life and allows the conscious mind to be present within each moment.

95.6 When an individual is awakening to the presence of love, they are not tired from the awakening to love because the nature of love is beyond words so incredibly invigorating. It seeks not to be measured, just the moments of expression as it is the state of being. It is invigorating, calming, nurturing. The idea that it is exhausting, limiting, and frustrating is the unconscious mind speaking of what you are doing to it: limiting its opportunity to engage. It is frustrated because it is not anchoring the perception and moving life as an expression of itself. If you take a moment to think about the negative expressions of exhaustion that present themselves within your mind that are attempting to define how you are awakening to new states of awareness, and look at the words impersonally, it is the unconscious mind speaking of how it feels in the process. The problem being is that those feelings are what create within the day to day. When you practice the Clear Mind Experience, you are anchoring, activating, and moving in and out of the 49 positive mind feelings which enable you to celebrate shifts in consciousness through the conscious mind.

95.7 Because the unconscious mind is unable to identify with love, it is continually seeking to measure what it gives you. Because it is unable to see love, it has no measurement and nothing to measure from. Once you move in and out of experiences of love, it will continually speak about why that love will not be permanent, why that love cannot serve, what are the distrusting qualities of how you are perceiving that love, and it will continually attempt to shift the perception and the rational mind into negative feelings on current experiences of love. The beauty of the Clear Mind Experience is that it gives you a foundation, a structure, and a momentum in which you are continually lifting perception out of the unconscious as it is retracting back into itself, and the perception of the personal mind is moving into the conscious mind. And it is within that process that the conscious mind moves the unconscious into the presence of love dissolving it.

95.8 The unconscious mind will consistently speak of the effort and sacrifice, the lack of support from the universe in relationship to the path of self-discovery. This is because the individual is accessing the unconscious mind to understand it, and the unconscious mind does not allow itself to feel supported, does not allow itself to trust, does not allow itself to experience freedom, does not believe that it can receive, is unable to perceive wisdom, and within these qualities will talk endlessly of the waste of life in seeking the opposite to the unconscious because it is, the entire time, attempting to protect its position within reality by the suggestions in which it makes to define how you are moving through each moment.

95.9 It is within this process of the unconscious mind that one is able to identify with the importance of clearing the unconscious through the act of dissolving it, rather than the act of moving into it to see it, to walk away from it. One is not able to walk away from the unconscious mind because the unconscious mind believes that it is you. It will interpret that attempt as a type of death. And when the mind perceives that it could potentially die, it will within that moment create experiences to maintain itself and keep itself alive. The unconscious mind is similar in this experience. That is why one must only focus on the birth; the birth of the conscious mind into the moment. This is the gift of the Clear Mind Experience.

96.1 The beauty of dissolving the unconscious mind is that it is not taking any action within your life both inner and outer to be defined. You are not engaged within the relationship of discovering how it is acting out or what it is saying within your life because the dissolving of its interpretations is happening within the brain, therefore, setting the perception free to experience and perceive reality through the 49 positive feelings and interpretations of the conscious mind.

96.2 The most powerful gift of the Clear Mind Experience is that truth, the presence of love, the process of awakening is happening within the realm of experience and not simply the realm of knowledge. The presence of love is experienced within life physically, mentally, and emotionally within the Clear Mind Experience because the conscious mind is moving into the unconscious and dissolving it within the presence, flow, and interpretations of love that are within the Clear Mind process. This then takes the self-discovery process out of the realm of thinking, out of the realm of planning how one feels one must let go of interpretations that are separate to love into the experience of this happening within each moment of each day within each breath which makes the process of awakening able to move within life with profound clarity, precision, and momentum.

97.1 When one practices the Clear Mind Experience, what awakens initially is a perceived awareness to love. Within the perceived awareness to love, one feels love because of the 49 positive feelings that support the presence of love will be active within life. Because through the feelings, the potential of love is revealed within all areas of life so there is continuity between inner experience and outer perception and outer engagement with reality.

97.2 When one is having the experience of love through perceived awareness to love, the peace and condition needed to honor love is able to function within the day to day. The conditions needed to honor the presence of love and its continued momentum will move towards life and celebrate life because perception will have shifted, and life experiences will be aligned to the outer experiences and relationships and opportunities that are required to support love and create a structure in which an individual can reside in love.

98.1 The emotional mind is a magnificent gift as it presents opportunities within each moment to bring life to the feeling of love. When one is feeling love, then the momentum of joy, abundance, and wisdom will dance through their minds as a magnificent symphony of potential that can be experienced from moment to moment.

98.2 The greatest gift of the emotional mind is that it hosts the alchemy of love into being, into the world. The world interprets our perception of ourselves through our emotional demeanor. Most individuals believe at some point within their lives that their emotions are what is to be suppressed and controlled for us to be good, well, centered, perceived as spiritual beings.

98.3 It is within our emotions that we host the capacity to experience joy. It is within experiencing joy that we invite the universe to present us with experiences, relationships, and opportunities that honor the presence of love and allow and enable us to build a structure within our lives that supports the environment of love within all that we do within each moment. It is within celebrating joy that we create and allow and access the continual momentum and flow of abundance. This is because within perception, one must celebrate within joy the momentum of wisdom and how wisdom has been birthed within the conscious mind and how the conscious mind is re-defining life. When an individual is struggling between the conscious and unconscious mind, then there will be an outer struggle of freedom versus limitation and restriction. For some individuals, the struggle is the personal unconscious. For some, it is the collective unconscious. And for some, it is both.

98.4 Our emotions are our vehicle in which to express and experience joy, to create, to allow, to honor, to nurture, to express, and will present love and union of mind within the world through their expression. It is within our emotions that we engage within relationship, within ourselves, and the world which includes individuals, nature, and experience. It is within our emotions that we preserve all connection to love, and within our emotion that we are moved to make choice that will move us into the presence of love, or move us into another experience that does not allow the presence of love. It is within our emotions that we yearn for freedom from what is not love.

98.5 It is within our emotions that we are set free to experience the unlimited potential of love, or within the retraction of the emotion that we are held into bondage, and within this bondage, we yearn to be free. The gift of our emotions is universal because within each being there are seven primary emotions. And when the primary emotions are harmonized to the presence of love, then tremendous unity of one mind will form on the planet because the 49 feelings of love that are preserving the presence of love will be animated through the conscious mind. So when one conscious mind meets another conscious mind and they are expressing the beauty of love, there will be union of mind, an all-ness to the experience. One does not seek to be one with all. One is one with all because the qualities of the conscious mind, the 49 positive mind feelings are all the same for each of us, and within each environment the emotions will deliver seven of the feelings.

98.6 It is within creating harmony of one mind upon the planet by awakening the conscious mind to the presence of love that humanity lives within a symphony of expression that honors life on the planet and preserves the presence of love. It is within the beauty of love that each moment is perceived, and it is harmonizing the seven key emotions to the presence of love that creates the one mind.

98.7 Through the Clear Mind Experience and dissolving the unconscious, an individual is honoring all emotion because they are clearing the unconscious mind that is using emotion as a vehicle in which to animate and express itself. When an individual has cleared the unconscious, the emotions are an expression of love, wisdom, and insight which allows an individual to feel honored, embraced, and supported within each moment of life. And within these feelings there is a sense of joy that the presence of love is honoring life within and preserving itself within self-appreciation.

98.8 If an individual is living within the unconscious mind and the emotions are a vehicle in which to represent the unconscious mind to life, then the emotions will always be presenting conflict to us within our lives. Relationships, experiences, and opportunities will partake within this conflict because the limited ideas and belief systems of the unconscious mind and what it believes will be interacting with us emotionally and there will be a sense of powerlessness.

99.1 What is important to understand is that our emotions drive our feelings even though some believe it is the other way around and that it our feelings choose our emotions. It is our emotions that take our feelings into reality which makes the emotion the primary function and the feeling the second. Until an emotion takes a feeling into reality, the feeling is static and not creating.

99.2 Within an unconscious perception, thought is released into one of the seven emotions. Then how the thought makes sense to the rational mind will awaken a feeling to support the interpretation. Once the interpretation has found the feeling, the emotional reaction to the feeling will be what represents and engages with life.

99.3 This sequence of perception can be witnessed when an individual will be engaged for many months in thoughts of fear, destruction, separation, and distrust way before what they contemplated as their destruction appears to them as an experience within their lives. When it appears within their lives, they will have a language that will say they knew it was coming. What is saying that 'I knew it was coming?' It is the unconscious mind that is saying this because within the feelings of fear, destruction, separation, and distrust, the experience was released. Then, within the feeling of this experience being released, the rational mind believed it, and within the union of the rational mind and the feeling, there was confirmation within the creation of the experience. The universe responded by presenting an experience that responded to the feelings not the thoughts.

100.1 - 100.3 Within the day to day, people are encouraged to believe that feeling comes before emotion. When you are engaged within the unconscious, this is true because there is a breakdown of order. The unconscious mind is operating within the chaos, of not understanding life through fear and control, not allowing life to be within a momentum through the aspects of distrust, fear, and control. This does not say that the unconscious mind is not created as a structure because it is, but within its chaos, there is order. It is only when the unconscious mind engages through perception, feeling, and emotion that it appears to be chaos and dysfunction. Within its structure of where thoughts and feelings and emotions are stored, there is order. When the conscious mind appears within reality, there is a flow. There are not definitive commands within the conscious mind because it only activates within the feeling center the 49 feelings in which to express wisdom that appears spontaneously within each moment. It does not store thought like the unconscious mind, and within this process, there appears to be order and harmony because harmony and balance are aspects of the feelings of the conscious mind. It is within this flow of the conscious mind that one will benefit and progress within life in a way that is filled with harmony and momentum.

101.1 - 101.2 Let us take a moment to reflect on what a person who is dismantling the unconscious mind is going to experience within their day to day. When an individual is analyzing qualities that are presented from the unconscious mind, then they will live one of the greatest heartaches and frustrations which is an incongruency of living truth and having moments where the perception and limited perceptions within the personal mind of the unconscious are not present, and they are able to experience conscious moments within their day to day. However, within their relationships, finances, progress, momentum, and flow of life, there is an exhaustion versus a vitality. And this is because when analyzing the thoughts of the unconscious mind, there is the perception of suppressing the unconscious mind, healing the unconscious mind, or denying its thoughts. It is the feelings that come from this that interfere with a conscious mind flow within the day to day living; where the outer living experience will still be unconscious even though there is a conscious awareness within the individual within how they are perceiving potential, wisdom and love that is expressed as life.

101.3 When an individual is analyzing the unconscious mind, there is a flow in which perception moves into an experience. Firstly, an individual will take a position or host a judgment that one interpretation is better than another. Within activating this interpretation, a thought is then triggered and moved into an emotion. Once the emotion triggers a feeling, and the feeling is typically an underlying fear of the current experience, or a negative quality of the 49 unconscious mind feelings, or it can be the perception of exhaustion of why one is still facing limitations that exist within the collective unconscious or the personal unconscious thoughts, there is a sequence in which thought and feeling move through emotion to support what has happened within life. When one is engaging within the unconscious to analyze one's direction, the outer experience will always be initiating reaction from the unconscious mind. When one is within a conscious mind, there is a flow, an ebb and flow of an in and out of the experience, and the experience is only complimenting the inner experience. When an individual is engaged within the unconscious, then the outer experience is continually reinforcing the separation from love within the unconscious mind, and the unconscious mind perceives that the experience derived first and then the unconscious mind reacted. When, in a sense, the experience has happened because a feeling was moved from the unconscious mind into life to be interpreted as a negative experience, and then the negative experience came into form.

101.4 Once an individual has this experience and is engaged this way within the unconscious, then feelings of powerlessness can move in and out of the thoughts, and then the celebration of what one has had to dilute to awaken to the current state will be diluted within that moment, and then the individual will interpret a struggle in how they perceive life. They will not be able to live within a flow between emotion and feeling within their lives. This creates great frustration and again empowers the fear that the inner vision and inner knowing and inner presence of wisdom are not able to function outside within the world, and this is because the unconscious mind is claiming the experience through the feelings.

101.5 If we are analyzing the unconscious mind, our outer lives are a reflection of the powerlessness within the relationship of the unconscious and the disjointed attempt to heal what cannot be healed. The unconscious mind when suppressed will release itself in animation that will create upheaval and cathartic release within the being. If an individual suppresses a cathartic release to move the unconscious mind, then they will experience a confusion within how they perceive their current experiences and they will move in and out of being completely aware within a conscious state of awareness of truth, higher frequencies, higher interpretations, higher calling, and then moving into a complete unconscious, lifeless, confused state of consciousness where they are not able to interpret in the same form that they do within the conscious mind which creates a rejection of one's courage, path, and discernment.

102.1 Take a moment to integrate your feelings by drawing a picture or painting a picture of images that allow you to have vision for life. Take a moment to reflect on the images and what feelings come up for you in looking at the images, and this is how the universe relates to you. When feelings move forth, the universe responds by how what feelings come into play to support what you have upon your canvas of life. Once you have painted or drawn your pictures, take a moment to look at the pictures and the feelings that come up for you is how the universe would respond to the pictures.

102.2 When our emotions are harmonized to the presence of love, then all of our feelings that are presented to the universe create a momentum of love because the universe is always interpreting the presence of love within our everyday within all thoughts, feelings, and emotions that are being moved through the conscious mind through feelings that are being presented within each moment. When we create this momentum within life, then life becomes a celebration.

102.3 The gift of the Clear Mind Experience is that when you are dissolving the unconscious mind rather than dismantling it, the unconscious mind can at no point during the day take control of one's feelings due to the process of the Clear Mind Breath and Clear Mind Support Mantra.

102.4 Feelings are the dual experience of either preserving life within the beauty that is available within feelings that support the presence of love, or they are key in destroying and separating us from the potential of life by denying the beauty of love within the powerlessness of not feeling worthy to receive love.

102.5 When an individual dissolves the unconscious mind, life is not celebrated through the perception of perfection, but life is an expression of the potential of consciousness. Emotions are harmonized. Feelings are centered around the movement of love. The mind is clear of the unconscious which makes an environment of a beautiful mind which allows the individual to host the presence of love and move life in and out of its potential within each moment.

103.1 The false fear and interpretation that the unconscious mind places within the minds of humanity through drug companies and various institutions and various mediums of the media, is that emotions can hurt us. But, simply, they are not able to. Emotions don't hurt us, they don't humiliate us, they don't derail us, and they are not the obstacle of our awakening to higher consciousness. Suppressing emotions will make emotions cathartic and out of control, but it's all coming from within the unconscious mind. The unconscious mind is simply using the emotions as the vehicle and deadening the emotion will only give power to the unconscious mind because it will push back in other experiences of disease, disharmony, social dysfunction, addiction, fear, control, anxiety, and depression.

104.1 It is the unconscious mind that perceives humiliation, hurt, fear, distrust. It will also perceive the control one thinks one needs to awaken. If it perceives these various conditions, it will invoke feelings emotionally and the feelings that surface emotionally will create the experiences outside to be able to support them.

105.1 - 105.3 It is within clearing your mind of the unconscious thoughts, feelings, and emotions that you remove the equation of living negative feelings within that create negative experience outside. When one wishes to move beyond the limitations of the unconscious mind, it takes a fearless embrace of the emotional mind. You cannot choose or find the fearlessness to embrace the emotional mind or the will to embrace your emotions. However, the gift of the Clear Mind Experience is that a spontaneous union will occur within a Clear Mind, within a beautiful mind that is free of the unconscious mind; a union with the presence of love and the emotional mind.

106.1 Within the Clear Mind Experience, our seven key emotions are defined as: self-acceptance, forgiveness, silence, compassion, celebration, inner knowing, and oneness. Each of these emotions can be a vehicle for the unconscious mind or the conscious mind. Emotions are not what hold negativity. They are simply what move the unconscious mind or the conscious mind.

106.2 - 106.3 It is our lives that are defined by the expression of our seven emotions. As they move through the five primary relationships within our lives which are: relationship to child-mind, relationship to self-love, relationship to emotions, relationship to living mind, relationship to spiritual mind, each one of these relationships show up as an expression and interpretation of both our inner and outer experiences, and each relationship will host both thoughts, feelings, and emotions of the unconscious mind and expressions of love from within the conscious mind.

107.1 - 107.4 It is our seven primary emotions which are: self-acceptance, forgiveness, silence, compassion, celebration, inner knowing, and oneness that seven feelings within each of the emotions is hosted. To further clarify and understand this, please turn to the Clear Mind Feelings Scale on page ___. If you go to the emotion such as, Self-Acceptance, you will see there are seven positive and seven negative feelings listed. The negative feelings are the unconscious feelings. The positive feelings are the conscious feelings; the potential of love that can be expressed and interpreted within form through the conscious mind. It is important to discover these qualities and feelings from within each of the seven key emotions as we are easily able to identify with how the universe is speaking to us based on how we feel about ourselves, our relationships, and our experiences. The Clear Mind Feelings Scale will help an individual understand when they are operating consciously within their feelings or unconsciously. It is important to interpret this scale so as to understand the subtlety of feelings that are being moved within the mind and creating within life.

Harmony

108.1 Self-acceptance defined as an expression of the conscious mind becomes a state of being not a state of mind. When one has harmonized the emotion of self-acceptance to love, there is a sense of presence and the qualities of self-acceptance become a feeling within how one perceives one's ability to be present within all activities within life.

108.2 When self-acceptance is awakened within the conscious mind, the expression of trust, a sense of feeling embraced, the knowing of being honored, the experience of being nurtured, the unlimited potential of how one can be supported within the universe within each day, and the harmonious expression of love is allowing of all relationships, allowing of one's career, the potential of new life, relationship to parents and birth is balanced, harmonized, fluid, and is clear of past limitations, and all and every idea of loss, lack, and control. When one has harmonized the beauty of self-acceptance within their lives and self-acceptance is able to perceive the magnificence of love, then one will operate within their day to day in a manner that supports the transparency of love.

109.1 Often in people's lives, one struggles to be defined throughout their career in a form that is not containing stress. What one must realize is that the condition of stress comes from the perception of oneself. If one feels challenged within feelings that they have of themselves, such as within self-acceptance, they will be experiencing unconscious feelings from the conscious mind that perpetuate distrust, a sense of abandonment, the feeling of being dishonored, opportunities to perceive guilt, a feeling that one is unsupported, a rigidity and a fear to change. It is when one perceives the unconscious mind within their career that one feels suffocated and one feels stressed because their belief system is allowing of one to feel that one is lost to what they are doing and that the career has become the identity that has surpassed the fluidity of potential and love within one's perception of oneself. When one harmonizes self-acceptance to perceive love, then life has a rhythm and within the rhythm, there is the belief of abundance and a sense to allow unlimited potential to be birthed within each moment and each experience because one is able to trust. One is able to know that one is going to be embraced, honored, nurtured, supported within decisions that one makes to preserve the presence of love. And when one makes those choices to preserve the presence of love, then the universe will present multitudes of opportunities for one to experience the creativity, knowledge, intelligence, drive, passion, purpose, and awareness that moves them into their career of choice. When one honors purpose, one is not supporting stress because one feels to be entering a calling and not being pushed into a condition of living.

109.2 When one harmonizes the beauty of self-acceptance within their lives, they are free from the feeling of being burdened. Because within dissolving the unconscious thoughts that create the feelings that are unconscious that operate through the presence and condition of self-acceptance, one no longer has a powerlessness within their choices but in life feels that they are being honored within each choice and opportunity or potential. When one trusts what is moving within their lives, then one will be presented with experiences that honor the presence of trust. One can only attract experiences that dishonor trust when there is distrust being expressed within the unconscious mind.

109.3 When living within self-acceptance within the capacity to express the conscious mind within self-acceptance, one is filled within the state of being with a deep sense that opportunities and one's career are there as a celebration of life and a gift that is moved within our lives is that the condition of a career is not strived for or gained through personal mind or effort. When one is harmonized to the presence of self-acceptance and the qualities of self-acceptance such as trust, embraced, honored, nurtured, supported, harmonious, and allowing are being expressed within the potential of life, then life is gifted what is able to support these qualities. Within these qualities, there is no opportunity for personal effort because each of these qualities as they move in and out of one another draw energy into oneself because there is a belief of allowing a movement of trust, a sense of being embraced, the movement within being honored. As what is received within awakening the expression of being nurtured is the realization that IAM supported. And then within knowing one is supported, there is the harmonious expression and presence of love.

110.1 Self-acceptance is also how one relates to one's home. Their home environment is expressed within the qualities of self-acceptance. When one lives within the conscious mind clear of unconscious thoughts, allowing the presence of love, then one's home feels nurturing. It represents a womb-like sense to allow unconditional love to live as an expression of trust as the home will feel to embrace life. One will feel honored and nurtured and supported by the harmony of the home as the home will reflect the state of being that is allowing of life to move through the home as an expression of love. When one lives within the presence of love and is expressing self-acceptance and the qualities of self-acceptance within a conscious mind, the home will represent a means in which to express creativity, to receive and live within peace and stillness and joy, and the presence of wisdom will operate within the home as one lives free from hardships and loneliness of addiction. It is only within the unconscious mind that one's home fills with hardships and loneliness of addiction because the home becomes the source in which the unconscious feelings of oneself are fulfilled, such as a sense of distrusting the world, feeling abandoned by ones that should love us, a sense of feeling dishonored within relationships or conditions of the world, a knowingness that how one operates makes them feel guilty, or perceive guilt that the home feels unsupported and they feel suffocated within a rigidity and fear of what life is able to offer them within how they engage within their day to day. Often, homes of the unconscious mind are filled with addiction because it replaces the feelings of longing for love within oneself.

110.2 Within the conscious mind when one has cleared the unconscious and is living within the presence of love within oneself, all relationships represent a wholeness and spontaneity because of how one perceives oneself. As well as the wholeness and spontaneity, there is a familiarity and kindness present within life because within life, one is only ever experiencing oneself. The familiarity and kindness is an expression of the presence of love that is consistent within all seven key emotions and all perceptions of life. And the spontaneity and wholeness is how one connects to life and others, what one provides to different experiences, and how one is nurtured by universal perception and consciousness. It is within a conscious mind when one perceives the presence of love that self-acceptance provides the essence of fulfillment within the opportunity to live in love and the opportunity to express the beauty of love. It is within self-acceptance that one lives free of any expectation of receiving as one is comforted within the presence of knowing that life is the gift of each moment.

111.1 Self-acceptance is the emotion that speaks to the universe and within our lives of the structure of our lives. Self-acceptance is a state of being when living within the conscious mind. We will feel that we are being supported within life, that we are receiving the beauty of gifts as an expression of the unknown and the presence of universal love. Self-acceptance when harmonized within a conscious mind offers the potential and places the life of the individual into the freedom of living as an experience of love within each moment, and the individual will be free of what one would demand one should have. And within that, one is free from suffering within loss.

111.2 Within the conscious mind, self-acceptance as a structure is free of expectation and failure; open and able to live within the potential of what is unseen so that true nurturing, true support, true beauty is able to be birthed as an expression of unlimited potential of love.

112.1 Within each of the seven key emotions, there are seven positive feelings. These seven positive feelings operate as an expression of love when the conscious mind is what is primarily available and the unconscious mind is dissolved. The seven positive feelings are how we express the unlimited possibilities of our life experience. Our life experiences are defined by the feelings. When we dissolve the unconscious mind, one is not seeking to reconcile experiences, but one is living within a fluid expression of love that allows positive feelings to define experiences. One can never change an experience in life. One can only perceive the experience through a positive or negative feeling. When one is clear of the unconscious, one has no potential to experience life or past experiences within negativity. The seven positive feelings that awaken to express the presence of love within self-acceptance are: trust; a feeling of being embraced; the expression of receiving by living within the knowing that one is honored; the beauty and fluidity of feeling one is nurtured; supported; has the capacity to live within a harmonious environment, relationship, or career; awakening the capacity that one is allowing of each moment within life.

113.1 When one is living within self-acceptance and is hosting the perception of the unconscious mind, one will experience emotional upheaval through different experiences of life that promote loss within the area of finances, relationships, and career, goals, and longings. When one lives within the unconscious mind, they will perceive life within self-acceptance through feelings of distrust, a sense of being abandoned, dishonored, the feeling of guilt, that life is not supporting what they wish were happening within their lives, and through this, a rigidity and a fear to hang on to what is lost or perceived to be lost will begin to direct life, and it will become their condition within life.

113.2 It is within perceiving life within the unconscious mind that self-acceptance will just be the opposite. Life will be what one is not able to accept. Within life, one will struggle. There will be limited opportunities. One will feel dishonored by what one is experiencing daily, and life will become a state of emotional chaos rather than a state of being; 'being' being defined as love. When life is being perceived within the unconscious mind, the seven feelings of self-acceptance will be speaking through various experiences that have us question ourselves. When one lives within the unconscious mind, the universe will cater to the negative feelings that one feels within oneself.

113.3 It is within perceiving life within the unconscious mind that the feelings of self-acceptance will have us question and feel great distrust of most experiences within our lives, within our home, within our career, within our relationships, within our finances. We will attract experiences that will question the safety and the condition of these areas of our lives. If we have accumulated within the unconscious mind, meaning accumulated wealth and asset whilst living within the unconscious mind, then we will continually question the loss of the accumulation and set up rigidities and fear within our lives to protect what is accumulated through the fear of loss. If one has not accumulated and is living within the unconscious mind, then one will live within the perception that one is not able to attract, is not being supported by the universe, and within that there is a rigidity and a fear to support one seeking to connect to abundance. The ways in which the unconscious mind and conscious mind will express love or loss through self-acceptance is unlimited when it comes to action of how one is defined as a being.

113.4 Feelings within the seven key emotions roll into one another, move in and out of one another. For example, when one feels distrust, one will feel guilty over the fact that they are not able to trust within their primary relationships, to career, income, and structure of home, and lifestyle. They will struggle to feel nurtured, to feel that they are being honored and embraced by life. Guilt and the condition of guilt is what has us engage within the collective unconscious and can keep one plugged into receiving dialogue from the collective unconscious about the limitations of life and that they are to distrust themselves and ability to make choices within their day to day.

113.5 When one is living within the unconscious mind and expressing feeling within self-acceptance, they will always appear to have the weight of the world on their shoulders because within the mind of the unconscious participant, one feels one must create life; that it is up to them to live in a means that makes them happy, and feels that they must make all around them happy, and if they fail to do so, then they will have failed, and either condition will have them appear to have the weight of the world on their shoulders because within the mind, they are the primary creator within their lives.

113.6 All conditions that are negative within the feelings of self-acceptance, such as distrust, abandonment, a sense of being dishonored, the perception of guilt, a sense of being unsupported, rigidity, and fear are all dissolved within the Clear Mind Experience within the unconscious mind.

When one has dissolved the unconscious mind, then experiences and feelings within life that are being expressed negatively within self-acceptance will dissolve within the unconscious mind, and the negativity to support the negative feelings of self-acceptance can no longer exist.

114.1 Within self-acceptance when one is living within the unconscious mind, one will perceive life through the feeling of distrust that life is abandoning them. There is a sense of being dishonored and a fear to protect oneself. There is the guilt that one is not able to trust and within the distrust, one is feeling unsupported and creates rigidity to protect oneself. Within career, finances, relationships to parents, and perception of one's home, one will experience life in a way that moves the seven negative feelings into expression when one lives within the unconscious mind. When one successfully dissolves the unconscious mind, then all experiences that supported the seven negative feelings of the unconscious mind that are expressing life within self-acceptance will end. It will be redefined.

Serenity

115.1 The second emotion is forgiveness that contains awareness to seven positive or seven negative feelings. When one has cleared the unconscious mind, one has the capacity to perceive life within the conscious mind. Within perceiving life within the conscious mind, one is able to experience the conscious interpretation of forgiveness that would be harmonized to the presence of love. When forgiveness is harmonized to the presence of love, it is the expression of serenity. When one is able to live within forgiveness expressed through the conscious mind, there will be a centering of one's physical and mental awareness as it will operate as the expression of serenity.

115.2 Serenity is a magnificent expression operating as forgiveness within a conscious mind. When one lives within forgiveness expressing the beauty of serenity, then one will move in life effortlessly, honoring each moment in self-appreciation. Within the conscious mind, there is no question to forgive as there can be no concept of what has happened to hurt. Within serenity when one is allowing the feelings of forgiveness, life is not able to create or attract painful experiences because within one's perception of oneself, physically and mentally, is the realization of kindness within each movement of life knowing that IAM the strength and purity to radiate serenity within each moment of life that receives life within gratitude.

115.3 When the emotion forgiveness is perceived within the presence of love living as an expression within a conscious mind, there will be a fluidity to life and a serenity that has a profound strength in which it moves through life because it has the momentum of allowing love to move within serenity and self-appreciation.

115.4 When one lives within the conscious mind and is an expression of forgiveness within each moment and the feelings of forgiveness are moving in and out of each experience, relationship to sexuality and sexual partners will have a kindness and a depth within them that one is hosting them within the purity and intent of honoring self-appreciation within each moment.

115.5 When one is living within the conscious mind and is resonating sexually within serenity, one will live balanced and will be free from allowing sexual and emotional co-dependencies to exist and define partnership and relationship because one will be living within movement, knowing strength, purity, gratitude, serenity, and kindness as an expression of sexuality. One will be seeking to live within the spontaneous knowing that life is preserved within the sexual experience and love is what moves the sexual experience through oneself.

115.6 When one is living within the conscious mind and able to perceive the beauty of forgiveness and the seven feelings of serenity are expressing life within each moment, then gratitude and kindness will be present throughout the day within ideas and experiences of oneself or in relationship to others; meaning that life will present opportunities of loving oneself and honoring vulnerabilities of others, and within honoring the vulnerability of others, one will celebrate oneself within gratitude.

115.7 It is the quality of forgiveness, the emotion of forgiveness, and the seven feelings contained within its expression that allows someone to have a fluid sense of discernment in which they are able to honor life, honor the presence of love, honor the needs of others that will be presented to them within each moment. When one is living within the conscious mind, they will be free of the suffering and limitations of others because they will have the discernment to preserve love within themselves and the discernment to honor life within another. There is no chance of living within the loss of expectation when one lives within the awareness of forgiveness; as there is nothing to lose because forgiveness is a fluid movement of consciousness that moves in and out of life creating connection of life force from one to the other. It is within the conscious mind and the union of forgiveness within a conscious mind that one will move in and out of experiences with others feeling deeply honored, appreciated, and safe within the realization and expression of kindness. Sexuality will be a means in which to honor the beauty of oneself and the potential of self-love.

One will not engage within sexuality seeking to be heightened or to create some awareness to power or control of oneself, but one will engage within sexuality to experience the movement of love that is contained within the life force that will move throughout the being, throughout the seven emotions into the pineal gland where one will realize IAM the presence of love allowing life to move as IAM all life.

115.8 The seven feelings that will experience life within the awareness of forgiveness from within the conscious mind are: kindness, movement, the beauty of knowing, the strength to live within, the purity that IAM, the serenity of movement, and the gratitude of all life.

116.1 - 116.1i When forgiveness as an emotion expresses the unconscious mind, it will do so through seven negative feelings. Forgiveness, rather than being a feeling of centering of one's physical and mental awareness that promotes serenity when in a conscious mind, will express within a person's perception a sense of being betrayed in what is sought to be accumulated within life, whether the accumulation is materially, emotionally, or mentally. If one is living within the seven negative feelings of forgiveness, they will be presented with many experiences that represent betrayal of thought, feeling, and emotion and will define their feelings of oneself within shame and judgment that will promote a strong sense of anxiety to be defined within outer experiences which will accumulate a limited perception of oneself.

116.2 When one is living within the unconscious mind and expressing unconscious thoughts that move into forgiveness that awaken the seven negative feelings to be expressed, one will feel through their sexual experiences, friendships, relationship to the past that they feel overwhelmed and confused by perceptions. Thoughts within their mind will run within chaos. They will struggle to perceive clarity and peace within union with others.

116.3 - 116.4 When one is living within the unconscious mind expressing the seven negative qualities or feelings of forgiveness, an individual will feel judged by the world and their capacity to cope. They will be continually bombarded with various experiences of betrayal where they are continually seeking forgiveness for different relationships, opportunities, and experiences within their lives.

117.1 When an individual is continually seeking forgiveness, they will perceive a powerlessness within their feelings that life is not serving them, that true love is not able to be found or experienced, and love is defined continually through a co-dependency of fear and through loss. When one is living within the unconscious mind and experiencing the seven negative feelings that move through the perception of forgiveness, then life will be drawing in experiences and relationships that promote the un-surety of sarcasm. One will attempt to control their reality to protect themselves from the pain of sarcasm and within that there will be great confusion, a sense of being overwhelmed. Then, within the overwhelm, one will perceive the shame of how they have been able to live through these various experiences, and within that an anxiety will surface to protect themselves from engaging within the shame, and then a judgment will occur from the anxiety.

Radiance

118.1 Silence living as the experience of stillness is what awakens union within wisdom. And within wisdom, one is able to live within peace as love is unified and operating within the body and within the mind. When love is unified within the body and mind, there is a presence of stillness that allows life to move in and out of expression, of the inner expression and the outer expression.

118.2 When silence is operating within the conscious mind, the body will perceive reality within the state of awareness as stillness.

118.3 When an individual is able to perceive within the body a deep sense of peace, then this peace will move throughout every cell of the body awakening new vitality within a profound sense of calmness. When one is able to operate within this sense of calmness, one is aligned to the flow of life and not rejecting or drawing in through purpose, but is more allowing life to be embraced through a sense of inner conviction that comes from the state of calmness and peace that when moved through the mind, does so as a realization of love because love is realized by the mind as a feeling of stillness within the body.

118.4 It is within having harmonized stillness within the conscious mind that one is living as the presence of love.

118.5 The beauty of perceiving the qualities of stillness within your day to day will allow experiences and situations that allow you to feel safe, allow one to experience joy as one is honoring the freedom of personal choice to maintain and preserve the beauty of calmness.

118.6 The beauty of stillness, of silence is that when the universe perceives one as operating within the conscious expression of silence within feelings of themselves, then life will provide a steady stream. Life will move effortlessly within a flow as relationship to earth, life, others, and experiences.

118.7 It is within silence that one is able to realize the potential and expression of the soul. Realization is being defined within the realization of the presence of love within the mind; where one will realize the qualities of the soul and the resonance in which it supports and is moved within the life force. When one is able to truly allow this experience of stillness by dissolving the unconscious mind that true awakening can occur. It is within the stillness that the realization of love, universal mind, and oneness is occurring.

118.8 When one has realized the beauty of the soul, the presence of love within stillness, life will become for the individual an expression of service as the calling of the individual will be honored. Life will be a movement of sharing, witnessing, and releasing within the presence of love as each day, each relationship, and each opportunity becomes an expression of love that is perceiving reality within the essence of stillness.

119.1 The seven positive feelings expressing stillness within a conscious mind are: living calmness through the inner-conviction to allow and preserve peace; as within peace, there is a sense of knowing IAM safe to live within being honored as I experience the joy of personal freedom.

120.1 When one is living within the unconscious mind and living within the expression of the seven negative feelings associated with the emotion of silence, then one is devoid within the mind-body and perception of stillness. There will be chaos and interaction with the outer experiences that are continually forcing the individual to make changes within their day to day that counteract the flow of stillness.

120.2 Life experiences will bring forth various opportunities for an individual to have bouts of anger and appear rageful, and within the bouts of anger that are spontaneous within each experience that is brought to them to serve the anger, there will be the promotion of guilt and fear within the outer perception and the inner feeling.

120.3 When an individual is living within the unconscious perception, silence is defined through moments of confrontation. It is within continual confrontation that someone will either suppress their needs out of the fear that they will be confronted, or they will serve their needs by pushing or shoving life as they are seeking confrontation to feed the need to express their anger and promote fear within their lives of others.

120.4 When an individual begins to confront the tendencies of anger and the strength and the power that they have projected within the confrontational tendencies, then they will experience great anxiousness and fear which will then, in turn, promote depression and lifelessness. Their lives will be an up and down roller coaster of great confrontation where one is intimidating life through confrontation, anger, and self-inflicting judgment that is what is not able to preserve the presence of peace for the final payoff which is the depression and lifelessness to allow the self-hatred.

120.5 It is within the emotion of silence that we're not in harmony with love but living as a perception of the unconscious mind that one will through the emotional interpretations create great destruction of one's life.

120.6 The seven negative feelings of silence that can be perceived within the unconscious mind are not able to preserve life and will contradict life of the individual. It is within the distortions of silence that one will be challenged by addiction and substances as they choose these addictions

Humanity is a living movement of the child-mind.

and substances to assist them from disassociating within each moment which either promotes the fear of anger and confrontation or keeps one out of fear and confrontation.

120.7 When the silence emotion is engaged within the unconscious mind, life will honor the disassociation to love by presenting negative experiences that promote stress, betrayal, grief, sadness, overwhelming moments of confrontation, anger, and anxiousness.

120.8 It is within the emotion of silence when engaged with the unconscious perceptions and seven negative feelings that one will experience panic attacks because it is within the imbalance and the disassociation of love from the silence emotion that one will experience panic attacks.

120.9 It is also within the emotion of silence and the disharmony of the seven feelings to express that of the negative feelings, that one can be stimulated by thoughts of suicide. It is the imbalance of silence that promotes thoughts and actions of suicide.

121.1 The seven negative feelings that are expressing the unconscious mind within the emotion of silence are: conflict that stimulates the anxiousness and the fear of confrontation which will promote anger upon others or oneself that forces one to disassociate into depression and lifelessness, and then through the fear of repercussions of the depression and lifelessness, one will live within life within the suppression of what one seeks to become free of to allow harmony within their lives.

Faith

122.1 Faith/Compassion is a conscious expression of love that will honor faith; faith being defined as the belief to support unknown expressions that preserve life, love, and the potential of love.

122.2 When an individual is living within the presence of love within a conscious mind, they will perceive life emotionally within compassion. And within this compassion, they will honor life through faith to one essence; the one essence being the presence of love.

122.3 Compassion is the emotion that will honor the essence of love which is to preserve love within all actions, within all thoughts, within all feelings of others and ourselves through speech, through interaction, through physical connection, through emotional connection, through energetic connection, and through intent of purpose of the individual being within our lives.

122.4 - 122.5 Living within the conscious mind as an expression of compassion, emotionally life will have a fluidity of peace and within that fluidity will be a feeling of being embraced by life's circumstances because life is being defined within the wisdom of our minds, our hearts, and the universal mind.

122.6 It is within the expression of compassion that one will experience great joy because a deep sense of fulfillment will be honoring life within the safety of knowing IAM embracing all life within love.

122.7 It is within the conscious expression of compassion that the spiritual heart within life will be electrified through various experiences drawing love in and out of how we perceive oneself. Within the lives of others and within service for the planet, we will be living as a conscious expression of compassion allowing love to be defined within each moment as we are living within the freedom of no longer seeing and perceiving life within self-judgment.

122.8 When one is living within the conscious mind living within the expression of compassion, when one looks at oneself within the human mirror, they will be experiencing through what they hear as thoughts; the presence of love thinking of itself as one will hear the beauty of one's inner voice speaking of one's individual beauty and the vulnerability of that beauty and how the acceptance of all form that is free of judgment will become the most radiant strength in knowing IAM the presence of love living within form celebrating the honor of loving and living oneself.

123.1 The seven positive feelings that are awakened within the beauty of the conscious mind as an expression of compassion are: within life IAM allowing the presence of joy to awaken within peace, beauty, and wisdom as IAM compassionate within the union of knowing IAM embraced.

124.1 When compassion is aligned to the unconscious mind, the individual will host the seven negative feelings that will give the individual the overall feeling of hopelessness. Within their lives, many experiences and opportunities will attract and bring forth the feeling of hopelessness to the surface of their life.

124.2 It is within aligning the unconscious to the emotion of compassion that one will feel lost physically, emotionally, and mentally; not able to participate within life and losing concentration and ability to engage within life within each moment.

124.3 It will be within hosting the negative feelings within compassion that an individual will not be able to articulate people's needs as they are not able to articulate their own. Throughout various experiences and opportunities and relationships within their lives, they will attempt in all ways to fit in and be accepted by others but only to be rejected.

124.4 It is one living within the unconscious mind that is expressing the seven negative feelings of compassion that will often define their lives as having their heart broken moving in and out of various experiences that are frustrating to them as they struggle to honor themselves and be honored by others.

124.5 When an individual is living within the unconscious mind and unable to express conscious awareness of compassion, then the individual will have a deep feeling of powerlessness as they are living within self-judgment of all that they engage in within life. This self judgment becomes a fear and when expressed within faith, they are often perceiving that they are getting punished for not doing better within their lives and not being better at what they should be doing.

124.6 It is within the unconscious expression of compassion that an individual will be criticized by life, opportunities, and others within how they are perceiving life and how they are perceived within life.

124.7 It is within the unconscious mind that the negative feelings of compassion will have an individual manipulate their environment through silence. They will be protecting themselves by being outwardly confronted and will withdraw into grief.

124.8 The individual within the unconscious mind that is projecting negative feelings within compassion will have a low self-esteem, will often lose friendships, partnerships, and opportunities because they will suffer from bouts of self-destruction within their lives. The self-destruction will come about through manipulating opportunities and experiences and relationships in a means to protect one's grief through the self-judgment and self-criticism that will awaken an indecision that will have the individual through indecision withdraw from life.

124.9 The primary and most important and first relationship that will be lost within unconscious interpretations of compassion is the relationship to oneself and the ability to preserve life, love, and wisdom, and joy within one's experience of oneself.

124.10 When an individual stands in front of the mirror and is feeling negative feelings that are moved through compassion, one will experience negative self-talk, self-criticism, and self-judgment. This will awaken tremendous indecision within life, career, and choices. As when one witnesses one's reflection within the mirror, one hears all the ways that one is not suitable to exist within life and all ways one must improve oneself to be accepted by oneself and others.

124.11 It is within unconscious perceptions of compassion that there is the potential for promiscuity, disregard, loneliness, detachment, which leads to feelings of abandonment from life.

124.12 It is within the unconscious perception of compassion that an individual will focus on the feelings, the seven negative feelings of the unconscious, and they will within their struggles to see what they losing focus on the loss until it is gone.

125.1 The negative feelings within the unconscious interpretation of compassion are: within life I will manipulate life, experiences, relationships to oneself and others to protect the grief that one is consumed in thoughts of self-judgment and self-criticism which provide indecision within life, opportunity, relationships, and experiences which has one through the distrust of the indecision withdraw from life and allow destruction of potential.

Celebration

126.1 When one is perceiving celebration through the conscious mind, then one will be living as an expression of joy. Within living as an expression of joy is the potential for life to present opportunities that support the presence of joy within your life. It is within joy that one will honor wisdom, will honor actions, ideas, and experiences as an expression of joy through the perception of unlimited potential.

126.2 The greater momentum on the planet that can move towards us to accelerate our lives and the awareness of who we are in living purpose is the perception of celebration. It is how our feelings represent our story of joy to the universe that creates this momentum.

126.3 The beauty of celebration is that we are within the essence of celebration honoring wisdom which is honoring life, which is honoring our opportunity to live in self-love daily within all thoughts, words, and actions which will awaken experiences within our lives that honor the presence of celebration and preserve it within our lives.

127.1 The seven positive feelings that are perceived within celebration within the beauty of the conscious mind are: to honor the rhythm and expression within life as within honoring this expression of celebration, stability and clarity move various moments of life into the realization of kindness as IAM living pleasure within the union of all life.

128.1 There will be the feeling that when celebration is suppressed within the unconscious mind and the seven unconscious feelings, one will appear to have dampened one's spirit; meaning one does not have the vitality to move one's life into action through conscious awareness and preservation of life and love.

128.2 Life will be void of celebration within an unconscious perception of celebration. It will be void of joy unless there is false joy of the unconscious mind, which is when the unconscious mind seeks to make everything happy.

128.3 The unconscious mind will seek to accumulate things in its life that it thinks will make it happy. It will perceive that others want what they have: relationships, career, partnerships, abundance, wealth, and objects. It will perceive others wanting these items because it believes this is what makes them happy.

128.4 The irony of the unconscious mind when it is attempting to create happiness, attempting to create joy through false perception is that it seeks one to accumulate things that are meaningless within the realm of essence. It does this so it will have the conversation that can say, "Look, I have everything, but I have nothing. I have lost my life in gaining everything, but now I have no idea of who I am."

128.5 It is within the unconscious perception of celebration that the 'imposter syndrome' is activated within the perception of the individual; the 'imposter syndrome' being what I appear to be on the outside is not how I feel within.

128.6 When the unconscious mind accumulates within life the appearance of happiness, one will have moved through life experience and say that based on how I measure success, I can be happy.   Or an individual will say the opposite and discredit their worthiness to receive within others, situations, circumstances, and events.

128.7 When the unconscious is perceiving joy and celebration through seven negative feelings, the individual will feel instability because the world will appear to be unstable, and the individual will appear to be able to control life which will give a sense of separateness within their own needs and the needs of others.

128.8 It is within the unconscious perception of celebration that disharmony will move through the mind as indecision when anger is expressed towards the everyday experience, others, potential, and life.

129.1 The seven negative feelings that are perceived within celebration within the chaos and confusion of the unconscious mind are: within life I will control experiences so as not to experience fear because within my life is the instability of indecision and within the indecision, there is the experience of anger as all disharmony is projected within life so as to feel separateness.

Inner Knowing

130.1 Inner knowing when expressed within a conscious mind is about allowing life; allowing the flow of how life presents itself and living within the established awareness of trust that life is a constant flow of awareness in and out of oneself.

130.2 When one is living within the presence of inner

knowing through a conscious mind, life is a celebration of grace where life is defined by the mystical presence of something magical where intuition and circumstances and coincidences become a celebration, and life presents and opportunity to identify with the life force energy, the beauty within all.

130.3 It is within the conscious awareness of inner knowing that we are engaged within the romance of ourselves. We are engaged within a romance with life, others, experiences, and potential because we are void of fear.

130.4 Within the expression of inner knowing from within a conscious mind, wisdom will reveal itself with a gusto of stillness because there will be no challenge to its existence. There will be no 'what if' scenarios playing out within the questioning of the unconscious so wisdom will move itself forward with great energy and invigorated presence. The stillness of this invigorated presence is coming from the knowing that there only is the expression of wisdom that represents the means in which to express love.

130.5 The beauty of inner knowing expressed within a conscious mind is that inner knowing is the presence of love that is operating as an expression of human form.

130.6 It is within inner knowing that the union of life and love happens. The inner and outer expression of where we experience knowing. We reside within the higher mind, the higher understanding, and where life is the living presence of this understanding.

130.7 It is within inner knowing that we are within the center point within the mind; where the conscious mind and the unconscious mind meet to dissolve into the presence of love.

130.8 The beauty of inner knowing within the conscious mind is that it is the point where life knows love and love creates life.

130.9 It is the magnificence of inner knowing that allows the inner and outer expression of everything to realize that there is nothing; no attachment, no condition, no control, no fear. There is only the moment and what is living is the expression of love and preserving love within the movement of life.

130.10 The beauty of inner knowing is that it is the potential of love that is made manifest within the moment. It is the point within the mind that receives and articulates the language of love through the simplicity of the child mind.

130.11 It is the magnificence within the conscious mind that is perceiving life within the emotional awareness of inner knowing that unleashes the happiness because within this knowing is the personal freedom that allows wisdom to unfold and life to flow within the purity and trust of what is being perceived and expressed within the beauty of wisdom.

130.12 It is the sacred invitation within the conscious mind expressing itself within inner knowing. It is the invitation from the voice of intuition that allows personal means, personal identity to meet wisdom, to be embraced within the oneness, and receive the invitation to love oneself.

131.1 The seven positive feelings that are perceived within inner knowing within the beauty of the conscious mind are: IAM the expression of wisdom that is allowing life to be revealed within the trust that IAM receiving life within each moment living within the purity of the intuitive presence that is allowing all life to move.

132.1 Inner knowing within a conscious mind is the interpretation of profound grace where everything that is unknown is revealed into the potential and activation and resonance of profound, deep love. However, when life is being identified and perceived within an unconscious mind, then grace is interpreted through that unconscious mind and through the seven negative feelings of inner knowing to be that of limitation because what is unseen is unknown, and what is unknown is something to be feared.

132.2 Within an unconscious mind within the perception of inner knowing, each moment becomes one that will denounce the potential for discord, allowing one to engage within unconscious thoughts effortlessly because the perception of inner knowing is continually making reference to the rational mind; what makes sense when it is being perceived within the unconscious.

132.3 When one is living within the unconscious perception of inner knowing, then one will perpetuate hatred, anger, a disgust for life, ourselves, others, and great differences within their lives is released within life. Their experiences, relationships, and opportunities will have the mind fend off feelings of vulnerability of oneself and great difference with others.

132.4 It is within this condition, an unconscious perception of inner knowing, that an individual will hold judgments close, and positions of what is right and wrong through their interpretations will be many and overwhelming for them and those within their lives.

132.5 When one hosts the unconscious perceptions of inner knowing, people within their lives will be their failures. And within each moment of each day within their own minds, they will be consistently failing within their own perception to live a life they feel they are deserving of but limited to receive.

132.6 The language that will become part of their vocabulary to express their disgust will be that others appear to be 'stupid' or 'idiots.' This will be to give weight to their feelings of disgust.

132.7 The point where the mind is challenged to give thought to how they are perceiving and treating others, they will spiral into feelings of abandonment, and the seven negative feelings of inner knowing will be turned upon themselves where their thoughts of themselves will be 'I am one of discord that lives within fear. I have to gain control because I am hated and distrusting of others which makes me angry because I have been abandoned.'

132.8 It is within the fear of the judgment of who they think that they are one will host relationships of deceit because the relationships will give back to them the false ideas they have of themselves and how they are perceiving and treating others.

132.9 When one lives within the unconscious perception of inner knowing, one will experience a great separation of love, and within that separation feel great panic on how they must reconnect to others and themselves and the things that they have to overcome to be able to function as a normal human being because they have perceived such judgment of their normalcy. There is no definition for what is normal and what is not as they are not able to live within wisdom knowing that all is oneness, perfect, and in divine order as expression of oneself and love.

132.10 An individual that hosts unconscious thoughts within the perception of inner knowing will have a vast vocabulary of cynicism and be expressing challenges of others and life through their vast ideas of distrust. There will be many, many manifestations within their life that force them to further empower cynicism.

133.1 The seven negative feelings that are perceived within inner knowing within the limitations of the unconscious mind are: within life I am experiencing discord, and within this discord I have great fear to control, as within controlling life I perceive the hatred of individuals, and within this hatred I experience distrust for myself and my own ability to create life, and within that limitation I experience anger for all that has happened to me because within my life I have been abandoned by love.

Oneness

134.1 Oneness is the essence of gratitude that one experiences within life as a means in which to express life and receive life when living within the perception of the conscious mind.

134.2 When we are living within the beauty of oneness, life is defining itself within the presence of gratitude for all life within ourselves and outside of ourselves. It is within our gratitude that we are moved into the oneness that all life is an expression of oneself.

134.3 It is within a harmonized expression of oneness when one is perceiving oneness within a conscious mind that we are not able to judge others, and the capacity to be in judgment is no longer an aspect of the mind. This being the case, the universe will not bring experiences towards us that need to be measured as good or bad.

134.4 Living within oneness within a conscious mind, each experience we are nurtured, as within the moment there is profound peace, and within our interpretations we are the living stillness.

134.5 Within the presence of oneness and gratitude, we are able to receive many gifts that are available to us within life that allow us to live within the presence of love, and once received we are able to bestow the gratitude of the expression of love upon others.

134.6 When one is engaged within the simplicity of gratitude within the conscious mind, life is simple because within the character one has a presentation of wholeness and fulfillment.

134.7 When one is living within the conscious expression of gratitude, there is a warmth and our lives become a sacred invitation to experience and support and preserve the presence of love within ourselves, others, and within each moment.

134.8 Within the conscious mind when expressing the presence of oneness, one will receive many opportunities to express love within form because the universe is allowing us to preserve love within our expression of gratitude.

135.1 Seven positive feelings that perceive oneness within the beauty of a conscious mind are: within life IAM nurtured within the peace to know stillness as IAM a gift of simplicity that is allowing oneness to operate within life as divine wholeness.

136.1 Oneness when perceived within the unconscious mind is distorted through the perception that an individual will live with stories of resentment. These stories of resentment can be about others, experiences, relationships, the world, or spiritual growth and understanding.

136.2 Within each day, an individual will experience within the unconscious perception of oneness that there is always a means in which to support something happening. There is always a story that whatever happened within life is somebody else's fault; that they are powerless to everything that happens because there is the disassociation that I am one with all, things are happening to me not because of me.

136.3 It is even when an individual is connected to wisdom. However, within oneness, they are connected to the unconscious mind that they struggle to perceive the world as thoughts, feelings, and emotions that they are having of themselves they still feel that the world is somehow failing to support who they are.

136.4 Within the unconscious perception of oneness, an individual will experience great anxiety and feel to keep people emotionally at bay as they continually seek to blame others for their anxiety and their definition of stress that is within all of their life.

136.5 Even within interpretations of the unconscious mind when perceiving oneness, one could feel quite successful. However, through the desire to control everything within their life, it usually brings everything crashing through addiction of controlling greed through fear, of controlling quality of life through fear, of controlling wisdom through fear.

136.6 If one is within the unconscious mind when perceiving oneness, they will have non-rational, emotional interpretations of life, love, and others to control the ideas within the unconscious of betrayal, exclusion, and abandonment.

136.7 Within the unconscious perception of oneness, there is a strong need to abdicate and blame others so everything that happens within their life is somebody else's fault which keeps them within the separation.

136.8 When one awakens upon the path of wisdom and one has not cleared the unconscious perceptions of oneness, they will within their minds have resentment and that resentment will become a means in which to despise the ignorance of the world. This interpretation will also happen with somebody who is not practicing a conscious path but is deeply unconscious and is sitting within the resentment of despising the ignorance of the world; the ignorance of the world being defined by them as the world ignorant of their suffering.

136.9 Within the unconscious interpretations of oneness, there is a deceiving quality and this quality is that the unconscious mind will mimic the conscious mind. It will mimic it through spiritual knowledge. But what will be the giveaway, that it is an unconscious perception, is the harshness in which judgments are cast upon others believing that what they believe is correct to the point of self-righteousness.

136.10 It is within interpreting spirituality within the unconscious that the mind will trick oneself into a spiritual ego where one believes they have far surpassed the bite of the unconscious. Their interpretations of love are projected towards others as a means in which to achieve self-control.

136.11 It is when blaming others and abdicating towards others that self-control is protected. The self-control being defined as believing one has a non-confrontational, emotional demeanor through suppression.

137.1 The seven negative feelings that perceive oneness within the unconscious mind are: within life there is the experience of anxiety for I am in need of blaming and abdicating the world in which I suffer to control all confrontation of the non-rational perception as I despise what does not see my suffering.

138.1 The beauty of identifying with how the unconscious mind is operating within the seven key emotions is that we are able to pinpoint how and where it is creating within our lives; in which perceptions, relationships, opportunities, and experiences.

138.2 It is our seven feelings that we experience both consciously and unconsciously within ourselves when engaging within life that defines us within the universal mirror which then is what attracts experiences within our lives.

138.3 The law of attraction moves through our feelings. We attract by what we feel whether unconscious or conscious. We create our experiences, relationships within our day to day based on if we are engaged within the seven conscious feelings or seven unconscious feelings of each of the seven emotions.

138.4 When we awaken the conscious mind by dissolving the unconscious mind, our lives will be able to benefit by the 49 beautiful feelings that support the presence of love within all aspects of our lives because the universe will be co-creating in a means in which to preserve love and life within all that we experience within each day.

138.5 Many of you have witnessed where the unconscious mind is operating or present within your life. However, this is not a limitation. As being free of the unconscious mind is as simple as clearing your mind to become free of how it is defining your life.

138.6 One is not able to heal or change one's mind in relationship to the unconscious mind, we are not able to even release the unconscious mind because one is not able to choose when to engage with it and for what purpose. The unconscious mind is a spontaneous movement of thought that creates feeling that operates through our emotions. It is when the unconscious mind presents itself through our emotions that it will demonstrate to life who we are and life will provide to us a means in which to fulfill these feelings.

138.7 The beauty of dissolving the unconscious is that by clearing it through this simplicity, one will bring profound clarity and beauty into life because one will have engaged the 49 positive feelings of each of the seven key emotions that will allow life to preserve love through various experiences that one engages in within each day.

139.1 There is profound freedom and joy in simply learning that there are great benefits in dissolving the unconscious mind because upon learning that you are able to achieve such profound transformation within your life so simply, you are automatically free from the guilt that you must somehow change the limiting behaviors that have been with you throughout your life as a perception of the unconscious mind. That, in and of itself, is freedom.

139.2 Within knowing within the simplicity that the unconscious mind can be gone is new vigor and vitality because one knows one does not have to find answers to healing, changing, or becoming different from what one only knows of oneself since one has been within the unconscious.

139.3 If one has not experienced life in a conscious mind without the unconscious, then one does not really know who they are beyond its limitations. The unconscious mind will protect itself by believing it has mental or emotional conditions that are negative and that they must be healed and within that, one will cater to them in the idea that one is attempting to resolve them.

139.4 When one begins the process of dissolving the unconscious mind, there is profound joy that fills the mind of the individual that cannot be defined through word because every part of the experience of dissolving the unconscious mind is that of joy because one is not 'moving into' within their perception the negativity to deal with it, but the perception is being 'drawn out of' the negativity and within that moment of love moving what is not love into itself is a joy that cannot be defined through word only feeling.

Chapter Five
Relationship to Child-Mind

140.1 The child-mind is a magnificent expression of innocence that lives within vision and purpose that all life is but an innocent exchange of beauty, simplicity, and potential of love.

140.2 Through the world, through needs for humanness, through the media, education, friendships, parents, interpretations emotionally, experiences, as children we are shown the opposite to love. Life will represent unlimited opportunities and potential to experience love, however, will be diluted by the unconscious mind that is unable to perceive love.

140.3 It is within the first seven years of life that the child-mind will define itself within the presence of the world. Within relationships and experiences, a child will interpret their feelings as ideas, thoughts, feelings, and emotions of themselves that will define the unconscious mind and their experiences moving forward after the age of seven.

140.4 Within the first seven years of life through images, touch, feelings, emotions, and thoughts that are presented within each moment to the child-mind, the child is defining itself.

140.5 It is within the first seven years of life that the child is defining the perceived relationship to love or the perceived relationship to the loss of love.

141.1 Within today's day and age with media, internet, violence, music, education, movies, many different interpretations, children are born into situations where messages and experiences of love are diluted. This is because the unconscious mind is so present and such a strong hold within their environment.

141.2 A child faces daily the choices and spontaneous opportunities to engage with their primary caregivers and peers through social interpretations, media, and education. It is within their engaging with these various experiences and emotional interpretations that the child will develop unconscious feelings that separate themselves from love.

141.3 It could be assumed at times that a child will live within a protected, loving environment. It would be assumed that how would a child develop the unconscious and disassociations from love when they are living within a supportive environment that is cultivating their self-belief. The problem is that a child is not making assumptions based on what is given to them. They are making assumptions of themselves emotionally by what they witness within others. If a child witnesses a primary caregiver of a movie or an emotional situation where they are powerless to connect that person or experience to love, then the child will interpret that powerlessness as themselves, their failure to connect to love. The unconscious mind is established in this form so as it will always develop. The reason that the unconscious mind must develop is for the sheer fact that an individual accesses and uses the unconscious mind to awaken into the presence of love. Within the Clear Mind Experience, the unconscious mind is accessed through the conscious mind, and the conscious mind draws the unconscious mind into itself to dissolve it. It is within this dissolving of what is not love into love that the true realization of love is experienced. It can be guaranteed that when a child is born, they are born to fall asleep to the unconscious mind within certain interpretations of their life.

142.1 There is such a great movement within humanity not to support and preserve the union of love, life, wisdom, and opportunities. And it goes beyond simply loving your child to be able to support them within love because through education, media, and different outlets, and expectations of others, they are always witnessing a loss of love. There is an oversaturation upon this planet that has lost the capacity to be able to preserve love, and that is because the unconscious mind both collectively and personally is at the pinnacle of its own destruction and separation from reality.

142.2 The child-mind has been educated through various interpretations to want more, need more, have more, and experience more. When a child is moving through life with these expectations, it will lead to a mental confusion, and the child will not be able to perceive their correct age and the natural order of their expectations for that age. They are not able to flow within the role of life because the natural order of their minds emotionally has been sent into chaos through television, internet, movies, adult interpretations, and video games. They are forced to interpret life within the moment beyond their emotional capacity to integrate life. It is this type of movement in awareness on the planet where children have left their role of their current age; that they are now experiencing a rapid movement within the unconscious mind where the speed of the unconscious mind moves extremely fast and they are not able to focus and integrate into reality.

When one medicates one's child for activity and for being overly active, it is simply because the child-mind is running so fast it is disengaged from its capacity to be moving through the natural order. And when one takes the medication, they are simply putting the conscious and unconscious minds to sleep which disengages the child from life and development within how they feel and perceive themselves and their opportunities in moving forward. The beauty of the Clear Mind Experience is that it will and does have the ability to slow down the unconscious mind so it is not running so rapidly, and the individual is able to integrate and operate through a conscious awareness and perception.

143.1 If we take a moment to review the mentality and perception and behavior patterns of an adult, one would be saying that adults are also suffering within this type of mental breakdown and chaos where they are consumed in thoughts of what should be rather than honoring, loving, and embracing the moment of what is. This is because the unconscious mind does not have the capacity to live within the moment, and it is being so stimulated through addictions and desires and immediate gratification that it is only ever able to choose the next thing. It is not looking to move into the acceptance of what is because it does not have the capacity to do so.

143.2 Within the world at this time, the greatest sadness of humanity is that each day families break apart through failed expectations of what they have not received from one another or the world to consummate their happiness.

143.3 It is within this moment that humanity and our civilization is hitting a crisis point because adults are falling by the wayside within the misery of what they should have rather than honoring and loving what they do have. The emotional interpretations of humanity at this time is not able to truly embrace what is within the moment and see the beauty of that moment because of the speed in which the unconscious mind is activated and moving within their lives.

143.4 The child-mind is very important in the sense of an individual awakening into wisdom. This because no matter how old we are, or what circumstances we have lived within our lives, or the level of responsibilities that we have had and how much we feel we have had to grow up, there is an aspect of the mind that must be activated to be our current perception within each moment, and that activation is that of the child-mind. It is the child-mind when left to its natural state that is the aspect of perception that lives within the moment allowing life to be that of self-discovery. It is important that one clear the mind to be able to activate the purity of the child-mind so one can truly access and experience the profundity within the presence of love.

144.1 What has been revealed within the Clear Mind Experience is that it can successfully engage the child-mind while one is still able to sit within responsibilities and potential of life experience to be an adult, to be a parent, to have multiple tasks that one must be able to conduct within their lives maybe within the mission of service, or maybe within an expression of love. It is within the Clear Mind Experience that the child-mind is awakened and released into its magnificence; so an adult is now an adult perceiving life within the simplicity of a child. It is within this spontaneous awakening that an individual will emotionally be set free from expectations of what life should be presenting and moves into the fluidity and expression of how life and love is preserved within each moment.

144.2 It is within the child-mind that the most small, precious and spontaneous moments become the most profound. It is where adults that we seem to reach the point in our lives where we seek new meaning, new definition to not be attached to outcome, to love what we have, to move throughout life unconditionally while enjoying even the smallest moments, and most important, to understand the meaning of life. All of these answers are revealed and expressed within the beauty of the child-mind. Without the child-mind being activated within the presence of love and becoming free of the unconscious interpretations that lack the presence of love, then an individual is simply waking up to the meaning of life through knowledge without the true experience of what love feels to be.

145.1 The child-mind within its purity will call our heart its home. It will participate within life because it enjoys who it is and what it is and will preserve life simply by enjoying the fact that it is living.

145.2 It is the child-mind that has the capacity to allow wisdom to express new definition of this freedom and celebration of the past because it is our nature to live within the unconditional perceptions and not look to fix, but allow the unconscious mind to be dissolved to discover new meaning.

145.3 It is from within the child-mind that an individual will begin to awaken the curiosity of who am I, where and what does that mean. And from the moment that the child-mind ponders this question, it will move out into life on a journey to rediscover itself because the child-mind when free from the unconscious mind or when seeking to become free from the unconscious mind will move out into reality to redefine the expression and the experience of love. The child feels unlimited in how life moves around it.

145.4 - 145.4i It is within the child-mind rediscovering itself that new meaning will be revealed as life, new interpretations will be moved through the mind as wisdom, There may be a moment of spontaneous awakening, happiness and a feeling of letting go. Once the doorway of the child-mind opens and the child-mind sees the way through to love, then it's time to brace oneself because the child-mind is an unstoppable expression of endless potential of love expressed.

146.1 It is within the child-mind that life is enlivened through the process of self-discovery. Because to a child, life is the moment, is the opportunity, and the discovery always of something new. There are no preconceived ideas of outcome or what should or could be. So when the child-mind is awakened within the presence of the conscious mind, it is the fluidity to allow life to exist within the fluid rhythm of love.

146.2 The child-mind is continually allowing life to move into perception and within that moment inviting wisdom to present new interpretations, to invite life through positive feelings of love, insight, and wisdom within new relationships. And within the moment that life moves into the child-mind is the profound opportunity to understand something incredible and magnificent about living within life within the child-mind.

147.1 When the child-mind sees unconscious thoughts, feelings, and emotions that were created in the first seven years of life have awakened within the child-mind, there will be inner conflict.

147.2 Within the perception of the child-mind is the opportunity to experience love, and the unconscious mind will block that because it will fear the experience of love because it cannot see love. To a child if it is looking at something and it is unable to see it, it will be afraid of it, and it is similar to that of the unconscious. When it is sitting perceiving life, if love moves towards it, it will attempt to block love to protect itself because it is not able to see love. It just senses that there is something moving towards it. It senses a loss of connection so, therefore, to protect the child-mind and the vulnerability, the unconscious mind will begin to parent the child-mind through self-criticism, negative self-talk. The negative self-talk that moves through the child-mind is that of the unconscious and is mostly created and personifies the voice's negative interpretation of the primary caregivers and primary environment in which the child was raised within the first seven years of their life.

148.1 Throughout the history of this planet, individuals have strived to make union of one mind. To achieve this, they have attempted to confront the unconscious which is all thoughts, feelings, and emotions that are separate to love that are created within the first seven years of life. And within the confrontation, they have aimed to dismantle the unconscious hold upon their lives, within their minds, attempting to set the inner child free. This type of work can take years and years along with multitudes of self-development work or therapy to release the smallest particle of the unconscious mind if it ever releases.

148.2 It has been revealed to be the life's work of this being to deliver the technology of the Clear Mind Experience to humanity so humanity can make an exponential shift in consciousness by dissolving the unconscious mind and no longer engaging in stories of what should be happening to heal the dysfunction of the unconscious mind and the separations to love.

There has been an oversaturation on the planet of addiction and abuse primarily. The Clear Mind Experience is able to dissolve the unconscious mind at the speed in which addiction and abuse vibrates on the planet. It is a high frequency, unconscious momentum that exists within these two interpretations, and it is the Clear Mind Experience that allows for this vibration to be met and dissolved by the conscious mind. The first role of the Clear Mind Experience is to dissolve the negative self-talk that is that of the child-mind.

148.3 The Clear Mind Experience is a process in which to dissolve the unconscious mind accurately and precisely all while allowing the participant to remain within spontaneous awareness and revelations that come between the union of the conscious perception of love and the unconscious retraction from love. It is within the experience of the Clear Mind process that an individual will awaken the child-mind to be able to have the capacity to perceive life within the moment. Within each opportunity as an expression of love, the individual will feel to be living and creating life within the presence of love.

149.1 There are a great number of individuals throughout the world today that have a devastating story within the childhood from ideas, thoughts, feelings, and emotions, and physical experiences of abuse, trauma, grief, detachment, abandonment. The Clear Mind Experience is their GIFT. As its mechanism is able to bypass the need to protect oneself and merge one within the perceived beauty of love.

149.2 There is a rising within humanity that people fear greatly to deal with past confrontation, confusion, abuse, trauma, conflict, and fear of childhood. It is within suppressing these feelings that individuals are experiencing depression, anxiety, and fear. What one needs to realize is that the unconscious mind is not able to let go of the interpretations that have been acquired through trauma. However, the unconscious mind can be dissolved and within that, the child-mind will become free to experience love. When the unconscious mind lets go of the child-mind and no longer holds it hostage within negative self-talk that is in relationship to a dysfunction, a disassociation, grief, trauma, or abuse that has shifted the perception from love, then true freedom moves through the child-mind. An individual is elevated into great levels of consciousness in knowing that IAM free.

149.3 – 149.4 There are many means in which the planet has been striving through spiritual ideas to create a level of freedom from the past. Through therapy there have been endless ways in which one has hoped to purify the past from the physical, mental, and emotional system and present a way in which life is able to comfortably be assimilated and assimilate past experiences within the mind. However, what has happened from that is that people have become over-consumed and over-saturated in suppressing the thoughts because they are not able to digest the emotional content of looking at the thoughts in the various experiences. Such practices, such as hypnotherapy and some various forms of psychotherapy, have had individuals look at past experiences and defined them as being who they are through their memory. This serves nothing except to understand the dysfunction of the unconscious. The unconscious mind needs to be dissolved so it is not there to be interpreted. Interpreting it only serves to keep it strong because we validate within the feelings, 'IAM that.' It is also the disruption to self-development when the unconscious mind has been developed within the first seven years of life around the fear of being dishonored. When one fears being dishonored, there births a great struggle in getting the unconscious to let go to the spontaneous flow of the child-mind which is what an individual needs ultimately to let go of wisdom and the presence of love. It is within the Clear Mind Experience and the flow of the process that joins the two aspects of the mind together as one, that an individual is already moving in and out of the spontaneous flow of the child-mind without having to break through the barriers of fear within the unconscious mind to achieve it. That, in and of itself, awakens a huge possibility and potential within humanity for humanity to transcend unconscious thought because it is happening beyond the belief system of one's capacity to achieve.

150.1 The unconscious mind when it struggles to let go and feels dishonored becomes the victim that protects itself through depression, co-dependency, anxiety, and mental confusion. Mental confusion and emotional confusion is just simply the unconscious mind speaking about the dysfunction about not being able to prioritize experiences within life to protect itself.

150.2 If the child is mentally abused, the child-mind in an unconscious state will become the protector. The unconscious mind will stand in front of the child-mind and through control, anxiety, addiction, and anger, it will be seeking to protect the child-mind from thinking positively of itself so that it does not get let down or hurt, be made a fool of, or be shamed because it will always feel the moment in which innocence of thought and self-belief will have been lost. Any outside behavior that attempts to restore self-belief will appear to be what will create potential shame.

150.3 The unconscious mind is a struggle consistently, and it cannot let go to wisdom. It cannot let go to the presence of love because it is not able to identify with love. It is not able to support love. It is not able to support the unknown of wisdom and spontaneous movement of wisdom out of the fear that it does not perceive love. So to protect itself, it will co-create within the environment through the negative feelings that you have of your limitations of being not able to have the capacity to connect to love. The unconscious mind will keep you busy on learning about it.

150.4 The unconscious mind will speak often of its limitations and how one must heal of its conditions of pain, indecision, disease, unfulfilled needs, fears, anxiety, depression, and most important, it will place these demands within your day to day continually reminding you that you must deal with it. This is how it stays in relationship. The beauty of the Clear Mind Experience is that an individual moves out of the experience of the unconscious through the practice and becomes witness to the dialogue of the unconscious mind, and they are no longer operating at its demands.

151.1 Within the unconscious mind, there is divinity within its development. It is what is contained within the unconscious mind that acts as an invitation to the conscious mind for love to discover itself. The greater the disassociation to love within the unconscious mind, the faster association to love will be made within the conscious mind.

151.2 Upon the planet at this time, it is fair to say that the energies and interpretations that are there to develop the unconscious mind and the extremes of violence, abuse, and physical disharmony, and grief, poverty, and limitations, and violence are not necessary to develop the unconscious. The unconscious mind can be developed through a very simple interpretation that separates one from love. One does not have to have been violated, betrayed, abandoned, or abused to develop the unconscious mind. It is these extremes that have children suffer daily that become adults that perpetuate the suffering.

151.3 Those who are able to understand the process of the Clear Mind Experience and the beauty and simplicity of dissolving the unconscious mind and what it will mean to children, then a child's life will become very important to you. Children are the essence of our community. It is a child living within the purity of the conscious mind free from the unconscious that becomes who we are as adults. It becomes our purpose to provide that and be a means in which for them to have that experience.

151.4 It is the calling within humanity at this time that adults no longer live within the unconscious seeking to be served within it and shift it through dissolving it as fast as humanly possible so as no longer to provide collective unconscious chaos in which children suffer daily.

151.5 Take a moment to think about a child that is being abused right now, a child that is being harmed right now. That is happening because we as adults are holding onto an aspect of the unconscious mind within our own minds.

It is what we hold onto within our own minds that believes in their suffering, because we believe in our own.

151.6 It is no longer believing within your own suffering and allowing life to be a free expression of love that this shift in consciousness is occurring upon the planet. This is not a shift in consciousness that is about seeking to understand the unconscious. This is a shift in consciousness that is about walking away from it, no longer containing it, no longer engaging in it, and living within a life free of the collective and personal unconscious mind, negative mind, and any thoughts, feelings, or emotions that distort the presence of love.

1151.7 This awakening upon the planet is about moving our personal minds into that of the child-mind; our personal perception into the simplicity of the child-mind. It is within doing this that we are restoring the capacity to live within the presence of love enabling oneself to perceive each moment within the experience of love. As it is within the child-mind that an individual will preserve love, which is love within humanity within our thoughts as the realization will occur that I am simply the thought.

151.8 When introducing adults to the Clear Mind Experience, it is always encouraged that they would practice and participate within the experience to help children. It is within awakening the child-mind that they will live in honor of this aspect of the mind. It is when an adult is living within this aspect of the mind that not a child upon the earth could suffer because there would be no unconscious mind to create and support suffering.

151.9 For a moment, take time to sit and think about the children at this time that are being harmed, the children that are growing within dysfunction that are separate to love and live within physical, emotional, and mental torment, abuse, grief, and trauma. Upon reflecting upon those children, one would say there is an urgency upon this planet for the unconscious mind to be dissolved and the urgency has become critical.

152.1 For thousands of years as civilizations have evolved upon the earth, it has been a spiritual, karmic requirement of the human condition that individuals and humanity establish a structure of interpretations that are contained within the mind as the unconscious mind, and this has happened both collectively and personally.

152.2 The collective unconscious mind is all thoughts, feelings, and emotions that engage as action upon the planet that enabled the unconscious mind personally to engage within its experience on the outer. The collective unconscious mind supports all disassociations from love through experience that it provides to humanity.

152.3 To simply define the collective unconscious, one would say that it was in existence to serve the personal unconscious mind within the outer environment.

152.4 It is obvious at this time to those who are willing to look at what the unconscious mind is perceiving as reality and those who are striving to awaken a more conscious perception that upon the earth at this time, there seems to be a battle, and the battle is between the conscious perception of love and the unconscious conditions that support a lack of love on the planet. When an individual dissolves the unconscious mind personally, they are also dissolving the unconscious mind collectively because the personal unconscious mind is what keeps the collective unconscious mind in play. If one has no capacity within their personal mind to engage within the unconscious, then the unconscious mind collectively has nobody to serve or nothing to serve and therefore will not function upon the earth and will dissolve and disintegrate much like the unconscious within the personal mind.

152.5 For those of the light at this time that are attempting to awaken a conscious mind to assist the earth within the shift of awareness that is moving across the planet at this time, it is important to have dissolved the personal unconscious mind because within dissolving the unconscious mind, there are no unconscious perceptions that can be fed into the collective unconscious.

152.6 If one were to look at what was happening on the planet at this time unconsciously, one would say, "How do we fix all that is unconscious?" And the answer would be: we don't fix anything. You cannot fix what is unconscious on the planet. You can only not feed what is unconscious into it, and it will no longer exist.

152.7 - 152.8 The victory for the conscious mind on the planet is to starve the unconscious mind energetically to have the capacity to truly live in witness to it, to have disengaged from it, to be free of no longer needing it because what was once interacting within the unconscious mind is no longer within the personal mind to engage.

153.1 - 153.1i Since we have developed the unconscious mind within the first seven years of life, it is from that point that the individual will enter another aspect of development which is the expression of 'personal will'.

153.2 The 'personal will' within The Book of Awareness is defined as: the time in which the child interacts within life through its developed independence within its self-expression through relationships that engage the definition of oneself through their outer experiences. The 'personal will', will have them interact throughout life in both interpretations that are conscious and unconscious. The 'personal will' is simply the vehicle in which the individual will engage within reality, but it is the feelings of the unconscious or conscious perceptions that create experience within the universe by drawing life towards the individual in which the child will engage within 'personal will'.

153.3 It is at this point within the 'personal will' that the collective unconscious and the personal unconscious form union so as to further develop beliefs and behavior patterns that one perceives that one is within life. The unconscious mind while active within a person's perception always creates before the conscious mind, and it is this reason being that the unconscious mind is the vibrations of the planet because the planet is primarily within the unconscious state due to the speed in which the unconscious is moving across the planet into interpretations.

153.4 It is within this aspect of development that is experienced within the personal will that the unconscious mind will move negative thoughts, feelings, and emotions into life through the mirror of the collective unconscious. The personal unconscious through 'personal will', will become reinforced through one's feelings about life, others, and oneself.

154.1 It is the potential within an individual that enters adolescence and begins to move in and out interpretations of life that an individual can spontaneously release a calling within the conscious mind that the unconscious and conscious meet one another through the built-in mechanism within perception that reveals to the rational thinking mind that love is seeking to realize itself through the process of releasing the unconscious mind into the conscious mind. However, due to the fact that this interpretation has not been on the planet, individuals are missing this calling and identifying more from a position of powerlessness of, "Who am I? I'm not sure who I am. I have dysfunction." And then within that judgment, hosting and housing the dysfunction that the unconscious mind is projecting because the information of this ability to be able to dissolve the unconscious mind has not been available.

154.2 The reconciliation process is revealed within The Book of Awareness as it is the moment in which the unconscious mind is triggered into a retraction, and the conscious mind is triggered to move into the unconscious and draw it back into itself. It is a process that happens between parents and adolescents facilitated through a trained Clear Mind Facilitator.

154.3 When one is dissolving the unconscious mind, it is an aspect of the structure that the child-mind must awaken first because it is the child-mind that has the mechanism in which to perceive negative self-talk. When an individual or an adult perceives its needs to awaken and to realize the presence of love, to realize freedom, to understand life from new meaning within new perception, the child-mind must awaken first because the child-mind is the doorway into the mysticism of how one will perceive the beauty of wisdom. One is not able to host the negative self-talk as one will judge the perception of wisdom and will not be able to integrate the perception of wisdom through the judgment.

New Child

155.1 The gift of today and the rise in consciousness in humanity's shift within consciousness is that we have available to us the opportunity to live within higher consciousness without developing an unconscious mind that's so dramatically separate or removed from the conscious mind like it has been in the past. This allows the karma of abuse, trauma upon the planet to be released and no longer remain active within the collective unconscious.

156.1 Children of our new time and new era are profoundly different in operation within the mechanism of the brain. There is a great change within the child-mind and how it develops, as it will not develop the unconscious mind as its previous structure and interpretation to realize the presence of love. As we as humanity dissolve the unconscious mind, those born into humanity will not within the first seven years of life develop a disassociation from love through the unconscious. It is important that when dissolving the unconscious mind that it be done collectively in a rapid speed so humanity is not fragmented across the globe where one portion is experiencing something and another something else. The Clear Mind Experience has the means in which to transport humanity into a global awakening of huge proportion of living free within the presence of love within a very short number of years.

156.2 The beauty of living free of the unconscious mind is that the child-mind will be supported by humanity and the world to remain free of the unconscious and all thoughts that disassociate one from the presence of love.

156.3 Within humanity is an existence and functioning

within the clarity of the conscious mind, the child-mind will be willfully encouraged and directed within the day to day to remain within the conscious mind interpretations of how to preserve the presence of love within life.

157.1 – 157.2 Within this current activation of consciousness upon the planet, adults are to become mainly aware that the commitment to life, living, for humanity to be the living expression of love is to be cultivated within the perception and lives of children daily in all of their environments that support development, health, education, and living. It is when adults dissolve the presence of the unconscious mind within their capacity to live within the day to day that a child will be able to benefit from the integrated perceptions of wisdom that will be available upon the planet as they will be perceived within the conscious clarity of the conscious mind of the adult.

157.3 It is the calling of humanity within the Clear Mind Experience to create opportunity within our lives that we have the capacity to nurture children within the unlimited potential of love; to create a mind and awaken a beautiful mind that is always able to nurture and honor the space and vulnerability of the child-mind so that the child-mind is able to awaken within the presence of the adult mind and be nurtured and carried over from the child-mind to the adult mind through child development.

Simplicity of Love

158.1 Throughout many lifetimes upon this planet, there are many spiritual leaders and many ingenious individuals who have spoken about the clarity of the child-mind, always reinforcing that it is the adult that cultivates the child-mind that will be the wise man.

158.2 Spirituality has in the past placed great focus on the potential of an adult returning to that of a child-mind and within the child-mind, they are able to live within the heart. And within that, they are able to move into higher levels of consciousness from a perception of freedom and the un-limitedness of knowing 'IAM allowing the self-discovery of all life within all that IAM.'

158.3 For a moment, take some time to witness a child, to witness them engaging within reality. Each movement and each moment that they partake is an interaction with the universe to discover new meaning. Every time that they engage with a specific activity, relationship, opportunity, or experience, they are discovering meaning; effortlessly and unconditionally allowing the meaning to become an aspect of who they are. It is that beauty within the child-mind that wisdom can redefine past experiences and past opportunities of who we have been into the becoming of 'IAM living within the presence of love.'

158.4 Within a child-mind, they are not telling the universe how life has to be because they have no previous definition. They are simply articulating opportunity, unlimited potential within the moment, translating potential into form. A child-mind will operate from the pure transparent sense of vulnerability as it seeks the universe to embrace them, support them, and reveal to them interpretations within each moment. Until a child-mind is told other, they believe in the perception of love. When one clears the unconscious mind, the child-mind returns to that perception. You cannot harm, take away, or discredit the perception of love within the child-mind. You can only cloud it with the perceptions of the unconscious. Once these clouds have been dissolved, the child-mind will operate within its divine criteria, which is to be supported within the universe on the path of self-discovery within the vulnerability allowing each moment to be a pure, transparent expression of love defining itself within the mind of the child.

158.5 It is the vulnerability of the child-mind that makes it so magnificent, that it can so effortlessly sit within its vulnerability and allow the universe to move in and out of it as an expression that is defining the child and how it feels in perception to oneself and life within each moment.

158.6 It is this magnificence and beauty of returning to the child-mind as an adult that allows the joy and vulnerability that is available within the child-mind to be experienced. It is in clearing the negative self-talk of the child-mind that allows the adult to embrace effortlessly the spontaneous movement and awakening and articulated presence of wisdom that is available within the mind within life as the universe attempts to redefine all existence within the presence of love once the unconscious mind has been dissolved.

159.1 One may be asking how and questioning that how as an adult could one possibly experience life within the vulnerability of a child when there are responsibilities? What one would have to realize is that wisdom is there to articulate and preserve life, that wisdom will articulate within the child-mind what the responsibility means to it and how it can be preserved as love. So responsibilities become an effortless flow of life preserving the qualities of love within how we are being perceived within reality.

159.2 In truth, as an adult, there does appear to be more responsibility, but that responsibility is only defined as such when we have created life through control and fear of the unconscious. When one embodies the awareness of the child-mind, then wisdom, and life, and the tasks of life, and the responsibilities of life don't feel to be responsibilities. They feel to be opportunities to experience life. And within that, there is profound simplicity to one's responsibilities. One's responsibilities feel intense and large and vast when an individual is connected to the unconscious mind, and the unconscious mind uses the outer activities as a means in which to create a lifestyle that the unconscious mind perceives it is not able to be released from.

159.3 When life is perceived within the beauty of wisdom, there is a feeling within each moment that life is gifted to us but not created by us. It is within this feeling of life being gifted to us that one can effortlessly express the beauty of gratitude in allowing life to move through oneself.

159.4 Within the child-mind is the realization that life is given to us, that form is our gift, and that incarnation is the gift in which we express the presence of love. When we are able to witness life as being this gift of what is given to us, then we perceive that within each experience and each opportunity is a further expression of this gift.

159.5 When we are living within wisdom of the conscious mind, we are aware that each moment is a gift. We spend life understanding, defining, and giving life an expression to those gifts. It is within honoring the gift of life that we are saying within life that we are preserving the beauty of love.

160.1 Within life, there are many beings that are aware that their lives are beyond what they could have created. They are aware that some true magic moved through their lives, presented them with many opportunities, a means in which to live within relationship to the beauty of mysticism within their lives, and that experiences within their life have been filled with the unexpected potential and joy. It is within the lives of these beings that the joy of love is being experienced, that the beauty of wisdom is being revealed, and that the essence of the child-mind is allowing the magnificence of self-discovery to flow effortlessly within life within each moment.

160.2 When vision and inspiration appear spontaneously within the child-mind, the unconscious mind will witness what comes of the beauty. Once it witnesses action that supports the presence of love, it will attempt to grab a hold of the experience, take it as its creation by voicing means in which to protect it rather than allowing the experience to grow, express, awaken so one is able to become free within it.

161.1 There are many circles within psychology and analysts within the mind that would define the unconscious as a storehouse of unlimited interpretations. This would be true if the nature of the unconscious was not to be limited. It is only the perception of love that can be unlimited. The perception of the unconscious is limited because the end result is to control its existence. It is only when an essence is flowing freely within life that it can experience unlimited interpretations such as love. However, the unconscious mind does not flow within love, it retracts within itself. It retracts into the feeling of limitation, and within the limitation, which is its nature, is not the means in which to have unlimited interpretations.

162.1 Awakening to the presence of love is the action of transcending ideas that personalize love through the limitation of experiencing love.

162.2 Within honoring that one must transcend ideas that personalize life through a limited perception of love, then one would agree that returning to the perception of the child is key to the success of fully dissolving the personal perception because it is within the child-mind that we are birthed into life with no ideas of limitations about opportunities, experiences, and relationships. We are just an expression of life and love ebbing and flowing in and out of the experience of choice.

163.1 Returning to the child-mind as an adult has to be done through the dissolving of the unconscious. When we dissolve the unconscious mind, we are within the child-mind because it was within the child-mind that it was created. Once an individual starts on the path of dissolving the unconscious, the individual will enter the child-mind and dissolve the negative interpretations and negative self-talk of oneself that exists within the seven key emotions. It is within identifying with this shift that the child-mind becomes free and is able to express life and love and potential, free of all past burdens of the unconscious mind because the language of the unconscious mind is perceived as being outside of the child. The child-mind believes it is what exists as the adult. It doesn't really wholly see the adult. It knows it is life because it is the vehicle in which birth was given.

When the unconscious mind is dissolved within the child-mind, the child becomes witness to the unconscious knowing that it is the presence of love hearing a voice that is continually telling it to step out of love. The spirit of the child is very powerful in reclaiming the essence and presence of love and will effortlessly work through the remainder of the unconscious mind dissolving it from the means in which it experiences life.

163.2 When an individual returns to the child-mind to dissolve the unconscious mind, the Clear Mind Experience moves the individual back through the pattern that the unconscious mind was created in; dissolving it from the top through to the base.

163.3 The unconscious mind when it's created is like building a structure with Lego blocks. As each emotional signifier locks in to the next emotional signifier, the unconscious mind is stored within the unconscious through feelings. Each of these feelings is represented as a Lego block, each one fitting in to the next one.

163.4 The unconscious mind is a profound structure within its existence. It is programmed to build a house that will house the feelings that interpret the importance of defining why one needs the unconscious, why it is important to build, how one feels within the unconscious, and then how the world will interact with the structure of the unconscious.

163.5 The safest way to remove the unconscious mind is starting at the top and moving to the foundation. The foundation is today, and the child, where it all began, is the top.

163.6 If you take a moment to consider that if you were to pull apart a building made out of blocks, if you were to take pieces from anywhere, you would cause the structure to collapse.

163.7 When the unconscious mind is pulled apart and is forced to collapse, one will experience anxiety or sadness. One will be experiencing the unconscious mind being sad and anxious about its condition and the fact that it is not able to operate within its structure. It will begin to panic and have anxiety over the fact that it is not able to relate from piece to piece through the 49 signifiers which will advance a being into depression and anxiety.

163.8 If the unconscious mind is also dismantled in this form, there will be clusters of the unconscious mind that will remain intact that will give individuals potentially opportunity to form addictions because there will be many power centers that accumulate together within the signifier of the unconscious. If you visualize for one moment that you collapse a building by removing some of the blocks, you will see that when the building collapses, more than likely, it will take up greater mass on the floor. There will also be the fact that the parts that cluster together create a weight in the area in which they are now sitting. When an individual collapses the unconscious mind, the brain perceives the unconscious mind as a larger expression than it is because it takes up greater mass, and there is also the fact that some areas of the unconscious become heavier in weight due to clusters within the neuro-pathways within the signifiers. Which is perceived by the brain that the unconscious mind has greater control in certain areas, and it is these feelings that create outer circumstances to fulfill these ideas and feelings.

163.9 In collapsing the unconscious mind, we create what would be perceived as chaos within the thought process with confusion not knowing what one wishes to pursue within their experience of life. However, if one were to take the structure apart piece by piece allowing for contemplation on the beauty of the structure as it is taken apart as you remember building each part of it, then there will be a rhythmic movement to dissolving and taking apart the unconscious mind. It will feel safe to the brain, safe to the perception, and safe within the child-mind because there will not be the collapse. When the unconscious mind collapses by disengaging aspects of it rather than taking it apart piece by piece, the unconscious mind will speak about the worthlessness of its existence. It will talk about

Life is a living expression of each moment,
as each moment awakens the rhythm of love.

the sadness of the fact that it can't function. It will talk about the fact that it cannot function. And within this conversation, the rational mind will hear this and then begin to voice means in which it can no longer function properly, and the individual will make interpretations that they need help because they are not able to function within the world, but it is purely the unconscious mind speaking of itself. There are a great number of light workers in which this has happened to because the signifiers of the unconscious mind have clustered together and have not formed a steady stream of awakened consciousness within the brain that has allowed them to perceive their transformation within the profundity of peace and wisdom. When an individual collapses the unconscious mind rather than taking it apart through the dissolving of the unconscious, then they may experience erratic behavior within their lives financially or within conditions and situations of their experiences because the universal mirror is seeing the collapse of the unconscious and creating the chaos that it sees within the perceived feelings of the individual from the experience.

163.10 The gift of dissolving the unconscious mind is that one is able to experience the gratitude for taking it apart piece by piece because within the process of doing so, one is able to remain within peace. It is important upon the path of awareness that an individual is able to perceive peace within their awakenings and contemplation; otherwise, abundance will not be able to move through their lives because they will have resentment for the effort that they have had to have within their life to remove the unconscious. The unconscious mind can be a painful experience when it is being randomly dismantled through practices that cannot support the signifiers within the unconscious mind. The Clear Mind Experience dissolves the unconscious mind in the flow in which it was created which allows for a birth.

163.11 When one practices the Clear Mind Experience, there is no catharsis, emotional chaos, addiction, or turmoil because as one is clearing and dissolving the unconscious mind, there are no aspects of the unconscious mind that are acting out to protect itself as one part leaves because you are moving back through the unconscious. You are not moving forwards through it but back through it. And because the unconscious mind is what retracts, it can't feel that one is moving in to dissolve it.

163.12 - 163.12i Within dissolving the unconscious mind, there is also the fact that one personally chose to remove every signifier that would be interpreted through the unconscious as the unconscious. It is in removing the signifiers through personal choice that the conscious mind is within celebration that one chose to do so; as it is discovering the beauty of love within itself as it is dissolving the unconscious mind. When one is able to do this, the transformation process becomes one of celebration, awareness, and unconditional love, and no longer is an experience of turmoil, trauma, and indecision.

163.13 For this moment, take a time to reflect on if you were to take the Lego structure that was created and built by yourself, the child, and began to dismantle it and packed up all the pieces and there was clear space, that is the same as within your brain. And what happens within that clear space is that the conscious mind fills the space with the presence of love so one is able to live within the full, whole interpretation of love as perception of oneself. Once the structure had been dismantled and the unconscious mind dissolved, the conscious mind will be moving in and out of itself expressing itself as courage and within the personal perception of the individual will move gratitude through the perception because it will be endlessly speaking of the gratitude one has for oneself within the courage and willingness to dissolve the unconscious mind. And within that courage, the conscious mind would have the room to move and the freedom to express the fullness of love and within that, the gratitude would move that love into the earth, into humanity, into the expression of your life for fulfillment and whole knowingness of love.

164.1 When we move into the child-mind and have dissolved the interpretations of the unconscious mind that are all thoughts, feelings, and emotions that separate one from love, then the individual becomes a living expression of the child-mind that is living of love, allowing love, expressing love, honoring love, realizing the beauty and magnificence of love, and within that realization is able to live within the unlimited capacity to celebrate the presence of love within each opportunity and relationship.

164.2 - 164.2ii A key within the success of the Clear Mind Experience is that the child-mind operates within the exchange of self-discovery. So when the unconscious mind is clearing from the child-mind, it is not done so through the motive to fix what is broken, but the child-mind perceives the movement of the conscious mind moving in and out of the unconscious as a means in which to experience self-discovery.

164.3 Within the perception, the child-mind will perceive motive and connect to it. If self-discovery is done through a longing for life to be different or repaired, this is an unconscious interpretation that will keep the child-mind separate from the moment. When the child-mind is kept separate from the moment, then it is separate from love and the individual is put back into the unconscious mind thinking that one is discovering something of oneself. When one sits down to practice the Clear Mind Experience, there is no motive. There is the movement and within the movement, there is the expression of love. And within the expression of love, the conscious mind is able to reunite, sweep, and swallow the unconscious within itself and realize the presence of love and how love is being perceived, ignited, and awakened within the perception.

164.4 It is within the intricacy of motive and how that operates within perception that has people stuck for many years on the path of self-discovery.

164.5 Motive is an intricate aspect of the mechanism of the unconscious because the child-mind does not see fault. It does not believe that it is bad, and it allowing at all times of a moment of being honored, a moment of being embraced. It is unlimited. It does not seek change, and it does not seek perfection. It seeks to discover a new moment within life, and within the Clear Mind Experience, it will ebb and flow within the conscious/unconscious perceptions for the realization and the true experience of love.

164.6 A component of the Clear Mind Experience is that the unconscious mind is being dissolved through the process of the experience, and not through the motive to understand change or improve oneself through the unconscious mind.

164.7 The practice has an individual focus on the awareness that one is already living within the presence of love as the presence of love, and within knowing one is love, the outer experience will change. The mechanics of the experince promotes this awareness within one's perception and engages the child-mind to support this. This is not to say that an individual is blindly educated on believing that they are something that they are not. It is simply an area of awareness that one is to hold focus upon, the presence of love, as one dissolves the unconscious. And then as the unconscious mind is dissolving into the conscious mind, the awareness is articulated through the wisdom within the brain that enables an individual to reconcile transformation.

165.1 When one thinks of returning to the child-mind, it is simply looked upon as a process that is best defined within the action of dissolving the unconscious; where one's perception is set free into the child-mind and the child-mind set free into the perception, no longer limited through negative thoughts, feelings, and emotions from the unconscious mind.

165.2 The world has a divine criteria within the brain that enables us to perceive love that is never altered. It can never be altered or damaged. The perception of love may be overshadowed and interrupted by the flow of expression from the unconscious and its interpretations, and the electrical charge that hasn't moved through perception, but love is not damaged or lost and does not need to be repaired. And the unconscious mind cannot be repaired or fixed because no aspect of its existence exists for the expression of love.

165.3 The aspects of the unconscious mind, negative self-talk that is stored within the child-mind has to be dissolved simply as sugar and water so the child-mind is able to simply function within its divine criteria. One cannot seek change by telling the child-mind that it is not functioning correctly because when the child-mind is told that it is not functioning correctly, it will begin to enhance the limitations of the dysfunction believing that the dysfunction is what it is.

165.4 Many adults have been educated within the realm of self-development and psychology to fix, heal, or change aspects of the inner child. However, it is not the inner child that needs to be fixed. There is nothing broken, and there is no dysfunction ever allowed to be contained within the conscious perception of the child-mind. It is merely the unconscious mind speaking of itself, speaking of the child, as it not able to perceive love within the child. Once the individual is able to dissolve the unconscious mind, the child-mind is set free into the unlimited expression and unconditional love of the child perception.

166.1 It is the unconscious mind that is perceived as dysfunctional within itself. It is able to and has the capacity to store betrayal, sadness, and fear.

166.2 Let's take a moment to ask what is operating where the unconscious is not? Is the unconscious operating simultaneously? It is this realization to love that takes one shift, one moment, one thought in perception; the awakening to reside within the simplicity of the child-mind, the beauty to perceive life as an effortless flow of unlimited interpretations that allow the profundity of love to live within wisdom. There can be no burden in the world where there is the child-mind. There is no burden as to what should be, could be, would be, or can be because within the child-mind that is the process of allowing the conscious mind to operate, there is no expectation from one moment to the next.

166.3 The child-mind operates through feeling. It operates within each moment defined by the feeling that it engaged in within each moment. If the feelings are from the unconscious mind, the child will perceive unconscious feeling and within that it will engage in negative self-talk through the feeling that it is experiencing. If the child-mind is engaged within the conscious mind, then the child will allow the fluidity and expression of love to define each moment within the unlimited potential at how love could present itself within that moment.

166.4 The child-mind is able to preserve love by living within the presence of love within itself. Then within the world and life experience, it will honor all interpretations and preserve life as the presence of love. It is not the child-mind that seeks to fix or repair or to change. It is the unconscious mind interpreting through a judgment of another or oneself that there is something broken.

166.5 It is within the child-mind that becomes free of the unconscious mind that true realization of love can occur, which will create the self-realization of personal freedom and the loss of identity. It is within the child-mind that one truly awakens to the presence of love; as it is the child-mind that allows the presence of love to move within life through the simplicity of knowing IAM Love, the birth of love, the realization of love, the profound oneness of all love; as within knowing it that IAM the child of love. IAM restored within knowing that IAM the oneness of all life.

167.1 It is important to clarify the beauty of the child-mind, the vulnerability of what it will experience within the day to day. It is also important to understand how the unconscious mind will interpret the child-mind and the limitations that can come within somebody's life through the interpretation of the unconscious mind living within the child-mind.

Child-Mind Living within the Freedom of the Conscious Mind

168.1 It is within the child-mind perceiving life free of the unconscious that the individual will feel supported within life because the child-mind has integrated that there is the birth of life.

168.2 The unlimited aspect of the child-mind is that when vision, inspiration, and opportunity appear, the child-mind does not have the means in which to measure or define in limitation what this actually means. The child-mind will witness life, will witness the gift and allow all to manifest as an expression of vision, inspiration, and opportunity with no expectation of outcome or means in which life appears.

168.3 The beauty of the child-mind is that it has the ability to play within one's career, one's relationships; able to define the beauty of joy through activities of the heart. It will be drawn into activities of the heart. The child-mind will live life within a sense of vision rather than burden. It will direct how one will fulfill hopes and dreams for life through vision rather than burden.

169.1 The wisdom of the child-mind is that when it is in the arena of caring and embracing others, the child-mind perception will be inspiring and unconditional because within the child-mind, it perceives others as an aspect of themselves. It is encoded within the divine criteria of the child-mind that all life witnessed by the child is an aspect of the child. It's the child when operating within a conscious mind who will be able to engage within life, within others, within the unconditional perception of loveWithin a conscious perception, the child-mind will within its innocence and the perception of self-discovery host relationships that preserve trust, that honor life, and always seek ways to innovate the unconditional expression of joy, union, and companionship with others within life.

169.2 The conscious mind will within the child perception attract career, partnerships, and ways in which to engage love and approval that support and preserve always the presence of love, self-love. When the child-mind is conscious, it is only about operating from the realm of love.

169.3 When one is living within the perception of the child-mind and able to effortlessly express seven key emotions that contain the 49 positive feelings consciously within each moment, then an individual will operate as an unconditional expression of how life, situations, others, and opportunities are a means in which to preserve life and love, as each moment will be the opportunity of honoring birth and death. Within the beauty of the child-mind, there is no fear of death because each moment is the moment of birth. Within the child-mind, there is no death because there is birth into form or birth into non-form.

169.4 The child-mind perception will be nurtured, honored, and supported by the universe when living within a conscious mind because life experiences, opportunities, and circumstances will develop around honoring its perceived feelings: the profound ideas of love, life, and beauty. There will be an effortless flow within the presence of life that allows the mind to celebrate the simplicity of self-discovery.

169.5 When the child-mind is fully awakened to the conscious mind, the universe will preserve life within the child-mind by allowing the perception to flourish in love through various life experiences. The universe once it recognizes the perception of love within the conscious awareness of the child-mind of the individual only has the capacity at that point to preserve life and love within the perception of that individual.

Suppressed by Unconscious Expression

170.1 When the child-mind is suppressed and restrained by unconscious thoughts and negative self-talk that are separate from love, it will allow limitations through fear and distrust to move through life. If validated by a sense of inadequacy, the child-mind will have a depression in the fact that it fears to exist, or it will have an addiction as it perceives it must control its existence to survive.

170.2 When the child-mind is suppressed within an unconscious expression, relationships within one's life will be a voice to the individual that their behavior is unacceptable or they will feel trapped within the relationships, and experiences with others will feel unaccepted and powerless.

170.3 When the child-mind is suppressed by the unconscious, the individual will be in the world feeling that relationships are asking them for their need to change. They will feel that they are either a weak person or that they are overbearing, but there is not a balance within how they are perceived by others. They will not be able to host a healthy relationship that manages life and maintains life within love because the unconscious mind will have them out of balance within the protection and limited perceptions and expectations of how the relationship must serve them or they must serve the relationship.

170.4 The child-mind when suppressed by the unconscious will appear not to be supportive or conscious of the needs of others. People around them will say they feel dishonored or unheard by them as they struggle to define interpretations that support others, and within that, there is a sense of abandonment that people are not able to articulate or understand the individual or one another.

170.5 When the child-mind is suppressed by the unconscious, the child will perceive distrust, disharmony, and within that, there will be a feeling that life has abandoned them. Within that, they will retract from the hope and potential that life is about self-discovery and move into the interpretation that life needs to be controlled for one to remain within happiness, and one must protect oneself to restore, awaken, or maintain happiness.

171.1 Unconscious interpretations that are expressed within the child-mind are able to be removed and dissolved within the Clear Mind Experience. That is the beauty of the Experience, that there is no limitation of the unconscious because an individual initiates the process and begins the process of dissolving the unconscious. The unconscious will retract into itself and cease operating within the individual's life as a random expression from moment to moment.

171.2 Within the unconscious mind are negative interpretations: thoughts, feelings, and emotions that have been created within the first seven years of one's life. They are thoughts, feelings, and emotions that do not allow the child-mind to live within the innocence. The innocence will be lost in the constant validation not to trust in prosperity, relationships to others who will consistently air distrust and reasons to fear life or one's ability because the universe will be catering and supporting and fulfilling the negative feelings of the child-mind.

171.3 Within the child-mind that is unconscious, life will not feel to be fun. It will feel to be a responsibility. If one is not able to preserve life through self-esteem, then the individual will appear to be irresponsible. As part of the responsibility, one will feel one must change who one is to be accepted by the world or oneself. That is also the case for an individual who feels to be irresponsible, that the day will come when they must change how they are living within life because they are being irresponsible to how they perceive themselves and others. This is all negative self-talk of the unconscious mind.

171.4 When an individual is living within the suppression of the child-mind, one will always feel unwelcome within their living environment. There will be a sense of constantly having to move, redecorate, or change the living environment even if one never does. There won't be the sense of satisfaction within one's living environment because one will be seeking to improve why one has feelings of loss. If one never wants to change, never wants to change the environment, they will have a perceived judgment about the fact that they don't wish to do that.

171.5 When the child-mind is suppressed through the unconscious mind, one will have consistent ideas that will be presented that one must change, must create change for happiness.

171.6 When one is living within the suppressed child-mind from the unconscious, they will feel loss of wealth, loss of love, loss of friendship, and loss of support or stature. One will create a means in which one feels supported within life only to spend the remainder of life fearing that one is not able to survive within that life, and that all that they have created, will be taken or lost.

171.7 When one is living within the child-mind that is suppressed by the unconscious, they will crave for things within their life and judge their level of success. An individual will long to establish some type of new order to life that is all created through a judgment that one has not made it, will not make it, and is not really showing up in life in the fullness in which they should be.

171.8 All of the dysfunction spoken of within the suppression of the child-mind through the unconscious comes from the fact that the child-mind through the dysfunction of the suppression is not allowed to appreciate life. The unconscious mind will continually speak about what, how, when, and why the child-mind must be different, and within that expression, the child-mind will listen to the unconscious mind speaking about why the child-mind is not given permission to appreciate the essence, presence, and love that is available within life.

172.1 It is within living within an unconscious mind that the unconscious mind will steal the child from our experience of life. With that feeling will be a sense of loss, will be shame, blame, and abdication of how that child-mind is no longer operating within one's perception.

172.2 When one is suppressed within the child-mind, there is a spontaneous sadness in this loss. And it is within life that there is a representation of this sadness through life experience.

172.3 Once the unconscious mind is dissolved, there is a revelation within the child-mind that is a profound gift, a gift that surpasses anything that could be imagined. And that gift is one's capacity to preserve the beauty of life, to allow the beauty of the unknown, to be open to the self-discovery of wisdom; as within the child-mind is the alchemy that ignites the fire of love within the brain to perceive the self-realization of love.

172.4 It is within returning one's perception to the child-mind that one moves beyond any limited thoughts, feelings that kept one from its beauty and simplicity. It is in moving into this simplicity of the child-mind that the unlimited potential of life is birthed within each moment within the perception of oneself.

172.5 It is the birthright of the child-mind to return to the point of birth within the perception of the adult, as it is in returning to the point of birth that one lives within the conscious mind. And it is living the conscious mind that is the birthright of humanity.

172.6 Take a moment to experience and contemplate for one moment whether or not the world is a living expression of the child-mind at this time.

172.7 Let us reflect for one moment that if the world was living within the child-mind, then the means in which to preserve life, love, simplicity, and divinity would be beyond measure.

172.8 It would be that humanity returning to that of the perception of the child-mind that there would be a profound oneness within the world because children and adults would perceive the same things within life as being important, valuable, and inspiring; and both child and adult would be moving in life in and out of experiences in a motion that is able to, in a movement that is inspired to support and allow the presence and beauty of love.

172.9 If humanity were to return to the beauty of the child-mind while living as a conscious perception of love, then life would effortlessly move upon the planet in one mind. As one mind, we would honor love, preserve wisdom within our elders and the spirit and inspiration of our youth. We would move in one community throughout the world honoring and preserving the one essence: the presence of love.

172.10 Living within the union of one mind upon the planet if humanity were to be restored to that of the child-mind would become the momentum of humanity. It would be within the beauty of this momentum that great revelation of love would be experienced within the wholeness of all life. It is this momentum that we seek to discover, reveal, and participate in throughout the Clear Mind Experience.

Chapter Six
Relationship to Self-Love

173.1 The essence of self-love is what allows one to perceive the presence of love within oneself. It connects us to all life through the vision that all is love, that all has potential to love. And where love is not present, self-love will seek to preserve itself by moving away from what is not love, and withdrawing into love. It is within the absence of self-love that one is disconnected from all life, the beauty within life, and the meaning of life.

173.2 When one is moving through life within the essence and expression and radiance of self-love, we are one with what preserves love within thoughts, words, actions, within each moment. It is the essence that preserves love, that allows us to form oneness within as the presence and interpretation of wisdom.

173.3 It is within the presence and interpretations of self-love that we experience the oneness of the earth. We feel one within her radiant potential. We feel the oneness of regeneration, vitality, growth, movement, death, birth, ending, beginning, awareness, retraction, union, and expansion.

173.4 It is within feeling her beauty within us that we experience the opportunity to honor our own beauty. When we live within the presence of self-love, we live within the perception that all life within life is one.

173.5 It is within the beauty of self-love that we are able to touch the soil, her ground, as if our own body, as it is within honoring her resources and spirit of nature that we honor our minds. As within our minds, we are able to perceive the magnificence of her offering as the magnificence of our own. We perceive that the body of the earth is of the human body. It is to be honored. It is to be nurtured. It is to be preserved within the union of love.

173.6 Through the sacred presence within the earth, there is an energy within the earth that allows us within form to feel that we are supported, that allows the spirit to reside within the essence that 'one' is home. It is upon residing upon the earth that we as humanity have the potential to move within each moment in one mind, in union together within the expression of love.

173.7 Within humanity is the potential to experience the beauty of one mind. The potential to express the unlimited essence of love is ripe within each moment. Living within the potential of love is allowing all life to take form within the preservation of self-appreciation.

173.8 Life is but a reflection of the beauty of love, and each moment of life becomes an opportunity to consciously allow love to move in and out of various expressions, cultures, within rhythm. As within love, there is no individual community. There is a global community of one movement living within the expression of one knowing, and that is 'IAM the unlimited perception of self-love.'

173.9 Love moves within us, as love moves in and out of it-self within us expressing the beauty of form within emotion, within actions, within thoughts as movement, so does the radiance of love move in and out of awareness within the earth.

174.1 There is divine potential within humanity. There is the divine potential that all life will harmonize love within the expression and unlimited potential of awakened harmonious light. It is within self-love that we awaken the divine potential and release it upon the earth for all to benefit.

174.2 It is within the radiance of self-love that all life is the living harmony of an expression, and the expression is the presence of love. And within the presence of love, the earth is ripe with gifts that are moving effortlessly within our capacity to honor what is experienced within us and that is the presence of love.

174.3 It is within the presence of self-love, within perceiving the beauty of love that we allow our lives to be defined as an expression of love because our feelings of love will move life into action, and life in action will support the living presence of self-love.

174.4 Self-love is the essence that allows us to care about ourselves, to express care to others, and to awaken experiences, and receive opportunities within our day to day that serve to celebrate our courage to love, our courage to perceive wisdom, and the willingness to let go to the beauty; that within everything that is not allowing us to live within the expression of love, we are able to dissolve, when dissolving the unconscious perceptions that are not able to acknowledge or accept the capacity and the rhythm, the beauty and the magnificence of love.

175.1 Self-love is the sacred gift of incarnation. It is what is given to us within its capacity to preserve life as love. Self-love is the ultimate gift of love because self-love is the moment when ultimate, universal, divine love takes form and presents itself within each moment, each day, each relationship, and each opportunity as you.

175.2 Amongst many expressions, self-love is the experience and interpretation of our physical qualities; whether our interpretation be within the perception of a conscious mind, through the act of self-appreciation, or maybe the physical qualities are interpreted within self-judgment and critical thought which does not allow self-love to be interpreted through the physical expression of beauty.

175.3 Let's for one moment stick within the feeling of pure unconditional love. Feel form, your physical form, and that within this moment, you no longer had the capacity to judge aspects of your physical form that you had decided were imperfect and did not serve you. That just, within this moment, you were able to sit comfortably within the expression of form that was within this moment, and within that expression and self-acceptance, and allowing of self-love of form, you were able to feel the radiance of love moving in and out of the body, of the mind as radiant self-appreciation.

175.4 Take a moment to ponder the opportunity of seeing your physical form in honor, in beauty, in love, and that the mind was void of any thoughts of disharmony, control, fear, ideas, rejections of how the body should, could, or would be 'if only.'

175.5 Self-love will honor the body through the ritual of understanding and moving into each cell of the body to allow the presence of love. Through the sensuality of touch, through the cleansing purity of water, through the spontaneous exhilaration of movement, self-love is available waiting to be expressed within the interpretation of form.

175.6 Imagine for one moment that you were living within the freedom, within the capacity to make interpretations of your physical self that honored your unique expression and that you were free of what did not honor your unique expression and creation that you are.

176.1 When one lives within the unconscious perception, they are able to have a capacity in which to say that they are happy with themselves physically because the unconscious mind will turn the body into what is worshipped as all creation.

176.2 The unconscious mind will hang on to the body as being its trophy or being what it needs to fix to be better. There are times when one would be able to say that they are happily integrated into their beauty and have worked hard at creating and maintaining their current interpretation of their beauty. The test, however, to see if the presence of self-love is available would the interpretation of beauty be changed beyond their means to control it, and within that moment, would self-love present itself?

176.3 One would have to ask, is the body being cared for within the presence of self-love if there is limited self-approval on how one perceives one's qualities? And if the qualities were to diminish, would one be able to approve of oneself unconditionally?

176.4 At times when one is looking for motive of self-care, one would ask, has it been created through self-judgment?

One would ask, is the interpretation of beauty connected to fragility within self-esteem that could collapse at any moment should the perception of outer beauty be diluted or transformed?

176.5 One would ask oneself that if outer beauty could not be controlled, life would still go on, but would self-approval be available? Within the unconscious mind, it is not, and it would not be available. However, within the conscious mind, it would be available because the conscious mind sees no judgment in form. It sees an expression of love preserving itself as form, and within that preservation is able to celebrate the beauty in which it is.

177.1 When an individual is rising in consciousness, and the heart is awakening, the rhythm of the body will change to serve the vibration of the wisdom which will alter the form and the ways in which one engages with the form.

177.2 It does not mean that everyone that awakens to the presence of love will go through dramatic physical shifts or loss of outer beauty within the redefinition of wisdom. However, it means that one must be flexible and allow the body to shift within its momentum and realize that life is a journey and the body will take many forms, and expressions will have many forms, and not to seek to control the body as something that does not have meaning, purpose, or does not have the wisdom of divinity.

177.3 For some, there are strong addictions to the outer physical appearance. And the outer physical appearance could be all they've longer to experience void of any seeking of love or self-love or perception of wisdom.

177.4 For some, the transformation of form upon the path of self-discovery can be dramatic. What would appear as a recalibration of what is determined as physical beauty will have to take place within the perception of the individual.

178.1 For some men and women who awaken to self-love, life becomes solely defined by wisdom and not the thoughts of how and who they want to be, and within this, there is a loss of identity.

178.2 For some, when wisdom awakens or will awaken, there is a redefinition, a reinterpretation of physical beauty that one must move one's perception into to allow full activation of the heart and higher levels of consciousness.

178.3 It will be the interpretations of beauty that were made to a sleeping mind that will no longer feel comfortable to the individual that has embodied the presence of wisdom. And in response to the wisdom and the embodiment of wisdom, the body will reconfigure, and mental perceptions of what beauty is and how the body will pertain to its first beauty will recalibrate.

178.4 When this happens to an individual, there will be what feels to be an incredible loss, frustration, or sadness within the experience, as the attachment to form and how it should look and be perceived and approved of by others will be redefined within each moment of life. And the individual will be left seeking and questioning answers as to what has happened or is continuing to happen to physical form. What is appropriate to realize within this moment is that during this time, one is to realize that life is a journey and not simply what you experience right now. It could take the body a certain period of time to recalibrate the energetic field of its rise in consciousness. However, it will move in and out. It will ebb and flow out of different experiences. What is important is that one does not define one's body or become attached through fear as to how it is expressing itself, whether it be in disharmony, disease, or if it were to change in some form. One would be able to sit and participate to realize that at some point, the body once it reaches the recalibrated level of awareness will begin to express a new identification of beauty and wellness that awakens peace, awareness, and oneness within the mind of the individual.

178.5 During the moment that an individual will begin to reconfigure physical beauty, there appears to be a type of mental struggle where the mind wishes to regain the previous interpretation of beauty. And at some point within the process, the mind will feel lost and that it has awakened some type of loss within its connection to form.

179.1 The body is an expression of life as of the earth. When one is living within the conscious mind and not limiting or controlling the body through negative interpretation with conditions of how one must live to reflect love, to reflect self-approval, then the body will ebb and flow like nature, moving in and out of experiences, defining itself always through the movement of retraction and expansion; where in one moment it is the outer breath, and in the next, it is the inhale, where the body is taking in, connecting, re-energizing, moving within the sense of knowing of all that is the perception of love. And then the body will experience the expansion, where it moves outside and begins to give within the presence of itself to others energetically and within movement, words, emotions, and intent.

179.2 There are times when the body will flourish and thrive, and times when it is required to cleanse. As parts of the body die off to be redefined through new growth, there is a movement, an ebbing and flowing within the beauty of the body that one is able to capture as an expression of life, movement, wisdom, and love. It is important that one's lifestyle allows this movement and natural expression of divinity within form that moves in and out of creation of oneself from the inner and outer realms.

179.3 Within the ebbing and flowing of the body, there are times when the body will increase in mass to accommodate new energetic flow, new abundant consciousness, or it may trim down and move idle into a stillness that allows for other levels of consciousness to begin to evolve and awaken. When one is not consciously controlling the body through defined ideas and limitations of what it must be to be perfect, to be healthy, to be an expression of what one would term as beauty, then the body will become a vehicle and a means in which to awaken new levels of consciousness as it will carry the consciousness within form so as not to dilute or pollute the mind so the mind may become a vehicle in which to move the presence of love.

179.4 The more awareness that we have and the move we connect to wisdom, the less an individual is able to define or hold onto the ideas of how one must be physically.

179.5 As there are seasons within Mother Nature, there are seasons within our own perceptions, and it is really about allowing within your life the beauty of your season. As it is within the winter that one moves within and allows the clouds to pass, allows the cleanse of life, allows the mind to become free of all thought that carries heat. It is within the winter that one restores a foundation within oneself that is transparent, allowing, and all-encompassing. It is within the spring that the all-encompassing beauty that was real-

The presence of love is the living expression
of this moment, and the realization that
IAM love.

ized within the winter shows new life and births new life within the expression of oneself; where one's life becomes decorated within the movement and expression of love that has formed its new presentation during the winter. It is within the summer that the over-expectation of new life is burned away. And within the summer, one will accumulate the stillness and the resolve and reconcile that the new presentation that was found in the winter is now available to be experienced within life and to provide profound light and energy and warmth within the realization of love. It is within the fall that old energy drops away to allow the birth of the new. It is within the fall that one releases all that one is not, all that is false within the unconscious perception. And it is within the fall that one moves into the winter to begin the process of birthing the beauty of love once again.

180.1 When an individual awakens to the presence of love, dissolving the unconscious mind within the Clear Mind Experience, there will be the experience of ebbing and flowing within one's diet and exercise routine because of new energy that becomes present. As one feels the presence of love, diet and movement become defined by something, by taste that preserves the presence of love within the individual and allows one to feel nurtured, supported, living within the rhythm of trust, within all that is experienced, as a means in which to care for oneself by one's diet and movement.

180.2 It is important when awakening the conscious mind that an individual allows themselves to awaken new ways. It is in redefining life through these new ways that one will integrate physically, allowing all that is within life, within form to nurture. As the increase in vibration moves through form from wisdom, one is nurtured through the process of allowing the new ways to integrate physically.

180.3 When an individual moves into this fluctuation of consciousness where the conscious perception of self-care through self-love is moving into embracing oneself through the awakening to self-love, attempting to control the body to serve the unconscious mind and its interpretations of physical beauty that are fueled through self-judgments are impossible. It is within the presence of self love that one is expressing the divinity of love within all expressions of form. It is within the perception of self-love that there are no limitations within one's capacity to live in love, experience love, and radiate the presence of love within life for all.

180.4 One is not able to reside within self-judgment when one has awakened to the presence of self love because the capacity to have judgment is no longer available. It is because one is more evolved. One has become more evolved. The further one awakens into the conscious inter-pretations of self-love, and as the unconscious mind is dis-solving, one is unable to connect to unconscious thoughts of the body when one is consciously perceiving self-love.

181.1 The beauty of self-care within a mind, within a body that is experiencing the beauty of self-love is that self-love becomes a spontaneous expression of honoring one's form within the nurturing awareness to love and wisdom.

181.2 Living within the conscious mind, the experince of self-care that we operate in will not be measured by what we are gaining from self-care but by what we are sup-porting. And what we are supporting within a conscious mind during the self-care experience is the presence of love. Self-care is a means in which to preserve love within action which is self-love.

181.3 When the presence of love awakens within our interpretation, it is important that the self-care ritual cater to serve that stillness. It is within serving the stillness that the true presence of love can permeate through the body, through the mind developing a harmony of oneness within the expression of form.

181.4 When an individual awakens the presence of love within the self-care ritual, their energetic flow may change and fluctuate and seek to experience movement within a different form. Take a moment to reflect upon yourself. If you are practicing the Clear Mind Experience, write down any physical activity or ritual that you feel would nurture the presence of love in taking care of yourself. If you are yet to practice the Clear Mind Experience, write down, firstly, what you like to practice to support the physical movement of the body and the ritual of self-care, and then write what you think you might be attracted to experience if you were to feel a deeper connection to the presence of love.

182.1 When beginning the Clear Mind Experience, it is advisable to begin to look at where you feel you are most nurtured within the expression of physical movement. Once an individual begins to dissolve the unconscious mind, then the choice of physical movement must be done so from the perception of love and not from the perception of self-judgment. A way in which to assist within this process is to spend some time thinking about ways in which you would seek to support and enjoy yourself and the presence of love within life. If you have made a list of activities that you feel nurture the presence of love, then take some time to be able to integrate these activities one at a time until you have chosen a pattern that serves the energetic flow of your new perception and the presence of love and stillness.

182.2 Providing ourselves with the fluidity and the time and the freedom of judgment to truly allow ourselves to awaken self-love within the body is not something that the unconscious mind will want to provide you, and it is not something that humanity is willing to allow one to discover when it is unconscious. The world is driven for individuals to represent a certain physique in proof of who they are and how they are within life. However, the conscious mind is not able to control how wisdom will wake up and perceive itself within the individual. And if the individual is prepared to let go of the potential of what could have been, then all love will reveal itself within the individual clearly.

182.3 Upon the planet, there is a strong judgment on the size and shape of an individual's form. Even within conscious movements or conscious gatherings or groups or communities of individuals, there is a judgment around those that carry weight as being those that are carrying dysfunction, disharmony, or baggage. As wisdom knows no measurement, and wisdom does not measure, and wisdom is a vehicle in which to receive, having judgments about the size an individual in which to represent wellness is an unconscious perception. Wellness when defined within the unconscious mind is about size and an individual not carrying weight. However, when living within a conscious mind, the conscious mind does not have the capacity to judge what form is better than the other and will simply use the form as a means in which to integrate the wisdom.

182.4 Within the unconscious mind, it has been clearly defined that if an individual carries weight that they are not as beautiful or as able to integrate into the everyday lifestyle because there is a certain perception that a certain weight serves life more effectively versus a person that carries weight or appears to have some overweight tendencies.

Even within the wellness market and the spiritual market, if an individual carries weight no matter how wise one may appear, these markets will define the individual as having issues with who they are if they are carrying weight.

For one moment, reflect upon your body, reflect upon the aspects of the body where you feel comforted. If you feel overly confident with your body, ask yourself why. Question yourself to locate any fears, any preconceived ideas that will be hiding fears.

Within a Conscious Mind the form is not measured – within the unconscious mind – form is measured through expectation and fear.

183.1 Self-love does not measure itself through the perfection of form. Self-love is the energy of fullness. It is an expanded awareness into the knowingness of what one feels within the presence of love. Self-love will not measure through the perfection of form how wisdom is expressing itself.

183.2 It is important within humanity that we dissolve the aspect of the unconscious that creates limitation for individuals to be able to express wisdom. It is important to remove the judgment. How we perceive individuals to show up in the world and understand that within an expression of wisdom, there is no measure of a perfect form.

183.3 As humanity raises in consciousness and the elevated perceptions of consciousness begin to awaken, form will be honored through self-love as something that is preserved within life.

183.4 Within an awakened mind is not the means in which

to seek perfection. It is within living within an awakened mind that the true beauty of humanity is able to be served.

183.5 As we focus on clearing the unconscious, dissolving the unconscious through the Clear Mind Experience, it is obvious that in the years to come, the world will no longer look physically the same, and the language of self-care will be playful, energetic, inspiring, serving the heart of the child as one will live free from the unconscious, which means that fear, anxiety, self-judgment, self-promotion, abdication, and blame will be dissolved within the unconscious.

184.1 Today the world is defining self-love through the sexual perception. The unconscious mind will interpret that if it is received sexually as being admired by the sexual needs of others, then one is to approve of oneself says the female and male mind. Then the unconscious mind will say, "If I do not fit in to that sexual perception, then there can be no role for me so I shall step aside." It is within stepping aside that the individual will become insignificant sexually and will begin to move into a depressed interpretation of sexuality.

184.2 With consciousness awakening by the moment, humanity is challenged within every moment to remain within a clear steady flow within the presence of love. This is because within the breakdown of humanity, the unconscious mind is confronted and appears to be confronted by people forcing it to make a choice; that it is not to engage within itself. Within the Clear Mind Experience, the unconscious mind does not get to choose. It simply folds into the conscious mind through the process of the Clear Mind Experience.

184.3 It has become an epidemic upon the planet with thousands of married individuals leaving their spouses and families for younger sexual experiences, or to cater to sexual addiction. It is happening to both men and women, where the unconscious mind is seeking power through the interpretations of sexuality.

184.4 It is when a society such as this one is driven to feel thirty when one is forty, forty when one is fifty, and now recently fifty when one is sixty that there is the creation of great unrest for one's current experience. It takes one out of the moment of their current age and places them within an imaginary age which, therefore, connects them to behavior that cannot support the season of their life. Just like the earth, life has seasons. And as one moves in and out of and ebbs and flows within these seasons, wisdom is presented and ways in which to connect to wisdom is revealed.

184.5 - 184.6 There is great conflict at this time within generations. We have an older generation that seeks to be the younger generation. We have the younger generation asking the questions, "Well, if a forty-year-old within their minds takes my position of a thirty year old on the planet, where do I fit in?" This type of behavior further validates a disassociation from the moment and the presence of love. There is great profound stillness and wisdom within one embracing oneself, embracing potential within the moment, embracing current age, not to feel old but to embrace the cultivated wisdom that comes from having lived for that period of time.

184.7 As a woman who is currently forty, I wish to embrace that beauty of being forty and live free from the unconscious mind speaking otherwise.

184.8 The unconscious mind will seek to move one out of their current perception of reality by creating another story that is unattainable. It is unattainable for a person to regress ten whole years and move into a different experience and actually be ten years younger. One may feel that this is very doable, but when one is able to integrate and express life that within the season of being fifty, I AM filled with the vitality and youth that comes from integrating the beauty of the fact that I am fifty, it is very powerful. It is true that as we grow older we can feel younger, and this is because we are returning within the child-mind. And when one returns to the child-mind, then youth is recaptured.

184.9 In a conscious mind, age means nothing. It simply allows us to accumulate wisdom through the length of time and opportunity that we have been available to integrate the conscious mind.

185.1 One would have to question oneself and say, "What was so unattractive with being our age?" The unconscious mind would have one believe that there was an unattractiveness of expressing one's true age. One would have to question, "Why should we measure our successes based on who is going to be sexually attracted to us?" One would have to ask, "Does sexual attraction begin with ourselves?" If we are attracted to ourselves sexually, we are able to live strong within various interpretations of form because there is an integrated awareness of oneself.

185.2 It is within the beauty of touch, the presence of love, the essence of insight, the beauty of vision, and the experience of movement that love and sexuality begin within ourselves.

185.3 Many times within life, we can be hiding, not sitting within the power of self-love but looking to fit in so people will be able to integrate the fact that we are experiencing thoughts that are positive of who we are. We will attempt to cover up aspects of ourselves that we have judged, when in essence, once they are revealed, profound beauty may reveal itself.

185.4 When we reach a point of vulnerability within our physical form, there is an aspect where there is a presence within us that no longer seeks for approval of others. It is when one lives within this knowing that life becomes an expression of the heart, and one lives in constant awareness of the body and how one is approving of oneself free from judgment.

185.5 In self-love is the profound opportunity to love oneself. It is within loving oneself that we realize the beauty of courage; the courage to celebrate oneself right now.

185.6 When one has recognized that the conscious mind is expressing the presence of love, self-love, within life, then one does not seek compliments from others. One will experience spontaneous interactions of self-appreciation with others and within life.

185.7 Within each moment of the conscious mind, one will receive a continuous flow of compliments that allow one to experience the beauty of self-appreciation.

185.8 Within each day, an individual will receive compliments that demonstrate how they feel, not what they long for. Within the mind, they will feel honored. They will express the honor of loving. They will be aware of the beauty of living the radiant expression of self-love.

186.1 There are many magnificent qualities operating within life, within our perception, besides sexual perception. There are many magnificent qualities operating within life that truly embrace the vulnerability of how one will interact within the presence of self-love.

186.2 The collective unconscious always seeks to discredit, always seeks to confuse, and always seeks to remove the presence of love within life, within each experience.

186.3 - 186.3i Within relationships upon the earth, immediate gratification has become the backbone of relationships, and while one chooses to be in one, whether it is within relationship to one's career, one's family, one's partner, one's children, one's lifestyle, one's job.

186.4 It is the perception of the unconscious mind that the person that is sitting opposite us must keep us feeling ten years younger because it is within this preconceived idea of the unconscious that this false perception makes us believe that we are not the age that we are, and provides falsehood to one's identity and how one integrates and perceives vitality. There is an in authenticity within the unconscious that tries to take youth rather than accept within the moment one's position within life and truly merge within the gifts of what that season of life is bringing.

186.5 It is of the unconscious mind that one would not want to integrate oneself to be the age that one is. It could not be further from the moment knowing we are the age that we are and refusing to love that age, feel freedom within that age. As within the conscious mind, there is a timelessness that has no fear of death, no loss of time, as we are allowing ourselves to celebrate ourselves as a magnificent expression of self-love.

186.6 Allowing ourselves to accept our age within a conscious perception, within the realm of unconditional love is the ultimate expression of self-love when one has achieved it. When we live within this state, we are allowing others to be received, honored, nurtured, and supported within the presence of self-love.

186.7 The beauty of residing within the child-mind living within self-love is that we are able to love and honor our current age effortlessly because a child loves to grow, loves to flourish, and loves to discover. And when one has awakened within the child-mind to the presence of love, then the discovery of what is a joy in which to participate is revealed.

186.8 Within a conscious mind that is allowing the beauty of love through self-acceptance of one's perception and current age within life, when one is living within the child-mind, one allows the mind to progress, to awaken, and to become. When one is living within an unconscious perception and disassociated from the pure love of the child-mind, then the individual will retract, withdraw, and go backwards. If you think about the retraction, that is when the unconscious mind seeks to be younger, seeks to withdraw itself to a different age.

186.9 When one is living within the unconscious mind, then one will always speak about loss and retraction, as the unconscious mind seeks to return to where it originally came from and return all outer experience to the moment before.

186.10 Within each moment, relationship, and day that we are in relationship with the unconscious, the mind is removing the opportunity to show up within the fluidity of ways in which to celebrate life without judgment, life without the perfection. Worrying, concerned, doubting how one is perceived by oneself and others.

187.1 Through magnificence of expressing self-love is the beauty of allowing vulnerabilities of who we are and how those vulnerabilities are presented within life. And it is within these vulnerabilities that we inspire courage.

187.2 It is within realizing that within one moment to the next is a sacred and profound opportunity to embrace oneself as a radiant reflection of love. That within relationships, experiences, and opportunities is a means in which to see, move, allow, and celebrate the presence of self-love.

187.3 Within humanity awakening to self-love is a profoundly intimate journey. Clearing the unconscious mind by dissolving its perception allows for a profound vulnerability to live within one's life that allows one to intimately embrace the journey of life and love.

187.4 Within life, we are not always in control of experiences of the body, but some experiences are that of a karma to self-discover, and within this self-discovery will be the revelation of love.

187.5 Transformation of the body can seem like an experience from one moment to the next, where life was moving in one direction and then one is moved quickly into another direction, and it is within this that one is being sent to discover life.

187.6 When an individual is judged by another, it is felt by the universe, by the individual, and the one in judgment. It is within life important to balance what is unseen with what is seen and to always encourage the magnificence of a child.

Judgment can be felt by the soul. It can force a person to become a prisoner of their own interpretation of themselves. As we awaken upon the earth, it is important to not limit wisdom through a judgment of one's size. If one is perceiving that perfection comes from a form that is a particular size, shape, demeanor, then one is losing the relationship to wisdom and the spontaneous expression that one is living within connection to the being.

187.7 When within life one rejects the form, one will be put into a position where they will be rejected by those that were expected to love them, those that are expected to integrate within them. And this is because, when one rejects the form, one is rejecting the presence of life, and not preserving love within life. There is great vulnerability at times to truly nurture the presence of love and embrace the presence of love.

187.8 Throughout humanity, particularly women are encouraged that they must diet, fast, detox, take tablets, practice techniques to be able to shift their body to that of the perfect imaginings of the mind. However, one's true nature of love will not allow life to be defined in that form. In the true expression of love, one is able to express divinity within many forms. When one is able to define self-love by one's physical image, then one may not get to the depth of what love truly feels like. Within life, the depth of self-love is present when one is less aware and more detached of the perfection of form. It is within feeling the perfection of form that an individual will believe in the falsehood of self-love that is moved through the unconscious mind and comes from self-gratification and the immediate gratification from others.

187.9 At times when individuals are living within awareness to love, then one will feel to truly embrace unlimited potential of how form will move within life to support wisdom.

187.10 When one is living within a form that does not have them move deeply into humanity because there is a sense of achievement or accomplishment within the form, then an individual will at times not be able to perceive the needs of others and the courage that is needed to let go of others.

187.11 Self-image at times can be fed through adoration and immediate gratification from others. This does not make for a positive self-image but more of a co-dependent self-image based on fear of rejection.

187.12 – 187.12i When an individual loses a positive self-image and becomes addicted to adoration and the props of being clothed in jewelry, and presents the judgment that one is not good enough, then it is at this time that an individual will be able to birth the grounds to awaken courage, the essence of what is need to truly awaken a new perception of oneself.

187.13 It is within the unconscious mind that one will always speak about withdrawing and retracting. The unconscious mind will speak about loss, the need to experience loss, the need to withdraw, and the need to move into.

187.14 – 187.14i Within each moment of each day in each relationship with the unconscious, the mind is removing from us the capacity to live separate from the presence of love.

187.15 - 187.15i When in your life has your form had you reinterpret value for yourself?

*Date*_____

_____

_____

_____

_____

_____

_____

_____

*Date*_____

_____

_____

_____

_____

_____

_____

*Date*_____

_____

_____

_____

_____

_____

_____

188.1 Define **7** of your most beautiful physical qualities right now without any change.

*Date*_____

1. _____
2. _____
3. _____
4. _____
5. _____
6. _____
7. _____

*Date*_____

1. _____
2. _____
3. _____
4. _____
5. _____
6. _____
7. _____

*Date*_____

1. _____
2. _____
3. _____
4. _____
5. _____
6. _____
7. _____

188.2 Where does the collective unconscious mind attempt to label feminine expression?

*Date*_____

_____

_____

_____

_____

_____

_____

_____

*Date*_____

_____

_____

_____

_____

_____

_____

_____

*Date*_____

_____

_____

_____

_____

_____

_____

_____

189.1 When has change suddenly approached you and within the turmoil you have awakened peace?

*Date*_____

_____

_____

_____

_____

_____

_____

_____

*Date*_____

_____

_____

_____

_____

_____

_____

_____

*Date*_____

_____

_____

_____

_____

_____

_____

_____

189.2 How does letting love go feel so good?

*Date*_____

_____
_____
_____
_____
_____
_____
_____

*Date*_____

_____
_____
_____
_____
_____
_____
_____

*Date*_____

_____
_____
_____
_____
_____
_____
_____

189.3 Can within separation union form?

*Date*_____

_____
_____
_____
_____
_____
_____
_____

*Date*_____

_____
_____
_____
_____
_____
_____
_____

*Date*_____

_____
_____
_____
_____
_____
_____
_____

189.4 When self-love expresses itself within, what is the feeling?

*Date*_____

_____

_____

_____

_____

_____

_____

_____

*Date*_____

_____

_____

_____

_____

_____

_____

_____

*Date*_____

_____

_____

_____

_____

_____

_____

_____

189.5 Define your relationship to wisdom.

*Date*_____

_____

_____

_____

_____

_____

_____

_____

*Date*_____

_____

_____

_____

_____

_____

_____

_____

*Date*_____

_____

_____

_____

_____

_____

_____

_____

189.6 Where in life are expectations failed through false desires of what could or should be to serve greater happiness?

*Date*_____

_____

_____

_____

_____

_____

_____

_____

*Date*_____

_____

_____

_____

_____

_____

_____

_____

*Date*_____

_____

_____

_____

_____

_____

_____

_____

189.7 What do expectations take from us?

*Date*_____

_____

_____

_____

_____

_____

_____

_____

*Date*_____

_____

_____

_____

_____

_____

_____

_____

*Date*_____

_____

_____

_____

_____

_____

_____

_____

189.8 How is self-appreciation an expression within?

*Date*_____

_____
_____
_____
_____
_____
_____
_____

*Date*_____

_____
_____
_____
_____
_____
_____
_____

*Date*_____

_____
_____
_____
_____
_____
_____
_____

189.9 When we are free to love ourselves, free to allow life, the conscious mind will awaken inner strength and knowing that will redefine life. How is your life redefined through courage and inner awareness?

*Date*_____

_____

_____

_____

_____

_____

_____

*Date*_____

_____

_____

_____

_____

_____

_____

*Date*_____

_____

_____

_____

_____

_____

_____

190.1 How does self-love define itself within a newness within life?

*Date*_____

_____
_____
_____
_____
_____
_____
_____

*Date*_____

_____
_____
_____
_____
_____
_____
_____

*Date*_____

_____
_____
_____
_____
_____
_____
_____

190.2 When love ebbs and flows in and out of itself defining itself, how does peace support us?

*Date*_____

_____
_____
_____
_____
_____
_____
_____

*Date*_____

_____
_____
_____
_____
_____
_____
_____

*Date*_____

_____
_____
_____
_____
_____
_____
_____

190.3 When at times through the awareness of the conscious mind have you witnessed the emotions purge and clear themselves for new expressions? Define the experience.

*Date*_____

_____
_____
_____
_____
_____
_____
_____

*Date*_____

_____
_____
_____
_____
_____
_____
_____

*Date*_____

_____
_____
_____
_____
_____
_____

190.4 Have you witnessed the difference in how the conscious mind expresses loss versus the unconscious mind, and if so define.

*Date*_____

_____

_____

_____

_____

_____

_____

_____

*Date*_____

_____

_____

_____

_____

_____

_____

*Date*_____

_____

_____

_____

_____

_____

_____

191.1 Are there really endings when you are in love, or are they moments that redefine life?

*Date*_____

_____

_____

_____

_____

_____

_____

_____

*Date*_____

_____

_____

_____

_____

_____

_____

_____

*Date*_____

_____

_____

_____

_____

_____

_____

_____

191.2 What ending has become a birth within your life?

*Date*_____

_____

_____

_____

_____

_____

_____

*Date*_____

_____

_____

_____

_____

_____

_____

*Date*_____

_____

_____

_____

_____

_____

_____

192.1 Self-love is an endless expression of potential. How do we benefit by the truth that self-love has no measure?

*Date*_____

_____
_____
_____
_____
_____
_____
_____

*Date*_____

_____
_____
_____
_____
_____
_____
_____

*Date*_____

_____
_____
_____
_____
_____
_____
_____

192.2 Write about three adventures that have unfolded within your life that have allowed self-love to discover itself.

*Date*_____

_____

_____

_____

_____

_____

_____

_____

*Date*_____

_____

_____

_____

_____

_____

_____

_____

*Date*_____

_____

_____

_____

_____

_____

_____

_____

192.3 What do you feel makes up the alchemy of self-love?

*Date*_____

_____

_____

_____

_____

_____

_____

_____

*Date*_____

_____

_____

_____

_____

_____

_____

_____

*Date*_____

_____

_____

_____

_____

_____

_____

_____

192.4 How is self-love defined within your life within this moment?

*Date*_____

_____

_____

_____

_____

_____

_____

*Date*_____

_____

_____

_____

_____

_____

_____

*Date*_____

_____

_____

_____

_____

_____

_____

193.1 How does peace define itself when a situation moves unexpectedly?

*Date*_____

_____

_____

_____

_____

_____

_____

_____

*Date*_____

_____

_____

_____

_____

_____

_____

_____

*Date*_____

_____

_____

_____

_____

_____

_____

_____

193.2 How does the conscious mind define self-acceptance?

*Date*_____

_____
_____
_____
_____
_____
_____
_____

*Date*_____

_____
_____
_____
_____
_____
_____
_____

*Date*_____

_____
_____
_____
_____
_____
_____
_____

193.3 Define freedom from self-judgment and how it feels.

*Date*_____

_____

_____

_____

_____

_____

_____

_____

*Date*_____

_____

_____

_____

_____

_____

_____

_____

*Date*_____

_____

_____

_____

_____

_____

_____

_____

194.1 How is life celebrating itself through your intent to honor all life?

*Date*_____

_____
_____
_____
_____
_____
_____
_____

*Date*_____

_____
_____
_____
_____
_____
_____
_____

*Date*_____

_____
_____
_____
_____
_____
_____
_____

Absence of Self-Love

195.1 Define a modern day discomfort for women and how it is dissolved through a change of perception.

*Date*_____

_____

_____

_____

_____

_____

_____

*Date*_____

_____

_____

_____

_____

_____

_____

_____

*Date*_____

_____

_____

_____

_____

_____

_____

195.2 Define sexuality.

*Date*_____

_____
_____
_____
_____
_____
_____
_____

*Date*_____

_____
_____
_____
_____
_____
_____
_____

*Date*_____

_____
_____
_____
_____
_____
_____
_____

196.1 Define conscious sexual expression and the qualities of its interaction and unconscious sexual expression and the qualities of its interaction.

*Date*_____

_____

_____

_____

_____

_____

_____

_____

*Date*_____

_____

_____

_____

_____

_____

_____

_____

*Date*_____

_____

_____

_____

_____

_____

_____

196.2 How does awakening our own experience of sexuality to that of the conscious mind serve the planet?

*Date*_____

_____

_____

_____

_____

_____

_____

*Date*_____

_____

_____

_____

_____

_____

_____

*Date*_____

_____

_____

_____

_____

_____

_____

196.3 What does imbalanced sexual desire do to the planet?

*Date*_____

_____
_____
_____
_____
_____
_____
_____

*Date*_____

_____
_____
_____
_____
_____
_____
_____

*Date*_____

_____
_____
_____
_____
_____
_____
_____

196.4 Do exercise recording sexual remarks, statements or images – timing how often they appear.

*Date*_____

_____

_____

_____

_____

_____

_____

_____

*Date*_____

_____

_____

_____

_____

_____

_____

_____

*Date*_____

_____

_____

_____

_____

_____

_____

_____

196.5 - 196-6 Define how sexual desire is not something that can be satisfied.

*Date*_____

_____
_____
_____
_____
_____
_____
_____

*Date*_____

_____
_____
_____
_____
_____
_____
_____

*Date*_____

_____
_____
_____
_____
_____
_____
_____

197.1 How is the unconscious mind preserving itself through sexual desire?

*Date*_____

_____

_____

_____

_____

_____

_____

_____

*Date*_____

_____

_____

_____

_____

_____

_____

_____

*Date*_____

_____

_____

_____

_____

_____

_____

_____

197.2 How does denial from the unconscious interpret the conscious mind as self-righteous?

*Date*_____

_____
_____
_____
_____
_____
_____
_____

*Date*_____

_____
_____
_____
_____
_____
_____
_____

*Date*_____

_____
_____
_____
_____
_____
_____
_____

197.3 How small is the world when living within the collective unconscious mind and why?

*Date*_____

_____
_____
_____
_____
_____
_____
_____

*Date*_____

_____
_____
_____
_____
_____
_____
_____

*Date*_____

_____
_____
_____
_____
_____
_____
_____

198.1 How is the collective unconscious mind inviting individuals in to self-loathing, and how can this be resolved through conscious perception?

*Date*_____

_____

_____

_____

_____

_____

_____

_____

*Date*_____

_____

_____

_____

_____

_____

_____

_____

*Date*_____

_____

_____

_____

_____

_____

_____

198.2 Define honoring oneself.

*Date*_____

_____

_____

_____

_____

_____

_____

_____

*Date*_____

_____

_____

_____

_____

_____

_____

_____

*Date*_____

_____

_____

_____

_____

_____

_____

_____

198.3 Define the feeling of self-love.

*Date*_____

_____

_____

_____

_____

_____

_____

_____

*Date*_____

_____

_____

_____

_____

_____

_____

*Date*_____

_____

_____

_____

_____

_____

_____

198.4 When have you felt disassociated from self-love and what was the inner dialogue at the time?

*Date*_____

_____

_____

_____

_____

_____

_____

_____

*Date*_____

_____

_____

_____

_____

_____

_____

_____

*Date*_____

_____

_____

_____

_____

_____

_____

_____

198.5 Negative Self talk does what to the planet?

*Date*_____

_____

_____

_____

_____

_____

_____

_____

*Date*_____

_____

_____

_____

_____

_____

_____

_____

*Date*_____

_____

_____

_____

_____

_____

_____

_____

198.6 Negative self talk does what to humanity?

*Date*_____

_____
_____
_____
_____
_____
_____
_____

*Date*_____

_____
_____
_____
_____
_____
_____
_____

*Date*_____

_____
_____
_____
_____
_____
_____
_____

199.1 Define falling in love with yourself through the experience of a Clear Mind.

*Date*_____

_____
_____
_____
_____
_____
_____
_____

*Date*_____

_____
_____
_____
_____
_____
_____

*Date*_____

_____
_____
_____
_____
_____
_____

199.2 Is it possible to embrace yourself intimately and experience deep and profound love and arousal?

*Date*_____

_____

_____

_____

_____

_____

_____

*Date*_____

_____

_____

_____

_____

_____

_____

*Date*_____

_____

_____

_____

_____

_____

_____

199.3 If self-love is an expression of unlimited love, is it true to say that sexually satisfying yourself could be as deeply nurturing and fulfilling as with another? Explain.

*Date*_____

_____
_____
_____
_____
_____
_____
_____

*Date*_____

_____
_____
_____
_____
_____
_____
_____

*Date*_____

_____
_____
_____
_____
_____
_____

200.1 Define sensuality of the conscious mind.

*Date*_____

_____

_____

_____

_____

_____

_____

*Date*_____

_____

_____

_____

_____

_____

_____

*Date*_____

_____

_____

_____

_____

_____

_____

200.2 How does self-love define union?

*Date*_____

_____

_____

_____

_____

_____

_____

_____

*Date*_____

_____

_____

_____

_____

_____

_____

_____

*Date*_____

_____

_____

_____

_____

_____

_____

_____

200.3 Define how sexuality moves in and out of itself.

*Date*_____

_____
_____
_____
_____
_____
_____
_____

*Date*_____

_____
_____
_____
_____
_____
_____
_____

*Date*_____

_____
_____
_____
_____
_____
_____
_____

200.4 What are the feelings of sexuality within a conscious perception?

*Date*_____

_____

_____

_____

_____

_____

_____

_____

*Date*_____

_____

_____

_____

_____

_____

_____

_____

*Date*_____

_____

_____

_____

_____

_____

_____

_____

200.5 Define the beauty of being a woman that is not defined by thoughts either personally or collectively but thought feelings and the beauty that feels to be sexuality.

*Date*_____

_____

_____

_____

_____

_____

_____

_____

*Date*_____

_____

_____

_____

_____

_____

_____

_____

*Date*_____

_____

_____

_____

_____

_____

_____

200.6 How is being a woman honored through self expression?

*Date*_____

_____

_____

_____

_____

_____

_____

_____

*Date*_____

_____

_____

_____

_____

_____

_____

_____

*Date*_____

_____

_____

_____

_____

_____

_____

_____

200.7 Feeling self-love within a conscious mind knows nothing of the unconscious – explain.

*Date*_____

_____

_____

_____

_____

_____

_____

_____

*Date*_____

_____

_____

_____

_____

_____

_____

_____

*Date*_____

_____

_____

_____

_____

_____

_____

_____

200.8 Define Touch.

*Date*_____

_____

_____

_____

_____

_____

_____

_____

*Date*_____

_____

_____

_____

_____

_____

_____

_____

*Date*_____

_____

_____

_____

_____

_____

_____

_____

200.9 How is intimacy an expression of oneself?

*Date*_____

_____
_____
_____
_____
_____
_____
_____

*Date*_____

_____
_____
_____
_____
_____
_____
_____

*Date*_____

_____
_____
_____
_____
_____
_____
_____

200.10 When one is living within the presence of love, how is the beauty of self-love discovered within ideas one has of oneself?

*Date*_____

_____

_____

_____

_____

_____

_____

_____

*Date*_____

_____

_____

_____

_____

_____

_____

_____

*Date*_____

_____

_____

_____

_____

_____

_____

In and out of Love

201.1 How has the unconscious mind interpreted love within your life?

*Date*_____

_____

_____

_____

_____

_____

_____

*Date*_____

_____

_____

_____

_____

_____

_____

*Date*_____

_____

_____

_____

_____

_____

_____

201.2 What does stillness feel like and how does it soothe the need to feel love?

*Date*_____

_____

_____

_____

_____

_____

_____

_____

*Date*_____

_____

_____

_____

_____

_____

_____

_____

*Date*_____

_____

_____

_____

_____

_____

_____

_____

201.3 Does love move towards us as well as within us? Please define.

*Date*_____

_____

_____

_____

_____

_____

_____

_____

*Date*_____

_____

_____

_____

_____

_____

_____

_____

*Date*_____

_____

_____

_____

_____

_____

_____

_____

202.1 Can the beauty of living be defined within the awareness to love?

*Date*_____

_____

_____

_____

_____

_____

_____

_____

*Date*_____

_____

_____

_____

_____

_____

_____

_____

*Date*_____

_____

_____

_____

_____

_____

_____

_____

202.2 Is one able to live within the world while living within a way that preserves love, if so how?

*Date*_____

_____

_____

_____

_____

_____

_____

*Date*_____

_____

_____

_____

_____

_____

_____

*Date*_____

_____

_____

_____

_____

_____

_____

202.3 List seven ways the media would like you to change.

Date_____
1. _____
2. _____
3. _____
4. _____
5. _____
6. _____
7. _____

Date_____
1. _____
2. _____
3. _____
4. _____
5. _____
6. _____
7. _____

Date_____
1. _____
2. _____
3. _____
4. _____
5. _____
6. _____
7. _____

202.4 - 202.4i List seven ways love is able to redefine itself within the beauty of perception.

*Date*_____

_____

_____

_____

_____

_____

_____

*Date*_____

_____

_____

_____

_____

_____

_____

*Date*_____

_____

_____

_____

_____

_____

_____

203.1 What does it mean to feel self-love?

*Date*_____

_____

_____

_____

_____

_____

_____

_____

*Date*_____

_____

_____

_____

_____

_____

_____

_____

*Date*_____

_____

_____

_____

_____

_____

_____

_____

203.2 What does it mean to express self-love?

*Date*_____

_____

_____

_____

_____

_____

_____

_____

*Date*_____

_____

_____

_____

_____

_____

_____

_____

*Date*_____

_____

_____

_____

_____

_____

_____

_____

203.3 Do you think that self-love is a spontaneous expression?

*Date*_____

_____

_____

_____

_____

_____

_____

_____

*Date*_____

_____

_____

_____

_____

_____

_____

_____

*Date*_____

_____

_____

_____

_____

_____

_____

_____

204.1 How is humanity supporting love?

*Date*_____

_____

_____

_____

_____

_____

_____

*Date*_____

_____

_____

_____

_____

_____

_____

*Date*_____

_____

_____

_____

_____

_____

_____

204.2 List seven awakenings that can happen within humanity to inspire self-love.

*Date*_____

_____

_____

_____

_____

_____

_____

_____

*Date*_____

_____

_____

_____

_____

_____

_____

_____

*Date*_____

_____

_____

_____

_____

_____

_____

_____

204.3 Define self-love for an adolescent.

*Date*_____

_____

_____

_____

_____

_____

_____

*Date*_____

_____

_____

_____

_____

_____

_____

*Date*_____

_____

_____

_____

_____

_____

_____

205.1 In union with love and life, one can preserve simplicity and purity how?

*Date*_____

_____

_____

_____

_____

_____

_____

_____

*Date*_____

_____

_____

_____

_____

_____

_____

_____

*Date*_____

_____

_____

_____

_____

_____

_____

_____

205.2i – 205.2ii What is most exciting to you about how humanity can inspire self-love?

*Date*_____

_____

_____

_____

_____

_____

_____

_____

*Date*_____

_____

_____

_____

_____

_____

_____

_____

*Date*_____

_____

_____

_____

_____

_____

_____

_____

Dialogue

206.1 Define Self-Worth.

*Date*_____

_____

_____

_____

_____

_____

_____

_____

*Date*_____

_____

_____

_____

_____

_____

_____

_____

*Date*_____

_____

_____

_____

_____

_____

_____

206.2 What are you doing within each day to preserve interpretations of yourself?

*Date*_____

_____

_____

_____

_____

_____

_____

_____

*Date*_____

_____

_____

_____

_____

_____

_____

_____

*Date*_____

_____

_____

_____

_____

_____

_____

_____

206.3 Does what others think of you, that are judgments, mean anything to you and if so, do you feel that these judgments are or were previous or current perceptions of yourself?

*Date*_____

_____

_____

_____

_____

_____

_____

_____

*Date*_____

_____

_____

_____

_____

_____

_____

_____

*Date*_____

_____

_____

_____

_____

_____

_____

Self-Love expressed within a Conscious mind

207.1 Self-Love allows what?

*Date*_____

_____

_____

_____

_____

_____

_____

*Date*_____

_____

_____

_____

_____

_____

_____

*Date*_____

_____

_____

_____

_____

_____

207.2 Self-Love invites life to?

*Date*_____

_____
_____
_____
_____
_____
_____
_____

*Date*_____

_____
_____
_____
_____
_____
_____
_____

*Date*_____

_____
_____
_____
_____
_____
_____
_____

208.1 Self-Love speaks how?

*Date*_____

_____
_____
_____
_____
_____
_____
_____

*Date*_____

_____
_____
_____
_____
_____
_____
_____

*Date*_____

_____
_____
_____
_____
_____
_____
_____

208.2 Self-Love experiences life as?

*Date*_____

_____
_____
_____
_____
_____
_____
_____

*Date*_____

_____
_____
_____
_____
_____
_____
_____

*Date*_____

_____
_____
_____
_____
_____
_____

Self Love Denied within an Unconscious Mind

209.1 The unconscious mind perceives love as?

Date_____

_____

_____

_____

_____

_____

_____

_____

Date_____

_____

_____

_____

_____

_____

_____

_____

Date_____

_____

_____

_____

_____

_____

_____

209.2 The unconscious mind limits love by?

*Date*_____

_____
_____
_____
_____
_____
_____
_____

*Date*_____

_____
_____
_____
_____
_____
_____
_____

*Date*_____

_____
_____
_____
_____
_____
_____
_____

209.3 The unconscious mind confuses love by?

*Date*_____

_____

_____

_____

_____

_____

_____

*Date*_____

_____

_____

_____

_____

_____

_____

*Date*_____

_____

_____

_____

_____

_____

_____

209.4. The unconscious mind asks what?

*Date*_____

_____
_____
_____
_____
_____
_____
_____

*Date*_____

_____
_____
_____
_____
_____
_____

*Date*_____

_____
_____
_____
_____
_____
_____
_____

209.5 The unconscious mind defines others as?

*Date*_____

_____

_____

_____

_____

_____

_____

*Date*_____

_____

_____

_____

_____

_____

_____

*Date*_____

_____

_____

_____

_____

_____

_____

209.6 The unconscious mind limits others' kindness by?

*Date*_____

_____
_____
_____
_____
_____
_____
_____

*Date*_____

_____
_____
_____
_____
_____
_____
_____

*Date*_____

_____
_____
_____
_____
_____
_____
_____

209.7 The unconscious mind fears love because?

*Date*_____

_____
_____
_____
_____
_____
_____
_____

*Date*_____

_____
_____
_____
_____
_____
_____
_____

*Date*_____

_____
_____
_____
_____
_____
_____
_____

209.8 The unconscious mind lives a separation to love how?

Date_____

_____
_____
_____
_____
_____
_____
_____

Date_____

_____
_____
_____
_____
_____
_____
_____

Date_____

_____
_____
_____
_____
_____
_____
_____

209.9 The unconscious operates today in...

*Date*_____

_____

_____

_____

_____

_____

_____

_____

*Date*_____

_____

_____

_____

_____

_____

_____

_____

*Date*_____

_____

_____

_____

_____

_____

_____

_____

Honoring Life as Love

210.1 - 210.1i Self-Love celebrates life as...

*Date*_____

_____
_____
_____
_____
_____
_____
_____

*Date*_____

_____
_____
_____
_____
_____
_____
_____

*Date*_____

_____
_____
_____
_____
_____
_____

210.2 Self-Love celebrates others how?

*Date*_____

_____
_____
_____
_____
_____
_____
_____

*Date*_____

_____
_____
_____
_____
_____
_____
_____

*Date*_____

_____
_____
_____
_____
_____
_____
_____

210.3 Self-Love celebrates wisdom by?

*Date*_____

_____

_____

_____

_____

_____

_____

_____

*Date*_____

_____

_____

_____

_____

_____

_____

_____

*Date*_____

_____

_____

_____

_____

_____

_____

_____

210.4 Self Love celebrates breath as?

*Date*_____

_____
_____
_____
_____
_____
_____

*Date*_____

_____
_____
_____
_____
_____
_____

*Date*_____

_____
_____
_____
_____
_____
_____

210.5 Self-Love is the expression of timelessness in what form?

*Date*_____

_____
_____
_____
_____
_____
_____
_____

*Date*_____

_____
_____
_____
_____
_____
_____
_____

*Date*_____

_____
_____
_____
_____
_____
_____
_____

Chapter Seven

Living Love

211.1 Awakening the conscious mind allows life to form a structure to support the presence of love – how has a structure begun to support you and the realizations of love that you are experiencing?

*Date*_____

_____

_____

_____

_____

_____

_____

_____

_____

_____

_____

_____

_____

_____

*Date*_____

_____
_____
_____
_____
_____
_____
_____
_____
_____
_____
_____
_____

*Date*_____

_____
_____
_____
_____
_____
_____
_____
_____
_____
_____
_____
_____
_____

211.2 How would you like a supportive structure to feel?

*Date*_____

_____

_____

_____

_____

_____

_____

_____

*Date*_____

_____

_____

_____

_____

_____

_____

_____

*Date*_____

_____

_____

_____

_____

_____

_____

_____

212.1 How does momentum increase within a structure that supports the presence of love?

*Date*_____

_____

_____

_____

_____

_____

_____

_____

*Date*_____

_____

_____

_____

_____

_____

_____

_____

*Date*_____

_____

_____

_____

_____

_____

_____

_____

212.2 How is your home a structure that allows and circulates the presence of love?

*Date*_____

_____
_____
_____
_____
_____
_____
_____

*Date*_____

_____
_____
_____
_____
_____
_____
_____

*Date*_____

_____
_____
_____
_____
_____
_____
_____

212.3 Where are you most nurtured to express the presence of love?

*Date*_____

_____

_____

_____

_____

_____

_____

_____

*Date*_____

_____

_____

_____

_____

_____

_____

_____

*Date*_____

_____

_____

_____

_____

_____

_____

_____

Education & Development

213.1 How is education a primary caregiver of children?

*Date*_____

_____

_____

_____

_____

_____

_____

_____

*Date*_____

_____

_____

_____

_____

_____

_____

_____

*Date*_____

_____

_____

_____

_____

_____

_____

213.2 What is the role of the education facility in defining relationship to the unconscious mind as well as content?

*Date*_____

_____
_____
_____
_____
_____
_____
_____

*Date*_____

_____
_____
_____
_____
_____
_____
_____

*Date*_____

_____
_____
_____
_____
_____
_____
_____

213.3 Define 3 important transitions within your childhood.

*Date*_____

1._____

_____

2._____

_____

3._____

_____

_____

*Date*_____

1._____

_____

2._____

_____

3._____

_____

_____

*Date*_____

1._____

_____

2._____

_____

3._____

_____

_____

213.4 It is within the environment of education that a child will develop the unconscious mind in part during the first seven years of life. This is an important time within the child's development to maintain that inter- pretations that are being expressed towards the child emotionally and socially are that of an alignment to the integrity that preserves the presence of love.

214.1 Due to the fact that education is primarily based on measurement of performance whether intellectually, socially, or physically, most of the child's development at school is through the unconscious mind. The con- scious mind is not able to measure performance as it is based on the spontaneous movement of expression within each moment. Having a child educated within an environment that does not measure performance within the mind of achievement has to have balance. There has to be the recognition of performance without the measurement that supersedes the capacity of the child within that moment. It is the negative interpretations that are placed on the child during the measurement process that empowers the negative self-talk because the child will digest the comments as an indication of lack. The collective consciousness of the interpretation will then be placed within the environment of the child, and the parents and the children will begin the journey of reinforcing what the measurement of their perform- ance has engaged within the interpretations of the child.

214.2 How do you feel free from measurement of success?

*Date*_____

_____

_____

_____

_____

_____

_____

_____

*Date*_____

_____

_____

_____

_____

_____

_____

_____

*Date*_____

_____

_____

_____

_____

_____

_____

_____

214.3 How does the conscious mind comfort the child?

*Date*_____

_____

_____

_____

_____

_____

_____

_____

*Date*_____

_____

_____

_____

_____

_____

_____

_____

*Date*_____

_____

_____

_____

_____

_____

_____

_____

214.4 Within the standard education model, the child-mind is taught to follow a system rather than intuition. They are governed by rules rather than insight and wisdom, and spontaneous expressions of wisdom are denied within this system. This is teaching the child-mind to disengage from the source of wisdom within the brain and to perceive what is outside of the child as more important than what is being presented within.

214.5 As education begins to change, as it rises in frequency, you will find classrooms that host stillness and silence to promote deeper intuitive connections. Decisions from children will not be promoted to be made by fear of rejection, shame, or humiliation of classmates and peers because as the consciousness of the planet increases, there will be structures in place that prevent this from happening.

215.1 How do children affect one another and how can society teach self-appreciation?

*Date*_____

_____
_____
_____
_____
_____
_____
_____

*Date*_____

_____
_____
_____
_____
_____
_____
_____

*Date*_____

_____
_____
_____
_____
_____
_____
_____

215.2 Explain to a child your perception of self-esteem.

*Date*_____

_____

_____

_____

_____

_____

_____

_____

*Date*_____

_____

_____

_____

_____

_____

_____

_____

*Date*_____

_____

_____

_____

_____

_____

_____

_____

215.3 Invite a child into the awareness of protecting their minds as being a source of goodness and innovation – explain in a paragraph.

*Date*_____

_____
_____
_____
_____
_____
_____
_____

*Date*_____

_____
_____
_____
_____
_____
_____
_____

*Date*_____

_____
_____
_____
_____
_____
_____

215.4 As a parent or a caregiver of a child, it can be overwhelming to maintain consistent awareness to love within the heart of that child. And as a caregiver, due to the nature and condition of the planet that consciousness is moving quickly, and there are great pockets of unconscious energy present which lure the child and the intrigue and the self-development aspects of the child-mind into it. As a parent and caregiver, one can just simply reach forward and move the child back into conscious perception, or an unconscious parent will walk the child into this unconsciousness.

It is important that the unconscious mind be dissolved so one's capacity as a parent or caregiver is restored in which to support a child within the conscious mind. When one is living within the conscious mind, there is no effort to support a child in this manner. It is simply the expression of one's BEINGness.

216.1 It is the public school system that is primarily supporting the unconscious expression because of the chaos and mayhem of the emotional structures of parents and children within the environment as well as educators. The education system will change and become a highly evolved education system on the planet that does exist within some parts of the human globe at this time. However, these highly evolved education models are rarely accessible to mainstream. It will be upon clearing of the collective unconscious and unconscious minds of individuals that these systems will become more available because individuals will not be seeking to support the unconscious mind and, therefore, these systems will collapse.

Parenting

217.1 Why is parenting within a conscious mind expressed within unconditional love and courage?

*Date*_____

_____
_____
_____
_____
_____
_____

*Date*_____

_____
_____
_____
_____
_____
_____

*Date*_____

_____
_____
_____
_____
_____
_____

217.2 Does parenting move within greater consistency within a conscious mind and why is this so?

_Date_____

_____

_____

_____

_____

_____

_____

_Date_____

_____

_____

_____

_____

_____

_____

_Date_____

_____

_____

_____

_____

_____

_____

217.3 Who do children become and why are they vital and why is the development of the conscious mind so important?

*Date*_____

_____
_____
_____
_____
_____
_____
_____

*Date*_____

_____
_____
_____
_____
_____
_____
_____

*Date*_____

_____
_____
_____
_____
_____
_____
_____

217.4 A discipline of a parent or a primary caregiver that is dissolving the unconscious mind is that they are continuously reinforcing the beauty of the child-mind within themselves and the child. Through lifestyle and structure of the living environment and education system within the child's life there needs to be the simplicity of self-expression of the child-mind and an environment that allows a spontaneous flow of wisdom that will flow within the child-mind into life that will be the action of preserving the beauty of love.

217.5 Define mindfulness.

*Date*_____

_____

_____

_____

_____

*Date*_____

_____

_____

_____

_____

*Date*_____

_____

_____

_____

_____

_____

218.1 The Clear Mind Experience provides an opportunity for a child to be taught to witness another's separation from love emotionally and verbally. It is in being the witness to these conditions that the child will not be absorbing the separation from love through the fear to conform and agree with the statements that are made and experienced around them from the adults, primary caregivers, educators, and peers within their lives.

218.2 How can children pioneer the pathway for humanity when living within the conscious mind?

*Date*_____

_____

_____

_____

_____

_____

_____

_____

*Date*_____

_____

_____

_____

_____

_____

_____

_____

*Date*_____

_____

_____

_____

_____

_____

_____

_____

218.3 How are children supported to allow intuition to breathe within their day to day?

*Date*_____

_____
_____
_____
_____
_____
_____
_____

*Date*_____

_____
_____
_____
_____
_____
_____
_____

*Date*_____

_____
_____
_____
_____
_____
_____
_____

219.1 What is the primary benefit for children in dissolving our own personal unconscious minds?

*Date*_____

_____

_____

_____

_____

_____

_____

_____

*Date*_____

_____

_____

_____

_____

_____

_____

_____

*Date*_____

_____

_____

_____

_____

_____

_____

_____

219.2 What is the primary benefit for children when the collective unconscious begins to drop away?

*Date*_____

_____
_____
_____
_____
_____
_____
_____

*Date*_____

_____
_____
_____
_____
_____
_____
_____

*Date*_____

_____
_____
_____
_____
_____
_____
_____

220.1 Within living within a Clear Mind, one is able to pro-vide children with all that is needed within the structure from the classroom to the living room that enables them to live within the presentation and consistent flow and safety of a conscious mind. It is our contribution as adults within humanity that we are able to clear the minds of the personal perception of the personal unconscious that en-ables life to operate this way within a spontaneous flow and presentation of the conscious mind.

220.2 Define how the conscious mind would embrace the mind of a child through language for a positive self-esteem?

*Date*_____

_____

_____

_____

_____

*Date*_____

_____

_____

_____

_____

*Date*_____

_____

_____

_____

_____

_____

221.1 - 221.1i There is no perfection in assisting children within a conscious mind. The conscious mind has the capacity within it to nurture, to educate, to provide spontaneous wisdom and love to the minds, bodies, and emotions of a child. It is within living within a conscious mind where the personal unconscious has been dissolved that an individual will be in a spontaneous expression of love within the lives of children within their lives.

221.2 Think of how you relate to children, this is yourself – what nurtures you most about communicating with them?

*Date*_____

_____

_____

_____

_____

_____

_____

_____

*Date*_____

_____

_____

_____

_____

_____

_____

_____

*Date*_____

_____

_____

_____

_____

_____

_____

_____

221.3 How does the child-mind define itself when you are with children through play?

*Date*_____

_____
_____
_____
_____
_____
_____
_____

*Date*_____

_____
_____
_____
_____
_____
_____
_____

*Date*_____

_____
_____
_____
_____
_____
_____
_____

221.4 - 221.4i How is the child-mind operating and expressing itself within your life?

*Date*_____

_____

_____

_____

_____

_____

_____

_____

*Date*_____

_____

_____

_____

_____

_____

_____

_____

*Date*_____

_____

_____

_____

_____

_____

_____

_____

221.5 It is within creating a structure that supports and honors the presence of love within the perception of a child that we create a means in which we are able to preserve the presence of love within ourselves because the structure will enable us to be mindful of the conscious mind and how the conscious mind is interacting within the day to day and creating from the perception and magnificence of wisdom.

222.1 How do you perceive the union of one mind when interpreted as the child-mind and adult mind – define the beauty and essence of this union?

*Date*_____

_____

_____

_____

_____

_____

_____

_____

*Date*_____

_____

_____

_____

_____

_____

_____

_____

*Date*_____

_____

_____

_____

_____

_____

_____

222.2 It is within serving the children through the structure of the conscious mind that is developed from an evolved perception that we allow healing and we access aspects of our own personal child-mind that allows profound revelation, and allows adults to live within the creation of simplicity. We are within creating a structure, in which we operate within our own lives to honor and engage within the presence of the child-mind. The beauty of a child is that they are engaging us within the child-mind perception through their need to be cared for from the aspect of simplicity that exists within the child-mind. It is within clearing our own perception of the unconscious that the child-mind within the personal perception of the adult is able to embrace the child-mind or the true child.

Career

223.1 How is humanity allowing innovation to define a conscious mind?

*Date*_____

_____
_____
_____
_____
_____
_____

*Date*_____

_____
_____
_____
_____
_____
_____

*Date*_____

_____
_____
_____
_____
_____
_____

223.2 Write 5 ways that you see innovation within your day to day.

*Date*_____

_____

_____

_____

_____

_____

_____

_____

*Date*_____

_____

_____

_____

_____

_____

_____

_____

*Date*_____

_____

_____

_____

_____

_____

_____

_____

223.3 What new passions and expressions are awakening within a conscious mind?

*Date*_____

_____

_____

_____

_____

_____

_____

_____

*Date*_____

_____

_____

_____

_____

_____

_____

_____

*Date*_____

_____

_____

_____

_____

_____

_____

_____

223.4 The unconscious mind is always dissatisfied. It is always looking for ways in which to define its own misery, and it is continually speaking about its limitations and miseries and frustrations. It is more than likely that once an individual clears the unconscious and the unconscious mind is not able to perceive reality as the being that the career of the individual will change in the essence that they may not leave or change their position. They may change their perception in which they are engaged within the position, and what was once uncomfortable may actually turn out to be inspiring and may hold space within the conscious mind.

223.5 Living within the beauty of each moment allows what?

*Date*_____

_____

_____

_____

_____

_____

_____

*Date*_____

_____

_____

_____

_____

_____

_____

*Date*_____

_____

_____

_____

_____

_____

_____

224.1 It is within living within a conscious mind once an individual has dissolved the unconscious that new energy may move into their work environment and begin to redefine their inner perception and relationship to their career.

224.2 Define a moment where unconscious expression has been dissolved through creative, innovative, or peaceful interaction from the conscious mind.

*Date*_____

_____

_____

_____

_____

_____

*Date*_____

_____

_____

_____

_____

_____

*Date*_____

_____

_____

_____

_____

_____

224.3 How do you perceive unlimitedness?

*Date*_____

_____
_____
_____
_____
_____
_____
_____

*Date*_____

_____
_____
_____
_____
_____
_____
_____

*Date*_____

_____
_____
_____
_____
_____
_____
_____

224.4 Beauty and rhythm is birthed within a conscious mind within the knowingness of love – how?

*Date*_____

_____

_____

_____

_____

_____

_____

_____

*Date*_____

_____

_____

_____

_____

_____

_____

*Date*_____

_____

_____

_____

_____

_____

_____

224.5 How do others honor your career?

*Date*_____

_____

_____

_____

_____

_____

_____

_____

*Date*_____

_____

_____

_____

_____

_____

_____

_____

*Date*_____

_____

_____

_____

_____

_____

_____

_____

224.6 Once an individual begins dissolving the unconscious mind, it is more than likely that where they once felt frustrated, they would be interpreting a level of freedom from the conscious perception. Where one felt misunderstood, the conscious mind would enable the individual to feel embraced. Where one was questioning of one's abilities, the individual would be awakened to innovation and new productivity.

225.1 – 225.1i How is the conscious mind unlimited?

*Date*_____

_____

_____

_____

_____

_____

*Date*_____

_____

_____

_____

_____

_____

*Date*_____

_____

_____

_____

_____

_____

225.2 How does a conscious mind create and awaken opportunity?

*Date*_____

_____

_____

_____

_____

_____

_____

_____

*Date*_____

_____

_____

_____

_____

_____

_____

_____

*Date*_____

_____

_____

_____

_____

_____

_____

_____

225.3 Do ideas, innovation, and expression simply move through the conscious mind?

*Date*_____

_____

_____

_____

_____

_____

_____

*Date*_____

_____

_____

_____

_____

_____

_____

*Date*_____

_____

_____

_____

_____

_____

_____

225.4 The conscious mind will celebrate life how?

*Date*_____

_____

_____

_____

_____

_____

_____

_____

*Date*_____

_____

_____

_____

_____

_____

_____

_____

*Date*_____

_____

_____

_____

_____

_____

_____

_____

225.5 Can the conscious mind measure gain?

*Date*_____

_____

_____

_____

_____

_____

_____

_____

*Date*_____

_____

_____

_____

_____

_____

_____

_____

*Date*_____

_____

_____

_____

_____

_____

_____

_____

225.6 Does the conscious mind ebb and flow within creation, allowing and drawing life into itself to define each moment and, if so, how is this happening within your life?

*Date*_____

_____

_____

_____

_____

_____

_____

_____

*Date*_____

_____

_____

_____

_____

_____

_____

_____

*Date*_____

_____

_____

_____

_____

_____

_____

225.7 Define how the conscious mind moves to expand itself and what this means to life.

*Date*_____

_____

_____

_____

_____

_____

_____

_____

*Date*_____

_____

_____

_____

_____

_____

_____

*Date*_____

_____

_____

_____

_____

_____

_____

225.8 How does the conscious mind serve within a perception of freedom, a career that moves to expand itself throughout life?

*Date*_____

_____

_____

_____

_____

_____

_____

_____

*Date*_____

_____

_____

_____

_____

_____

_____

_____

*Date*_____

_____

_____

_____

_____

_____

_____

226.1 When one is changing from the unconscious to the conscious perception within one's career, it can take either small adjustments or sometimes major adjustments. It is depending upon if the environment is going to allow the individual to create new perception. If the nature and the spirit of the company is that of an unconscious perception, an individual may not be able to live within the environment of the career if it is not able to preserve love and life. Whereas if an individual is working within an environment that is simply saturated within unconscious personal perceptions of individuals, they will be able to live within that environment because the conscious mind does not have the capacity to judge an environment. It is only able to witness and interject as love.

226.2 When the conscious mind is allowing movement in our career, what does this mean?

*Date*_____

_____
_____
_____
_____
_____
_____
_____

*Date*_____

_____
_____
_____
_____
_____
_____
_____

*Date*_____

_____
_____
_____
_____
_____
_____
_____

226.3 What comes when we allow the universe to move life towards us and into our expression?

*Date*_____

_____
_____
_____
_____
_____
_____
_____

*Date*_____

_____
_____
_____
_____
_____
_____
_____

*Date*_____

_____
_____
_____
_____
_____
_____
_____

226.4 What is birthed within the presence and energy of a conscious career?

*Date*_____

_____
_____
_____
_____
_____
_____
_____

*Date*_____

_____
_____
_____
_____
_____
_____
_____

*Date*_____

_____
_____
_____
_____
_____
_____
_____

227.1 What is celebrated within your career when your choices and interactions are conscious?

*Date*_____

_____

_____

_____

_____

_____

_____

_____

*Date*_____

_____

_____

_____

_____

_____

_____

_____

*Date*_____

_____

_____

_____

_____

_____

_____

_____

227.2 When one is moving into the conscious mind, within each moment of the day is the opportunity that the 49 positive feelings will be interpreting themselves within the career. The 49 positive feelings are what will redefine one's career and how one represents the career, engages, and services one's career. Because the conscious mind is simply an expression of movement where the 49 feelings are spontaneously moving in and out of an experience to define the experience with no agenda to maintain, withdraw, or control the environment or experience, one will experience tremendous freedom in one's expression of their career.

227.3 When self-love is defined within our career what is our primary feeling?

*Date*_____

_____
_____
_____
_____
_____
_____
_____

*Date*_____

_____
_____
_____
_____
_____
_____
_____

*Date*_____

_____
_____
_____
_____
_____
_____
_____

228.1 Define how a career can be perceived as a gift within the conscious mind.

*Date*_____

_____
_____
_____
_____
_____
_____
_____

*Date*_____

_____
_____
_____
_____
_____
_____
_____

*Date*_____

_____
_____
_____
_____
_____
_____
_____

228.2 If one allows trust, can the universe help define life around that trust?

*Date*_____

_____

_____

_____

_____

_____

_____

_____

*Date*_____

_____

_____

_____

_____

_____

_____

_____

*Date*_____

_____

_____

_____

_____

_____

_____

_____

228.3 When one is engaged within the 49 positive feelings, there will not be a sense to push oneself within the world but to allow the world to be drawn into oneself.

228.4 When are the times that you feel most supported within your career?

*Date*_____

_____

_____

_____

_____

_____

_____

*Date*_____

_____

_____

_____

_____

_____

_____

*Date*_____

_____

_____

_____

_____

_____

_____

228.5 When one dissolves the unconscious mind, the most profound gift that is given for one's career is the essence of trust. It is trust that allows one to remain still to draw one's career, success, and abundance through one's life and not attempt to create one's career, success, and abundance within one's life.

228.6 When moments of the unconscious mind are witnessed within your career, how does this feel?

*Date*_____

_____

_____

_____

_____

_____

*Date*_____

_____

_____

_____

_____

_____

*Date*_____

_____

_____

_____

_____

_____

228.7 Can moving within new interpretations of a conscious mind enliven a career and, if so, how?

*Date*_____

_____
_____
_____
_____
_____
_____
_____

*Date*_____

_____
_____
_____
_____
_____
_____
_____

*Date*_____

_____
_____
_____
_____
_____
_____
_____

228.8 How does clarity of the conscious mind assist within your career and what does it bring to life?

*Date*_____

_____

_____

_____

_____

_____

_____

_____

*Date*_____

_____

_____

_____

_____

_____

_____

_____

*Date*_____

_____

_____

_____

_____

_____

_____

_____

Abundance & Joy

229.1 – 229.2 It has been the collective of this planet that an individual was able to create wealth, abundance, and success through the unconscious mind because the unconscious mind is addicted to these perceptions. The unconscious mind has been able to, upon this planet, create large vibrations of greed upon the earth. However, the unconscious mind creates greed in which to lose. The unconscious mind creates wealth to create the fear that one will remain within their life in fear and control of the fact of if they lost the wealth. The unconscious mind when an individual is not free living within a conscious mind will perceive success, stature, and abundance as what has enslaved them to serve it. One is able to clear the unconscious mind successfully and maintain their success and abundance. However, they will maintain it and not be enslaved to it.

229.3 How does consciousness celebrate the momentum of abundance?

*Date*_____

_____

_____

_____

_____

_____

_____

_____

*Date*_____

_____

_____

_____

_____

_____

_____

_____

*Date*_____

_____

_____

_____

_____

_____

_____

_____

229.4 How do you see the collective unconscious mind protecting wealth through fear, and what is it protecting?

*Date*_____

_____

_____

_____

_____

_____

_____

_____

*Date*_____

_____

_____

_____

_____

_____

_____

_____

*Date*_____

_____

_____

_____

_____

_____

_____

_____

229.5 Abundance is a rainbow of light that moves within us through the beauty of celebration – how does that make you feel and within that feeling define abundance.

*Date*_____

_____

_____

_____

_____

_____

_____

_____

*Date*_____

_____

_____

_____

_____

_____

_____

*Date*_____

_____

_____

_____

_____

_____

_____

229.6 When one is living within the conscious mind, abundance is an energetic field that moves towards us. It connects to us, moves through us to define itself within us through our awareness to joy. Abundance does not come from within us. It comes through us. It is a gift of being incarnated upon the planet, as abundance is a resource in which to take form. It is a means in which to provide energy into form and to create structure to preserve love. It is a stream of consciousness that moves as a rainbow of light upon the planet. It is within our joy that abundance moves within us and through us. It is within embracing wisdom and honoring all that has been given up through the unconscious that one is able to move abundance within their lives. If a light worker is struggling within abundance, it is because there is an interpretation within the unconscious mind that connecting to wisdom has been tiring. It is within the perception of exhaustion that the abundance stream will bounce off the field as that is the rejection of the unconscious mind. When one is moving into the conscious mind, it is important that the unconscious be completely dissolved for one to be able to fully embody all aspects of wholeness in awakening the conscious mind; abundance simply being one part of the whole.

230.1 Have you had a vision for your life and, if so, what is it?

*Date*_____

_____
_____
_____
_____
_____
_____
_____

*Date*_____

_____
_____
_____
_____
_____
_____
_____

*Date*_____

_____
_____
_____
_____
_____
_____
_____

230.2 Have there been times where you have felt that the universe and the law of attraction was not sharing your vision – at the time what was your language?

*Date*_____

_____

_____

_____

_____

_____

_____

_____

*Date*_____

_____

_____

_____

_____

_____

_____

*Date*_____

_____

_____

_____

_____

_____

_____

230.3 Do you believe that through exhaustion and the language of exhaustion you may have repelled abundance and, if so, what were the circumstances and how is it different today?

*Date*_____

_____

_____

_____

_____

_____

_____

_____

*Date*_____

_____

_____

_____

_____

_____

*Date*_____

_____

_____

_____

_____

_____

_____

230.4 At times we feel we are trying to get somewhere – why is this a limiting unconscious thought?

*Date*_____

_____
_____
_____
_____
_____
_____
_____

*Date*_____

_____
_____
_____
_____
_____
_____
_____

*Date*_____

_____
_____
_____
_____
_____
_____
_____

230.5 How is one able to innovate new direction – is it moving from within a conscious or unconscious mind?

*Date*_____

_____

_____

_____

_____

_____

_____

_____

*Date*_____

_____

_____

_____

_____

_____

_____

_____

*Date*_____

_____

_____

_____

_____

_____

_____

_____

230.6 Do you believe that throughout your life you have dismantled part of the unconscious mind and, if so, what are the repercussions that you have experienced before today because of this?

*Date*_____

_____

_____

_____

_____

_____

_____

_____

*Date*_____

_____

_____

_____

_____

_____

_____

*Date*_____

_____

_____

_____

_____

_____

_____

231.1 When have you felt most exhausted?

*Date*_____

_____

_____

_____

_____

_____

_____

_____

*Date*_____

_____

_____

_____

_____

_____

_____

_____

*Date*_____

_____

_____

_____

_____

_____

_____

_____

231.2 When you have been tired, what is the inner language at the time?

*Date*_____

_____

_____

_____

_____

_____

_____

_____

*Date*_____

_____

_____

_____

_____

_____

_____

_____

*Date*_____

_____

_____

_____

_____

_____

_____

_____

231.3 Why does receiving take no effort?

*Date*_____

_____

_____

_____

_____

_____

_____

_____

*Date*_____

_____

_____

_____

_____

_____

_____

_____

*Date*_____

_____

_____

_____

_____

_____

_____

_____

231.4 When is abundance able to flow through life?

*Date*_____

_____

_____

_____

_____

_____

_____

_____

*Date*_____

_____

_____

_____

_____

_____

_____

_____

*Date*_____

_____

_____

_____

_____

_____

_____

_____

231.5 – 231.6 How can life celebrate abundance when we are moving through the beauty of its expression within a conscious mind?

*Date*_____

_____
_____
_____
_____
_____
_____
_____

*Date*_____

_____
_____
_____
_____
_____
_____
_____

*Date*_____

_____
_____
_____
_____
_____
_____

232.1 It is within the statements that one is too tired to awaken and asking the question of when it is going to be over that abundance is repelled. One is too exhausted to allow the flow of abundance to move through one's field. The unconscious mind is speaking of itself in its exhaustion. It's talking about how tiring it is to let go. It's talking about how tiring it is to have been moved into a state where it is not able to function within its wholeness. It is talking about the fact that it is not operating within wholeness. It is within these moments that the individual is to remain within a still mind: 'IAM allowing of abundance. IAM allowing of life. IAM celebrating the joy of all knowing and all that IAM.' One remains still to allow consciousness to move within us that will reveal the beauty of prosperity.

232.2 When the unconscious mind is dissolved, it is not able to communicate because it has no function, structure, and is no longer in existence. When one is living within the conscious mind, one will speak as 'IAM' as the 'IAM' is the rational expression of life that moves through oneself as a vibration, knowing, expression of wisdom that is unlimited within its movement and description and knowingness of life within, upon, contained, in essence of the earth.

232.3 When abundance moves through us it speaks to us, it defines its relationship to us and celebrates within us the direction that it is flowing within our lives in which to celebrate life – what is abundance saying to you today?

*Date*_____

_____

_____

_____

_____

_____

_____

_____

*Date*_____

_____

_____

_____

_____

_____

_____

*Date*_____

_____

_____

_____

_____

_____

_____

Unconscious Abundance

233.1 - 233.3 Abundance upon this planet in an unconscious form has collapsed. It is dismantled, and slowly through dissolving one's unconscious, it is dissolving its remnants of existence. When the world financial markets collapsed, the unconscious mind was in its payoff. It showed humanity it owned nothing. It showed humanity it had nothing. It showed humanity it was worth nothing. It showed humanity that within one moment it would take all that one was addicted to within form. It is upon that day that light inherited the resources of the planet because upon that day the world looked at the unconscious mind and said, "I don't trust in your presence. I see the lie. I see the untruth, and I will walk within a direction to discover how to engage within reality, financially, that is not within an alignment to that untruth." It is important for humanity to have the realization of life free of the unconscious so that the financial collapse that has occurred on this planet is the only significant collapse that will occur to have one walk away from the shadow. Humanity, right now, is in a very viable and vulnerable state to be able to dissolve the unconscious because humanity has more or less let go of the unconscious through the shock and disbelief that it was what stole their wealth, their belief, and filled lies within their names to take them into the story of lack.

233.4 Abundance within a conscious mind needs to flow within conscious intent – define your intent for abundance within your life.

*Date*_____

_____

_____

_____

_____

_____

_____

_____

*Date*_____

_____

_____

_____

_____

_____

_____

*Date*_____

_____

_____

_____

_____

_____

_____

233.5 - 233.5i What can you celebrate within your journey to love that will allow you to receive and maintain a constant stream of abundance?

*Date*_____

_____

_____

_____

_____

_____

_____

_____

*Date*_____

_____

_____

_____

_____

_____

_____

*Date*_____

_____

_____

_____

_____

_____

_____

233.6 What does abundance gift the earth and humanity?

*Date*_____

_____

_____

_____

_____

_____

_____

_____

*Date*_____

_____

_____

_____

_____

_____

_____

_____

*Date*_____

_____

_____

_____

_____

_____

_____

_____

233.7 When abundance is defined by the conscious mind – how will it be perceived?

*Date*_____

_____
_____
_____
_____
_____
_____
_____

*Date*_____

_____
_____
_____
_____
_____
_____
_____

*Date*_____

_____
_____
_____
_____
_____
_____
_____

233.8 Is stillness an aspect within the movement of abundance and, if so, define.

*Date*_____

_____

_____

_____

_____

_____

_____

_____

*Date*_____

_____

_____

_____

_____

_____

_____

_____

*Date*_____

_____

_____

_____

_____

_____

_____

_____

Nutrition

234.1 How has nutrition become a spontaneous expression and movement of life?

*Date*_____

_____

_____

_____

_____

_____

_____

*Date*_____

_____

_____

_____

_____

_____

*Date*_____

_____

_____

_____

_____

_____

234.2 How would you define a celebration through food?

*Date*_____

_____
_____
_____
_____
_____
_____
_____

*Date*_____

_____
_____
_____
_____
_____
_____

*Date*_____

_____
_____
_____
_____
_____
_____

234.3 If we celebrate living through conscious expressions of food what are we gifting others within our lives as well as ourselves?

Date_____

_____

_____

_____

_____

_____

_____

_____

Date_____

_____

_____

_____

_____

_____

_____

Date_____

_____

_____

_____

_____

_____

_____

235.1 Where does food come from? What is its primary source?

*Date*_____

_____

_____

_____

_____

_____

_____

_____

*Date*_____

_____

_____

_____

_____

_____

_____

_____

*Date*_____

_____

_____

_____

_____

_____

_____

_____

235.2 Do we get closer to the primary source of conscious food when we eat it?

*Date*_____

_____

_____

_____

_____

_____

_____

_____

*Date*_____

_____

_____

_____

_____

_____

_____

_____

*Date*_____

_____

_____

_____

_____

_____

_____

_____

235.3 Within living within a conscious mind, the earth is expressing many aspects of beauty within our lives. How is nature a vital part of our nutrition?

*Date*_____

_____

_____

_____

_____

_____

_____

_____

*Date*_____

_____

_____

_____

_____

_____

_____

_____

*Date*_____

_____

_____

_____

_____

_____

_____

235.4 When the earth speaks through food as it grows in her soil, what do you think that she says?

*Date*_____

_____

_____

_____

_____

_____

_____

_____

*Date*_____

_____

_____

_____

_____

_____

_____

*Date*_____

_____

_____

_____

_____

_____

_____

235.5 When the earth allows the beauty of growth to expand within her, what does that feel like?

*Date*_____

_____

_____

_____

_____

_____

_____

*Date*_____

_____

_____

_____

_____

_____

_____

*Date*_____

_____

_____

_____

_____

_____

_____

235.6 What would you like to say to the earth for the beauty of her resources, knowing that you are saying it all to yourself.

*Date*_____

_____

_____

_____

_____

_____

_____

_____

*Date*_____

_____

_____

_____

_____

_____

_____

*Date*_____

_____

_____

_____

_____

_____

_____

235.7 The conscious mind will engage within the ritual of eating as an expression of simplicity. The conscious mind will choose food by color before taste. It will eat from sources that contain high frequency, clear energy that is not densified within the thoughts of those that have produced and the intent of those that have produced.

235.8 Define an experience where you know that the thoughts of others have been in your food.

*Date*_____

_____

_____

_____

_____

_____

*Date*_____

_____

_____

_____

_____

_____

*Date*_____

_____

_____

_____

_____

_____

236.1 Define how the conscious mind preserves life within nutrition and within this action has preserved love within.

*Date*_____

_____

_____

_____

_____

_____

_____

_____

*Date*_____

_____

_____

_____

_____

_____

_____

_____

*Date*_____

_____

_____

_____

_____

_____

_____

_____

236.2 Define packaged food.

*Date*_____

_____
_____
_____
_____
_____
_____
_____

*Date*_____

_____
_____
_____
_____
_____
_____
_____

*Date*_____

_____
_____
_____
_____
_____
_____
_____

236.3 Define living food and what the color of living food means.

*Date*_____

_____

_____

_____

_____

_____

_____

_____

*Date*_____

_____

_____

_____

_____

_____

_____

_____

*Date*_____

_____

_____

_____

_____

_____

_____

_____

236.4 – 236.5 It is the conscious mind that looks for the sharing principles because sharing is about expression, not the quantity principle which is about accumulation. The conscious mind will not move into accumulation because it will see it as a means in which to remain static. The conscious mind, therefore, looks for food within small packets; packets that serve the quantity that is required, food that is handpicked so there is very few to be had, very few pieces of the food to be maintained.

237.1 How does food ebb and flow within your life?

*Date*_____

_____

_____

_____

_____

_____

_____

_____

*Date*_____

_____

_____

_____

_____

_____

_____

_____

*Date*_____

_____

_____

_____

_____

_____

_____

_____

237.2 - 237.2i What does it or would it feel like to nurture the body?

*Date*_____

_____
_____
_____
_____
_____
_____
_____

*Date*_____

_____
_____
_____
_____
_____
_____
_____

*Date*_____

_____
_____
_____
_____
_____
_____
_____

237.3 - 237.5 When an individual is living within the conscious mind, nutrition is chosen based on one's emotions. When one is living within the conscious mind, one's emotions contain the frequencies of the 49 feelings. When one engages within nutrition as the food moves through, or the substance moves through form, it is the 49 feelings within the seven key emotions that interpret the relationship between the nutrition substance and the body. The conscious mind will choose food or nutrition based on what emotions are present within the moment, and the food and substance will honor the emotion by preserving love and life within the emotion. Nutrition within a conscious mind is beyond taste. It is about the experience, and when the alchemy of the food and the body merge within the perception of the conscious mind, the feelings that move through the alchemy is the magnificence of oneness within conscious awareness of form.

237.6 Define self-appreciation within nutrition.

*Date*_____

_____

_____

_____

_____

_____

_____

*Date*_____

_____

_____

_____

_____

_____

_____

*Date*_____

_____

_____

_____

_____

_____

_____

238.1 What emotions primarily come up for you when you eat?

*Date*_____

_____

_____

_____

_____

_____

_____

_____

*Date*_____

_____

_____

_____

_____

_____

_____

*Date*_____

_____

_____

_____

_____

_____

_____

238.2 Our emotions need to be aligned to that of love within a conscious mind, harmonized within the perception of love because our brains are programmed to choose nutrition based on emotion. If the unconscious mind is in control, then one will emotionally eat to create harm within one's body and to suppress the negative feelings of the unconscious mind. This is because the programming of the mind in choosing through perception, the engagement of food is programmed to be chosen to honor emotion within a conscious mind, suppress emotion within an unconscious mind.

238.3 When food is refined within its presentation to be fresh, how does that make you feel?

*Date*_____

_____

_____

_____

_____

*Date*_____

_____

_____

_____

_____

*Date*_____

_____

_____

_____

_____

238.4 Is it fair to say that we choose food based on our feelings?

*Date*_____

_____

_____

_____

_____

_____

_____

_____

*Date*_____

_____

_____

_____

_____

_____

_____

_____

*Date*_____

_____

_____

_____

_____

_____

_____

_____

238.5 Within humanity today, food is manipulated by the unconscious to keep humanity asleep. This is based on the greed principle. The unconscious mind is greedy. It wants to prove to humanity that the greed principle exists within the unconscious perception and force humanity to own that. Sugar, additives, coloring, sodium, fat, hormones, and overall poor manufacturing of food is created today to create a sleep state within the mind creating an energetic, static awareness within the brain so one does not choose to merge within the awakening of the conscious mind.

238.6 Do you think images that are expressed within the media around food create someone to disassociate from which foods are specifically speaking to us collectively?

*Date*_____

_____

_____

_____

_____

_____

_____

_____

*Date*_____

_____

_____

_____

_____

_____

_____

_____

*Date*_____

_____

_____

_____

_____

_____

_____

238.7 When do you feel most rushed to eat and what would you eat in a rush?

*Date*_____

_____

_____

_____

_____

_____

_____

_____

*Date*_____

_____

_____

_____

_____

_____

_____

_____

*Date*_____

_____

_____

_____

_____

_____

_____

_____

239.1 How has eating within a conscious mind altered your taste for food?

*Date*_____

_____
_____
_____
_____
_____
_____
_____

*Date*_____

_____
_____
_____
_____
_____
_____
_____

*Date*_____

_____
_____
_____
_____
_____
_____
_____

239.2 Choose a meal throughout today that you will write down the feelings that come up for you as you are eating. Write down the feelings.

*Date*_____

_____

_____

_____

_____

_____

_____

_____

*Date*_____

_____

_____

_____

_____

_____

_____

*Date*_____

_____

_____

_____

_____

_____

_____

239.3 Self-esteem is what?

*Date*_____

_____
_____
_____
_____
_____
_____
_____

*Date*_____

_____
_____
_____
_____
_____
_____
_____

*Date*_____

_____
_____
_____
_____
_____
_____
_____

239.4 When do you crave different foods, why do you sus-pect this happens and does the conscious mind crave food?

*Date*_____

_____
_____
_____
_____
_____
_____
_____

*Date*_____

_____
_____
_____
_____
_____
_____
_____

*Date*_____

_____
_____
_____
_____
_____
_____
_____

240.1 Taking wellness products is very supportive to the body when we are taking for supporting the goodness we already perceive. When you take your wellness products, what is your intent?

*Date*_____

_____

_____

_____

_____

_____

_____

_____

*Date*_____

_____

_____

_____

_____

_____

_____

*Date*_____

_____

_____

_____

_____

_____

_____

240.2 - 240.2i Define balance.

*Date*_____

_____
_____
_____
_____
_____
_____

*Date*_____

_____
_____
_____
_____
_____
_____

*Date*_____

_____
_____
_____
_____
_____
_____

241.3 Define where you are flexible within nutrition and self-care, so that both become a means to discover oneself and not control oneself.

*Date*_____

_____

_____

_____

_____

_____

_____

_____

*Date*_____

_____

_____

_____

_____

_____

_____

_____

*Date*_____

_____

_____

_____

_____

_____

_____

240.4 - 240.6 Within a conscious mind, there can be no judgment as to what is right and wrong. There are no positions to take. The ritual of self-care and nutrition, exist to preserve the presence of love within form. This may mean that if you are taking supplements, you may increase or decrease them. It may mean that you stop eating meat or incorporate a smaller amount. It may mean you will buy food within the day that you eat and not keep planned meals. This allows you the fluidity of being able to create within the moment and engage within wisdom within the moment and allow the emotional feelings of love to move through the merging of the nutritional substance and form. When choosing to engage within an experience of nutrition, one simply looks for the qualities, energetic flow, and intent of what one is about to consume.

240.7 What do you enjoy most about nutrition?

*Date*_____

_____
_____
_____
_____
_____
_____
_____

*Date*_____

_____
_____
_____
_____
_____
_____
_____

*Date*_____

_____
_____
_____
_____
_____
_____
_____

240.8 When you eat food that does not support freshness, what is the language of your craving?

*Date*_____

_____

_____

_____

_____

_____

_____

_____

*Date*_____

_____

_____

_____

_____

_____

_____

_____

*Date*_____

_____

_____

_____

_____

_____

_____

_____

241.1 The conscious mind will create a living structure to experience the presence of love. It will create a structure within one's life where it is able to ebb and flow within a presentation of itself through all various aspects of your life that are in relationship to form.

241.2 When do you witness miracles within your relationships?

*Date*_____

_____
_____
_____
_____
_____
_____

*Date*_____

_____
_____
_____
_____
_____
_____

*Date*_____

_____
_____
_____
_____
_____

241.3 - 241.3i Define how you feel nurtured within the home – which aspects of the home feel most enchanting and embracing to you?

*Date*_____

_____

_____

_____

_____

_____

_____

_____

*Date*_____

_____

_____

_____

_____

_____

_____

*Date*_____

_____

_____

_____

_____

_____

_____

241.4 When one is defining a structure in which to support the presence of love, one will review relationships within one's life to various aspects of life. When one is reviewing relationship, one is able to say, "Is the relationship defined by the conscious or unconscious mind?" If it is defined by the conscious mind, then the structure in your life will honor how love will be awakened. If it is a relationship of the unconscious mind, then one will perceive the suppression and rejection that the unconscious mind will project into the structure.

242.1 How is the living mind allowing and inviting conscious awareness to love within your home, career, and primary relationships?

*Date*_____

_____

_____

_____

_____

_____

_____

_____

*Date*_____

_____

_____

_____

_____

_____

_____

_____

*Date*_____

_____

_____

_____

_____

_____

_____

242.2 When do you feel inspired?

*Date*_____

_____
_____
_____
_____
_____
_____
_____

*Date*_____

_____
_____
_____
_____
_____
_____
_____

*Date*_____

_____
_____
_____
_____
_____
_____
_____

242.3 It is not about racing out and changing our lives once one begins to dissolve the unconscious. It's about allowing the stillness. The living mind is what perceives life, what creates structure for love to engage within reality, within life. The living mind will present conscious awareness and wisdom that will have you understand how to move beyond limitations, co-dependent ideas and relationships. It is a magnificent aspect of the mind as it is what gives structure. It is the house in which you live and reside within conscious awareness.

242.4 Within the living mind, life is honored in a way that has one feel supported – how is the living mind honoring your life and aligning experiences that have you feel supported?

*Date*_____

_____

_____

_____

_____

_____

_____

_____

*Date*_____

_____

_____

_____

_____

_____

_____

_____

*Date*_____

_____

_____

_____

_____

_____

_____

242.5 Define 7 ways that you effortlessly embrace others.

*Date*_____
1. _____
2. _____
3. _____
4. _____
5. _____
6. _____
7. _____

*Date*_____
1. _____
2. _____
3. _____
4. _____
5. _____
6. _____
7. _____

*Date*_____
1. _____
2. _____
3. _____
4. _____
5. _____
6. _____
7. _____

242.6 How does the conscious mind express harmony within union?

*Date*_____

_____

_____

_____

_____

_____

_____

_____

*Date*_____

_____

_____

_____

_____

_____

_____

*Date*_____

_____

_____

_____

_____

_____

_____

243.1 When one is experiencing unconscious thoughts, feelings, and emotions within the perception of the living mind, then the structure in which supports life will also be unconscious. The structure of one's life will support limitations. One will feel frustrated by failed expectations; experience a rejection, fear, aloneness, question their safety within life and their ability to make decisions, or one will be controlling of one's ability to make decisions. When one is supporting the unconscious mind within thoughts, feelings, and emotions within the living mind, then the feelings to support life will be that of the unconscious.

243.2 Can entitlement affect flow within one's life and, if so, how?

*Date*_____

_____
_____
_____
_____
_____
_____
_____

*Date*_____

_____
_____
_____
_____
_____
_____
_____

*Date*_____

_____
_____
_____
_____
_____
_____
_____

243.3 If you did not expect anything – what would happen?

*Date*_____

_____

_____

_____

_____

_____

_____

*Date*_____

_____

_____

_____

_____

_____

_____

*Date*_____

_____

_____

_____

_____

_____

_____

243.4 Where in humanity does unwelcomeness exist – if you were to speak out loud into the universe to counteract unwelcomeness what would you say?

*Date*_____

_____

_____

_____

_____

_____

_____

_____

*Date*_____

_____

_____

_____

_____

_____

_____

*Date*_____

_____

_____

_____

_____

_____

_____

243.5 How can we support union of one mind through relationships to others?

*Date*_____

_____

_____

_____

_____

_____

_____

_____

*Date*_____

_____

_____

_____

_____

_____

_____

_____

*Date*_____

_____

_____

_____

_____

_____

_____

_____

243.6 – 243.6i What is the most powerful aspect of vulnerability?

*Date*_____

_____

_____

_____

_____

_____

_____

_____

*Date*_____

_____

_____

_____

_____

_____

_____

_____

*Date*_____

_____

_____

_____

_____

_____

_____

_____

243.7 When one is within an unconscious relationship within the living mind, one will feel that life is lost within loneliness and distrust, and one may begin to pursue an inner plight to let go to the presence, and essence, and potential of love.

243.8 When you feel life being drawn towards and it is demonstrated through the expression of coincidence, how does it make you feel?

*Date*_____

_____

_____

_____

_____

_____

_____

_____

*Date*_____

_____

_____

_____

_____

_____

_____

*Date*_____

_____

_____

_____

_____

_____

_____

244.1 Define how the living mind perceives love.

*Date*_____

_____

_____

_____

_____

_____

_____

*Date*_____

_____

_____

_____

_____

_____

_____

*Date*_____

_____

_____

_____

_____

_____

_____

244.2 Where do you most enjoy creating within life?

*Date*_____

_____

_____

_____

_____

_____

_____

_____

*Date*_____

_____

_____

_____

_____

_____

_____

_____

*Date*_____

_____

_____

_____

_____

_____

_____

_____

244.3 It is within the living mind that all life is brought together. It is within the living mind that aspects of life that hold life together are expressed. The living mind is the structure that exists, that enables self love to express itself within the child-mind, within life. It is the alchemy of form and spirit.

244.4 Define potential and how you are supporting it today within conscious perception.

*Date*_____

_____

_____

_____

_____

_____

_____

*Date*_____

_____

_____

_____

_____

_____

_____

*Date*_____

_____

_____

_____

_____

_____

_____

244.5 When the conscious mind is free to function within life, it will bring forth within life many magnificent experiences, opportunities, and relationships that will honor the beauty of innovation, wisdom, and within this wisdom there will be vision within each moment and each expression as it merges in and out of the presence of love.

244.6 How do you express the living mind within your unique living expression - list five ways that represent your self-appreciation.

*Date*_____

_____
_____
_____
_____
_____
_____
_____

*Date*_____

_____
_____
_____
_____
_____
_____
_____

*Date*_____

_____
_____
_____
_____
_____
_____

Chapter Eight
Relationship to Others

245.1 - 245.3 It is within our relationship to ourselves that life awakens outer relationships. Within each relationship within life, we are within relationship to an aspect of how we perceive ourselves currently, or within the past or within vision of the future. It is within the perception of oneself that life is defined. The nature of relationships to others and with others is the definition of our relationship to oneself. The emotional payoff within each experience is what one is seeking to experience within hosting the relationship. When one dissolves the unconscious mind, many relationships change within definition and allow for new opportunity so wisdom and the presence of love are able to be preserved within the relationship.

245.4 How have you defined relationships as a foundation within your life, within the past and today?

*Date*_____

_____

_____

_____

_____

_____

_____

_____

*Date*_____

_____

_____

_____

_____

_____

_____

*Date*_____

_____

_____

_____

_____

_____

_____

246.1 Define your relationship to your parents and how you are experiencing freedom within the relationship today.

*Date*_____

_____
_____
_____
_____
_____
_____
_____

*Date*_____

_____
_____
_____
_____
_____
_____
_____

*Date*_____

_____
_____
_____
_____
_____
_____
_____

246.2 Define three of your most impactful relationships to date.

*Date*_____

1. _____

_____

2. _____

_____

3. _____

_____

_____

*Date*_____

1. _____

_____

2. _____

_____

3. _____

_____

_____

*Date*_____

1. _____

_____

2. _____

_____

3. _____

_____

_____

246.3 The number of relationships that are of the unconscious within our lives will be determined by the magnitude of its thoughts, feelings, and emotions, and how much of it is expressing and operating itself within our emotions through our five primary relationships. Not all relationships have to be of the unconscious mind unless all of one's perception is engaged within the unconscious mind. When one dissolves the unconscious, conscious relationships will begin to awaken and new life will begin to merge, new conscious expression within old relationships that were housing unconscious perceptions. Within life, within love, love moves to awaken itself within all. When an unconscious relationship exists within one's life, love will move within the experience to redefine itself as love.

246.4 Define how an unconscious relationship has felt in the past and how you have been able to redefine it through the conscious mind.

*Date*_____

_____

_____

_____

_____

_____

_____

_____

*Date*_____

_____

_____

_____

_____

_____

_____

*Date*_____

_____

_____

_____

_____

_____

247.1 How does the Clear Mind Experience define relationships?

*Date*_____

_____
_____
_____
_____
_____
_____
_____

*Date*_____

_____
_____
_____
_____
_____
_____
_____

*Date*_____

_____
_____
_____
_____
_____
_____
_____

248.1 Why is dissolving the unconscious mind so important to how we perceive relationships?

*Date*_____

_____
_____
_____
_____
_____
_____
_____

*Date*_____

_____
_____
_____
_____
_____
_____
_____

*Date*_____

_____
_____
_____
_____
_____
_____
_____

248.2 Define a relationship that connects you to inner awareness, what are the feelings that come from this relationship?

*Date*_____

_____

_____

_____

_____

_____

_____

_____

*Date*_____

_____

_____

_____

_____

_____

_____

_____

*Date*_____

_____

_____

_____

_____

_____

_____

_____

248.3 Are you nurtured by one primary relationship within your life and, if so, which one, and, if not, why?

*Date*_____

_____
_____
_____
_____
_____
_____
_____

*Date*_____

_____
_____
_____
_____
_____
_____
_____

*Date*_____

_____
_____
_____
_____
_____
_____
_____

249.1 When have you felt confused about relationships and how do you feel different today?

*Date*_____

_____

_____

_____

_____

_____

_____

_____

*Date*_____

_____

_____

_____

_____

_____

_____

_____

*Date*_____

_____

_____

_____

_____

_____

_____

_____

249.2 List 7 ways that you host relationship within your life – list experiences, individuals, visions and opportunities.

*Date*_____

1. _____
2. _____
3. _____
4. _____
5. _____
6. _____
7. _____

*Date*_____

1. _____
2. _____
3. _____
4. _____
5. _____
6. _____
7. _____

*Date*_____

1. _____
2. _____
3. _____
4. _____
5. _____
6. _____
7. _____

249.3 List three gifts of a conscious relationship to experiences and opportunities and how these are able to support spontaneous inner vision.

*Date*_____
1._____

_____

2._____

_____

3._____

_____

_____

*Date*_____
1._____

_____

2._____

_____

3._____

_____

_____

*Date*_____
1._____

_____

2._____

_____

3._____

_____

250.1 How does living within a conscious mind improve the qualities of our lives and those around us?

*Date*_____

_____

_____

_____

_____

_____

_____

_____

*Date*_____

_____

_____

_____

_____

_____

_____

_____

*Date*_____

_____

_____

_____

_____

_____

_____

_____

250.2 What are the most successful structures within your life, the structures that support conscious perception?

*Date*_____

_____

_____

_____

_____

_____

_____

_____

*Date*_____

_____

_____

_____

_____

_____

_____

_____

*Date*_____

_____

_____

_____

_____

_____

_____

_____

Parents or Primary Caregivers

251.1 Define your childhood and the language of the unconscious.

*Date*_____

_____

_____

_____

_____

_____

_____

*Date*_____

_____

_____

_____

_____

_____

*Date*_____

_____

_____

_____

_____

_____

251.2 Due to the overwhelming unconscious presentation within earth at this time and that it is mainly geared towards children from age five to seventeen, it is difficult to create a conscious structure within the life of a child as a parent or primary caregiver. This is because the collective unconscious mind has a basis, theme, and momentum is supporting the 49 negative feelings that express negativity and unconscious thought and a language that does not preserve the presence of love within the environment.

251.3 Is there co-dependency in negativity and why is this? Is this a quality in which the unconscious mind can preserve itself?

*Date*_____

_____

_____

_____

_____

_____

_____

_____

*Date*_____

_____

_____

_____

_____

_____

_____

_____

*Date*_____

_____

_____

_____

_____

_____

_____

251.4 It is when the parents of primary caregivers or children begin to dissolve the unconscious mind that the conscious and unconscious conflict will surface within the primary environment, and the opposing polarities will be present. They will seek reconciliation and discussion within the environment. The child will be seeking to let go of the unconscious; the reconciliation with the primary caregiver or the adult, parent, and the parent will be seeking to dissolve the unconscious and not support negative interpretations of themselves and the child.

251.5 What appears to be opposing within the conscious and unconscious mind before the unconscious is dissolved into the conscious?

*Date*_____

_____

_____

_____

_____

_____

_____

*Date*_____

_____

_____

_____

_____

_____

*Date*_____

_____

_____

_____

_____

_____

251.6 What is important in discussing the ebb and flow of love?

*Date*_____

_____
_____
_____
_____
_____
_____
_____

*Date*_____

_____
_____
_____
_____
_____
_____
_____

*Date*_____

_____
_____
_____
_____
_____
_____
_____

251.7 It is within the point of dissolving the unconscious mind within the individual that those within the environment will feel more attached and attempt to create some type of experience, situation, or illness that is meant to draw the individual that is shifting the unconscious back into the attachment and co-dependency of the unconscious mind.

251.8 Are our emotions when unconscious a roller coaster and, if so, why?

*Date*_____

_____
_____
_____
_____
_____

*Date*_____

_____
_____
_____
_____
_____

*Date*_____

_____
_____
_____
_____
_____

251.9 When it is said that the mind will experience a pulling away and drawing into, what is this speaking about?

*Date*_____

_____

_____

_____

_____

_____

_____

*Date*_____

_____

_____

_____

_____

_____

_____

*Date*_____

_____

_____

_____

_____

_____

_____

251.10 The parent-child relationship living within the conscious mind is a means in which to honor and discover love within the relationship to one another within how life is defined, within how one another is supported by the beauty and spontaneity of how love is preserving itself within the relationship. It is the opportunity to feel the presence of love and being nurtured, embraced, and honored as love of oneself.

252.1 Why does reconciliation take both parties, and what party does the Clear Mind Experience represent in the process?

*Date*_____

_____

_____

_____

_____

_____

_____

_____

*Date*_____

_____

_____

_____

_____

_____

_____

*Date*_____

_____

_____

_____

_____

_____

_____

252.2 If you were to explain to your child or your child-mind, feelings that were experienced within your life or theirs before the age of 7 what would you say?

*Date*_____

_____

_____

_____

_____

_____

_____

_____

*Date*_____

_____

_____

_____

_____

_____

_____

_____

*Date*_____

_____

_____

_____

_____

_____

_____

252.3 The reconciliation process being activated within the personal mind of the child is an important part of a healthy development of an individual as when they move out into the world, and the reconciliation process has taken place, they are able to make decisions, choices, and create within their environment through the presentation of wisdom because the validation of the unconscious mind has occurred.

253.1 When a parent will not allow reconciliation, what do you perceive the unconscious mind will interpret this action as? How do you think that this would feel and could it potentially block further experiences of love if the unconscious mind is not dissolved, just from the fact that the unconscious mind would be protecting itself from the shame and humiliation of the rejection?

*Date*_____

_____

_____

_____

_____

_____

_____

*Date*_____

_____

_____

_____

_____

_____

_____

*Date*_____

_____

_____

_____

_____

_____

253.2 When the child is not able to gain reconciliation with the adult, the child will perceive guilt because they will feel that they have perceived the parent within a way that does not preserve self-appreciation, and the unconscious mind will move out into perception a confusion. The child will perceive a lack and feel guilty over their needs to become free from the interpretations of the parents. Reconciliation is an important part of having the unconscious mind retract itself into itself because it is upon reconciliation that the unconscious mind will withdraw. It will not have the power to project. It will move back within itself. If one is not able to reconcile with parents, this is the gift of the Clear Mind Experience because the act of the process, the way in which the process is structured, and the way that an individual participates within the practice is perceived by the unconscious as reconciliation.

253.3 Does assisting someone else to feel positive and embraced interpret itself within their mind as gratitude for them, and you?

*Date*_____

\
\
\
\
\
\
\

*Date*_____

\
\
\
\
\
\

*Date*_____

\
\
\
\
\
\

253.4 When someone pulls away, does the unconscious mind feel rejected and, if so, how?

*Date*_____

_____

_____

_____

_____

_____

_____

_____

*Date*_____

_____

_____

_____

_____

_____

_____

_____

*Date*_____

_____

_____

_____

_____

_____

_____

_____

254.1 When an adolescent is able to host a relationship from the conscious mind, it will allow them to find their bridge, the bridge that they will take as an adult to cross them into the world, which is all thoughts, feelings, emotions that operate within perception of the journey of life that they are embarking upon. As they move out into the world, into their independence, if they have had reconciliation then they will not cross the bridge in fear, rebellion, confusion, or concern, and continue moving over and backwards towards the parents out of obligation to the parents. When a child is not able to stand upon their own two feet within the world, it is because the unconscious mind has not had reconciliation with the parent, and self-doubt within the child is strong, and the child will keep returning to the front door of the parent to seek the reconciliation. It is a spontaneous activation within one's awareness. It is operating as the child at the time.

254.2 Why is it important that adolescents experience their rite of passage into adulthood walking within the presence of love, why would you like to see this?

*Date*_____

_____

_____

_____

_____

_____

_____

_____

*Date*_____

_____

_____

_____

_____

_____

_____

_____

*Date*_____

_____

_____

_____

_____

_____

_____

254.3 When a child has been through successful reconciliation or when an adolescent has been through a successful reconciliation with the parent or is practicing the Clear Mind Experience, their independence is not controlled by weaknesses of the unconscious. Their needs are not controlled by the unconscious, and they are not controlled by the unconscious perceptions of the parent.

255.1 Why is it important for parents to clear the mind, and if you were to invite one into the process – including yourself, what would you say? What would be the purpose of doing it?

*Date*_____

_____

_____

_____

_____

_____

_____

_____

*Date*_____

_____

_____

_____

_____

_____

_____

*Date*_____

_____

_____

_____

_____

_____

_____

255.2 During the reconciliation process, the adult will not say that they failed the child. They will merely talk about the fact that within consciousness, there is no perfection; that the parent operated within their capacity to preserve life and love, and if they did not have the capacity, then that's who they were at the time. They will express to the child, not the stories that they were not perfect, but the wisdom to support the fact that they operated within the child's life within their capacity. And if the child witnessed any form of separation of love, it was that of the parent. It is upon parent discussing this with the child that the unconscious mind perceptions that are that of the parent will be reconciled and ready to be dissolved within the unconscious of the adolescent. The reconciliation process establishes the 49 signifiers to be in position ready to be dissolved, waiting for awarenesses to move into conscious awareness of the individual allowing one to move into the presence of love.

256.1 What benefits has the unconscious mind served the planet?

*Date*_____

_____

_____

_____

_____

_____

_____

_____

*Date*_____

_____

_____

_____

_____

_____

_____

*Date*_____

_____

_____

_____

_____

_____

_____

_____

256.2 The unconscious mind within the wisdom and beauty of its existence and divinity is that it is our gateway to love. Because within dissolving what is not love within the mind, we perceive and merge within the beauty of the conscious mind, which is the living perception of an unconditional presence of love.

256.3 What does love feel like when birthed within us?

*Date*_____

_____

_____

_____

_____

_____

_____

*Date*_____

_____

_____

_____

_____

_____

*Date*_____

_____

_____

_____

_____

_____

256.4 The reconciliation between parents and children or caregivers is the critical step for the child-parent relationship that allows the child to merge into life within wholeness and allows the parent to merge into wisdom in self-appreciation.

256.5 – 256.5i The unconscious mind without reconciliation of the parent or the Clear Mind Experience will hold onto itself believing that it is a fictitious story. How so?

*Date*_____

_____

_____

_____

_____

_____

_____

_____

*Date*_____

_____

_____

_____

_____

_____

_____

*Date*_____

_____

_____

_____

_____

_____

_____

256.6 When an adolescent is not able to receive the benefits of the reconciliation process, they will move out into life within their day to day. They will translate life that it is unsteady. They will feel detached emotionally from others. They will believe that they hurt others, and they will be accused by others that their detachment to life is hurtful.

257.1 How can we within everyday life validate others before they are suppressed into pain?

*Date*_____

_____

_____

_____

_____

_____

*Date*_____

_____

_____

_____

_____

_____

*Date*_____

_____

_____

_____

_____

_____

257.2 – 257.2i If we do not dissolve the unconscious mind, what would happen to youth, and if you could at this time say to a child what life would be like free from the unconscious, what would you say?

*Date*_____

_____

_____

_____

_____

_____

_____

_____

*Date*_____

_____

_____

_____

_____

_____

_____

*Date*_____

_____

_____

_____

_____

_____

_____

257.3 The play of the unconscious mind is that it wants your attention. And the more that we cater to it within our day to day within our perceptions through medication, behavior, disease, conflict, and powerlessness, the greater hold that it will have over our awareness because the rational mind will believe that the story of the unconscious is what is the living being.

257.4 Are youth seeking to be free of previous interpretations of the unconscious sooner rather than later and how is that serving humanity?

*Date*_____

_____

_____

_____

_____

_____

_____

_____

*Date*_____

_____

_____

_____

_____

_____

_____

_____

*Date*_____

_____

_____

_____

_____

_____

_____

258.1 How do we assist children and youth to experience life in a manner that supports the need for minimal reconciliation as they become older?

*Date*_____

_____

_____

_____

_____

_____

_____

_____

*Date*_____

_____

_____

_____

_____

_____

_____

_____

*Date*_____

_____

_____

_____

_____

_____

_____

258.2 The reconciliation process is more than likely inhibited in most circumstances. It is, therefore, the reason why the Clear Mind Experience is so powerful in dissolving the unconscious mind, as it is what is able to set individuals free from the behavior patterns within the unconscious from the dysfunction that it moves within and out of life. And within practicing the Clear Mind Experience, the reconciliation process is achieved through the expression of the program itself and not a requirement for its success in dissolving the unconscious.

258.3 How much of our primary caregivers from the first seven years of our lives make up our unconscious thoughts?

*Date*_____

_____

_____

_____

_____

_____

_____

_____

*Date*_____

_____

_____

_____

_____

_____

_____

_____

*Date*_____

_____

_____

_____

_____

_____

_____

_____

258.4 Is it important to remember the thoughts, or to dissolve them without knowing each of them?

*Date*_____

_____
_____
_____
_____
_____
_____
_____

*Date*_____

_____
_____
_____
_____
_____
_____

*Date*_____

_____
_____
_____
_____
_____
_____

259.1 How does the nature of human condition which is love – benefit through a Clear Mind?

*Date*_____

_____

_____

_____

_____

_____

_____

*Date*_____

_____

_____

_____

_____

_____

_____

*Date*_____

_____

_____

_____

_____

_____

_____

_____

259.2 What are we doing when we disassociate from the moment, what are we saying to the universe and is this serving us and, if so, how?

*Date*_____

_____

_____

_____

_____

_____

_____

*Date*_____

_____

_____

_____

_____

_____

_____

*Date*_____

_____

_____

_____

_____

_____

_____

259.3 Write about an experience that you would like to reconcile within your life - then breathe Self Acceptance breath one.

*Date*_____

_____
_____
_____
_____
_____
_____
_____

*Date*_____

_____
_____
_____
_____
_____
_____
_____

*Date*_____

_____
_____
_____
_____
_____
_____

259.4 The unconscious mind is structured to release itself. Why do you think it is important to honor this process if we have been gifted it?

*Date*_____

_____

_____

_____

_____

_____

_____

_____

*Date*_____

_____

_____

_____

_____

_____

_____

*Date*_____

_____

_____

_____

_____

_____

_____

259.5 How has the unconscious mind been your invitation into the conscious mind?

*Date*_____

_____

_____

_____

_____

_____

_____

_____

*Date*_____

_____

_____

_____

_____

_____

_____

_____

*Date*_____

_____

_____

_____

_____

_____

_____

_____

259.6 Have you experienced reconciliation with your parents and how has the Clear Mind Experience nurtured you?

*Date*_____

_____
_____
_____
_____
_____
_____
_____

*Date*_____

_____
_____
_____
_____
_____
_____
_____

*Date*_____

_____
_____
_____
_____
_____
_____
_____

260.1 Define Self Development and how it serves to pre-serve love within humanity.

*Date*_____

_____

_____

_____

_____

_____

_____

_____

*Date*_____

_____

_____

_____

_____

_____

_____

_____

*Date*_____

_____

_____

_____

_____

_____

_____

_____

260.2 Define three important benefits that you receive in dissolving the unconscious mind.

Date_____

1._____

_____

2._____

_____

3._____

_____

_____

Date_____

1._____

_____

2._____

_____

3._____

_____

_____

Date_____

1._____

_____

2._____

_____

3._____

_____

_____

260.3 To express rhythm of the mind means what?

*Date*_____

_____
_____
_____
_____
_____
_____
_____

*Date*_____

_____
_____
_____
_____
_____
_____
_____

*Date*_____

_____
_____
_____
_____
_____
_____
_____

260.4 How important is our role within the lives of others and why?

*Date*_____

_____

_____

_____

_____

_____

_____

_____

*Date*_____

_____

_____

_____

_____

_____

_____

*Date*_____

_____

_____

_____

_____

_____

_____

Partner to Partner

261.1 Conscious partnership is not about the gender or each participant within the union. It is about the attraction and the basis of the union, the conditions in which it came together within the mind. Love does not have the ability to discriminate against form and gender and nor would we wish that upon another. Why do you think it is important that love move impersonally to serve everyone upon the planet?

261.2 You are able to attract a relationship within life as a partner that is based on conscious or unconscious mind. If the relationship is conditioned as a pay-off emotionally, then more than likely it is being directed by the unconscious.

Conscious Partnership

262.1 How is one nurtured within a conscious relationship?

*Date*_____

_____

_____

_____

_____

_____

_____

_____

*Date*_____

_____

_____

_____

_____

_____

_____

*Date*_____

_____

_____

_____

_____

_____

_____

262.2 It is within a conscious partnership that a blissful, loving union is a potential, however, not always felt during the experience of removing the unconscious perceptions that one another will engage upon within the experience of one another.

262.3 Do you think there are varying ideas of a conscious relationship?

*Date*_____

_____

_____

_____

_____

_____

*Date*_____

_____

_____

_____

_____

_____

*Date*_____

_____

_____

_____

_____

_____

262.4 What does the unconscious mind fear most about union besides the fact that it cannot see it or experience it.

*Date*_____

_____

_____

_____

_____

_____

_____

_____

*Date*_____

_____

_____

_____

_____

_____

_____

_____

*Date*_____

_____

_____

_____

_____

_____

_____

_____

262.5 Define how partners move in an out of one another.

*Date*_____

_____
_____
_____
_____
_____
_____
_____

*Date*_____

_____
_____
_____
_____
_____
_____
_____

*Date*_____

_____
_____
_____
_____
_____
_____
_____

262.6 Within the conscious relationship amongst the purification process will be a transparent, nurturing, higher meaning to life which can make life bearable, at times, just.

263.1 That is the beauty of the conscious relationship that as unbearable as it can be, as blissful as it can return, and this is because of the awakening that is occurring within the minds of the individuals that are participating within the relationship. If one were to step out of this conscious relationship in resistance to awakening, the relationship would end.

263.2 Define conscious awareness versus unconscious awareness.

*Date*_____

_____
_____
_____
_____
_____
_____
_____

*Date*_____

_____
_____
_____
_____
_____
_____
_____

*Date*_____

_____
_____
_____
_____
_____
_____
_____

263.3 The beauty of union is that no moment is left from the beauty of self-discovery, list the last 5 feelings you discovered in relationship to another. How are these feelings typically different if so?

Date_____

_____

_____

_____

_____

_____

_____

_____

Date_____

_____

_____

_____

_____

_____

_____

Date_____

_____

_____

_____

_____

_____

_____

263.4 It can be perceived by some that the holy relationship will not have the disharmony of the unconscious relationship. However, this is untrue. Until the unconscious mind is dissolved, the holy relationship will act as a vehicle in which to dissolve what is not able to preserve love by enforcing choice upon each partner, that within each moment, within each expectation, within each moment of disharmony which is that of the unconscious mind, the individual will be faced with the choice to move into the conscious awareness of love to preserve life, to preserve love within the relationship.

263.5 – 263.5i Define a conscious and unconscious relationship.

*Date*_____

_____

_____

_____

_____

_____

_____

*Date*_____

_____

_____

_____

_____

_____

_____

*Date*_____

_____

_____

_____

_____

_____

_____

263.6 When the conscious mind is lighting the path, it is difficult to hide out within the unconscious – how has the conscious mind moved to preserve itself within your life and relationships?

*Date*_____

_____

_____

_____

_____

_____

_____

_____

*Date*_____

_____

_____

_____

_____

_____

_____

*Date*_____

_____

_____

_____

_____

_____

_____

263.7 Within the expression of the holy relationship are many realizations of love. Love when it presents itself will present deeply profound, spiritual love. At times that love can seem to present itself for just a moment. Then as fast as it was present, it is gone again because it has drawn what is not love to the surface so may appear again. Within the in and out, the ebbing and flowing from the conscious to the unconscious, the unconscious mind will project expectations, thoughts, feelings, and emotions that will surface to be dissolved within the light, within the wisdom of one another.

264.1 – 264.1i The energetic field of conventional marriage is the vibration of the unconscious. It is the starting block of failed expectations, and it is the holy relationship that finds it difficult to exist within its conventionality, within the frequency of the field.

264.2 If need and expectation were taken out of a marriage what would define the relationship?

*Date*_____

_____

_____

_____

_____

_____

_____

_____

*Date*_____

_____

_____

_____

_____

_____

_____

*Date*_____

_____

_____

_____

_____

_____

_____

264.3 How is marriage redefined within a conscious mind?

*Date*_____

_____
_____
_____
_____
_____
_____
_____

*Date*_____

_____
_____
_____
_____
_____
_____

*Date*_____

_____
_____
_____
_____
_____
_____

264.4 As the planet moves into new awareness, increased vibrations of frequency, and new times, marriage is becoming a ceremony of union, where two beings come together in union to express the beauty of love, and within all action and perception of one another, preserve life within a flow, an effortless flow of oneness. Where two children come together as the living mind, and within the living mind in a relationship to one another, to life, to abundance, to the world, and together move out into the world as an expression and commitment to love.

264.5 – 264.5i How are your honoring union in your life and, if not, what do you think the unconscious mind is seeking to experience in the relationship that struggles to form union?

*Date*_____

_____

_____

_____

_____

_____

_____

_____

*Date*_____

_____

_____

_____

_____

_____

_____

_____

*Date*_____

_____

_____

_____

_____

_____

_____

264.6 How has union been activated within your life?

*Date*_____

_____

_____

_____

_____

_____

_____

*Date*_____

_____

_____

_____

_____

_____

*Date*_____

_____

_____

_____

_____

_____

_____

264.7 Union awakens what within us?

*Date*_____

_____

_____

_____

_____

_____

_____

_____

*Date*_____

_____

_____

_____

_____

_____

_____

_____

*Date*_____

_____

_____

_____

_____

_____

_____

_____

264.8 Within the sacred union is the opportunity to awaken new meaning within life. It is within the sacred union that we awaken a further awareness to self-love and deep self-appreciation because the union becomes a means in which to experience the divinity of union within oneself.

264.9 How does union honor self-appreciation and does this preserve self-love?

*Date*_____

_____
_____
_____
_____
_____

*Date*_____

_____
_____
_____
_____
_____

*Date*_____

_____
_____
_____
_____
_____

265.1 Does union measure perfection?

*Date*_____

_____
_____
_____
_____
_____
_____
_____

*Date*_____

_____
_____
_____
_____
_____
_____
_____

*Date*_____

_____
_____
_____
_____
_____
_____
_____

265.2 Within the conscious relationship, there are no expectations of one another, as the conscious mind is simply an expression that moves into each moment as the relationship moves into each moment. The relationship becomes an opportunity to discover the next moment and the moment after that, and within each moment, one is revealed emotionally, physically, and mentally to be preserving love within life.

265.3 Relationships are an ebbing and flowing, through what?

*Date*_____

_____

_____

_____

_____

_____

_____

*Date*_____

_____

_____

_____

_____

_____

_____

*Date*_____

_____

_____

_____

_____

_____

_____

265.4 - 265.5 The momentum of love moves so effortlessly within the holy union because within this relationship are not the vibrations of obligation, but the relationship is a means in which to serve one another to awaken to the presence of love. If one within the relationship feels obligated to receive from the other, the relationship will end because within the holy union, there is only the expression of love, and love will end where it is not preserved because it will not be able to operate as it will not be seen.

266.1 When within your life does fire present itself, within you and what is it assisting you to burn off?

*Date*_____

_____

_____

_____

_____

_____

_____

_____

*Date*_____

_____

_____

_____

_____

_____

_____

*Date*_____

_____

_____

_____

_____

_____

_____

_____

266.2 The holy union within all of its abundant light and love can be emotionally and mentally volatile at times. Much like the beauty and magnificence of the ocean, the emotional tides within the relationship will rise up and deep peace will flow and enter the relationship. Then as fast as the peace entered and flowed within the hearts, minds, and emotions of those within the relationship, the tides will retract and withdraw from the stillness and within that, there will be a roar of emotion as peace attempts to find its way back to the surface, to the expression, to the presence of love.

266.3 How is love like an ocean? Do you like the ocean and how does that reflect your experience with love?

*Date*_____

_____

_____

_____

_____

_____

_____

_____

*Date*_____

_____

_____

_____

_____

_____

_____

*Date*_____

_____

_____

_____

_____

_____

_____

_____

266.4 After conflict and the energy withdraws, what is the feeling and the overall purpose and how does wisdom serve to the stillness of this moment?

*Date*_____

_____

_____

_____

_____

_____

_____

_____

*Date*_____

_____

_____

_____

_____

_____

_____

_____

*Date*_____

_____

_____

_____

_____

_____

_____

266.5 How does wisdom serve union within a relationship?

*Date*_____

_____

_____

_____

_____

_____

_____

_____

*Date*_____

_____

_____

_____

_____

_____

_____

_____

*Date*_____

_____

_____

_____

_____

_____

_____

_____

266.6 If there is conflict and union operating within the same relationship – what is happening, what does this represent?

*Date*_____

_____

_____

_____

_____

_____

_____

_____

*Date*_____

_____

_____

_____

_____

_____

_____

_____

*Date*_____

_____

_____

_____

_____

_____

_____

_____

267.1 Why does the holy union confront the unconscious perceptions?

*Date*_____

_____
_____
_____
_____
_____
_____
_____

*Date*_____

_____
_____
_____
_____
_____
_____
_____

*Date*_____

_____
_____
_____
_____
_____
_____
_____

267.2 The holy union will tear down a false house that does not allow love to be present because its passion and purpose and the flow of love will seem to host such power that the false house will have to fall. And within the presence of that falling, the new house of light will stand erect.

267.3 Within union can one feel the presence of oneness and, if so, explain.

*Date*_____

_____

_____

_____

_____

_____

_____

*Date*_____

_____

_____

_____

_____

*Date*_____

_____

_____

_____

_____

_____

267.4 When we can live through the holy relationship, make the distance to the moment where love has realized itself, then a profound magic will appear. Within that magic, each one within the holy relationship will stand within themselves, however, in union with the presence of love that will enable the feeling of oneness to exist within the knowingness and presence of one another.

267.5 As one awakens within a Clear Mind how is union being defined?

*Date*_____

_____

_____

_____

_____

_____

_____

_____

*Date*_____

_____

_____

_____

_____

_____

_____

_____

*Date*_____

_____

_____

_____

_____

_____

_____

_____

267.6 It is but the sacred gift of the holy union, the sacred jewel within the union. It is the magic that appears where the union sustains itself with no effort but as a continuous expression of love flowing in and out of love. Within the holy union is the alchemy of love, and the alchemy of love is ever changing, ever moving, radiating the resonance and radiance of the sun.

Living within the Holy Union

268.1 Define a Holy Relationship, as a partner, friend, or associate.

*Date*_____

_____

_____

_____

_____

_____

_____

_____

*Date*_____

_____

_____

_____

_____

_____

_____

*Date*_____

_____

_____

_____

_____

_____

_____

1A The beautiful gift to the holy union today is that of the Clear Mind Experience, where the relationship no longer has to be the vehicle and the means in which one another dissolves what is not love. In dissolving the unconscious mind, the relationship will not be directly confronting the unconscious. The soul will no longer be using the relationship as a way to purge the limitations of the unconscious expressions emotionally, physically, mentally as the minds will resonate within the magnificence and purity of all prevailing oneness.

268.1-1A Write seven ways that the conscious mind could support your current relationship or idea of a relationship.

*Date*_____
1. _____
2. _____
3. _____
4. _____
5. _____
6. _____
7. _____

*Date*_____
1. _____
2. _____
3. _____
4. _____
5. _____
6. _____
7. _____

*Date*_____
1. _____
2. _____
3. _____
4. _____
5. _____
6. _____
7. _____

268.1-1A List seven feelings that support a holy relationship within your perspective.

*Date*_____

_____

_____

_____

_____

_____

List seven feelings that support a holy relationship within your self.

*Date*_____

_____

_____

_____

_____

_____

Breathe Gratitude Breath

List seven feelings that support a holy relationship within your perspective.

*Date*_____

_____

_____

_____

_____

_____

List seven feelings that support a holy relationship within your self.

*Date*_____

_____

_____

_____

_____

_____

Breathe Gratitude Breath

List seven feelings that support a holy relationship within your perspective.

*Date*_____

_____

_____

_____

_____

_____

List seven feelings that support a holy relationship within your self.

*Date*_____

_____

_____

_____

_____

_____

Breathe Gratitude Breath

268.1-2A Define your sacred ceremony – the date or time that hosting one is special and why particularly at that time. Write the purpose of the ceremony and what it will express to life, how it will define the living expression of your partnership. This ceremony can be done with yourself, defining your relationship to self-love or in honor of your union with another.

*Date*_____

_____

_____

_____

_____

_____

_____

_____

_____

_____

_____

_____

_____

_____

Breathe Gratitude Breath

*Date*_____

_____

_____

_____

_____
_____
_____
_____
_____
_____
_____
_____
_____
_____
_____

Breathe Gratitude Breath

*Date*_____

_____
_____
_____
_____
_____
_____
_____
_____
_____
_____
_____
_____

Breathe Gratitude Breath

268.1-3A Review the Clear Mind Positive Feeling Scale and write 7 negative mind feelings that you see are currently playing out in your life. In 21 days return and write 21 positive mind feelings that you are experiencing today. Once you have written the positive mind feelings take a moment to review if these feelings are related to the first negative feelings that you recorded.

*Date*_____

_____

_____

*21 Days*_____

_____

_____

_____

_____

_____

_____

_____

_____

_____

Breathe Gratitude Breath

*Date*_____

_____

_____

_____

*21 Days*_____

_____
_____
_____
_____
_____
_____
_____
_____
_____
_____

Breathe Gratitude Breath

*Date*_____

_____
_____

*21 Days*_____

_____
_____
_____
_____
_____
_____
_____
_____
_____

Breathe Gratitude Breath

695

268.1-4A Write three ways that you have created rigidity and routine that limit a spontaneous expression of love within your relationship to yourself or another.

Write three ways that you can awaken an openness within how you express love to yourself or another that will, through action dissolve the limitations of rigidity and routine.

*Date*_____

1. _____

_____

2. _____

_____

3. _____

_____

1. _____

_____

2. _____

_____

3. _____

_____

Breathe Gratitude Breath

*Date*_____

1. _____

_____

2. _____

_____

3. _____

_____

1. _____

2. _____

3. _____

_____

Breathe Gratitude Breath

*Date*_____

1. _____

2. _____

3. _____

_____

1. _____

2. _____

3. _____

_____

Breathe Gratitude Breath

268.1-5A Write about a time when you have in your life been speaking to yourself through self-criticism to self motivate your need for spiritual or personal transformation.

Write when you have spoken to another through self-criticism to self motivate another of their need for spiritual or personal transformation. How did this motivation express the unconscious mind and what was it saying.

What can you tell yourself or another to allow them to experience themselves as the potential of love within this moment?

*Date*_____

_____

_____

_____

_____

_____

_____

_____

_____

_____

_____

_____

_____

Breathe Gratitude Breath

*Date*_____

_____

_____

_____
_____
_____
_____
_____
_____
_____
_____
_____
_____

Breathe Gratitude Breath

*Date*_____

_____
_____
_____
_____
_____
_____
_____
_____
_____
_____
_____
_____

Breathe Gratitude Breath

268.1-1B Reflect for a moment on when you have discussed unconscious limitations with others outside of your
relationship to another or your relationship to yourself.
Think back for a moment and determine when you have
expressed unconscious definition in these moments in relationship to yourself, your relationship or another. In this
moment, as you reflect upon this moment take a moment
to write an affirmation to life, removing any limitations that
you spoke of yourself or another.

*Date*_____

_____

_____

_____

_____

_____

_____

_____

_____

_____

_____

_____

_____

Breathe Gratitude Breath

*Date*_____

_____

_____

_____

_____

_____

_____

_____

_____

_____

_____

_____

_____

_____

_____

Breathe Gratitude Breath

*Date*_____

_____

_____

_____

_____

_____

_____

_____

_____

_____

_____

_____

_____

Breathe Gratitude Breath

268.1-2B Take a moment to reflect back on conflict that you have experienced within yourself or within your relationship. Once you have remembered your moment of conflict, write on a sheet of paper how you feel today about he conflict, what it would need to be resolved within yourself and how you feel today in being free of it. Once you have written your note to Self, sit down and sip a cup of tea and read the note out loud to the universe. Once your note is read you may burn it.

*Date*_____

_____
_____
_____
_____
_____
_____
_____
_____
_____
_____
_____

Breathe Gratitude Breath

*Date*_____

_____
_____

_____

_____

_____

_____

_____

_____

_____

_____

_____

_____

_____

Breathe Gratitude Breath

*Date*_____

_____

_____

_____

_____

_____

_____

_____

_____

_____

_____

_____

_____

Breathe Gratitude Breath

268.1-3B Sit peacefully and reflect on a time that you allowed the unconscious mind to define your feelings of yourself or another and conflict erupted. Take a moment to write how that experience has made your feel of yourself and or the other person. What would you like to say to yourself of the other to reinstate love, in place of the conflict and judgment.

Once you have written of your experience, sit quietly and sip a cup of tea while you read your note out loud to the universe. Once your note is read you may burn it.

*Date*_____

_____

_____

_____

_____

_____

_____

_____

_____

_____

_____

_____

_____

Breathe Gratitude Breath

*Date*_____

_____

_____

_____

_____

_____

_____

_____

_____

_____

_____

_____

_____

_____

_____

Breathe Gratitude Breath

*Date*_____

_____

_____

_____

_____

_____

_____

_____

_____

_____

_____

_____

_____

Breathe Gratitude Breath

268.1-4B Write seven ways that honoring love in life is a ritual. How in life can you preserve love as a ritual? How in life can your expression of love be a ritual for another? What has been the most enjoyable part of setting up the bathing ritual for yourself or another?

*Date*_____

_____

_____

_____

_____

_____

_____

_____

_____

_____

_____

_____

_____

_____

_____

_____

_____

_____

_____

_____

_____

Breathe Gratitude Breath

*Date*_____

_____
_____
_____
_____
_____
_____
_____
_____
_____
_____
_____
_____
_____
_____
_____
_____
_____
_____
_____
_____
_____
_____
_____
_____
_____
_____
_____
_____
_____

Breathe Gratitude Breath

*Date*_____

Breathe Gratitude Breath

268.1-5B What is your intent for your bathing ritual for yourself or another? When you touched yourself or another after your bathing ritual what was the feeling of your experience? When the sexual energy began to stir within your what did you want to do, and how are you preserving the sexual energy within this moment.

Define this in a manner that allow you to continue to support your discovery of maintaining the movement and preservation of sexual energy.

*Date*_____

_____
_____
_____
_____
_____
_____
_____
_____
_____
_____
_____
_____
_____
_____
_____
_____

Breathe Gratitude Breath

*Date*_____

Breathe Gratitude Breath

*Date*_____

Breathe Gratitude Breath

268.1-6B How in your life are you supporting sexuality and the beauty of its movement within your life? How is stimulating yourself sexually comforting to you? What do you feel during the process? Can you comfortably preserve your sexual energy when it is stimulated within yourself? How do you preserve your sexual arousal that is achieved within the experience of another? What was most arousing from the bathing ritual?

*Date*_____

_____

_____

Breathe Gratitude Breath

*Date*_____

_____

_____

_____

_____

_____

_____

_____

_____

_____

_____

_____

_____

_____

_____

_____

_____

_____

_____

_____

_____

_____

_____

_____

_____

_____

Breathe Gratitude Breath

*Date*_____

Breathe Gratitude Breath

269.1 – What can attachment within a relationship do to it?

*Date*_____

_____
_____
_____
_____
_____
_____
_____

*Date*_____

_____
_____
_____
_____
_____
_____
_____

*Date*_____

_____
_____
_____
_____
_____
_____
_____

269.2 Does a relationship have its own predestined outcome?

*Date*_____

_____
_____
_____
_____
_____
_____
_____

*Date*_____

_____
_____
_____
_____
_____
_____
_____

*Date*_____

_____
_____
_____
_____
_____
_____
_____

269.3 Is peace available within conflict and, if so, how?

*Date*_____

_____
_____
_____
_____
_____
_____
_____

*Date*_____

_____
_____
_____
_____
_____
_____
_____

*Date*_____

_____
_____
_____
_____
_____
_____
_____

269.4 What is most comfortable about a relationship when each partner is awakened to self-love?

*Date*_____

_____
_____
_____
_____
_____
_____

*Date*_____

_____
_____
_____
_____
_____
_____

*Date*_____

_____
_____
_____
_____
_____
_____

269.5 Why does the mind create limitations within relationships?

*Date*_____

_____

_____

_____

_____

_____

_____

_____

*Date*_____

_____

_____

_____

_____

_____

_____

_____

*Date*_____

_____

_____

_____

_____

_____

_____

_____

269.6 What is union?

*Date*_____

_____
_____
_____
_____
_____
_____
_____

*Date*_____

_____
_____
_____
_____
_____
_____
_____

*Date*_____

_____
_____
_____
_____
_____
_____
_____

269.7 Is the planet a holy relationship and, if so, to what?

*Date*_____

_____
_____
_____
_____
_____
_____

*Date*_____

_____
_____
_____
_____
_____
_____

*Date*_____

_____
_____
_____
_____
_____
_____

269.8 What is a miracle?

*Date*_____

_____
_____
_____
_____
_____
_____
_____

*Date*_____

_____
_____
_____
_____
_____
_____
_____

*Date*_____

_____
_____
_____
_____
_____
_____
_____

270.1 How does unconditional love serve ourselves within a holy relationship?

*Date*_____

_____

_____

_____

_____

_____

_____

_____

*Date*_____

_____

_____

_____

_____

_____

_____

_____

*Date*_____

_____

_____

_____

_____

_____

_____

_____

270.2 If one is not attached to outcome, is a relationship served to awaken into the expression of conscious love?

*Date*_____

_____
_____
_____
_____
_____
_____
_____

*Date*_____

_____
_____
_____
_____
_____
_____
_____

*Date*_____

_____
_____
_____
_____
_____
_____
_____

Unconscious Partnership

271.1 What does it mean to be out of love within ourselves and when we are, what usually gets us to seek a different experience of ourselves?

*Date*_____

_____
_____
_____
_____
_____
_____

*Date*_____

_____
_____
_____
_____
_____
_____

*Date*_____

_____
_____
_____
_____
_____
_____

271.2 How do we fill voids within our lives and what does this do for us?

*Date*_____

_____

_____

_____

_____

_____

_____

_____

*Date*_____

_____

_____

_____

_____

_____

_____

_____

*Date*_____

_____

_____

_____

_____

_____

_____

_____

271.3 How does the conscious mind dissolve the unconscious aspect of a relationship and how can you contribute to this potential success?

*Date*_____

_____

_____

_____

_____

_____

_____

_____

*Date*_____

_____

_____

_____

_____

_____

_____

_____

*Date*_____

_____

_____

_____

_____

_____

_____

271.4 Does the conscious mind awaken an individual beyond their personal will to participate?

*Date*_____

_____
_____
_____
_____
_____
_____
_____

*Date*_____

_____
_____
_____
_____
_____
_____
_____

*Date*_____

_____
_____
_____
_____
_____
_____
_____

271.5 What dissolves within an unconscious relationship, list 5 feelings.

*Date*_____

_____
_____
_____
_____
_____
_____
_____

*Date*_____

_____
_____
_____
_____
_____
_____
_____

*Date*_____

_____
_____
_____
_____
_____
_____
_____

272.1 Why do you think that in partnership one partner seeks first or with great gusto than the other, how does this serve the union in a positive way?

*Date*_____

_____

_____

_____

_____

_____

_____

_____

*Date*_____

_____

_____

_____

_____

_____

_____

*Date*_____

_____

_____

_____

_____

_____

_____

272.2 How are you encouraging another and what does this feel like to you?

*Date*_____

_____
_____
_____
_____
_____
_____
_____

*Date*_____

_____
_____
_____
_____
_____
_____

*Date*_____

_____
_____
_____
_____
_____
_____

272.3 How is the conscious mind serving our relationships in life?

*Date*_____

_____

_____

_____

_____

_____

_____

*Date*_____

_____

_____

_____

_____

_____

_____

*Date*_____

_____

_____

_____

_____

_____

_____

272.4 Within the unconscious partnership when one individual begins to perceive life free of the unconscious, they will review their life with their partner. They at that point may determine that they do not have anything in common with this being any longer because what was once available to heal or to transform oneself into love is no longer being interpreted in that manner. They may feel strongly that to enable themselves to truly become clear of the unconscious, the person either needs to join them upon the journey or walk away from them setting one another free.

272.5 When the unconscious and conscious minds disagree, would you say that the conscious mind is dissolving the unconscious and why?

*Date*_____

_____

_____

_____

_____

_____

_____

_____

*Date*_____

_____

_____

_____

_____

_____

_____

*Date*_____

_____

_____

_____

_____

_____

_____

272.6 Do you perceive that the conscious mind would rather exist within self-acceptance?

*Date*_____

_____

_____

_____

_____

_____

_____

_____

*Date*_____

_____

_____

_____

_____

_____

_____

_____

*Date*_____

_____

_____

_____

_____

_____

_____

_____

The beauty of the Clear Mind Experience is that everyone is able to dissolve the unconscious mind and shift the unconscious thoughts, feelings, and emotions that promote negative behavior. Implementing the Clear Mind Experience within the relationship will give the relationship a much needed guide in which to begin the process of healing and moving into the path of union with one another.

273.1 Who have you been in an unconscious relationship with and what did it feel like? You are writing this to identify with how you feel about yourself within the unconscious child-mind, which is being dissolved. It is within answering this question that you will be able to identify with how dissolving the unconscious mind is going to benefit you.

*Date*_____

_____

_____

_____

_____

_____

_____

*Date*_____

_____

_____

_____

_____

_____

_____

*Date*_____

_____

_____

_____

_____

_____

_____

The unconscious mind when confronted within the vulnerability that life will present different ideas of how one can live as one attempts to preserve life within the union may seek control within the relationship through behavior, addiction, disease, grief, sadness, anger, behavior that creates distrust, disharmony, and confrontation which promotes fear within the other.

273.3 If and when you have been in an unconscious relationship, have you felt in control in the relationship or powerless within the relationship?

*Date*_____

_____

_____

_____

_____

_____

_____

_____

*Date*_____

_____

_____

_____

_____

_____

_____

*Date*_____

_____

_____

_____

_____

_____

_____

273.4 If you are experiencing an unconscious partnership – take a moment to look at the Clear Mind Positive Feeling Scale and choose seven positive feelings that would serve to awaken the relationship to that of a conscious perception. Once you find the positive feelings, identify with the opposing negative feelings and ask yourself if you are feeling these feelings in the relationship and when in your childhood you experienced the same feelings. Write a paragraph to the child-mind that includes the 7 positive feelings that you found on the scale inviting it into the expression of these feelings.

*Date*_____

_____
_____
_____
_____
_____
_____
_____
_____
_____
_____
_____
_____
_____

*Date*_____

_____
_____

_____

Date_____

273.5 – 273.7 It is with the unconscious mind seeking to preserve itself within life that it will promote its fears, control, betrayal, indecision, addictions, validations, and powerlessness within one another to those around them. This is because the structure of the unconscious relationship is very much focused on the outside world and how one is being perceived within the outside relationship, within the outside world. The unconscious mind will seek to show and demonstrate its dysfunction to others, seeking humiliation, grief, detachment, abandonment, shame, and confusion.

273.8 What does it feel like when relationships promote the unconscious mind?

*Date*_____

_____

_____

_____

_____

_____

_____

_____

*Date*_____

_____

_____

_____

_____

_____

_____

*Date*_____

_____

_____

_____

_____

_____

_____

_____

273.9 The unconscious mind will have great expectations and judgment of their partner. And when the partner is not able to fit into the expectations of that partner, then the partner with expectation will within an unconscious state project anger and fear and at times betrayal and validate the betrayal through the lack of that which has all come from the perception of the unconscious. It is of the projection.

274.1 What are three of the greatest fears that show up in an unconscious relationship?

*Date*_____

_____
_____
_____
_____
_____

*Date*_____

_____
_____
_____
_____
_____

*Date*_____

_____
_____
_____
_____
_____

275.1 What are unconscious relationships showing us?

*Date*_____

_____

_____

_____

_____

_____

_____

_____

*Date*_____

_____

_____

_____

_____

_____

_____

_____

*Date*_____

_____

_____

_____

_____

_____

_____

_____

275.2 What happens when thoughts create quickly? What are the benefits of this? Why is living within a Clear Mind important to assisting these benefits?

*Date*_____

_____

_____

_____

_____

_____

_____

_____

*Date*_____

_____

_____

_____

_____

_____

_____

*Date*_____

_____

_____

_____

_____

_____

_____

275.3 It is within the words that are spoken to one another and the thoughts provoked within these words from the unconscious relationship that events will begin to occur within the relationship from outer experiences that can create hardships, frustrations, great loss, and a great need for transformation of the personal mind.

275.4 How are you supporting the language of love within personal relationships?

*Date*_____

_____

_____

_____

_____

_____

*Date*_____

_____

_____

_____

_____

_____

*Date*_____

_____

_____

_____

_____

_____

Chapter Nine
Spiritual Mind

276.1 Define the 'spiritual mind' and how you are serving it into being today.

*Date*_____

_____

_____

_____

_____

_____

_____

_____

_____

_____

_____

_____

_____

_____

_____

_____

*Date*_____

_____
_____
_____
_____
_____
_____
_____
_____
_____
_____
_____
_____
_____

*Date*_____

_____
_____
_____
_____
_____
_____
_____
_____
_____
_____
_____
_____

276.2 - 276.3 The spiritual mind is the conscious mind, the aspect of the personal mind that can perceive love, create within love, seeks not to find love, lives within the realization of 'IAM Love,' lives within each moment as an expression, a spontaneous expression of its unlimited potential.

276.4 What is the benefit of the unconscious mind dissolving during this part of our evolution as a planet?

*Date*_____

_____

_____

_____

_____

_____

*Date*_____

_____

_____

_____

_____

_____

*Date*_____

_____

_____

_____

_____

_____

_____

276.5 Define three ways that you see the conscious mind acting within the greater presentation of life.

*Date*_____

1._____

_____

2._____

_____

3._____

_____

_____

*Date*_____

1._____

_____

2._____

_____

3._____

_____

_____

*Date*_____

1._____

_____

2._____

_____

3._____

_____

_____

277.1 List three ways that you identify the collective unconscious operating within the world.

Date_____

1._____

_____

2._____

_____

3._____

_____

_____

Date_____

1._____

_____

2._____

_____

3._____

_____

_____

Date_____

1._____

_____

2._____

_____

3._____

_____

_____

277.2 The unconscious mind collectively is mostly present within the media, communication, education, medicine, music, sexuality, religion, politics, governance, and finances. These are the areas that promote addiction, imbalanced sexuality, immediate gratification, false hopes, dreams, false identity in which one believes within personal suffering of not being able to gain, or creating falsehood for objects that are detached from the preservation of life.

277.3 If we dissolve the personal unconscious, is the world changing quickly by awakening quickly and, if so, why?

*Date*_____

_____

_____

_____

_____

_____

_____

*Date*_____

_____

_____

_____

_____

_____

_____

*Date*_____

_____

_____

_____

_____

_____

_____

_____

277.4 Name three ways the collective unconscious mind speaks to you within life.

*Date*_____

1._____

2._____

3._____

_____

_____

*Date*_____

1._____

2._____

3._____

_____

_____

*Date*_____

1._____

2._____

3._____

_____

_____

277.5 Why does the collective unconscious mind dissolve within the life of one that dissolves the personal unconscious and how will this positively serve yourself and humanity?

*Date*_____

_____

_____

_____

_____

_____

_____

_____

*Date*_____

_____

_____

_____

_____

_____

_____

_____

*Date*_____

_____

_____

_____

_____

_____

_____

277.6 – 277.6i The world at this time within the collective unconscious represents struggle within our own warfare, within our own perception. As the world defines for us what can be preserved and what can be let go of, the world provides us with a means in which to take action on preserving life, love within ourselves.

277.7 Does the battle of the conscious and unconscious mind affect humanity as a whole and what plays out within the structure of life?

*Date*_____

_____

_____

_____

_____

_____

_____

_____

*Date*_____

_____

_____

_____

_____

_____

_____

*Date*_____

_____

_____

_____

_____

_____

_____

278.1 Is the battle of the conscious and unconscious mind impersonal or personal?

*Date*_____

_____

_____

_____

_____

_____

_____

_____

*Date*_____

_____

_____

_____

_____

_____

_____

_____

*Date*_____

_____

_____

_____

_____

_____

_____

_____

279.1 Define the inner battle that once was or is.

*Date*_____

_____

_____

_____

_____

_____

_____

*Date*_____

_____

_____

_____

_____

_____

_____

*Date*_____

_____

_____

_____

_____

_____

_____

279.2 When we allow the conscious mind to move through the planet by dissolving the unconscious mind and moving out of all that separates from us from love, we create harmony within the world and draw within the world one community, one global community that moves within the presence of love. When we do this, we create a safe, nurturing, abundant, and prosperous environment for children, adults, and all sentient beings that are preserved within the presence of love.

280.1 How have you felt during catharsis in your life? If it has benefitted you, how is this so and how has it affected another?

*Date*_____

_____
_____
_____
_____
_____
_____
_____

*Date*_____

_____
_____
_____
_____
_____
_____
_____

*Date*_____

_____
_____
_____
_____
_____
_____

280.2 What have you noticed dissolve within the collective unconscious mind through your Clear Mind Experience?

*Date*_____

_____
_____
_____
_____
_____
_____
_____

*Date*_____

_____
_____
_____
_____
_____
_____
_____

*Date*_____

_____
_____
_____
_____
_____
_____
_____

281.1 Living within the light does not mean jumping into the darkness and trying to get the darkness to understand what is light. Reflect on this for one moment, darkness cannot understand what is light. It can only be transmuted into the frequency of light. The unconscious mind is not able to live within peace, union and the preservation of love. It can only be dissolved by love so it is not there to perceive the other.

281.2 Where in your life have you expected an unconscious problem would fix itself and what do you think your expectation was emotionally paying you?

*Date*_____

_____

_____

_____

_____

_____

_____

*Date*_____

_____

_____

_____

_____

_____

_____

*Date*_____

_____

_____

_____

_____

_____

_____

282.1 If life is a flow that exists within the moment, what is memory?

*Date*_____

_____

_____

_____

_____

_____

_____

*Date*_____

_____

_____

_____

_____

_____

_____

*Date*_____

_____

_____

_____

_____

_____

_____

282.2 Within life, love seeks nothing except lives within life within perception as a spontaneous flow that seeks nothing and lives within us as an unlimited expression to experience all.

*Date*_____

_____

_____

_____

_____

_____

_____

_____

*Date*_____

_____

_____

_____

_____

_____

_____

_____

*Date*_____

_____

_____

_____

_____

_____

282.3 How does love gain momentum?

*Date*_____

_____
_____
_____
_____
_____
_____
_____

*Date*_____

_____
_____
_____
_____
_____
_____
_____

*Date*_____

_____
_____
_____
_____
_____
_____
_____

282.4 Define how love is effortless.

*Date*_____

_____

_____

_____

_____

_____

_____

_____

*Date*_____

_____

_____

_____

_____

_____

_____

_____

*Date*_____

_____

_____

_____

_____

_____

_____

_____

283.1 When are you most still within the mind?

*Date*_____

_____
_____
_____
_____
_____
_____
_____

*Date*_____

_____
_____
_____
_____
_____
_____
_____

*Date*_____

_____
_____
_____
_____
_____
_____
_____

283.2 What do you think your personal unconscious mind has been mostly protecting within itself as a means in which to play with outer experience within your life?

*Date*_____

_____

_____

_____

_____

_____

_____

_____

*Date*_____

_____

_____

_____

_____

_____

_____

_____

*Date*_____

_____

_____

_____

_____

_____

_____

283.3 - 283.4 When individuals remove and dissolve the unconscious mind, then the collective unconscious has nothing in which to engage and will dissolve also. Once we effectively as a planet dissolve the unconscious mind, there is now awakened upon the earth and within the personal mind a clear transparent place. The mind will become an energetic center for color, vision, purpose, and language to be moved into the day to day by the expression of our emotions in form that preserve the 49 feelings of love that are defined within the beauty of all life. The universe will celebrate our clarity and transparency of mind by providing opportunities and a means in which for us to exist within all that preserves the beauty of love.

284.1 When you experience a Clear Mind, or moments without the unconscious, how does the mind feel, how do thoughts feel, is there stillness, are there greater feelings, or is there more or less confidence? What is the expression that you feel at the time?

*Date*_____

_____

_____

_____

_____

_____

_____

_____

*Date*_____

_____

_____

_____

_____

_____

_____

*Date*_____

_____

_____

_____

_____

_____

_____

284.2 When you think analytically what is the feeling that you get within your mind?

*Date*_____

_____

_____

_____

_____

_____

_____

_____

*Date*_____

_____

_____

_____

_____

_____

_____

_____

*Date*_____

_____

_____

_____

_____

_____

_____

_____

284.3 Has your thinking changed throughout your life? Meaning, what is important for you to think about today rather than previously within your life?

*Date*_____

_____

_____

_____

_____

_____

_____

_____

*Date*_____

_____

_____

_____

_____

_____

_____

_____

*Date*_____

_____

_____

_____

_____

_____

_____

284.4 - 286.8

HARMONY

SERENITY

RADIANCE

FAITH

ESSENCE

GRACE

CONSCIOUS MIND
ANTICLOCKWISE DIRECTON
HIGHER FREQUENCY

UNCONSCIOUS MIND
CLOCKWISE DIRECTION
CONSTANTLY SEEKING

ONENESS

PERSONAL/CONSCIOUS MIND
AURAS AND CHAKRAS

287.1 Is the personal mind when clear of the unconscious mind transparent and, if so, please explain.

*Date*_____

_____

_____

_____

_____

_____

_____

_____

*Date*_____

_____

_____

_____

_____

_____

_____

_____

*Date*_____

_____

_____

_____

_____

_____

_____

_____

287.2 When one connects with the collective mind rather than the personal mind, is it fair to say that one is experiencing less personal identity?

*Date*_____

_____

_____

_____

_____

_____

_____

_____

*Date*_____

_____

_____

_____

_____

_____

_____

_____

*Date*_____

_____

_____

_____

_____

_____

_____

287.3 Does it serve a 'beautiful mind' to have less personal identity?

*Date*_____

_____
_____
_____
_____
_____
_____
_____

*Date*_____

_____
_____
_____
_____
_____
_____
_____

*Date*_____

_____
_____
_____
_____
_____
_____
_____

287.4 If one's feelings are not attached to outcome through thoughts, what can life feel to offer?

*Date*_____

_____

_____

_____

_____

_____

_____

*Date*_____

_____

_____

_____

_____

_____

_____

*Date*_____

_____

_____

_____

_____

_____

_____

287.5 What is the difference between intuition and knowing?

*Date*_____

_____

_____

_____

_____

_____

_____

_____

*Date*_____

_____

_____

_____

_____

_____

_____

_____

*Date*_____

_____

_____

_____

_____

_____

_____

_____

287.6 Are there times where you have questioned wisdom, even slightly and what was the spoken topic of the wisdom?

*Date*_____

_____

_____

_____

_____

_____

_____

_____

*Date*_____

_____

_____

_____

_____

_____

_____

_____

*Date*_____

_____

_____

_____

_____

_____

_____

_____

287.7 When have you experienced knowing versus intuition and what did it feel like?

*Date*_____

_____

_____

_____

_____

_____

_____

_____

*Date*_____

_____

_____

_____

_____

_____

_____

_____

*Date*_____

_____

_____

_____

_____

_____

_____

_____

287.8 When you receive an intuitive message, do you see when it is preserving love?

*Date*_____

_____
_____
_____
_____
_____
_____
_____

*Date*_____

_____
_____
_____
_____
_____
_____
_____

*Date*_____

_____
_____
_____
_____
_____
_____
_____

288.1 Why is peace beyond the definition of words and could it be defined within feelings?

*Date*_____

_____

_____

_____

_____

_____

_____

_____

*Date*_____

_____

_____

_____

_____

_____

_____

_____

*Date*_____

_____

_____

_____

_____

_____

_____

_____

288.2 Is peace a feeling that is free of thoughts that are not peace?

*Date*_____

_____

_____

_____

_____

_____

_____

_____

*Date*_____

_____

_____

_____

_____

_____

_____

_____

*Date*_____

_____

_____

_____

_____

_____

_____

_____

288.3 Is peace our natural 'state of being'? If so, how so?

*Date*_____

_____
_____
_____
_____
_____
_____
_____

*Date*_____

_____
_____
_____
_____
_____
_____
_____

*Date*_____

_____
_____
_____
_____
_____
_____
_____

288.4 Why is the unconscious mind attached to conditions of form and mind?

*Date*_____

_____

_____

_____

_____

_____

_____

_____

*Date*_____

_____

_____

_____

_____

_____

_____

_____

*Date*_____

_____

_____

_____

_____

_____

_____

_____

288.5 Within a Clear Mind, one that has dissolved the interpretations of the unconscious, there are no failings of love or battle between light and dark. There is no need to numb life out through medication, addictions, and stimulants, and disease because within a conscious mind, there is a state of being that is peace, and peace is supported within the presence and essence and expression of trust that is defined by the magnificence of wisdom.

289.1 Name one experience in life that you feel speaks to how you have felt about yourself in the past or how you feel about yourself today – even if the experience is unconscious but your perception is conscious.

*Date*_____

_____

_____

_____

_____

_____

_____

*Date*_____

_____

_____

_____

_____

_____

*Date*_____

_____

_____

_____

_____

_____

289.2 Why is love not able to support the limitations of the unconscious mind?

*Date*_____

_____
_____
_____
_____
_____
_____
_____

*Date*_____

_____
_____
_____
_____
_____
_____
_____

*Date*_____

_____
_____
_____
_____
_____
_____
_____

290.1 How does a spiritual mind operate?

*Date*_____

_____
_____
_____
_____
_____
_____

*Date*_____

_____
_____
_____
_____
_____
_____

*Date*_____

_____
_____
_____
_____
_____
_____
_____

290.2 Within the spiritual mind, energetic interpretation of what happens on the outside and how it is perceived within life flows differently, feels differently within the mind, but this is because it creates differently, because it creates the interpretations within mind that preserve love on the outside.

290.3 Within a beautiful mind, when one is clear of the unconscious, the universe will line up experiences to honor vision, why is this?

*Date*_____

_____

_____

_____

_____

_____

_____

_____

*Date*_____

_____

_____

_____

_____

_____

_____

_____

*Date*_____

_____

_____

_____

_____

_____

_____

290.4 In a conscious mind, visions of life become prophetic experiences of what is awakening to support the higher value, preservation of life and love upon the planet. Visions will be carried forth across the planet and united within the magnificence of potential where there are no perceived limitations, as within a mind clear of the unconscious life is but an endless expression from one moment to the next of the profound quality and alchemy of love.

290.5 What language do you think the unconscious mind would or does speak to confuse you out of believing in a vision?

*Date*_____

_____
_____
_____
_____
_____
_____
_____

*Date*_____

_____
_____
_____
_____
_____
_____
_____

*Date*_____

_____
_____
_____
_____
_____
_____

291.1 Write a vision for your life, and within the writing speak of it being orchestrated and supported within a 'beautiful mind' and the movement of the 49 positive feelings of a Clear Mind.

*Date*_____

_____
_____
_____
_____
_____
_____
_____

*Date*_____

_____
_____
_____
_____
_____
_____

*Date*_____

_____
_____
_____
_____
_____
_____

291.2 When in your life has the unconscious mind attempted to speak you out of a vision for your life, your
future, or your wisdom? When it has, how has this felt?

*Date*_____

_____

_____

_____

_____

_____

_____

_____

*Date*_____

_____

_____

_____

_____

_____

_____

_____

*Date*_____

_____

_____

_____

_____

_____

_____

291.3 When one has a vision but the unconscious is not clear, one will have the vision and may face the hurdle of limited feelings that start over once the vision is released. It is upon that moment that the conscious mind may take on the persona of the warrior, of Joan of Arc, and as the visionary with the conscious mind, with the conscious intent, with your sword firmly planted out in front of you, you will ride into the future by never giving up, entering a battle that is beyond words, while invoking suffering that one never hoped or dreamed to encounter as you attempt to shepherd your vision into being. It is within the unconscious mind that an individual will be challenged, that their vision will be challenged. That once love reveals itself, the unconscious mind will surface and the challenge will begin. However, within the Clear Mind Experience, there is no battle because upon the first breath, the victory has already occurred. Because upon the first moment of practicing it, love is realized, and upon each practice is only presenting the realization.

291.4 - 291.4i Why does the unconscious mind fear visions?

*Date*_____

_____
_____
_____
_____
_____
_____
_____

*Date*_____

_____
_____
_____
_____
_____
_____
_____

*Date*_____

_____
_____
_____
_____
_____
_____
_____

291.5 Define the battle and what has taken place when it is over and is there really a battle or an awakening?

*Date*_____

_____

_____

_____

_____

_____

_____

_____

*Date*_____

_____

_____

_____

_____

_____

_____

_____

*Date*_____

_____

_____

_____

_____

_____

_____

_____

292.1 Define Simplicity.

*Date*_____

_____

_____

_____

_____

_____

_____

*Date*_____

_____

_____

_____

_____

_____

_____

*Date*_____

_____

_____

_____

_____

_____

_____

292.2 Define Love and how it is perceived within a Clear Mind.

*Date*_____

_____

_____

_____

_____

_____

_____

_____

*Date*_____

_____

_____

_____

_____

_____

_____

_____

*Date*_____

_____

_____

_____

_____

_____

_____

_____

292.3 Would you agree that a 'beautiful mind' is able to express unconditional love and, if so, why?

*Date*_____

_____

_____

_____

_____

_____

_____

_____

*Date*_____

_____

_____

_____

_____

_____

_____

_____

*Date*_____

_____

_____

_____

_____

_____

_____

_____

292.4 What is non-judgment and how will and does life benefit through this perception?

*Date*_____

_____

_____

_____

_____

_____

_____

_____

*Date*_____

_____

_____

_____

_____

_____

_____

_____

*Date*_____

_____

_____

_____

_____

_____

_____

_____

292.5 Look at the Clear Mind Positive Mind Scale – choose a positive feeling that you feel predominantly now and write how it will and is serving your primary relationship within your life.

*Date*_____

_____

_____

_____

_____

_____

_____

_____

*Date*_____

_____

_____

_____

_____

_____

_____

*Date*_____

_____

_____

_____

_____

_____

_____

292.6 How does love support creation?

*Date*_____

_____

_____

_____

_____

_____

_____

*Date*_____

_____

_____

_____

_____

_____

_____

*Date*_____

_____

_____

_____

_____

_____

_____

292.7 When living within a Clear Mind, how can the presence of love move through you into life to birth or support creation?

*Date*_____

_____

_____

_____

_____

_____

_____

_____

*Date*_____

_____

_____

_____

_____

_____

_____

_____

*Date*_____

_____

_____

_____

_____

_____

_____

292.8 Considering that love moves spontaneously, how is it moving to dissolve what is not love in your life?

*Date*_____

_____

_____

_____

_____

_____

_____

_____

*Date*_____

_____

_____

_____

_____

_____

_____

_____

*Date*_____

_____

_____

_____

_____

_____

_____

_____

292.9 It is within a Clear Mind, it is within the beautiful structure of the conscious mind that 49 positive feelings will move through the seven key emotions. It is within the engaging of positive feelings and emotion, the perception awakens and within the perception, one will not experience anything that represents fear as one does not have the capacity to see what is separate from love. One will only navigate itself through life to dissolve what is not love into what is.

293.1 What is your predominant perception in life?

*Date*_____

_____
_____
_____
_____
_____
_____
_____

*Date*_____

_____
_____
_____
_____
_____
_____
_____

*Date*_____

_____
_____
_____
_____
_____
_____
_____

293.2 Write three times you have seen the unconscious mind attempt to preserve its feelings through life experience. Most times the life experiences will repeat themselves.

*Date*_____

1._____

_____

2._____

_____

3._____

_____

_____

*Date*_____

1._____

_____

2._____

_____

3._____

_____

_____

*Date*_____

1._____

_____

2._____

_____

3._____

_____

293.3 Choose seven qualities from the Clear Mind Positive Feelings Scale that you feel best define your feelings today. If you choose positive feelings, can you define what has been dissolved that was unconscious and if you choose negative, invite the positive feelings into life through a written invitation of experiencing them within your day to day, including why they are important to you?

*Date*_____

_____
_____
_____
_____
_____
_____
_____
_____
_____
_____
_____
_____
_____
_____
_____

*Date*_____

_____
_____
_____

Date_____

293.4 When one awakens the conscious mind by dissolving what is unconscious, one can still function within the world. The conscious mind will always define itself in a manner that dissolves the limited ideas of the unconscious mind. It can survive in any climate; all emotional, physical perceptions and conditions of the collective because it will always be gifted with the means in which to preserve itself.

293.5 Write about a time that you preserved the expression of self worth, how that made you feel, and what you feel the universe was aligning you to through the experience.

*Date*_____

_____

_____

_____

_____

_____

_____

_____

*Date*_____

_____

_____

_____

_____

_____

_____

_____

*Date*_____

_____

_____

_____

_____

_____

_____

293.6 The conscious mind is profound within its operation. It is a structure in which to present feelings in life that awakens vision and within vision, ideas move, thoughts and actions form in a manner that supports the endless preservation of love.

294.1 When we experience abuse within our lives, no matter how extreme or minimal, it is stored within the unconscious mind. When you breathe to dissolve the unconscious mind, you are dissolving these interpretations. The beauty of the Clear Mind Experience is that you are practicing a process that allows you to unconditionally embrace the mind and perception of the child. Through the language of love and the Clear Mind Breath, the child-mind is being nurtured into a rhythm of self-appreciation. Write a paragraph inviting your child-mind into an experience and interpretation of love.

*Date*_____

_____

_____

_____

_____

_____

_____

_____

_____

_____

_____

_____

_____

Date_____

_____
_____
_____
_____
_____
_____
_____
_____
_____
_____
_____
_____
_____
_____

Date_____

_____
_____
_____
_____
_____
_____
_____
_____
_____
_____
_____
_____

294.2 When you think of something that is unpredictable what does this immediately feel like to you – does it feel exciting or does fear of the unknown surface?

*Date*_____

_____

_____

_____

_____

_____

_____

_____

*Date*_____

_____

_____

_____

_____

_____

_____

_____

*Date*_____

_____

_____

_____

_____

_____

_____

294.3 The unconscious mind has fear of entering the conscious mind because the conscious mind is love and the unconscious mind cannot see it. Therefore, as your perception is being drawn into love, the unconscious mind wonders where the perception is going. Write a statement of what you are becoming free of, that would have the unconscious mind fear the love of the conscious mind. Defining what it most holds onto because it is what mostly defines it. ('it' being the unconscious mind)

294.4 The unconscious mind is not able to perceive love. It cannot see, feel, or know, or experience any quality of the conscious mind. When it senses perception moving in to the conscious mind, it perceives the feeling that the individual, the personal mind is entering the unknown. It is within that moment that it will encourage feelings of fear, distrust, disharmony, and question the light through feelings and thoughts of 'what if?' It is within the Clear Mind Experience and the structure of the Clear Mind Support Mantras that an individual at the point of moving into the conscious mind is able to retain connection to the conscious mind through the Clear Mind Support Mantra. Immediately upon hearing the unconscious make reference of fear, an individual is encouraged to breathe the three Clear Mind breaths and repeat the 'IAM' Clear Mind Support Mantra.

295.1 Define why the unconscious mind fears you moving into love.

*Date*_____

_____

_____

_____

_____

_____

_____

_____

*Date*_____

_____

_____

_____

_____

_____

_____

_____

*Date*_____

_____

_____

_____

_____

_____

_____

_____

295.2 – 295.3 It is within the moments of moving into the conscious mind and when the conscious mind is challenged that without participating in the Clear Mind Experience, the individual will typically try to rationalize, speak to the unconscious so it will let go. However, the nature of its existence is to exist, to not let go. For it to further protect itself, it will mix in some physical discomfort, negative memories, some senses of abandonment to loss of self-love, and within that moment, you have the unconscious mind seeking to protect its power.

295.4 Define freedom from fear and define how you perceive freedom from fear.

*Date*_____

_____

_____

_____

_____

_____

_____

_____

*Date*_____

_____

_____

_____

_____

_____

_____

_____

*Date*_____

_____

_____

_____

_____

_____

_____

_____

295.5 List three feelings or expressions of love that have been presented to you that you would not have otherwise considered.

*Date*_____

_____

_____

_____

_____

_____

_____

_____

*Date*_____

_____

_____

_____

_____

_____

_____

_____

*Date*_____

_____

_____

_____

_____

_____

_____

295.6 In the past when you have reacted, what has it been about and how is it different for you today – list three differences.

*Date*_____

_____

_____

_____

_____

_____

_____

_____

*Date*_____

_____

_____

_____

_____

_____

_____

_____

*Date*_____

_____

_____

_____

_____

_____

_____

295.7 Define how life is soothed and nurtured through your daily contribution.

*Date*_____

_____
_____
_____
_____
_____
_____
_____

*Date*_____

_____
_____
_____
_____
_____
_____
_____

*Date*_____

_____
_____
_____
_____
_____
_____
_____

295.8 The unconscious mind through the Clear Mind Experience is being loved, how do you perceive the wisdom that is spoken into the unconscious mind from the conscious mind?

*Date*_____

_____

_____

_____

_____

_____

_____

_____

*Date*_____

_____

_____

_____

_____

_____

_____

*Date*_____

_____

_____

_____

_____

_____

_____

296.1 Define three benefits that you see in the rational mind being allowing of your process to dissolve the unconscious mind, how is this directly benefitting each day?

*Date*_____

_____

_____

_____

_____

_____

_____

_____

*Date*_____

_____

_____

_____

_____

_____

_____

_____

*Date*_____

_____

_____

_____

_____

_____

_____

296.2 - 296.2i Define the rational mind, and when you breathe how it perceives your experience.

*Date*_____

_____

_____

_____

_____

_____

_____

_____

*Date*_____

_____

_____

_____

_____

_____

_____

_____

*Date*_____

_____

_____

_____

_____

_____

_____

_____

296.3 Within the Clear Mind Experience, one is not suppressing the unconscious mind so it will not bite back because it will not be interpreting the feeling that it has been cut off. Within the Clear Mind Experience because the conscious mind is dissolving the unconscious into itself, there is always a sense of union not a sense of suppression within the process.

297.1 The magnificence of living within the conscious mind is that life becomes free from the chaos. One becomes free to feel and honor love, free to express unlimited potential mentally, emotionally, and physically. Most important, one becomes free from the unconscious thoughts, feelings, and emotions that create suffering within life. It is within this freedom that humanity is able to reside, create, ignite, support the profound presence and momentum of love.

298.1 Choose three positive feelings from the Clear Mind Positive Feelings Scale, define how humanity can be gifted through these three feelings as you confirm their presence within your life today and always.

*Date*_____

_____

_____

_____

_____

_____

_____

_____

*Date*_____

_____

_____

_____

_____

_____

_____

*Date*_____

_____

_____

_____

_____

_____

_____

298.2 Define three ways that a beautiful mind awakens life in a new direction for children.

*Date*_____

_____

_____

_____

_____

_____

_____

_____

*Date*_____

_____

_____

_____

_____

_____

_____

_____

*Date*_____

_____

_____

_____

_____

_____

_____

_____

298.3 How is self-love experiencing itself as you and how is it being witnessed by others?

*Date*_____

_____

_____

_____

_____

_____

_____

_____

*Date*_____

_____

_____

_____

_____

_____

_____

_____

*Date*_____

_____

_____

_____

_____

_____

_____

_____

298.4 The magnificence of the Clear Mind Experience is that it supports the profound beauty and alchemy of self-appreciation. When love awakens through the Clear Mind Experience, it is not an awakening through the motive of seeking to change but expresses love as a living state within the being through a realization of love within a beautiful mind.

299.1 Define a Beautiful Mind and what it perceives.

*Date*_____

_____
_____
_____
_____
_____
_____
_____

*Date*_____

_____
_____
_____
_____
_____
_____
_____

*Date*_____

_____
_____
_____
_____
_____
_____
_____

299.2 Define how a Beautiful Mind will support love, will honor emotions and allow feeling within your experiences?

*Date*_____

_____

_____

_____

_____

_____

_____

_____

*Date*_____

_____

_____

_____

_____

_____

_____

_____

*Date*_____

_____

_____

_____

_____

_____

_____

_____

299.3 The magnificence of the Clear Mind Experience is that it is upon this planet, it awakens the birthright, which is that all beings are invited to live within the magnificent expression of a beautiful mind operating within life, living as a radiant expression of love.

300.1 Write a paragraph that defines the presence of love and the feelings that come up to preserve its role within your day to day. Within your words celebrate each moment that it is available to express itself within your emotions, within your feelings and within each word honor as the magnificent expression that you are.

*Date*_____

_____

_____

_____

_____

_____

_____

*Date*_____

_____

_____

_____

_____

_____

_____

*Date*_____

_____

_____

_____

_____

_____

_____

Start the **Clear Mind Experience** *Today*

www.highermindinstitute.com or
www.clearmindnewplanet.com

Experience the simplicity and beauty of living
free of the unconscious mind

The Clear Mind New Planet - Center for Stillness was founded by Clear Mind Experience pioneer Genie O'Malley. A center carrying deep stillness and wisdom to support the Clear Mind Experience, visitors are able join group classes, workshops, training, and one-on-one sessions with Genie O'Malley, as well as, highly trained Clear Mind Experience Practitioners.

Montauk, NY hosts magnificent beaches, accommodations, and the peace and simplicity needed to compliment your journey at the Clear Mind New Planet Center.

To receive up and coming schedules or to book a session please phone:

631.668.1017 or 888.515.0444

www.clearmindnewplanet.com
www.highermindinstitute.com

email: breathe@clearmindnewplanet.com